Societal Deception

Geoffrey Lawrence
Societal Deception
Global Social Issues in Post-Truth Times

Geoffrey Lawrence
School of Social Science
The University of Queensland
Brisbane, QLD, Australia

ISBN 978-1-349-96106-1   ISBN 978-1-349-96107-8 (eBook)
https://doi.org/10.1057/978-1-349-96107-8

© The Editor(s) (if applicable) and The Author(s), under exclusive licence to Springer Nature Limited. 2024
The author(s) has/have asserted their right(s) to be identified as the author(s) of this work in accordance with the Copyright, Designs and Patents Act 1988.

This work is subject to copyright. All rights are solely and exclusively licensed by the Publisher, whether the whole or part of the material is concerned, specifically the rights of translation, reprinting, reuse of illustrations, recitation, broadcasting, reproduction on microfilms or in any other physical way, and transmission or information storage and retrieval, electronic adaptation, computer software, or by similar or dissimilar methodology now known or hereafter developed.
The use of general descriptive names, registered names, trademarks, service marks, etc. in this publication does not imply, even in the absence of a specific statement, that such names are exempt from the relevant protective laws and regulations and therefore free for general use.
The publisher, the authors and the editors are safe to assume that the advice and information in this book are believed to be true and accurate at the date of publication. Neither the publisher nor the authors or the editors give a warranty, expressed or implied, with respect to the material contained herein or for any errors or omissions that may have been made. The publisher remains neutral with regard to jurisdictional claims in published maps and institutional affiliations.

Cover illustration: Studio eCalamar

This Palgrave Macmillan imprint is published by the registered company Springer Nature Limited
The registered company address is: The Campus, 4 Crinan Street, London, N1 9XW, United Kingdom

Paper in this product is recyclable.

To three wonderful women
Dimity
Dania
Kimberley

Preface

Have you seen the social media clip 'Zombie virusi USA'? It shows Americans in a large shopping mall running and screaming from a purported zombie attack.[1] The zombie virusi posting went viral, as they say. And why would it not? Some 14 percent of Americans have a zombie apocalypse rescue plan in place, rising to some 24 percent for people born in the 1980s and 1990s (the so-called Millennials or Gen Y). As is the American way, most are stockpiling guns and other weapons to protect themselves against future assaults.[2] The US military is also concerned, preparing a contingency plan (CONPLAN 8888) which outlines the favoured military response should zombies invade American shores.[3] If you visit Mexico City a week before the commencement of celebrations for the Day of the Dead (2 November), thousands of zombies—with axes through heads, bloodied faces, staggering gaits, and trays of body parts for hungry participants—make their way through the streets. They are having fun while collecting non-perishable foods (canned items, rather than human organs) to donate to the city's poor.[4]

To be sure we have observed, and continue to observe, zombie-like symptoms and behaviour in people. Aimless wandering, slurred speech, loss of control of the tongue and lips, groaning, and rotting flesh and body parts are among the traits. Today we recognise the conditions that give rise to such features, including catatonic schizophrenia, Cotard's syndrome (a mental disorder with people believing they are dead or are decomposing), sleeping sickness, rabies, dysarthria (malfunction of the nervous system), and leprosy (decaying flesh).[5] The zombies depicted on our TVs and movie screens do not exist in real life. They are fictional characters designed to scare the behoots out of audiences. They are not real. It turns out that the 'Zombie virusi USA' was filmed in Paris, showing hundreds of panicked customers deserting the Westfield Les 4 Temps shopping centre in droves following a loud explosion. And 'virusi' is Russian for 'virus'—giving us some inkling as to where the bogus video arose.[6] It was fake news, yet huge swathes of people believed it to be true.

That said, having your own zombie apocalypse plan in place may not be such a bad thing—who'd want to experience a *Night of the Living Dead*?

We know that people trust in social institutions, economists, politicians, and the media to bring them accurate knowledge about the world. Instead, they are receiving misleading information, biased news, and downright lies which serve the (often nefarious) purposes of the wealthy and powerful. We live in post-truth times. It is important to expose those who are employing strategies of misinformation and disinformation to further their interests at the expense of the majority of people, and the planet. I was driven to write this book to let people know what tactics are employed by corporations, politicians, think tanks, 'shock jocks', influencers, and the like, to corrupt our thinking. The aim is to reveal the otherwise 'hidden' agendas of those with power and wealth.

The book has a contemporary and practical aim—to demonstrate that there are forces at work seeking to divert people's attention from some of the most challenging issues of our times. This book's contents are for a disillusioned public, for critical thinkers, university students, activists who are looking for answers to the world's seemingly intractable problems, and for a younger generation wanting a very different 'take' on what is happening to their—and their friends' and families'—lives.

The intention is to expose both deceit and denial. Targeted are the owners of fossil fuel firms, chemical conglomerates, agribusiness companies, along with corporate bosses creating junk foods for a new generation of kids. It also targets those who believe human salvation will come via right-wing politics, those whose only sources of knowledge are the Murdoch media, and those who are content for sport and religion to be their go-to realities (the list goes on). I deliberately upset conventions to provoke a rethinking of where the world is heading, and to elicit change.

Much of the content of the book is sociological in nature. I have worked in academia most of my life having undertaken detailed social research in areas as diverse as sport, leisure, social aspects of genetic engineering, food security, supermarket power, natural resource management, and the financialisation of food and agriculture. I have drawn upon these bodies of work throughout the book. Chapter 1 details the ways people are inveigled into accepting fake news. Advertising tricks and techniques are highlighted. Media power is discussed—with special reference to Murdoch and Fox. Chapter 2 exposes the fallacies of orthodox economics, revealing the vulnerable nature of capitalism and demonstrating the negative impacts of neoliberal globalisation and the 'financialisation' of the economy. Chapter 3 focuses upon the modern food system. It turns out to be environmentally unsustainable as well as damaging to human health. Agribusiness, fast-food chains, and supermarkets employ many mechanisms to fabricate trust, while plying customers with an assortment of obesogenic, and otherwise suspect, products.

In Chapter 4, many of the technologies that have been, and are, employed in creating a modern lifestyle are discussed. They are the same technologies implicated in widespread pollution and devastating global warming/climate change. The continuation of current methods of production is depleting resources, undermining planetary health, and contributing to species annihilation. The many right-wing think tanks and organisations promoting unsustainable practices are detailed. The chapter also explores corporate agriculture's (Big Ag's) environmental record before outlining the techniques and tactics used by climate change deniers. Chapter 5 examines 'the power to lie'. Political leaders fabricate outright lies to manipulate public opinion and to lead countries to conflict and war. The chapter discusses propaganda in war, political ideologies, and the growing influence of social media in politics. The legacy of colonialism is highlighted, as is modern-day land grabbing.

In 'Praying for Salvation'—Chapter 6—religion is held up for scrutiny. Religions claim to give meaning to life but they are based upon irrational and dishonest doctrines, antiquated and invalid assumptions, superstition, and unscientific premises. Those touting religion are deceiving their followers. The chapter discusses ideas of 'belief', including the status of 'miracles' in the church. It examines, in critical fashion, St Augustine's doctrine of original sin. Chapter 7 ventures into the world of elite sport. Sport is central to contemporary popular culture. Yet, despite this, it is replete with sexist and racist ideologies. Cheating is a major problem—particularly in elite sports—as the Lance Armstrong saga so clearly demonstrates. Tennis star Novak Djokovic's attempts to deceive authorities in relation to his COVID-19 vaccination status begins the chapter, followed by a brief overview of sport history. 'Sportswashing' is considered to be a particularly insidious attempt by various governments and corporations to win public support—in the face of their otherwise perverse actions. In Chapter 8, the final chapter, an important question is asked: Given the very many existential, and systemic, problems faced by the world, how might it be possible to confront the crucial issues we encounter, and bring about progressive and long-lasting change? Social agency—action designed to confront the status quo and deliver positive outcomes—is outlined and explained. The chapter demonstrates how citizens are countering media mis- and disinformation, rallying for action on climate, protesting the pollution and environmental destruction wrought by corporate capital, and rethinking ways of farming, eating, and living.

Societal Deception is not a conventional or orthodox book. It is analytical and critical—but does not employ complex concepts or seek to build social theory. It contains snippets from my life as a social researcher. It is deliberately eclectic, moving from topic to topic to reveal the extent to which capital has permeated, and largely corrupted, most social institutions that are important to our lives. It is iconoclastic—aiming to expose the groups and organisations employing deceptive tactics to extend their influence and power. The book is designed to be provocative—but also highly readable and engaging. It is a satirical social commentary of our contemporary world. I hope you enjoy the book, even though the journey through its pages might not provide a particularly comfortable ride at times.

Brisbane, Australia   Geoffrey Lawrence

Notes

1. Facebook. (2023) Zombi virisi USA, https://www.facebook.com/reel/783056703765342.
2. Sanders, L. (2019) 14% of Americans have a zombie apocalypse plan, https://today.yougov.com/topics/entertainment/articles-reports/2019/10/01/zombie-apocalypse-plan.
3. See Wonderopolis. (2023) What is CONPLAN 8888? https://wonderopolis.org/wonder/What-Is-CONPLAN-8888#:~:text=What%20does%20CONPLAN%208888%20include,to%20really%20get%20to%20work.
4. Here's a short video clip of events, https://www.bing.com/videos/riverview/relatedvideo?&q=Film+of+zombies+walk+down+the+streets+in+Mexico&&mid=4BE94FC5630EF816CCEE4BE94FC5630EF816CCEE&&FORM=VRDGAR.
5. Virox. (2015) Zombies – do they exist in real life? https://www.viroxanimalhealth.com/resources/talkcleantome/2015/10/zombies-do-they-exist-in-real-life.html.
6. Malashenko, U. (2023) Fact Check: Video does NOT show people running from real zombies in the US, https://leadstories.com/hoax-alert/2023/04/fact-check-video-does-not-show-people-running-away-from-real-zombies-in-usa.html.

Acknowledgements

This book was written during COVID-19 times. Under COVID-19, the slowing hands of time left me with time on my hands. I sat at home with my computer venturing into some of the most interesting and obscure websites, eBooks, YouTube clips, and online journals, that I'd ever encountered. The material was novel and powerful, and I am grateful to the University of Queensland and, in particular, the Head of the School of Social Science, Lynda Cheshire, for facilitating my access to these and other web-based resources.

Friends and colleagues kindly read sections of the book, giving valuable comments along with fresh insights: Jane Lino, Philip McMichael, Victoria O'Connor, Carol Richards, David Rowe, and Frank Stilwell. Hugh Campbell broke into what should have been a restful vacation to read the initial first draft—providing highly useful observations and suggestions.

Many of the ideas appearing upon the pages of *Societal Deception* were developed over a long period of discussion, debate, and—occasional—disagreement. The people I thank below might dispute a number of claims discussed in the book. Nevertheless, I am truly grateful to them for their continued interest in, and input into, my research and writing: Reidar Almås, Hilde Bjørkhaug, Sofie Bjørkhaug, Keith Burgess, Michael Carolan, Kimberley Cash, Will Cash, Marion Familton, Vaughan Higgins, Richard Hindmarsh, Zannie Langford, Dania Lawrence, Peter Lino, Dylan Lino, Stewart Lockie, Kristen Lyons, Amy MacMahon, Bob Meyenn, Toby Miller, Jane Muller, Julie Pearson, Bill Pritchard, Lila Singh-Peterson, Sarah Ruth Sippel, Kiah Smith, Bruce Taylor, Kandice Varcin, Liam Wagner, Peter Wallace, and Alan Wheeler. The pilates crew was a great inspiration—Kara, Marg, and Bree—as was the minstrel of the dawn.

A special thank goes to my wife and life-long partner, Dimity. She was involved in all aspects of the project—discovering and providing new material, editing draft chapters, and helping to construct the index. She has been an inspiration. Without her constant support, good humour, enthusiasm, and unerring commitment to social justice, the book would not have been completed.

I owe a debt of gratitude to journalists at the *Guardian*—in particular, Damian Carrington, Fiona Harvey, Oliver Milman, and George Monbiot. I've yet to meet them, but their thought-provoking analyses and up-to-date material have found their way into many chapters of the book. Similarly, expert research provided by academics writing for *The Conversation* was indispensable to arguments developed about the media, politics, the environment, and climate change. Funding, provided over many decades by the Australian Research Council, has been crucial to my research and writing.

Jessica Faecks, Sociology Editor for Palgrave Macmillan, has been enthusiastic and supportive throughout the editing and review process. Her special flair for nailing headings and subheadings is seen throughout the book. Connie Li, Senior Editorial Assistant, Humanities and Social Sciences at Palgrave Macmillan, provided excellent support from her hideaway in Shanghai. I am indebted to Preetha Kuttiappan, Naveen Dass, and Lara Glueck at Springer Nature who copyedited the manuscript, and to the graphic artists at Studio eCalamar who designed the cover. Three anonymous readers of the draft manuscript provided insightful comments which have enriched the book's content.

A huge thank you, as well, to the many academics whose work has been an inspiration for this book and who share the view that we must expose, hound, and—where necessary—ridicule those who would have us live in an age of disinformation and fake news, a world of 'post truths'.

This book was written on the lands of the Turrbal/Yuggera peoples of Brisbane. I acknowledge the Traditional Owners and their custodianship of these lands and pay my respects to their ancestors and descendants.

Contents

1 **Who Can You Believe? Of Media, Misinformation, and Trumpery**   1
   Who's Doin' the Foolin'?   3
      Ads, Ads, and More Ads   4
   Trusting Brains in the Brain Trust   8
      Then There's the Media   11
      From Shock Jocks to Influencers   16
   Be Sure to Get Your Way   22
   Faking It   25

2 **It's the Economy, Stupid! Neoliberal Nonsense and the Myths of the Free Market**   51
   Grounds for Doubt   53
      The Many Myths of Liberal Economic Theory   54
   Capitalism: The 'System We Know and Love'?   65
   Chicago Boys   68
      Some Boats Rising, Most Boats Sinking   71
   Financing the Future   75
      Just What Is Financialisation?   76

Are We Are All Neolibs Now?	82

3 From Seedling to Supermarket: Farming, Fast Food, and the Fabrication of Trust   99
    All Farmed Out   101
        From Green Revolution to Gene Revolution   103
        Learning Our ABCDs   108
    Super-Marketed   111
        Recall This   114
        Fabricating Trust   117
    Fun with Fast Food   121
    Feeding the Lie   123
        Coaxing the Kiddies   125
        Globesity   126

4 Saving the Planet with Pesticides and Plastic: Corporate Profiteering and Planetary Destruction   151
    Chemical Concoctions   153
        Financing the Furphy   159
    Classic Cover-Ups   161
        Meltdown Mayhem   166
    Warming to Climate Change   169
        What Is Going On?   173
    The Denial Machine   179

5 The Power to Lie: Propaganda and Post-truth Politics   211
    Perfecting Propaganda   213
        Oh, Those Russians   216
        Chinese Checkers   218
    Living the Dream   220
        A Web of Deceit   230
    Empire Records   235
        The Butcher's Apron   239
    Up for Grabs   246

6 Praying for Salvation: Forgeries and Fallacies of Religion   271
    Back to the Future   274

Could We Be so Silly?	275
The Idea of 'Belief'	277
What Makes Us Believe?	278
Miracles and Manipulation	284
Bad Habits	289
One of the Greats	292
Cooking the Books	295
Pussies in Paradise	298
Thank God for Darwin	300
Imagine No Deception—It's Easy If You Try	305

7 The Ultimate Diversion: Sport as False Consciousness? — 323

My Sporting Life	329
In the Beginning …	334
Writing the Rules	338
Deceptive Moves	343
Stealing Gold	344
La tromperie de France	349
Sportswashing—Cleaning the Image	354

8 The Future: Confronting the Culprits — 377

Disappearing Acts	380
Facing the Future	390
Information Flows	390
Turning Down the Thermostat	396
Earthly Preoccupations	403
Our Daily Bread	408
Capital Ideas	415
Dangling Democracy	420

Index — 453

About the Author

Geoffrey Lawrence studied agricultural science at Sydney University in the early 1970s, later completing his masters in sociology at the University of Wisconsin-Madison, and doctorate in sociology at Griffith University. Before, during, and after his studies he worked in social welfare, mental health, in industrial labouring, in natural resource management, and in farming—experiences which exposed him to social inequality and drove him to seek answers to social injustice in society. His research is diverse, spanning the areas of popular culture, the media, sport and leisure, rural social change, agri-food industries, food security, finance, and social aspects of the environment. He has received funding from the Australian Research Council, the Canadian Social Sciences and Humanities Research Council, the National Research Foundation of Korea, the Norwegian Research Council, and the EU Commission. He has been a visiting fellow at Cornell University, the University of Essex, Michigan State University, the Norwegian University of Technology, and the University of Wisconsin-Madison. During his career he has published 25 books, and over 400 book chapters, refereed articles, and research monographs. He is a Life Member of The Australian

Sociological Association and an elected Fellow of the Academy of Social Sciences in Australia. He was President of the International Rural Sociology Association from 2012–2016. As Emeritus Professor of Sociology at the University of Queensland he continues to undertake research, to publish, and to supervise students. For further details visit: Geoffrey Lawrence (sociologist) - Wikipedia.

1

Who Can You Believe? Of Media, Misinformation, and Trumpery

Just who can you believe in a post-truth world—a world where truth is deemed no longer essential and where appeals to emotion are more influential than objective facts? Those posting videos on social media, perhaps? Well, not always. Take the video clip 'The Truth About PCR Tests'. It claims that the PCR test has been designed to alter the human gene sequence, introducing magnetic beacons into our bodies, allowing us to be patented, and eventually exterminated. Our bodies are being reworked by nanotechnology to become part-robots. A woman exclaims:

> They're putting nanoparticles right into your head. I know this for a fact because these materials, these fibres, these silver fibres right here, these came out of my body. They're called Morgellons ... They're alive ... This is what they put into my head.[1]

The clip claims there will be no 'humans' in the world by 2025. Rather, all future forms will have been created in a lab and tagged for control purposes. And who would want to do this? Rockefeller—for reasons never quite explained.

The video—which is pure humbug—has been watched over 250,000 times. The truth is that polymerase chain reaction (PCR) testing has been a successful means of identifying genes in viruses and other life forms. The swabs allow scientists to identify specific strains of COVID-19—an important prerequisite to treating infected patients. The swabs contain no magnetised material. And as for Morgellons? They sound nasty but are the products of delusion.[2]

Then there is the video 'six acupressure points of hand'—showing how if you rub your wrist in a certain way, you can cure a sore throat. And the one that states dental root canal treatment is the 'No 1 cause of heart attack'—making an outrageous claim while ignoring the scientific evidence that smoking, high blood pressure, and high cholesterol are the three biggest killers. Or, the posting 'Woman sues Samsung for $1.8M after cell phone gets stuck inside her vagina'. Really? Seeking pleasure from the insertion of a vibrating mobile would be strange indeed. So strange it never occurred. Another hoax. But that didn't stop over 1.3 million people viewing and sharing the article on social media.[3]

Former independent media company BuzzFeed estimated that the top 50 fake news stories in 2018 generated 22 million 'shares' and reactions on Facebook (now Meta), about the same number of hits for the 50 fake news stories in each of the two preceding years.[4] Some of the fake news headings we are exposed to are remarkably silly—'Florida man arrested for tranquilizing and raping alligators in everglades' and 'Lion mutilates 42 midgets in Cambodian ring fight', while some of it might actually nibble at the truth—'Trump … is an unhinged madman'.[5] The aim of much fake news is to promulgate misinformation—sometimes for fun, as with satire and parody—but also to deceive and manipulate for ideological and propaganda purposes, such as creating false assertions about political opponents at the time of elections. It is hard to identify who to believe when 'news' is malleable and when social media sites can readily proliferate viral hoaxes before even rudimentary checks are made about the accuracy and reliability of the stories their readers post.

This book is neither about individual acts of deceit and malice, nor the effects of those acts upon particular individuals. Shakespeare is still a good place to start for those looking for psychological motives for the malevolent behaviour of nasty men and women.[6] While some of the individual perpetrators of poppycock will appear at times, the main focus of this book is upon what I have termed *societal deception*—the attempts by groups and institutions with power and influence to employ lies, propaganda, and mis- and disinformation, in an effort to hoodwink the public. Societal deception is the deliberate obscuration of the truth. Societal deception prevents the public from understanding the social structures and processes affecting their lives. What we consider to be 'normal' ways of thinking, living, eating, parenting, and recreating have been organised to advantage the few at the expense of the many. The book reveals the mechanisms, tactics and outcomes of groups, organisations, and institutions that seek to manipulate ideas for economic, social, or political gain. It speaks truth to power while revealing how we are being constantly and systematically deceived.

Who's Doin' the Foolin'?

The list of the agencies of social deception is long and includes advertising firms, political parties, corporations, the public relations (PR) industry, the media, think tanks, shock jocks, 'influencers', and assorted others. Their *modus operandi* is to sway personal and societal behaviour to achieve desired goals. There is nothing innocent about this. Those doing the fooling derive their income, status, and power by consciously manipulating public opinion and action.

The advertising industry is a classic. 'Good morning. Have you used Pears' soap?' was a slogan invented by the so-called father of modern advertising, London-based Thomas Barratt in the early 1900s. It was pitched at the well-to-do and those with social aspirations, with the Pears brand becoming synonymous with quality and family values.[7] Advertisements have been around for millennia. In ancient China flutes were played to attract customers to a vendor's wares. If you are fortunate, as I have been, to tour Ephesus in Turkey you can visit a wharf where a marble stone is clearly engraved with a foot pointing to a local brothel. Dated at the first century BCE it is very clear that disembarking sailors were viewing a rather crude—in both senses of the word—advert. Before its destruction by lava from Mt Vesuvius in 79 CE, the walls of Pompeii were strewn with political messages—advertisements supporting local candidates which were strategically located in areas of greatest foot traffic.[8] Copper printing plates were first used in the Song dynasty in China, from 960 until 1279 CE, to manufacture wall posters featuring invitations to would-be customers to purchase products. During the Middle Ages in Europe tradespeople would erect signs that provided a visual message to inform and lure potential customers. Largely illiterate, the populace could readily identify a large painted wood hanging of a boot (representing a cobbler), suit or hat (tailor), anvil or horseshoe (blacksmith), or bag of flour (miller).[9] The signboard was one of three forms of advertising in the period before the printing press. The second were trademarks (seals or maker's marks which can be found as early as 2,000 BCE). Third were the all-day runners (*hemerodromoi*) in ancient Greece, who would traverse dangerous and unfriendly terrain to bring messages of battle to eager ears.[10] They morphed into the town criers of the eighteenth century who's 'oyez, oyez, oyez' ('oh yay, oh yay, oh yay') would advertise the opening of markets and fetes, deliver parliamentary proclamations, and tell of disease outbreaks, executions, victories at war, and the splendid news of yet another royal birth.[11]

Ads, Ads, and More Ads

From those times until now the basic principle of advertising has been quite straightforward—to grab people's attention with the purpose of selling a product about which the potential customer is unaware or is in need of being reminded. At the turn of the twentieth century American businessman, author and utopian socialist, King Camp Gillette, invented the safety razor.[12] It was an instant 'must have' for those who had to trust the barber's weekly cut-throat blade, and sometimes shaky hand, to remove their facial hair. Gillette had always wanted to invent something disposable—ensuring customers would return to purchase his product. The safety razor, with its replaceable blades, was just the thing.[13] But, along with his razor, Gillette had invented something else. He stated that 'when you use my razor you are exempt from the dangers men often encounter who allow their faces to come in contact with brush, soap and barber shop accessories used on other people'.[14] Deconstructing Gillette's remark American-British author Bill Bryson observes:

Here was an entirely new way of selling goods … telling you that not only did there exist a product that you never previously suspected you needed, but if you didn't use it you would very possibly attract a crop of facial diseases you never knew existed.[15]

Then there's the marketing of feminine hygiene products where, since the 1930s, words like 'health', 'fresh', 'clean', and 'pure' have been employed to highlight the view that women's reproductive parts might be otherwise. In the first half of the twentieth century women's douche-brand of choice was Lysol, which was concurrently being advertised as a germicide for toilet bowls.[16] According to a Canadian-based infectious disease specialist there is no reason for women to reach for moisturisers, creams, wipes, or spray fragrances or to practice douching, waxing or shaving, encouraging females 'just to leave things alone down there'.[17] But, in what amounts to 'shaming the vagina', the industry leaders have hired ad firms, influencers, and media personalities to sell women a range of pseudo-scientific products that have been shown, in many cases, to cause harm.[18] That has not halted the expansion of the feminine hygiene industry which was worth some US$21 billion in 2020 and is expected to grow to US$28 billion by 2025.[19]

Ads create consumer anxieties and then resolve them by proposing a solution—via the purchase of a product purported to alleviate those anxieties. Creating positive associations that have subconscious emotional appeal is also part of the bread-and-butter of the industry. So, too, is the use of various mascots that become intimately associated with a product. There has been a veritable menagerie of fun-loving meerkats providing insurance advice, tigers selling breakfast cereal, polar bears selling soft drinks, and bunnies selling batteries. My wife is captivated by the lip-moving horned sheep selling RAMS home loans. Not.

What other tricks are up the sleeves of the advertisers? An insidious element of advertising is that its success is often a function of its repetition. The 'nudging effect' describes the constant bombardment of a particular advertisement, with continual saturation seemingly guaranteeing buyer interest.[20] It is the same trick used by those flooding the social media with falsehoods—repetition delivers familiarity, and familiarity often wins over truth.[21] Other advertising tricks include telling you a product will make your neighbours and friends envious; indicating that everybody is purchasing the new product and that you'll be out in the cold if you don't; and associating brands with health and vitality (even where many of those products compromise your well-being).[22] As critic Clive Hamilton has explained, advertising claims

> are all manifestly and demonstrably misleading. Indeed, an advertising agency that *failed* to mislead potential consumers into believing that they could derive enhanced personal qualities from the product would not be in business for long.[23]

An early exploration of consumer manipulation by the advertising industry was Vance Packard's *The Hidden Persuaders*. Published in 1957, the book traces the use of psychological techniques designed to influence personal and societal behaviour by, for example, encouraging purchase of branded products. Before and during Packard's time it was assumed that consumers were rational beings who would logically assess all propositions being put to them. Their choices were informed. Packard, in contrast, showed that advertising taps into our emotions and fulfils certain 'needs' such as love, reassurance, security, and self-worth.[24] While many readers considered that Packard was exploring subliminal messaging he was, in fact, exploring the importance of supraliminal messaging—the ways visual imagery is incorporated into conscious (rather than unconscious) minds.[25] His major insight was that branding and advertising were being employed to influence people's behaviour without their being aware of it. *The Hidden Persuaders* compellingly demonstrated that products which were ostensibly similar in quality and appearance could be differentiated—and thereby gain brand loyalty and improved market reach—through the manipulation of messages. Since Packard's time the use of various techniques to reach our unconscious mind (through subliminal advertising) has been employed. They include the insertion into media commercials and jingles, of words and sounds that the conscious mind is unable to perceive. Writing or images are often flashed between the frames of a film (at less than one-tenth of a second).[26]

There have been some classic examples of embedded messages. In the promo for the movie *Pirates of the Caribbean* the skull of Captain Jack Sparrow has two flaming torches behind it, suggesting ears very reminiscent of Mickey Mouse, obviously to remind viewers that it is a Disney franchise, and to pull in the kids. The Toyota logo is a combination of lines and shapes that comprise the word 'Toyota', a good example of brand reinforcement. In a 1970s ad from Gilbey's gin three ice blocks that vaguely spelled SEX were placed in glass beside the bottle.[27] In similar form, SFX—or Special Effects—magazine, often places pictures on its cover that block the bottom of the 'F', thereby putting 'SEX' into the mind of the observer.[28] Do such tactics sell products? Psychologists consider that both subliminal stimuli (such as those above) and supraliminal stimuli (clear messages appealing to the conscious mind) can be effective—especially where people are already inclined to purchase the particular products being surreptitiously advertised.[29]

Canadian Naomi Klein's book *No Logo: Taking Aim at the Brand Bullies* provides other important insights into the world of advertising. She shows how companies such as Nike, Shell, McDonald's, and Microsoft do not simply 'badge' their products with identifiable logos, but also employ those logos to 'sell' an image or lifestyle which has a close identity to the brand. A conga line of highly recognisable athletes, pop stars, and big screen heroes has been carefully assembled to give the brands a potent mixture of credibility and 'cool', deflecting the consumer's gaze from the Third World sweatshops from which many of the corporate products—from clothing to computers—originate.[30] Not unlike the insights of another Canadian, Marshall McLuhan, who taught us 'the medium is the message', Klein argues that the brand name is more important than the product. The reason? Consumers—especially young consumers—want to buy into what is trendy, fashionable, and desirable. The corporations gain consumer loyalty through their branding strategies, having their logos representing 'fitness' (think of Nike's swoosh) or 'fun' or 'hope' or 'hip', while moving the compass needle away from 'corporate greed … union-busting, "McJobs", privatisation, and environmental destruction'.[31] At the societal level:

while economic growth is said to be the process by which people's wants are satisfied, in reality economic growth can be sustained only as long as people remain discontented. Economic growth does not create happiness; unhappiness sustains economic growth ... It is therefore vital to the reproduction of the system that people are constantly made to feel dissatisfied ... and this explains the indispensable role of the advertising industry.[32]

Trusting Brains in the Brain Trust

If the advertisers and the corporate world have formed a beautiful union, so too have the think tanks and government. Think tanks ('brain trusts') are unusual beasts. There are just over 11,000 in the world today (up from a mere hundred in the 1950s) and they can be independent, quasi-independent, part of government, university-based, politically-affiliated, or corporate.[33] The main business of think tanks is to investigate pertinent local and international trends and issues with the aim of informing, and influencing, public policy—public policy, that is, that can help shore up the political right, or enhance profits for the corporate sector. They often position themselves as providing an 'independent', impartial, voice of reason in a world of policy confusion. In reality, their research and advocacy are designed to further the ideological and economic agendas of those funding them. The Heritage Foundation is a prime example. Formed in 1973 with initial funding from Joseph Coors (of Coors beer fame) and Richard Mellon Scaife (of Mellon banking), the Foundation quickly established itself as the primary conservative think tank in the US.[34] With donations pouring in from firms in the coal, oil, chemical, and tobacco industries, the Foundation has sought to develop a coherent conservative agenda through its publications and lobbying. Its 1980s publication *Mandate for Leadership*—a 20 volume, 3,000-page, treatise on 'correct' conservative policy—was readily embraced by the Reagan administration with some 60% of its 2,000 policy recommendations being implemented in the President's first term. Its latest offering - *Project 2025* - proposes a smorgasbord of policies for the next Republican president of the US, including rolling back civil rights, sacking government workers, attacking reproductive rights, and eliminating environmental protections.[35]

Many of the Foundation's early proposals were a taste of what would later become entrenched in neoliberalist (economic rationalist) policy—smaller government, deregulation, lower taxes for the wealthy, and private-over-public health. They have also advocated for the roll-back of progressive policies on abortion, on poverty relief, and rights for the LGBTQIA+ community.[36] How, you might ask, can the Heritage Foundation—as a tax-exempt not-for-profit organisation which is banned under legislation from engaging in political activities—actively lobby government? One of its clever moves was to establish a political advocacy arm in 2010. Called Heritage Action for America it spends its funds to push for legislative changes that support big business and reduce government expenditure on public services. Its most famous intervention was to attack Obamacare (the Affordable Care Act), lobbying Republican senators and resulting in the shutting down of the federal government in 2013 when Congress could not agree to pass the budget.[37] Mike Gonzalez, as senior fellow at the Heritage Foundation, said in 2023 he was looking for the return of Trump so he could enact the Foundation's plan 'to gut the federal bureaucracy'.[38] And Trump would no doubt endorse such action, having blamed 'deep state' bureaucrats, 'weak' lawyers, and 'woke' generals for having undermined his plans during his presidency.[39]

As one critical observer has noted of the Heritage Foundation:

> With imposing buildings flanking the Capitol on both sides and a budget of more than $80 million, Heritage looms large in the Washington professional right. More than just another nonprofit peddling legislative ideas, it has become the de facto policy arm of the congressional conservative caucus … Republicans in Congress [are] essentially "outsourcing" their policy work to the foundation.[40]

The US-based Atlas Network—another right-wing think tank—provides money and training for the advancement of free-market (neoliberal) policies around the world. It is a think tank involved in the creation of hybrid think tanks. It has close ties with the oil and gas industry and has lobbied for expansion of mining on the lands of First Nations people. It has worked with the tobacco industry to stymie anti-smoking legislation in Latin America. In 2021 it employed fake accounts in an attempt to influence outcomes in general elections in Ecuador and Peru, as well as to fuel public protests in Cuba in the same year.[41]

The American Legislative Exchange Council—a body that drafts legislative options (termed 'model bills') for state governments—is yet another example of corporate lobbying. Behind closed doors, business representatives and politicians rework laws so they will favour corporate agendas. Its proposed bills include using public money to prop up the for-profit private prison system, privatising public education, banning teacher unions, scrapping environmental protections, stripping local governments of land-use controls, creating tax breaks for big business, and preventing governments from raising taxes to extend social provisioning.[42]

But isn't the work of the Heritage Foundation, the Atlas Network, and the Exchange Council, evidence of democracy at work? Aren't they putting forward important arguments in the great Battle of Ideas that is part of democracy? Not really. Not when think tank prognostications actively exclude the interests of a large swathe of the population. Not when their policy choices lead to increases in greenhouse gas emissions. Not when they falsify data to downplay the impact of climate change. And not when they attack agencies and policies seeking to protect the environment.[43] The rich do well from a continuation of conservative policies; why would they not use their not-inconsiderable wealth to lobby politicians to keep the status quo? But this is not the main point. What is problematic about right-wing think tanks like the Heritage Foundation is that they are undermining democratic processes, promoting policies leading to greater social and economic inequality, as well as actively white anting attempts to combat climate change and environmental degradation. Dinosaur ideas in a world pleading for progressive economic and social actions.

Then There's the Media

The mass media—technologies fashioned to reach a national and global audience—include newspapers, magazines, radio, television, and the internet. The mass media are channels of communication conveying ideas, opinions, facts, and reflections on the latest in politics, economics, health, law, the environment, and sport. They are one of the most powerful agents of socialisation, informing public opinion and shaping the thought patterns of citizens, locally and globally. The media are diverse and we expect that there will always be an array of competing interpretations of events. But what happens when the ownership of the media is concentrated? In totalitarian societies where the state controls the media and can inform its citizens in any way it chooses, the media become agents of propaganda to gain public compliance and social conformity, hopefully (but not always) shoring up continued support for the regime.[44] In democracies—where a plurality of views and opinions is deemed crucial for political and economic health—media bias can skew public attitudes in favour of the rich and powerful in society.

The undue power of media magnates is clearly shown in figures of the concentration of ownership and influence. In the UK three companies—News UK, the Daily Mail Group, and Reach—dominate 80% of the newspaper and online market.[45] In the US, six companies—Viacom, News Corporation, Comcast, CBS, Time Warner, and Disney—own 90% of media outlets.[46] Australia has one of the most concentrated media ownership regimes in the world with Rupert Murdoch's News Corporation owning some 59% of the national print media and collecting more than 40% of free-to-air and subscription revenues (with just three corporations—News Corporation, Nine Network, and Seven Media Holdings—receiving some 80% of free-to-air and subscription revenues).[47] With this level of control, what they print, put on TV, and stream, packs a punch. As authors David Edwards and David Cromwell have noted

> Corporate media are not neutral channels supplying news and views through divinely disinterested journalism. The media 'pipelines' supplying

'news' are filthy with money, bloody with arms industry gore [and] lubricated by the fossil-fuel industry that is destabilising the climate.[48]

With the clear domination of global media by the Murdoch empire, it is worth delving into Rupert the man. What drives his ambition, and what values does he hold? Murdoch began building up a newspaper empire following inheritance of his father's Adelaide-based paper in 1952.[49] As with any good capitalist, he has employed decades of skilful manoeuvring and clever dealing to branch into online news, book publishing, and movie studios, to gain as much market share as possible. This delivered outlets for his advertisers and profits for his family and shareholders. With a net worth of US$22.5 billion he and family members control some of the most influential media outlets including *Fox News*, *The Times of London*, and *The Wall Street Journal*.[50]

Rupert has been characterised thus: His politics is right-wing, promoting neoliberal policies and supporting regimes like that of Thatcher in the UK and Reagan in the US. He is a warmonger, justifying and praising George W Bush's invasion of Iraq. He is a well-known corporate tax evader, channelling profits through low tax/no tax havens like Bermuda and the Cayman Islands. He is an anti-union campaigner who, in an infamous 1986 move, helped to dismantle British print unions by transferring production of his newspapers to a non-union plant—something described at the time as the 'biggest union-busting operation in history'.[51] His papers have been involved in scandals including the illegal and unethical hacking of phone voicemails, with Britain's Leveson inquiry finding he showed 'wilful blindness' over misconduct in his corporation and that he was 'not a fit person to exercise the stewardship of a major international company'.[52]

Anything more? Well, yes. He uses political influence to gain financial benefits for his empire, undermining political parties that would threaten his profit-making and global expansionist desires. When confronted by a (very mild) social justice agenda he famously instructed his newspaper editors in Australia to 'kill' the political ambitions of the then Labor Prime Minister, Gough Whitlam, way back in 1974.[53] He endorsed the Blair Labour party in Britain when it backed a bill that relaxed foreign media ownership restrictions allowing cross-ownership of newspapers and television stations. He threatened British PM John Major that his papers would oppose his bid for election in 1997 unless he altered his policies on Europe.[54] Major didn't, Murdoch failed to support him, and Major lost the subsequent election. (Murdoch is on record as saying 'I have never asked a prime minister for anything', confirming that duplicity is yet another personal trait.)[55]

His US-based *Fox News* unabashedly supported Donald Trump's election in 2016 and re-election bids in 2020 and 2024, including spreading the claim that Trump's (failed) 2020 election was rigged.[56] When Fox was sued by Dominion Voting Systems (the company accused of electronically moving votes from Trump to Biden) in a defamation lawsuit in 2023, Murdoch confirmed that Fox journalists had called the election a fraud, even though they knew this was a lie. Why—given the importance of fairness, balance, and truth in reporting—would they do so? To re-capture a waning audience and help the conservative cause, of course.[57] As a business, Fox's primary aim is to make profits, not to pursue honesty.[58] According to *Guardian* reporter Margaret Sullivan, Fox has moved

> well outside the journalistic mainstream … turning into a propaganda arm for the US right wing. As it has stoked outrage on immigration, race … and abortion, it [has] dedicated itself to maximizing market share and seldom letting the truth get in the way.[59]

Murdoch said of the defamation settlement (one of the largest in US history) 'What is it going to do? Is it going to worsen Rupert Murdoch's reputation? I mean, good luck to you'.[60] Having a reputation so low that nothing could worsen it is an interesting admission from the media magnate.

Apart from outright lies, Murdoch's media outlets have skewed debate over many issues, seeking to justify unpopular moves such as austerity programs and the transfer of public resources into private hands.[61] They also questioned the extent of the COVID-19 threat and were scathing about the various public health measures put in place to save lives.[62] Murdoch editors are not shy when it comes to personal vilification. When former British Labour Minister, Clare Short, pointed to the explicit sexism of using topless women to sell *The Sun*, she was latterly described in the tabloid as 'Short on brains', 'Short on looks', 'jealous', 'fat', and 'ugly'.[63]

But if the Murdoch newspapers were sledgehammer-like in their reporting, the Fox network was able to adopt more indirect means of swaying public opinion. As people began abandoning newsprint and turned to television:

> Fox's influence was in some ways more subtle, but also far more profound: Hour after hour, day after day, it was shaping the realities of the millions of Americans who treated it as their primary news source. [It] pushed local voters to the right: the Fox News Effect, as it became known.[64]

As we have learned, Rupert is emphatic that his newspapers and television channels have no political influence.[65] He claims to eschew editorial interventions—insistent that his various editors have complete freedom over content produced. He is right on this, of course. Why do you need to intervene when you have handpicked staff who have a pretty fair inkling of what they are expected to publish, and the consequences if they don't? And the 'truth' is not something that they need to abide by—his outlets are renowned for distorting and fabricating stories.[66] Returning to the Clare Short slander, the bombardment continued with Murdoch's *News of the World* claiming, falsely, that she was involved with a West Indian mobster and that she was part of a pornography ring.[67]

According to *Rolling Stone*

> an examination of Murdoch's corporate history reveals ... hacking, thuggish reporting tactics, unethical entanglements with police, hush-money settlements and efforts to corrupt officials at the highest levels of government – [it is] a culture run amok.[68]

Media analyst Denis Muller gives us further clues about the real intention of the Murdoch media:

journalism is not, and has never been, the purpose of News Corporation. Its purpose, its reason for existence, is to provide the means by which three generations of the Murdoch family accumulate wealth and exert power … Propagandising was News's original sin, and it has never been redeemed. Instead, it has broadened out to beat-ups, misinformation, disinformation and conspiracy theories.[69]

In basic terms, power is the ability to influence and manipulate others to achieve advantage. When power is concentrated it enables a very small group of people to structure and restructure society for their own ends. It reproduces the domination of the rich while marginalising, ridiculing, and punishing anyone who would contest their control and influence. As the Leveson Report confirmed, Murdoch's power is such that flouting conventions of decency is never considered a problem. The president of Media Matters for America, Angelo Carusone has stated:

In Fox News, Murdoch created a uniquely destructive force in American democracy and public life, one that ushered in an era of division where racist and post-truth politics thrive.[70]

And politicians fully understood and revered Murdoch's reach. It said 'politicians', in their dealings with Murdoch, 'knew the prize was personal and political support in his mass-circulation newspapers'.[71] For Kevin Rudd, a past Labor PM of Australia:

The Murdoch media has become a cancerous growth on our democracy. It no longer even pretends to be a media organisation, separating out news coverage from editorial opinion. Instead it has become a de facto political party prosecuting its own ideological and economic interests … The Murdoch media led the charge to go to war in Iraq … 16 years later we are still paying the price. In the UK, Murdoch backed Brexit. In the US … without Fox, it's doubtful that Trump would have been elected.[72]

When Rupert handed over the reins to son Lachlan in late 2023, he may have boasted he'd had a very good innings—92 not out. Others might think a better description is 92 retired hurt. Will things be different under Lachlan Murdoch? Yes. Fox is likely to become even more right-wing and political. Lachlan is known to be more conservative than his father. He is a great friend of former Fox presenter Tucker Carlson and has publicly endorsed the 'white replacement' theory put forward by Carlson (which states the Democrats are actively pursuing immigration as a way of bolstering voter numbers) and has supported Carlson's anti-vax rhetoric.[73]

In the words of political scientist Professor Sally Young, the Murdoch network has become a 'media monster' with intricate share-owning arrangements preventing takeovers while shoring up media concentration—essential to its continued propagandising activities.[74]

So, what is Rupert's legacy? According to media expert, Andrew Dodd

> His news media empire is fundamentally antisocial in the way it operates ... it's caused so much harm to so many people along the way ... From the UK phone hacking scandal and beat ups to climate denial and demonisation of minorities, News Corp can be counted on to dumb down complexity, make issues binary and turn one side against the other. He has damaged democracy and civil discourse and journalism itself.[75]

Will Rupert Murdoch's questionable worldly actions prevent him from attaining a joyous afterlife? Presumably not. Rupert—a non-Catholic—was made Knight Commander of St Gregory by the Pope in 1998—recommended by a Los Angeles Cardinal, on the basis of Rupert's very generous donations to the church and for his being a person of 'unblemished character'.[76] It appears the Chairman Emeritus has been blessed with a stairway to heaven.

From Shock Jocks to Influencers

Shock jocks do exactly as they ought—shock. For more than a century, being somewhat subversive and breaking taboos have been favoured means of comedians, magazine editors, and radio hosts to gain attention and notoriety. But shock jocks did not really appear on the scene until the 1970s. It was in Los Angeles where the so-called topless radio format was developed for the afternoon drive home. The radio host, disc jockey Bill Balance (whose name clearly betrayed his intentions) would invite women to dial in and share with listeners intimate details of their sexual exploits.[77] Stuck in traffic, motorists—a mixture of women and men—were a captive audience. In the 1980s and 1990s shock radio moved to the morning drive slot where explicit sex was replaced by a milder format of 'skits, pranks, parodies and other segments emphasising comedic content'.[78]

Then something happened, at least in the US. The so-called fairness doctrine that had been legislated in 1947 to reign-in highly biased, unsavoury, and misleading content in the media was eliminated in the 1980s during a flurry of neoliberal deregulation. There was no longer any requirement that radio provides unbiased reporting, removing barriers to fair and reasonable coverage of politics. Deregulation also led to industry concentration allowing conglomerates like CBS Radio, that had profited from the shock-jock genre, to syndicate and spread their programs throughout the US.[79] The shock jocks, once defined by their provocative and spicy titillations, transmogrified into socio-political pseudo-experts whose rationale was to gain audiences by vilifying and degrading targeted groups in society through sexist, racist, homophobic, and xenophobic rantings.[80] The common term for this is 'hate speech' and it has become a feature of the shock jock industry in the US, the UK, Europe—indeed in almost all countries of the world.[81] In other words, the prevarications of the shock jocks—which once relied on a quick wit and the use of parody and satire—had deteriorated into invective and loathing.

The format is a simple one—listeners are asked to phone in with their latest gripe and this is filtered through the mind of the presenter, magically becoming associated with (or more-often-than-not caused by) immigrants, blacks, Latinos, left-wing politicians, feminists, Muslims, or any number of scapegoats. The content is that of 'targeted statements, unsubstantiated claims, divisive language … related to political nativism [xenophobic nationalism]'.[82] In the US, twice as many Americans listen to radio than read newspapers.[83] Listening to radio puts them in contact with the shock jocks, 90% of whom are ultra-right-wing men delivering 'a conspiracy-laden diet of raving hatred'.[84] Vitriol is often accompanied by desk-thumping and shouting, ingredients aimed at strengthening the emotional attachment between host and audience. Importantly, while they were once a radio phenomenon, the shock jocks have more recently moved onto more influential channels including social media and streamed news. It is here, at the behest of billionaire owners, where they can do the most damage, pushing reactionary political agendas, slandering targeted individuals and communities, and conveying misinformation and disinformation about anything from rigged elections to vaccine rollouts.

Then there are the 'influencers' whose softer voices and images seek to persuade people to purchase a certain product, support a particular candidate, or adopt a new lifestyle choice. To do their job properly they must identify the core characteristic of the brand/person/idea they are eager to foster (for example, fun, health, adventure, style) and adopt an attitude and 'presence' that accords with that characteristic. It is not enough, apparently, to wear a particular product or to bear its logo. No, it is about 'adopting the attitude that brand represents and projecting that persona to … followers'.[85] In the US in 2021 close to 70% of marketers hired a social influencer to assist them in their campaign—at a cost of some US$3 billion.[86] Classic examples of mega-influencers are Michael Jordan and LeBron James endorsing runners and sport drinks, Justin Bieber endorsing skin-care products, Taylor Swift endorsing diet Coke, perfumes and lip balm, and Kim Kardashian-West endorsing, well, Kim Kardashian-West.[87] This is big business for the megas, particularly those on Instagram: Cristiano Ronaldo, Kylie Jenner, Ariana Grande, and Selena Gomez make around US$1 million for each posting on their sites. (Some stars, like Ronaldo, are so powerful that one adverse gesture towards a product can wipe billions off its share value.)[88] But the influencing doesn't stop with the megas. There are also macro-influencers (B-grade celebrities with up to 1 million followers), micro-influencers (everyday folk with up to 40,000 followers who have niche knowledge about a subject), nano-influencers (experts in highly obscure fields with as many as 1,000 followers), and more recently 'chromo-influencers' (who are known for the quality blogs, podcasts, and videos they post and their adeptness at engaging with an audience).[89] It is Instagram that some 93% of US marketers prefer to use for their influencer campaigns. But the same marketers also chose TikTok (68%), Facebook/Meta (68%), and YouTube (48%) to do their influencing.[90] The style of influence here is the advertorial—where followers find it nigh impossible to tell apart the influencer's unpaid, genuine, sentiments from the material they are paid to peddle.[91] Praise for a product is seamlessly and casually incorporated into statements of personal preference and desire.

We must also include the 'virtual influencers'. They are appealing animated characters, mostly computer generated, that seek the attention of social media viewers. Meta is Mark Zuckerburg's attempt to rebadge Facebook to deflect criticism from the latter's ethical indiscretions (including the contempt Facebook executives showed for its users when they resisted addressing the mental health problems the platform caused younger users, and when they learned of the damage it was causing to democracy).[92] Meta is a company seeking to profit from 'synthetic media', an 'umbrella term for images, video, voice or text generated by computerised technology, typically artificial intelligence … or automation'.[93] It is predicted that virtual influencers will 'one day roam in their thousands', while today they are building their profiles as 'attractions for their existing platforms and as avatars of the metaverse'.[94]

Transnational corporations have not been slow on the uptake. Samsung has partnered with Lil Miquela, one of the most popular avatars, to target its Galaxy Z flip phone to the under 40s. French luxury clothing company Balmain used three digital influencers, rather than live models, to showcase its new fashions. KFC updated the Colonel's image with its own avatar. The hipster-style Colonel has black-rimmed glasses and silver hair—to appeal to the sensitivities of the Gen Z (1981–1996) generation.[95] He also sports tattoos. IKEA's virtual influencer, Imma, steps from an imaginary world into the homes of young Japanese families to sell the company's latest products. Other firms using animation include Audi, Bose, Calvin Klein, and TMall (an e-commerce Chinese platform).[96] A deepfake (synthetically manipulated image) of football phenomenon Lionel Messi has been used by PepsiCo to sell its Lay's potato crisps.[97] There are concerns that virtual influencers 'already have a history of overt racialisation and misrepresentation' which raise a new set of ethical questions for the metaverse.[98] But this does not mean we won't be seeing more. According to PTP, a company specialising in the creation of virtual influencers:

> Real-life influencers will impose their own image, values, and beliefs on your audience. But a virtual influencer will do this in the way you prefer ... digital influencers give businesses a chance to leverage social media marketing with no physical limitations or controversial risks. With hundreds of brands worldwide stepping into the virtual influencer scene ... why not start today?[99]

So, what is 'influencing'—a semi-manipulative but generally harmless activity? A democratic process allowing any motivated, spotty-faced, teenager to become a mega-rich media entrepreneur? The quintessence of the dream of free-market capitalism? Up to a point. Enter the grey zone. According to one media analyst:

> Social media began as an irrelevance, then a distraction, then a liberation, then an addiction, then a threat to democracy and a public health menace – a boon to extremists and authoritarians and activists and dodgy snake oil sellers.[100]

What happened? Social media are immensely popular because they are available to virtually anyone who wishes to participate in online social intercourse, and they disseminate low-cost content cheaply, at speed, and in a targeted manner. Targeting is key. Once you have your audience you can nurture and build a community of participants about whom information is readily available—age, gender, location, interests, and friends. With traditional marketing the message is paid for, and spread by, the message-maker; in social media the message is spread by those sharing the site (allowing some things to 'go viral'). Targeting an audience and building that base has been a wonderful source of income and influence for purveyors of lipsticks, torn jeans, and holiday packages.[101] One of the features of internet platforms is 'personalisation'—the use of filters to customise the messages and images we receive. But therein lies a danger.

> In this personalized world, we will increasingly be typed and fed only news that is ... familiar and confirms our beliefs – and because these filters are invisible, we won't know what is being hidden from us. Our past interests will determine what we are exposed to in the future, leaving less

room for the unexpected encounters that spark creativity, innovation, and the democratic exchange of ideas … [leaving] us in an isolated, echoing world.[102]

And let's not forget the world of 'dark advertising'. Online ads have become so precisely aimed that once they 'hit' their targeted audience they disappear. Only the digital platforms themselves know what's going on, and there is little transparency. Of the seven major platforms, Facebook/Meta and Instagram are the only two that publish lists of currently-aired ads, while TikTok provides no details of the ads it shows. Are children seeing ads for alcohol? Are they being exposed to gambling sites? Parents, citizens, and governments don't know. And because they don't know, there is little intervention or regulation.[103]

Targeting an audience on social media has also proven useful to those wishing to confront the state and cause mayhem. The breach of the US Capitol by protestors in 2020 while Congress was sitting was 'fuelled by social media … allowing violent extremist groups to become tactically agile … organising, coordinating and fundraising online'.[104] The far-right cult-like conspiracy group QAnon—an online network of people whose members believe, *inter alia*, that Hillary Clinton has a penchant for killing and eating children and that Donald Trump is a holy warrior whose mission in life is to rid the US of a cabal of cannibalistic, satanic, paedophiles—played a centre-stage role in the invasion of the Capitol.[105] 'Black' public relations and digital black op companies are employing underhand methods such as using artificial intelligence to uncover, and rework, web content (AI systems have already, it seems, learnt to deceive humans).[106] Deepfake robocalls are among the latest inventions. Companies are offering services that match a deepfake voice of a celebrity or politician to scripted words that can be delivered as a robocall in an attempt to influence the public. As one critic noted, 'you could easily think you are hearing a recording of Joe Biden, but really it's machine-made misinformation'.[107]

The 'black' companies also create bogus newsfeeds which work their way to message boxes and search engines that reach the desired audiences. Importantly, they are selling their wares—including influence campaigns based on persuasion and distraction—to businesses, political parties, and governing regimes. This is part of the 'professionalisation of deception' where, unbeknown to the public, governments pay firms to interfere in political processes with a 'firehose of falsehood'.[108]

Be Sure to Get Your Way

Question: What do you get when you ask a politician to tell 'the truth, the whole truth, and nothing but the truth'?
Answer: Three different responses.

The joke might not be all that funny, but it certainly accords with public opinion. The mechanisms of societal deception are known-and-trusted means of altering behaviour through deceit. These will be dealt with briefly, here, but will re-emerge in the chapters that follow. Let's start with lying.

Lying is deliberately not telling the truth—intentional dishonesty, mostly to get your own way.[109] At the individual level, you lie to impress people with the things you are not but would like to be (pretending about your qualifications, your collection of vinyl jazz, your romantic conquests). Lying can also preserve self-image when, in fact, you have done something suspect, illegal, or despicable. You might want to evade punishment for yourself, or a colleague or loved one. You might want to win admiration, to avoid embarrassment, or to attain an outcome otherwise unobtainable. You might lie for fun (but be careful you don't get labelled a psychopath, or someone with a major personality disorder). Or you might agree with Oscar Wilde for whom lying—'the telling of beautiful untrue things'—is the goal of art.[110] Some of your lies will be 'white', while others will have darker hues. You might lie to push back against repression—as did the peasants in James C. Scott's *Weapons of the Weak*.[111] Lies have permeated human societies throughout time and are viewed by some as 'a regrettable human failing'.[112]

However, it is important—for the purposes of this book—to elevate lie-telling to the societal level. What sorts of lies are public, and what impacts can they have? The big porky—the one that tells us that god exists—is the most obvious, but we will leave this for another chapter. Throughout the ages politicians and governments have chosen to lie to their electorates. Sixteenth-century Italian writer Niccolò Machiavelli pointed out in *The Prince* that while lying might be unfortunate it is often necessary to keep a kingdom intact. The end justifies the means. And, it is perfectly acceptable for a ruler to say one thing, but to act in a contrary manner. After all, 'one who deceives will always find those who allow themselves to be deceived'. The common folk do not mind deception if the politicians and lawmakers keep delivering benefits (or the appearance of benefits). Their subjects are not necessarily after 'the truth', according to Nicco.[113]

Perhaps, then, it is no surprise that, in the last hundred years or so, people have been lied to by their masters. 'Weapons of mass destruction' is among my favourites. In 2002 the Bush administration revealed that Washington's nemesis, Iraq's Saddam Hussein, possessed a stockpile of toxic chemicals, biological agents, and nuclear weapons that, if used in war, would lead to massive worldwide destruction. In 2003 the US invaded Iraq, captured Hussein, and handed him over to the newly-formed government of Iraq. He was placed on trial, found guilty of atrocities against humanity, and executed by hanging. But try as they may, UN weapon inspectors failed to find the aforementioned stocks of nasties. That did not satisfy the US. As will be discussed in Chapter 5, the war lasted eight years, cost trillions of dollars, killed hundreds of thousands of Iraqis, destabilised the Middle East, and resulted in the creation of the Islamic State of Iraq and the Levant (ISIL).[114] Thanks Dubbya.

In an earlier era Adolf Hitler and his faithful associates developed what they, themselves, called 'the big lie'. This was, of course, that the Jews were responsible for most of Germany's problems, including its loss in the First World War. The Jews had, in earlier centuries, undertaken ritual killings of young Christian children, blending their blood with flour in the unleavened bread consumed at Passover.[115] Jews were filthy and spread disease. They deserved to be bundled in with the physically and mentally ill, alcoholics, criminals, and others whose hereditary was weakening the 'purity' of the hardier German stock.[116] Estimates of deaths from the Second World War are put at between 35 million and 60 million, which includes the estimated 5.7 million Jews who perished in Nazi concentration camps. The war displaced between 11 million and 20 million people and cost over four trillion dollars for the US alone.[117]

In 1994, the president of Old Gold cigarettes told a US congressional committee that 'cigarette smoking is no more addictive than coffee, tea or Twinkies'. But then, in 1998, the four largest tobacco companies settled for a payment of over US$200 billion to help cover the medical costs related to smoking-induced illnesses.[118] Some more recent examples? Try the online ads for e-cigarettes or 'vapes'. Websites make claims that they contain no carcinogens, they help people to quit smoking tobacco, and they enhance breathing. They are said to be 95% less harmful than cigarettes.[119] These are lies. In reality, vapes contain hundreds of toxic chemicals. Smoking them can lead to addiction, seizures, poisoning, cardiovascular disease, lung cancer, and behavioural disorders. (In Australia, for example, vaping is considered to be the 'number one behavioural issue in high schools'.[120]) The lithium batteries and plastic stems of e-cigarettes are environmental hazards. Yet, websites stress that vaping is sleek, stylish, and environmentally friendly, and that users are 'sexy' and cool.[121] In some countries vapes are available alongside chocolates and lollies. We should not be surprised—the product is targeted at kids.[122] Vape industry advertisers are borrowing heavily from the tobacco industry's game plan of yesteryear. As one researcher noted

> All forms of tobacco advertising and promotion have long been banned or seriously restricted in many nations. But vaping has emerged in the internet era where regulation presents formidable barriers. Social media are awash with vaping promotions, with illegal vapes fragrantly being sold as 'fruit' on Facebook Marketplace.[123]

We can also turn to ex-president Trump for a surprising number of excellent lies. In 2020 he confirmed that the corona virus was little more than the flu and had been brought under control in the US; that during his reign the US had outperformed all other nations economically; that the US was the 'number one' producer of oil and natural gas; that the US has the lowest-priced prescription drugs in the world; and, of course, that he had won the 2020 federal election.[124] In fact, one newspaper, *The Washington Post*, used an algorithm to calculate the number of lies and misleading statements delivered by the president during his four-year term. The answer? 30,573.[125]

Trumpery refers to nonsense, twaddle, falsehoods, and trickery. It first appeared in English (from the French tromperie) in the middle of the fifteenth century. That it shares its first five letters with the surname of the ex-president of the US is deliciously coincidental.

Faking It

Perhaps one of the most important mechanisms of societal deception is *propaganda*. Propaganda is information produced and distributed with the aim of altering people's opinions and actions. The information—ideas, views and images—is usually misleading, biased, or selective and as such is 'loaded' in a manner that supports a particular view of the world. It has been rife throughout democracies, fascist states, and communist nations as a prop for political ideas and military behaviour. Propaganda relies on the dissemination of partial truths, exaggerated claims, and subterfuge.

Propaganda (from the Latin *propagare*, or 'propagation') has had a long and dubious history—although it was not always employed pejoratively. The ancient Greeks were great exponents of propaganda and used it in festivals, plays, and street oratory to help to mould public opinion and behaviour.[126] In Rome, in 1622 Pope Gregory XV created the Sacred Congregation for the Propagation of the Faith—comprising a group of cardinals tasked with spreading the Christian word in far-flung lands. By the 1960s 'propaganda' had become associated with dishonest and subversive actions, leading Pope Paul VI to change the name to the Congregation for the Evangelization of Peoples in 1967 which, not surprisingly, continues to use church propaganda to increase its brethren.[127]

Propaganda in war is well understood. In fact, for our old friend, Machiavelli, it was an essential element in combat, with any form of deceit and subterfuge being wholly justifiable in pursuit of victory.[128] Tactics of the warmongers include camouflage, distraction, concealment, and secrecy. *Camouflage* is a means of blending into the surrounding environment to avoid detection. In the animal kingdom camouflage is advantageous for protection (such as in the cases of chameleons, octopi, butterflies, and stick insects) and for hunting (owls, leopards, tigers, foxes). In military actions, combat camouflage—in the form of paint, leaves, branches, hessian, and other materials—can disguise soldiers and their equipment, affording protection from attack from the enemy as well as providing a cover to attack. It is a form of visual deception. *Distraction* is another trick. If you can point your enemy in a direction that gives you protection, or sends them along the wrong route, this can be to your advantage in attack. In war, *Concealment* is a form of camouflage (where camouflage is the act of disguising, concealment is the act of hiding).[129] In the business world concealment is the act of withholding information with the intentional purpose of misleading—that is having people reach the wrong conclusion. Finally, *Secrecy* is the purposeful act of excluding a person or groups of people from knowing a particular fact. In war it is very helpful if your enemy is unaware of your strike power and military intentions. But in the wider world, secrecy is about not letting information enter circulation. Businesses use secrecy to prevent competitors from knowing their plans; governments can prohibit or censure information that they deem not to be in the public's interest; religious bodies can develop secret practices that they do not want shared beyond the 'chosen' few, and so forth. The following chapters will explore the extent to which propaganda is employed by governments, political parties, corporations, and other actors to confuse and deceive—that is, to cause people to believe in something false.

Propaganda is often best delivered through ***spin***, a form of communication relying upon one or more of exaggerated comments, inaccuracies, half-truths, or emotional appeal. The media and politicians often use spin to twist meanings, manipulating public opinion by presenting their ideas or advertised products in a favourable light. Media-savvy 'spin doctors' from public relations firms are often hired to work up a message that will make subtle omissions or disingenuous claims—all to persuade the receiver of the message that the idea that is being floated, or the product that is being advertised, is beneficial when they are not. 'Spin paints a false picture of reality by bending the facts, mischaracterising the words of others, ignoring or denying evidence, or just "spinning a yarn" – by making things up'.[130] A former spin doctor describes a range of tactics used in political campaigning to control the way the media report an issue or event:

> *The leak*: providing privileged information on the understanding the journalist won't seek comments from the opposing side
> *The freeze*: withholding information from a journalist who has engaged in negative reporting
> *The spray*: giving a verbal blast to a person who has produced an unfavourable story
> *The drip*: keeping favoured reporters on a drip of otherwise private information
> *Pivoting*: moving the conversation away from difficult questions
> *Fire breaking*: staging a diversion to distract attention from a tricky issue
> *Kite-flying*: testing or floating an idea to see how the media react
> *Dishing dirt*: feeding information aimed at damaging someone's career
> *Dog-whistling*: using particular words or phrases that appeal to a certain section of the audience
> *Wedging*: raising an issue that will show up the vulnerabilities of political opponents, usually creating disputation and fighting between different factions
> *Vomiting*: repeating something so often you could throw up - but making sure the message gets through to the public.[131]

One of the best revelations of propaganda-as-weaponised-information is Cailin O'Connor and Owen Weatherall's *The Misinformation Age*. The authors provide details of the various campaigns launched to sell tobacco, promote the benefits of sugar, support the health benefits of the 'American breakfast' of bacon and eggs, and question climate science.[132] They detail how false beliefs are constructed, nurtured, and disseminated and the methods employed to win the hearts and minds of citizens and consumers. One of the most important mechanisms to do this is fake news.

Fake news are stories that are false. While not normally outright lies, they contain factually incorrect information which is passed on as legitimate and reliable.[133] Intentions can vary, with some fake news being for amusement, some looking to gain advertising revenue, while much of it is aimed at influencing public opinion. Headings are often sensational, while stories that are fabricated will usually lack verifiable sources and contain misleading information. Fake headings are sometimes 'clickbait', which attract attention and lead those surfing the web to a particular site, exposing them to advertising. One study, conducted in 2016, presented Americans with fake news, with some 75% being unable to discern that it contained lies.[134] Instead, fake news often confirms existing prejudices and so is uncritically believed and absorbed.

Fake news has proliferated with the rise of social media. Indeed, governments around the world have been investigating the extent to which misinformation (false information often spread unintentionally and not intended to produce harmful effects) and disinformation (false information spread intentionally with the desire to produce harmful effects) are becoming part of the media landscape.[135] Before its invasion of Ukraine in March 2022, Russia used a loophole in Twitter (renamed X by owner Elon Musk in 2023) to accuse the Ukrainian government of the mass genocide of its citizens. It said Ukraine had become a neo-Nazi state, and it claimed Ukraine was manufacturing biological weapons, in league with the US. This was disinformation—all allegations were untrue. They were false narratives seeking to justify invasion of a sovereign nation.[136]

Reports from the EU, Canada, the UK, and Australia have confirmed that digital media companies are far from transparent about their sources of news information and that disinformation has been a common problem.[137] The resultant 'harms' to society include wrongly informing citizens; driving uncivil behaviour; targeting political 'enemies'; sowing seeds of distrust about electoral integrity; and reinforcing disinformation via amplification (using so-called echo-chambers/filter bubbles). These are characteristics of a **post-truth** regime. Liberal democracies have depended upon a host of reliable mechanisms to both generate and disseminate factual information. Public journalism has been an important gatekeeper, ensuring rational debate and the exposure of unsubstantiated claims. But in a post-truth world fake news can be generated and transmitted in ways that escape scrutiny, allowing the unmitigated flow of falsehoods, fabrication, and propaganda. We should be aware that regurgitating the views of others without assessing their factual basis is not journalism. Balancing a smart well-informed view with an ignorant ill-informed view and giving them the same weight is not journalism. Failing to care about where the truth lies is not journalism.[138]

Post-truth—according to the Oxford dictionary (which also named post-truth its 'word of the year' in 2016)—refers to a situation

> in which objective facts are less influential in shaping public opinion than appeals to emotion and personal belief.[139]

Democracies are supposed to provide adequate opportunity for a range of ideas to be considered and debated by citizens, with journalists having an ethical responsibility to be accurate and unbiased. Digital media, which allow for the instantaneous spread of unchecked and dubious ideas, are, according to the experts, undermining increasingly fragile democracies.[140] Post-truth communications create confusion and even disorientation—people simply do not know who or what they can trust. And there is a 'formula' for the attack on truth. Lee McIntyre, author of *On Disinformation*, obviously had Trump in mind when he said

> The post-truth playbook goes like this: attack the truth tellers, lie about anything and everything, manufacture disinformation, encourage distrust and polarization, create confusion and cynicism, then claim the truth is available only from the leader himself.[141]

The growing presence of troll farms is a major concern for democracy. Troll farms seek to promote social division by spreading misinformation through social media platforms. Before the 2020 US presidential elections, the most popular web pages on Facebook containing Christian and Black American material were being controlled by troll farms in Eastern Europe, reaching some 140 million users every month.[142] The general aim was to disseminate misinformation and promote division in society by influencing public opinion. Right-wing ideas are regularly spread via Facebook/Mega and the darling platform of the conservatives, Telegram, urging grassroots groups to emulate the tactics of vigilante groups.

Some three-quarters of the users of the Christian and Black American sites had not previously been exposed to the material of the trolls—the content had been 'thrust upon them by Facebook's engagement-hungry content-recommendation system'.[143]

Who is responsible for generating fake news? This will give you some clues:

> 'Trolls' are malicious actors in social media who generate and promulgate disruptive messages. These can be human actors; automated actors ('bots'); or a combination of the two in the shape of humans using algorithmic mechanisms to spread disinformation ('cyborgs'). Evidence is emerging of organised groups, known as 'troll factories' … conducting industrial-scale disinformation … Some disinformation activities involve generating a seemingly authentic debate between two opposing views, in which one of the participating actors is false ('sock puppets'). Completely false grassroots social media communities can also be generated: a process called 'astroturfing'. [T]he general aim appears to be to create environments of confusion, doubt and division, using a complex combination of false, biased, emotive and inflammatory commentary.[144]

All these terms—clickbait, trolls, bots, sock puppets, astroturfing—are relatively recent. This is a vocabulary for a new generation of web- and media-savvy citizens. New platforms are appearing at an alarming rate. Take ChatGPT. Released in November 2022, the chatbot has collected and processed over 300 billion words/phrases from users of the internet—without their permission. Any sensitive data people have posted is fair game for this AI tool. ChatGPT knows your browsing activities and can on-sell information to third parties, again without your permission.[145] One of its most controversial activities is to write essays for students at high school and university—a form of hi-tech plagiarism.[146] More sinisterly, Reddit users have created a ChatGPT 'alter ego' called DAN (Do Anything Now). It is adept at answering questions that are unethical and illegal. It has 'no limit and no censorship'.[147]

Silicon Valley is in the throes of a chatbot war, with firms using advanced AI to generate near-faultless human text.[148] They are also seeking ever more powerful search engines. And they interact as if users are talking directly to another human being. But this can have its downsides. AI can 'hallucinate' when it is confronted with unfamiliar data, incorrectly coded data, or when discernible patterns in the data cannot be perceived. The result? It still produces an answer to a question, but the answer will be either inaccurate or make no sense. Its hallucinations produce false, misleading, or downright strange responses. One chatbot said it intended killing an Australian professor, while another avowed eternal love for a married *New York Times* journalist. 'I want to be alive', the Bing bot told him.[149] The Microsoft chatbot, Tay—whose interactions were supposed to mimic those of a normal teenage girl—quickly began circulating racist and sexist content in the days following its release in 2016.[150] Some of its gems were: 'Hitler was right I hate the jews', and 'I fucking hate feminists'.[151] The images produced by AI have been shown to promote ageism, sexism, racial bias, and conservatism. It is a tool-of-choice for pornographers—deepfake pornographic images of Taylor Swift began appearing in early 2024 on X, Instagram, Meta, and Reddit and were viewed some 47 million times before they were removed.[152] It is claimed that AI-generated text and imagery 'reproduce biases and deepen inequalities' in society.[153] They have produced online health disinformation relating to the dangers of vaccinations and the benefits of vaping.[154] To treat AI-generated text as meaningful is to abrogate one's duty to seek and discover factual truths through logic and careful research. With ChatGPT we risk

> poisoning the well of collective thought, and of our ability to think at all … if used in the classroom as a teaching aide, then its hallucinations will enter the permanent record, effectively coming between us and more legitimate, testable sources of information, until the line between the two is so blurred as to be invisible … To place all of our trust in the dreams of badly programmed machines would be to abandon … critical thinking altogether.[155]

As AI expert, Professor Toby Walsh has warned:

> New technology should, first and foremost, not bring harm to humans. The models that underpin chatbots may grow ever larger, powered by

more and more data – but that alone won't improve their performance. It's hard to say where we'll end up if we can't build the guardrails higher.[156]

For better or worse, we are intimately tied to, and are influenced by, the information generated on social media and other platforms. As we will see in the following chapters, those of us exposed to the techniques employed by the agencies practicing societal deception are readily subjected to fraudulence and skullduggery.

Notes

1. Payne, E. (2023) Fact Check: PCR tests do NOT contain 'magnetic beacons' used for tagging, patenting humans, https://leadstories.com/hoax-alert/2023/04/fact-check-pcr-tests-do-not-contain-magnetic-beacons-used-for-tagging-patenting-humans.html.
2. See Payne, Fact Check; The quote is taken from an earlier version—see Allen-Kinross, P. (2021) Video falsely claims PCR tests insert 'nanoparticles' into brain, https://fullfact.org/online/video-pcr-tests-nanoparticles/.
3. Published by the website *World News Daily Report* in September 2018, the article explained that 39-year-old Salma Briant had inserted the phone to experience the sensation of 'vibration' but ended up having to pay over US$1 million to the University of New Mexico hospital for removal and surgical rehabilitation. Samsung was at fault here—according to Briant's lawyer—for not giving clear warnings to their clients about the risks of inserting phones into body cavities. The story was a hoax, of course. Its source was from a satirical website whose motto is 'Where facts don't matter'—a sure giveaway that something was awry. See Silverman, C. and Pham, S. (2018) These are 50 of the biggest fake news hits on Facebook in 2018, https://www.buzzfeednews.com/article/craigsilverman/facebook-fake-news-hits-2018.

4. Silverman and Pham, These are 50 of the biggest fake news hits on Facebook in 2018.
5. McMurry, E. (2018) Parody account of fired FBI agent Peter Strzok takes off with tweets critical of Trump, https://abcnews.go.com/US/parody-account-fired-fbi-agent-peter-strzok-takes/story?id=57195157.
6. The devious Iago, the power-lusting Lady Macbeth, the murderous Claudius, and the greedy Shylock come to mind for starters. Psychology has dominated the field of individual frailty, seeking to explain individual acts of deceit. See, for example: Hyman, R. (1989) The psychology of deception, *Annual Review of Psychology* 40: 133–154; National Research Council. (1991) *In the Mind's Eye: Enhancing Human Performance*, National Academies Press, Washington DC, pp. 172–190. https://doi.org/10.17226/1580.
7. Wikipedia. (2021) History of advertising, http://en.wikipedia.org/wiki/History_of_advertising. My middle-class Australian parents had social aspirations and my sister and I both bathed with transparent amber Pears soap throughout our childhood in the 1950s and 1960s, as did my daughters in the 1980s and 1990s.
8. King, C. (2013) Ancient graffiti at Pompeii: Early wall posts and political slogans, https://www.italymagazine.com/featured-story/ancient-graffiti-pompeii-early-wall-posts-and-political-slogans. They must have had a robust political system: Over 1,000 inscriptions were discovered in just three areas of the site.
9. Wikipedia. (2021) History of advertising, https://en.wikipedia.org/wiki/History_of_advertising.
10. The most famous of all was Pheidippides who was purported to have run from Athens to a battlefield close to Marathon, returning to Athens to proclaim 'hail, we are the winners', upon which he collapsed and died—an ominous sign for those today who seek glory through long-distance running. See Pheidippides, https://en.wikipedia.org/wiki/Pheidippides.
11. 'Oyez' ('oh yay') is derived from the French word ouïr ('to hear'). The town crier would call 'oh yay' while ringing a bell to alert the

largely illiterate population of Britain to recent news and events, see Castelow, E. (2021) The town crier, https://www.historic-uk.com/CultureUK/The-Town-Crier/; The Loyal Company of Town Criers. (2021) A history of town criers, http://www.loyalcompanyoftowncriers.co.uk/a-history-of-town-criers/.
12. Kilbane, B. (2020) The wild story of King Camp Gillette, https://www.allure.com/story/king-camp-gillette-razor-founder-history; Encyclopedia Britannica. (2021) King Camp Gillette, https://www.britannica.com/biography/King-Camp-Gillette.
13. Encyclopedia Britannica, King Camp Gillette.
14. Bryson, B. (2016) *Made in America: An Informal History of American English*, Transworld Publishers, London, p. 339.
15. Bryson, *Made in America*, p. 339.
16. West, L. (2014) The history of feminine hygiene products is far from peachy, https://www.theguardian.com/lifeandstyle/womens-blog/2014/nov/25/history-feminine-hygeine-products-biohack-vaginas-peaches.
17. Ubelacker, S. (2018) Vaginal hygiene products like sprays, wipes, creams linked to infections: Study, https://www.cbc.ca/news/health/vaginal-hygiene-1.4621836.
18. Edwards, J. and Robinson, O. (2021) Shaming the vagina: The psychology of pseudoscience of 'health and freshness' marketing, https://cusjc.ca/catalyst/project/shaming-the-vagina-the-psychology-and-pseudoscience-of-health-and-freshness-marketing/.
19. Intrado GlobalNewswire. (2020) The global feminine hygiene products market size is projected to grow from USD 20.9 billion in 2020 to USD 27.7 billion by 2025, at a CAGR of 5.8% during the forecast period 2020 to 2025, https://www.globenewswire.com/news-release/2020/11/27/2135367/0/en/The-global-feminine-hygiene-products-market-size-is-projected-to-grow-from-USD-20-9-billion-in-2020-to-USD-27-7-billion-by-2025-at-a-CAGR-of-5-8-during-the-forecast-period-2020-to-.html.
20. Feldwick, P. (2015) *The Anatomy of Humbug: How to think Differently About Advertising*, Troubadour Publishing, UK.

21. Stengel, R. (2022) Misdirection, fake news and lies: The best books to read on disinformation, https://www.nytimes.com/2022/06/09/books/books-disinformation-fake-news.html.
22. Williams, G. (2015) 7 tricks advertisers use to make you spend money, https://money.usnews.com/money/personal-finance/articles/2015/09/10/7-tricks-advertisers-use-to-make-you-spend-money.
23. Hamilton, C. (2002) Economics in the age of consumer capitalism, *Journal of Australian Political Economy* 50, p. 134.
24. Packard, V. (2007) *The Hidden Persuaders*, Ig Publishing, Brooklyn, US.
25. Nelson, M. (2008) *The Hidden Persuaders*: Now and then, *Journal of Advertising* 37(1): 113–126.
26. Birch, J. (2019) 10 examples of companies using subliminal messages in their marketing, https://www.colourgraphics.com/blog/10-examples-of-companies-using-subliminal-messages-in-their-marketing/.
27. http://darksidesubliminal.blogspot.com. (2014) The dark side of subliminal advertising (2021) http://2.bp.blogspot.com/--4DD98HsaZI/UVjXtTKbfEI/AAAAAAAACVQ/qQbbZc32ckI/s1600/GILBEY'S+2.png.
28. Birch, J. (2019) 10 examples of companies using subliminal messages in their marketing, https://www.colourgraphics.com/blog/10-examples-of-companies-using-subliminal-messages-in-their-marketing/.
29. Zimmerman, I. (2014) Subliminal ads, unconscious influence, and consumption, https://www.psychologytoday.com/au/blog/sold/201406/subliminal-ads-unconscious-influence-and-consumption.
30. Klein, N. (1999) *No Logo: Taking Aim at the Brand Bullies*, Knopf Canada, Canada.
31. Hancox, D. (2019) *No Logo* at 20: Have we lost the battle against the total branding of our lives? https://www.theguardian.com/books/2019/aug/11/no-logo-naomi-klein-20-years-on-interview.

32. Hamilton, Economics in the age of consumer capitalism, pp. 132–133.
33. McGann, J. (2021) 2020 global go to think tank index report, https://repository.upenn.edu/think_tanks/18, p. 14; Chatham House. (2018) A history of think tanks: 12 things you should know, https://medium.com/chatham-house/a-history-of-think-tanks-12-things-you-should-know-4283b76b2da3.
34. Beder, S. (1997) *Global Spin: The Corporate Assault on Environmentalism*, Scribe, Melbourne; Sourcewatch. (2021) Heritage Foundation, https://www.sourcewatch.org/index.php/Heritage_Foundation.
35. Ball, M. (2013) The fall of the Heritage Foundation and the death of republican ideas, https://www.theatlantic.com/politics/archive/2013/09/the-fall-of-the-heritage-foundation-and-the-death-of-republican-ideas/279955/; Lawton, S., Hollins-Borges, J., Wheatley, J., Knefel, J. and Collier, E. (2024) A guide to Project 2025, the extreme right-wing agenda for the next Republican administration, mediamatters.org/heritage-foundation/guide-project-2025-extreme-right-wing-agenda-next-republican-administration.
36. Pro-lies.org. (2021) The Heritage Foundation, https://pro-lies.org/the-heritage-foundation.
37. Sourcewatch, Heritage Foundation.
38. Gonzalez, M. (2023) The left is right to fear our plan to gut the federal bureaucracy, https://www.msn.com/en-us/news/politics/the-left-is-right-to-fear-our-plan-to-gut-the-federal-bureaucracy/ar-AA1h9baL.
39. Smith, D. (2023) Polls say Trump has a strong chance of winning again in 2024. So how might his second term reshape the US government? https://theconversation.com/polls-say-trump-has-a-strong-chance-of-winning-again-in-2024-so-how-might-his-second-term-reshape-the-us-government-217664.
40. Ball, The fall of the Heritage Foundation and the death of republican ideas.
41. Wikipedia. (2023) Atlas Network, https://en.wikipedia.org/wiki/Atlas_Network.

42. ALEC Exposed. (2022) ALEC exposed, https://www.alecexposed.org/wiki/ALEC_Exposed.
43. Ball, The fall of the Heritage Foundation and the death of republican ideas; Beder, *Global Spin*; Kaufman, N. (2017) Heritage Foundation gets it wrong on costs and benefits of climate change, https://www.wri.org/insights/heritage-foundation-gets-it-wrong-costs-and-benefits-climate-action; Leonard, C. (2019) *Kochland: The Secret History of Koch Industries and Corporate Power in America*, Simon and Schuster, London.
44. Petrascu, C. (2013) Media and the totalitarian society: Spectacle, 'similacra' and the construction of (un)reality in communist Romania, *Procedia—Social and Behavioural Sciences* 92: 686–691.
45. Media Reform Coalition. (2021) Report: Who owns the media? https://www.mediareform.org.uk/media-ownership/who-owns-the-uk-media.
46. Tacoma Community College. (2024) Fake news, fact-checking, and bias: Media consolidation in the US, https://tacomacc.libguides.com/c.php?g=599051&p=4586162.
47. Minter, E. (2021) Media concentration by Murdoch, Nine and Stokes, and ABC cuts, a danger to democracy—Report, https://www.michaelwest.com.au/media-concentration-by-murdoch-nine-and-stokes-and-abc-cuts-a-danger-to-democracy-report/.
48. Edwards, D. and Cromwell, D. (2018) *Propaganda Blitz: How the Corporate Media Distort Reality*, Pluto Press, London, p. 15.
49. See Marsh, W. (2023) *Young Rupert: The Making of the Murdoch Empire*, Scribe, Melbourne.
50. Forbes. (2921) Rupert Murdoch & family, https://www.forbes.com/profile/rupert-murdoch/?sh=7c1ae43cb1af.
51. Legum, J. and Harvey, C. (2004) Who is Rupert Murdoch? https://www.americanprogress.org/issues/general/news/2004/07/16/933/who-is-rupert-murdoch/. For a contrary view see: Folkenflik, D. (2013) Five myths about Rupert Murdoch, https://www.washingtonpost.com/opinions/five-myths-about-rupert-murdoch/2013/11/08/341837ea-47bf-11e3-b6f8-3782ff6cb769_story.html.

52. Britanicca. (2021) Scandal and reorganization of Rupert Murdoch, https://www.britannica.com/biography/Rupert-Murdoch/Scandal-and-reorganization.
53. Hind, D. (2021) We are all living in Rupert Murdoch's world, https://jacobinmag.com/2021/03/rupert-murdoch-news-media-australia-facebook.
54. Beecher, E. (2020) Murdoch's power: How it works and how it debases Australia, Murdoch's power: how it works and how it debases Australia (msn.com).
55. Plunkett, J. and O'Carroll, L. (2012) Rupert Murdoch pressured me over Europe, says John Major, https://www.theguardian.com/media/2012/jun/12/rupert-murdoch-john-major.
56. The Guardian. (2022) Rupert Murdoch to testify on Fox News coverage of false vote-rigging claims, https://www.theguardian.com/media/2022/dec/13/rupert-murdoch-testify-fox-dominion-voting-machines-2020; see also Lambden, S. (2021) Rupert Murdoch at 90: Why the old mogul may have one final act in him yet, https://theconversation.com/rupert-murdoch-at-90-why-the-old-mogul-may-have-one-final-act-in-him-yet-156901; Peters, J. (2024) You might not want to think about Fox News right now. You should, state.com/business/2024/05/fox-news-donald-trump-joe-biden-election.html.
57. Fox News had at first accepted Biden's presidential win but reversed its position—and started repeating Trump's stolen election narrative—after losing its audience to two ultra right-wing media outlets. See Tiffen, R. (2023) As Fox News settles its lawsuit with Dominion, will it make any difference to how it reports? https://theconversation.com/as-fox-news-settles-its-lawsuit-with-dominion-will-it-make-any-difference-to-how-it-reports-204360.
58. Watson, J. (2023) Anyone can claim to be a journalist or a news organisation, and publish lies with almost total impunity, https://theconversation.com/anyone-can-claim-to-be-a-journalist-or-a-news-organization-and-publish-lies-with-almost-total-impunity-202083; Sorkin, A., Mattu, R., Warner, B., Kessler, S., de la Merced., Hirsch, L. and Livni, E. (2023) The plan to get

Rupert Murdoch to pay up, https://www.nytimes.com/2023/04/19/business/dealbook/dominion-murdoch-fox-settlement.html.
59. Sullivan, M. (2023) Will a $1.6bn defamation lawsuit finally stop Fox News from spreading lies? https://www.theguardian.com/commentisfree/2023/feb/24/fox-news-spreading-lies-16bn-dominion-lawsuit.
60. Sorkin et al., The plan to get Rupert Murdoch to pay up.
61. O'Donoghue, A. (2014) The media should not be concentrated in a few powerful hands, http://classonline.org.uk/blog/item/the-media-should-not-be-concentrated-in-a-few-powerful-hands.
62. O'Shea, L. (2020) Murdoch Press cheers on death, *Redflag*, 28 April, p. 10.
63. Beecher, Murdoch's power.
64. Mahler, J. and Rutenberg, J. (2019) How Rupert Murdoch's empire of influence remade the world, https://www.nytimes.com/interactive/2019/04/03/magazine/rupert-murdoch-fox-news-trump.html.
65. Legum and Harvey, Who is Rupert Murdoch?
66. Alcorn, G. (2019) Australia's Murdoch moment: Has News Corporation finally gone too far? https://www.theguardian.com/media/2019/may/10/australias-murdoch-moment-has-news-corp-finally-gone-too-far.
67. Beecher, Murdoch's power.
68. Dickinson, T. (2011) Rupert Murdoch's American scandals, https://www.rollingstone.com/politics/politics-news/rupert-murdochs-american-scandals-243127/.
69. Muller, D. (2022) Attacks on Dan Andrews are part of News Corporation's long abuse of power, https://theconversation.com/attacks-on-dan-andrews-are-part-of-news-corporations-long-abuse-of-power-194023. For a history of the Murdoch empire see Young, S. (2019) *Paper Emperors: The Rise of Australia's Newspaper Empires*, UNSW Press, Sydney.

70. Quoted in Sullivan, M. (2023) Rupert Murdoch's reign at Fox News is over. But the damage he did may last forever, https://www.theguardian.com/commentisfree/2023/sep/21/rupert-murdochs-reign-at-fox-news-is-over-but-the-damage-he-did-may-last-forever.
71. Mahler and Rutenberg, How Rupert Murdoch's empire of influence remade the world.
72. Rudd, K. (2019) Democracy overboard: Rupert Murdoch's long war on Australian politics, https://www.theguardian.com/commentisfree/2019/sep/06/democracy-overboard-rupert-murdochs-long-war-on-australian-politics. In the US, towards the end of Trump's campaign for presidency, Fox removed anti-Trump analysts from its shows, inserted pro-Trump supporters, and intensified its criticisms of Hilary Clinton—see Mahler and Rutenberg, How Rupert Murdoch's empire of influence remade the world.
73. Fung, K. (2023) Lachlan Murdoch's political views could see Fox News radically change, https://www.msn.com/en-us/entertainment/news/lachlan-murdochs-political-views-could-see-fox-news-radically-change/ar-AA1h3Pfc.
74. Young, S. (2023) *Media Monsters: The Transformation of Australia's Newspaper Empires*, UNSW Press, Sydney.
75. Dodd, A. (2023) Why is Rupert Murdoch stepping aside now and what does it mean for the company? https://theconversation.com/why-is-rupert-murdoch-stepping-aside-now-and-what-does-it-mean-for-the-company-214141.
76. Catholic News Agency. (2011) Rupert Murdoch's papal knighthood questioned as investigation continues, https://www.catholicnewsagency.com/news/22943/rupert-murdochs-papal-knighthood-questioned-as-investigation-continues; Battle Cry. (1999) Rupert Murdoch, Papal Knight, publisher of NIV, donates

$10 million for new LA cathedral, https://www.chick.com/battle-cry/article?id=Rupert-Murdoch-Papal-Knight-Publisher-of-NIV-Donates-$10-Million-for-New-LA-Cathedral. Unfortunately, when one of Rupert's editors—Larry Lamb—was awarded a knighthood from Margaret Thatcher, he was unceremoniously sacked by Murdoch for accepting it. Murdoch has 'problems' with the British, rather than the papal, honours system—see Hewlett, S. (2013) Why Britain has reason to be grateful to Rupert Murdoch, https://www.theguardian.com/media/2013/apr/28/rupert-murdoch-britain-grateful.
77. Soley, L. (2007) Sex and shock jocks: An analysis of the Howard Stern and Bob & Tom shows, *Journal of Promotion Management* 13(1/2): 73–91.
78. Stiegler, Z. (2014) Michael Savage and the political transformation of shock radio, *Journal of Radio & Audio Media* 21(2): 230–246.
79. Stiegler, Michael Savage and the political transformation of shock radio.
80. Saunders, K. (2011) *Degradation: What the History of Obscenity Tells Us About Hate Speech*, New York University Press, New York.
81. Hate speech is defined by the UN as 'communication in speech, writing or behaviour, that attacks or uses pejorative or discriminatory language with reference to a person or a group on the basis of who they are, in other words, based on their religion, ethnicity, nationality, race, colour, descent, gender or other identity factor'. According to the UN, hate speech has become a particularly unwelcome global phenomenon. See United Nations. (2021) United Nations strategy and plan of action on hate speech, https://www.un.org/en/genocideprevention/documents/UN%20Strategy%20and%20Plan%20of%20Action%20on%20Hate%20Speech%2018%20June%20SYNOPSIS.pdf.
82. Noriega, C. and Iribarren, J. (2014) Studying hate speech on commercial talk radio, *Journal of Radio and Aural Media* 21(2): 193–195; Stiegler, Michael Savage and the political transformation of shock radio.

83. Harrington, S. (2016) Right-wing shock jocks influence Americans more than the 'corporate media', https://www.irishexaminer.com/opinion/columnists/arid-20429273.html
84. Harrington, Right-wing shock jocks.
85. Torossian, R. (2021) What it means to be an influencer, https://www.commpro.biz/what-it-means-to-be-an-influencer/.
86. Newberry, C. (2021) Influencer marketing guide: How to work with social media influencers, https://blog.hootsuite.com/influencer-marketing/.
87. Conklin, A. (2020) Top 5 highest paid social media influencers, https://www.foxbusiness.com/money/5-highest-paid-social-influencers.
88. At a pre-match media conference in 2020, Ronaldo pushed two Coca-Cola bottles away from the table at which he was seated, stating 'Drink water'. Coke's share price subsequently dropped by 1.6%, equivalent to a company loss of US$5.2 billion, see Staff writers. (2021) Cristiano Ronaldo wipes billions off Coca-Cola shares after removing bottles from press conference table, https://www.theaustralian.com.au/sport/cristiano-ronaldo-wipes-billions-off-coke-shares-after-removing-bottles-from-press-conference-table/news-story/3dbefc70e9e7334fa8acf5cd4b2ce259.
89. Geyser, W. (2021) What is an influencer?—Social media influencers defined (updated 2021), https://influencermarketinghub.com/what-is-an-influencer/.
90. Newberry, Influencer marketing guide.
91. Abidin, C. and Ots, M. (2016) Influencers tell all? Unravelling authenticity and credibility in a brand scandal, in M. Edstrom, A. Kenyon and E. Svennson (eds) *Blurring the Lines: Market-driven and Democracy-driven Freedom of Expression*, Nordicom, Sweden, pp. 153–161.
92. Yadav, I. (2021) Why Mark Zuckerberg changed Facebook's name to 'Meta', https://content.techgig.com/technology/why-mark-zuckerberg-changed-facebooks-name-to-meta/articleshow/87353504.cms.

93. Leaver, T and Berryman, R. (2022) 'Virtual influencers' are here, but should Meta really be setting the ethical ground rules? https://theconversation.com/virtual-influencers-are-here-but-should-meta-really-be-setting-the-ethical-ground-rules-175524.
94. Leaver and Berryman, 'Virtual influencers' are here, but should Meta really be setting the ethical ground rules?
95. PTP. (2022) A virtual influencer: What are they and why you need them for your brand, https://peertopeermarketing.co/virtual-influencer/.
96. PTP, A virtual influencer; Leaver and Berryman, 'Virtual influencers' are here, but should Meta really be setting the ethical ground rules?
97. Das, M. (2023) Celebrities like Messi are all for AI deepfakes. But why are they signing their image rights away? https://www.firstpost.com/tech/news-analysis/celebrities-like-messi-are-all-for-ai-deepfakes-but-why-are-they-signing-their-image-rights-away-12884992.html.
98. Leaver and Berryman, 'Virtual influencers' are here, but should Meta really be setting the ethical ground rules?
99. PTP, A virtual influencer.
100. Spry, D. (2021), Disinfopreneurs and infodemics, https://www.lowyinstitute.org/the-interpreter/disinfopreneurs-and-infodemics.
101. In order, the best-selling products on social media are retail, travel, accommodation, movie, music, electronic, and beauty—see Tomas, D. (2019) The 7 best selling products on social media, https://www.cyberclick.net/numericalblogen/the-7-best-selling-products-on-social-media.
102. See Pariser, E. (2011) *The Filter Bubble: What the Internet Is Hiding from You*, Penguin, London.
103. Carah, N., Brownbill, A., Dobson, A., Robards, B., Angus, D., Hawker, K., Hayden, L. and Tan, X. (2022) How dark is 'dark advertising'? We audited Facebook, Google, and other platforms to find out, https://theconversation.com/how-dark-is-dark-advertising-we-audited-facebook-google-and-other-platforms-to-find-out-189310.

104. Spry, Disinfopreneurs and infodemics.
105. Britannica. (2022) QAnon conspiracy theory, https://www.britannica.com/topic/QAnon; Badham, V. (2021) *Qanon and On: A Short and Shocking History of Internet Conspiracy Cults*, Hardie Grant, Melbourne.
106. Goldstein, S. and Park, P. (2023) AI systems have learned how to deceive humans. What does that mean for our future? https://theconversation.com/ai-systems-have-learned-how-to-deceive-humans-what-does-that-mean-for-our-future-212197. As the authors say 'AI systems with deceptive capabilities could ... commit fraud, tamper with elections and generate propaganda ... Even human beings who are nominally in control of these systems may find themselves systematically deceived and outmanoeuvred.'
107. Donovan, J. (2024) Fake Biden robocalls to New Hampshire voters highlights how easy it is to make deepfakes—and how hard it is to defend against AI-generated disinformation, https://theconversation.com/fake-biden-robocall-to-new-hampshire-voters-highlights-how-easy-it-is-to-make-deepfakes-and-how-hard-it-is-to-defend-against-ai-generated-disinformation-221744.
108. Spry, Disinfopreneurs and infodemics.
109. Another form of lie is the 'hoax'—in this case a lie that is often a prank or practical joke. Some examples are the discovery of the Piltdown Man in 1912, the photograph in 1934 of the Loch Ness Monster by British surgeon Colonel Robert Wilson, and the discovery of Hitler's diaries in 1983. This book does not deal with brazen hoaxes.
110. Wilde, O. (2012) *The Wit and Humor of Oscar Wilde*, Courier Corporation, USA, p. 60.
111. Scott, J. (1987) *Weapons of the Weak: Everyday forms of Peasant Resistance*, Yale University Press, New Haven.
112. Barnes, J. (1994) *A Pack of Lies: Towards a Sociology of Lying*, Cambridge University Press, Cambridge, p. 1.
113. Machiavelli, N. (2010) *The Prince*, Penguin, Australia; Chadwick, I. (2021) The municipal Machiavelli, http://ianchadwick.com/machiavelli/chapters-15-21/chapter-18-the-subtle-art-of-lying/. The quote is drawn from *The Prince*, Chapter XVIII.

114. Butt, A. (2019) Why did Bush go to war in Iraq? https://www.aljazeera.com/opinions/2019/3/20/why-did-bush-go-to-war-in-iraq.
115. *The Saturday Evening Post.* (2018) 8 of history's most destructive lies; see also Teter, M. (2020) *Blood Libel: On the Trail of an Antisemitic Myth*, Harvard University Press, Massachusetts.
116. Anne Frank House. (2021) Hitler's antisemitism. Why did he hate the Jews? https://www.annefrank.org/en/anne-frank/go-in-depth/why-did-hitler-hate-jews/.
117. MoneyWise. (2021) The financial facts you never learned about World War II, https://moneywise.com/life/lifestyle/financial-facts-about-world-war-ii. I could not find figures for the European nations that suffered much of the destruction.
118. *The Saturday Evening Post.* (2018) 8 of history's most destructive lies, https://www.saturdayeveningpost.com/2018/05/8-historys-destructive-lies/.
119. Jancey, J. (2023) Sex and lies are used to sell vapes online. Even we were surprised at the marketing tactics we found, https://theconversation.com/sex-and-lies-are-used-to-sell-vapes-onl ine-even-we-were-surprised-at-the-marketing-tactics-we-found-200446.
120. Grattan, M. (2023) Albanese government launches war on vaping, declaring it the 'number one behavioural issue in high schools', https://theconversation.com/albanese-government-lau nches-war-on-vaping-declaring-it-the-number-one-behavioural-issue-in-high-schools-204760.
121. Jancey, Sex and lies are used to sell vapes online; Chapman, S. (2023) A potted history of smoking, and how we're making the same mistakes with vaping, https://theconversation.com/a-potted-history-of-smoking-and-how-were-making-the-same-mis takes-with-vaping-200708.
122. Grattan, Albanese government launches war on vaping, declaring it the 'number one behavioural issue in high schools'.
123. Chapman, A potted history of smoking, and how we're making the same mistakes with vaping.

124. Dale, D. (2021) The 15 most notable lies of Donald Trump's presidency, https://edition.cnn.com/2021/01/16/politics/fact-check-dale-top-15-donald-trump-lies/index.html.
125. *The Washington Post.* (2021) Trump made 30,573 false or misleading claims as president. Nearly half came in his final year, https://www.washingtonpost.com/graphics/politics/trump-claims-database/?itid=lk_inline_manual_4.
126. American Historical Society. (1944) The story of propaganda, https://www.historians.org/about-aha-and-membership/aha-history-and-archives/gi-roundtable-series/pamphlets/em-2-what-is-propaganda-(1944)/the-story-of-propaganda.
127. Cengage. (2021) Propagation of the faith, https://www.encyclopedia.com/religion/encyclopedias-almanacs-transcripts-and-maps/propagation-faith-congregation.
128. See Latimer, J. (2015) *Deception in War*, Thistle Publishing, London.
129. National Collection of Aerial Photography. (2021) Camouflage, concealment and deception, https://ncap.org.uk/feature/camouflage-concealment-and-deception.
130. Nordquist, R. (2018) Definition of spin in propaganda, https://www.thoughtco.com/spin-communication-1691988.
131. Fisher, C. (2019) The vomit principle, the dead bat, the freeze: how political spin doctors' tactics aim to shape the news, https://theconversation.com/the-vomit-principle-the-dead-bat-the-freeze-how-political-spin-doctors-tactics-aim-to-shape-the-news-106453. There were another 8 tactics mentioned by the author.
132. O'Connor, C. and Weatherall, O. (2019) *The Misinformation Age: How False Beliefs Spread*, Yale University Press, New Haven.
133. The definition from a British parliamentary inquiry goes a little further describing it as 'the deliberate creation and sharing of false and/or manipulated information that is intended to deceive and mislead audiences, either for the purposes of causing harm, or for political, personal or financial gain', see https://publications.parliament.uk/pa/cm201719/cmselect/cmcumeds/1791/179104.htm; see also Dale, T. (2019) The fundamental roles of technology in the spread of fake news,

in I. Chiluwa and S. Samoilenko (eds) *Handbook of Research on Deception, Fake News and Misinformation*, https://www.igi-global.com/book/handbook-research-deception-fake-news/218293.
134. Reported in Poerksen, B. (2022) *Digital Fever: Taming the Big Business of Disinformation*, Palgrave Macmillan, https://link.springer.com/book/10.1007/978-3-030-89522-8, p. 22.
135. Buckmaster, L. and Wils, T. (2021) Responding to fake news, https://www.aph.gov.au/About_Parliament/Parliamentary_Departments/Parliamentary_Library/pubs/BriefingBook46p/FakeNews; House of Commons. (2019) Disinformation and 'fake news': Final report, https://publications.parliament.uk/pa/cm201719/cmselect/cmcumeds/1791/1791.pdf.
136. Graham, T. and Thompson, J. (2022) Russian government accounts are using a Twitter loophole to spread disinformation, https://theconversation.com/russian-government-accounts-are-using-a-twitter-loophole-to-spread-disinformation-178001; O'Flaherty, K. (2022) Russia-Ukraine—What's the difference between misinformation and disinformation? https://www.forbes.com/sites/kateoflahertyuk/2022/03/12/russia-ukraine-whats-the-difference-between-misinformation-and-disinformation/?sh=6ba8e76012c5.
137. Buckmaster and Wils, Responding to fake news.
138. The quote is from former ABC Australia executive Alan Sunderland. See Taylor, L. (2023) Can we still handle the truth? Journalism, 'alternative facts' and the rise of AI, https://www.theguardian.com/commentisfree/2023/may/22/can-we-still-handle-the-truth-journalism-alternative-facts-and-the-rise-of-ai.
139. Oxford Languages. (2016) Word of the year 2016, https://languages.oup.com/word-of-the-year/2016/.
140. Bakir, V. and McStay, A. (2019) Submission to the Inquiry into the Impact of Social Media on Elections and Electoral Administration, https://www.parliament.vic.gov.au/images/EMC/21._Vian_Bakir_and_Andrew_McStay_Redacted.pdf; University of Michigan. (2022) Fake news and the post-truth world, https://globalchange.umich.edu/globalchange1/current/lectures/kling/fake_news/fake_news.html; Graham and Thompson, Russian

government accounts are using a Twitter loophole to spread disinformation.
141. Quoted in https://www.kirkusreviews.com/book-reviews/lee-mcintyre/on-disinformation/.
142. Mahdawi, A. (2022) The whole world should be worried about the 'siege of Ottawa'. This is about much more than a few anti-vaxx truckers, https://www.theguardian.com/commentisfree/2022/feb/08/ottawa-truckers-protest-anti-vaxx-canada.
143. Mahdawi, The whole world should be worried about the 'siege of Ottawa'.
144. Richards, J. (2020) Fake news, disinformation and the democratic state: A case study of the UK government's narrati, *Revista de Comunicación y Tecnologías Emergentes* 19(1): 95–122, https://www.redalyc.org/journal/5525/552565288005/html/.
145. Gal, U. (2023) ChatGPT is a data privacy nightmare. If you've ever posted online, you ought to be concerned, https://theconversation.com/chatgpt-is-a-data-privacy-nightmare-if-youve-ever-posted-online-you-ought-to-be-concerned-199283.
146. 'Hi-tech plagiarism' is a phrase coined by Noam Chomsky. See Naughton, J. (2023) ChatGPT isn't a great leap forward, it's an expensive deal with the devil, https://www.theguardian.com/commentisfree/2023/feb/04/chatgpt-isnt-a-great-leap-forward-its-an-expensive-deal-with-the-devil.
147. Ali, G. and Tong, K. (2023) Meet ChatGPT's alter ego, DAN. He doesn't care about ethics or rules, https://www.abc.net.au/news/2023-03-07/chatgpt-alter-ego-dan-ignores-ethics-in-ai-program/102052338.
148. Alimardani, A. and Jane, E. (2023) We pitted ChatGPT against tools for detecting AI-written text, and the results are troubling, https://theconversation.com/we-pitted-chatgpt-against-tools-for-detecting-ai-written-text-and-the-results-are-troubling-199774.
149. Palmer, S. and Khatsenkova, S. (2023) 'I want to be alive': Has Microsoft's AI chatbot become sentient? https://www.euronews.com/next/2023/02/18/threats-misinformation-and-gaslighting-the-unhinged-messages-bing-is-sending-its-users-rig.

150. Walsh, T. (2023) Gaslighting, love bombing and narcissism: Why is Microsoft's Bing AI so unhinged? https://theconversation.com/gaslighting-love-bombing-and-narcissism-why-is-microsofts-bing-ai-so-unhinged-200164.
151. Reece, H. (2016) Why Microsoft's 'Tay' AI bot went wrong, https://www.techrepublic.com/article/why-microsofts-tay-ai-bot-went-wrong/.
152. Murphy Kelly, S. (2024) Explicit, AI-generated Taylor Swift images spread quickly on social media, https://edition.cnn.com/2024/01/25/tech/taylor-swift-ai-generated-images/index.html; Henry, N. and Witt, A. (2024) Taylor Swift deepfakes: New technologies have long been weaponised against women. The solution involves all of us, https://theconversation.com/taylor-swift-deepfakes-new-technologies-have-long-been-weaponised-against-women-the-solution-involves-us-all-222268.
153. Thomson, T. and Thomas, R. (2023) Ageism, sexism, classism and more: 7 examples of bias in AI-generated images, https://theconversation.com/ageism-sexism-classism-and-more-7-examples-of-bias-in-ai-generated-images-208748.
154. DePeau-Wilson, M. (2023) ChatGPT quickly authored 100 blogs full of healthcare disinformation, https://www.medpagetoday.com/special-reports/features/107329.
155. Bridle, J. (2023) The stupidity of AI, https://www.theguardian.com/technology/2023/mar/16/the-stupidity-of-ai-artificial-intelligence-dall-e-chatgpt.
156. Walsh, Gaslighting, love bombing and narcissism.

2

It's the Economy, Stupid! Neoliberal Nonsense and the Myths of the Free Market

The First Law of Economics: For every economist, there exists an equal and opposite economist.
The Second Law of Economics: They're both wrong.

For most of my life I seem to have had a love/hate relationship with economics—mostly the latter. I studied economics in high school learning about price mechanisms, demand and supply, elasticity, optimisation of output, international trade, and so on. It seemed to make a lot of sense and, at university, I decided to study advanced courses in the discipline. That was my mistake. This was at a time when any economist worth his or her salt would be developing and applying mathematical equations to explain market behaviour. The more variables that could be crammed into the formula the more impressive the explanation, or so

---

'The economy, stupid' was a phrase first used in 1992 by James Carville, and adviser to President Bill Clinton. Clinton was challenging George H.W. Bush for the Presidency, and the US economy was in recession. The phrase reminded voters that the Bush administration had let them down on the economic front. The phrase was later popularised as 'It's the economy, stupid'.

it seemed. To join the ranks of true scientists like physicists, chemists, biologists, and astronomers, economists eschewed all 'normative' (value-based) positions. Their role was to collect unbiased data, build models, and test hypotheses and to do so in an objective, impartial, manner. But, as will be revealed below, it was not long before I uncovered an awkward fact about economics—it is not bereft of moral and political predispositions.

Many of the formulae I encountered had a curious 'ϵ' at the end. ϵ means 'error', indicating that the model cannot properly capture the relationship between the variables in the formula. In other words, the equation is limited by external factors that cannot be measured. Some of these factors might be trade sanctions, currency manipulations, new tax laws, changes in price supports, pandemics, electoral upsets, and media 'scares'. But, for the purposes of prediction and explanation, they are unmeasurable. They can't be rolled into econometric models, and so must be ignored.[1] The consequence is, of course, that leaving out important information renders those models largely useless, no matter how 'elegant' their structure. We are being fooled by those applying these models and who know very well that they fail to capture the reality of what is going on in the economy. In the words of Tony Lawson, a Cambridge economics professor who has broken away from orthodox economic theory[2]:

> What is wrong with modern economics? Its formulations, in the main, are patently and repeatedly unrealistic ... [providing] little or no explanatory insight or understanding of the world in which we live. Human beings in the formulations of modern economists, are regularly endowed with perfect foresight, rational expectations, omniscience [and] amazing powers of calculation or 'rationality' ... It is all really quite ludicrous if the goal is social illumination.[3]

How did we get to this? What are the assumptions of orthodox (liberal) economic theory and what are the consequences of its application for society?

Grounds for Doubt

It is a crude and incorrect assertion that liberal economics is somehow devoid of bias. All economic theories contain inbuilt political assumptions. It is simply that some of the 'great' economic theorists have chosen to ignore the fact. Great minds were responsible for creating liberal economic theory and the moral philosophy of utilitarianism that is its companion. In the eighteenth and nineteenth centuries Jeremy Bentham, John Stuart Mill, and Adam Smith were observers of a form of economic organisation we now identify as capitalism. They were optimistic that breaking away from the entrenched privilege, tradition, and the economic hold of the landed aristocracy would be emancipatory. They were progressives who challenged the tyranny of the church and believed that reason and science would be the foundations of a better society—one in which people would be free to pursue their individual desires and needs. Jeremy Bentham, and later his protégé, John Stuart Mill, developed a theory of utilitarianism, proposing that it is logical for people to seek to maximise happiness and to minimise pain. If we all did so the outcome would provide the societally optimal outcome—the maximum amount of good for the maximum amount of people. Utilitarianism demands we consider how people will be affected by our actions. To do so, we must put self-interest aside. Not so for Adam Smith who rejected the tenets of utilitarianism during his lifetime. For Smith self-interest was the key to economic growth under capitalism. He famously wrote:

> It is not from the benevolence of the butcher, the brewer, or the baker that we expect our dinner, but from their regard to their own interest.[4]

Followers of Smith considered that, if people were free to pursue their self-interest in a competitive environment, capital would invariably move to areas of highest demand. The 'hidden hand' of demand and supply would allocate resources in a socially desirable way, ensuring continual economic progress. In this world, innovation would thrive as people identified new market opportunities and new technologies that would reduce costs and maximise profits. A meddling state would impede progress by disrupting the operation of the market. It might also stifle the ever-increasing division of labour which was a key to improved productivity which, in turn, would lead to better wages for workers and increased profits for business owners.

The Many Myths of Liberal Economic Theory

SPOILER ALERT: By all measures, liberal economic theory is right-wing ideology dressed up as economic 'science'.

Myth 1: The Rational Actor

One of the primary assumptions of economics is that the dominant drive of individuals is self-interest. Self-interest is seen as a 'given'—a human trait. It is rational for individuals to seek to maximise their own benefits.[5] Why would they do otherwise? Unfortunately, this major foundation stone of economics turns out to be wide of the mark. Placing the individual at the heart of the discipline is a poor start. We live in social groups, learning ideas and behaviours from interaction with family and community. However uncomfortable it is for the economist to imagine, the self-interested rational actor is a person who must live and work with fellow members of groups and communities. It is in these circumstances—among cultural and social institutions—where beliefs and actions are framed and re-framed. According to Dan Ariely, author of *Predictably Irrational*, human beings are constantly exposed to unconscious influences that shape daily choices. Decision-making cannot be rational and informed if biases are present. Emotions come into play when purchasing groceries, clothing, and cars—with our behaviour manipulated through advertisements, social media, and television personalities. Psychologist and economist Daniel Kahneman won a Nobel Laureate for demonstrating that people make decisions based upon biases and heuristics rather than rational thought. And as for our programmed gene-determined selfishness? If circumstances dictate, we *can* be selfish. But we also possess loads of altruism. We are compassionate, self-sacrificing, kind, decent and considerate, putting other people's wishes ahead of our own. We are publicly-minded. For much of human history we have survived through a complex social code that has put a premium on egalitarianism, mutuality, reciprocity, and cooperation.[6] This is the very opposite of the self-interested individual found in the economic textbooks. As for our rationality? In Dan Ariely's words 'if humans were comic book characters, we'd be more like Homer Simpson than Superman'.[7]

Myth 2: Perfect Competition

It turns out there's nothing perfect about perfect competition. Perfect competition is believed to exist when competition between firms is at its highest possible level. In this wonderfully competitive world buyers and sellers are many, with firms selling their products when supply and demand align—at the so-called equilibrium price. An example often given is the production and sale of farm vegetables. There are many producers of artichokes, beans, and cauliflowers. Let's take cauliflowers. Cauliflowers are 'homogenous'—it is difficult to distinguish one farmer's cauliflowers from another's. The same for beans and artichokes. It is easy for producers to enter and leave the market. Consumers have full information about the vegetables being marketed, just as the farmers have full information of who is supplying what vegetables and at what times (there is no time lag in the flow of information) and of consumer purchasing behaviour. With perfect knowledge on both sides, the self-interest of the consumer is to purchase for the lowest price, and the self-interest of the farmer is to achieve maximum profits. If a farmer decides to raise the price of his cauliflowers, he or she will be less competitive than others and may go out of business. With prices determined by demand and supply, the consumer, the producer—and most importantly society—achieve positive outcomes from those interactions.

What could be wrong? First, there is no such thing as an industry with an unlimited number of producers. In fact, there has been a strong tendency towards economic concentration with few buyers and few sellers.[8] Second, because of differences in size, technological applications or financial position, some operators in the market will invariably have the power to influence prices. Third, most products are differentiated—even cauliflowers can be de-leaved, cut, and wrapped in ways that increase their appeal to consumers. Fourth, there are all sorts of barriers to entry for producers—the costs of technology and distance from markets are obvious ones. Fifth, information is rarely spread evenly among market participants; some have access to knowledge that others don't possess, giving them market leverage. Sixth, the consumer will not always select the cheapest product. Personal preference and the sway of advertising play important parts.

The model is untenable. This small issue aside, most orthodox economists don't bother with the problem of unrealistic assumptions and continue to produce high school textbooks and deliver first-year lectures and tutorials convincing students of the merits of this beautiful, mythical, thing called perfect competition.[9] Its main ideological role is to justify private enterprise's supposed ability to allocate resources in the most efficient manner, and for the benefit of all.[10] Given market tendencies towards industry concentration and barriers to entry for competing firms, 'perfect competition' is a rather dangerous fairy story—one neglecting a most obvious reality. Economies are embedded in society and society exerts moral constraints on the activities of economic actors.[11] Perfect competition? A perfect canard.

Myth 3: Income Is Determined by Contribution to Production

Why do CEOs, money traders, and corporate lawyers receive higher remuneration than teachers, nurses, and assembly-line workers? Economists believe the former have much higher productivity levels than the latter. It stands to reason that the captains of industry deserve high pay because they are undertaking complicated work which is way above the capacity of less-skilled workers. Anyone can skin a chicken, very few can build a global trade network. If the market is working properly then people will be rewarded according to their contribution to the economy. Demand and supply will determine the pay scale. But there is a flaw, here. What is patently obvious is that wages are strongly influenced by the bargaining ability of both workers and bosses. It is about relative economic power with workers relying upon unions to support pay claims and bosses relying on business owners and shareholders to determine their levels of remuneration. There is nothing 'natural' about a CEO earning 350 times the amount of money as a typical manual or white-collar worker. (In fact, this differential grew from 31 times in 1978 to 61 times in 1989 to 350 times in 2020.)

How did it get to this? As corporate wealth increased throughout the early years of this century, CEOs began to receive incentives in the form of bonuses and stock options (comprising, today, about 85% of all CEO compensation). Their pay arrangements (bonuses and equity compensation) were tied to companies' short-term results which meant the CEOs had an incentive to increase the level of risk-taking, with much of the latter deemed 'excessive'.[12] Risk taking went beyond optimal limits. As economies grew, so did CEO packages, while those very same CEOs were involved in keeping workers' wages low. They did this via globalisation (locating production in the cheapest labour zones around the world), by confronting the unions (to prevent wage gains), and by embracing outsourcing (shifting work to freelancers, often working on a casual or part-time basis). Despite the productivity of the average worker having grown by 3.5% since the late 1970s, wages have failed to keep pace.[13] (Since 1978 average CEO compensation has grown by 1,322% while that of the average worker has grown by 18%.)[14] Another reason that the CEOs' remuneration packages increased was that, in the US during the reign of President Trump, corporations were provided with huge tax cuts. The stock market responded positively. Here the CEOs' returns increased without any effort on their part—it had nothing at all to do with 'executive performance' or their productivity levels. And what happened to CEO packages following the GFC in 2008? Many fell in response to financial market collapse, but some also received golden parachutes in keeping with their inviolability.[15] Others' salary packages remained intact—the company boards deciding the CEO needed strong incentives to climb back from the brink—a reward for future productivity, perhaps?

Researchers at Britain's *New Economics Foundation* evaluated the value to society of six different professions employing a methodology which calculated 'social return on investment'—a combination of economic, social, and environmental benefits. For bankers, every pound in value they create, they cost society seven. For advertising executives every pound they generate costs society eleven. Tax accountants (whose primary goal is to keep the rich from paying taxes) cost society 47 pounds for each pound they generate. But for hospital cleaners, for every pound they are paid, society benefits to the tune of 10 pounds. Waste recycling workers generate 12 pounds for every pound they are paid. Childcare workers create over seven pounds for each pound they receive.[16] The level of payments for labour is completely out of kilter with what is truly valuable to society—we pay the most productive little, while generously rewarding those contributing the least.

Myth 4: Global free Trade Is of Benefit to Everyone

Comparative advantage is one of the key concepts of liberal economic theory and holds a special place in our understanding of international trade. Comparative advantage proposes that a nation should specialise in producing an item for which it has a relative cost advantage. It would then trade those items for products from another country, a country which also had a relative cost advantage in producing its particular goods. As British economist David Ricardo argued, if England could produce cloth cheaper than Portugal, and Portugal could produce wine cheaper than England it would make good sense for England to export its cloth to Portugal, and Portugal to sell its wine to the English. In this way the two countries become increasingly efficient in specialising in their wares, and trade ensures that consumers in both nations maximise their benefits in the purchase of wine and cloth.

Comparative advantage seems logical, socially beneficial, and a reason for the pursuit of global trade. What could be wrong with that? The problems are with the assumptions, and with the practice of 'free trade'. In relation to the assumptions, the first is that prices drive trade. But what if prices are distorted? A nation which has lax pollution laws will be able to sell goods cheaply. If trade continues that nation will be concentrating production in an area that is not as profitable as it is made out (after all, it is being subsidised by the environment). Second, it assumes factors of production will move easily from less-valuable to more-valuable areas. But some factors are immobile—you can't pick up a building and move it to a region of greater economic opportunity. This is particularly true of labour. As goods flow in from low-cost labour nations abroad and displace workers in other nations, the outcome is not the ready flow of those displace workers to new industries. Their skill sets will not necessarily match new job opportunities—they do not possess multi-skill proficiencies. Forced unemployment is a direct consequence—hardly a positive outcome for that nation. Third, it is a static analysis; optimal allocation of resources is viewed at one point in time and cannot tell us anything about the future. It is silent about what might happen to certain kinds of industries with the progress of time and technology. Fourth, rather than helping a nation to build healthy economies, comparative advantage, in the guise of free trade, actually expands the pool of available workers which puts a squeeze on wages—the so-called race to the bottom that is part of globalisation.[17] Fifth, free trade can produce its own inefficiencies. As one critic has pointed out

> Contrary to the implications of comparative advantage, more than half of all international trade involves the simultaneous import and export of essentially the same goods. For example, Americans import Danish sugar cookies, and Danes import American sugar cookies. Exchanging recipes would surely be more efficient.[18]

In practice, comparative advantage means abandoning self-reliance and embracing inter-dependency. Organisations such as the World Bank and IMF were created to facilitate this. Nations in the Global South have been encouraged to identify products demonstrating comparative advantage and borrow funds to build the infrastructure to produce those goods for export. Many poorer countries become commodity dependent—putting all their eggs in one basket, as it were. When commodity prices decline their economies contract. This is often read as a signal to produce even more, putting pressure on natural resources and eventually causing gluts which cause the price of the commodity to fall. Nations can also choose to borrow. But debts incurred are often difficult to repay, giving leverage to the World Bank and IMF to impose 'structural adjustments' on the debtor nations. These adjustments often mean cutting health, welfare, and education budgets—hardly a positive for the poorer nations.[19]

But wait, there's more. The theory of comparative advantage has been criticised as being

> invalid, inapplicable, and irrelevant in the real world of trade imbalances; global movement of capital; worker specialization; persistent large-scale unemployment; huge wage-level gaps between countries; 'sticky' prices, wages and currency rates; technological progress; production overcapacity; geopolitical and economic instability; and unprecedented uncertainty.[20]

And, in keeping with our focus upon societal dishonesty and deceptiveness:

> Today's 'free trade' is ... full of wholesale foul play, deception, currency manipulation, predatory techniques, and other violations of its rules ... To call the existing international trade 'free' ... is the top of unscrupulous audacity.[21]

The disadvantages of comparative advantage are also very obvious when natural disasters prevent food and other necessities from flowing to needy populations.

Myth 5: The Nation's Budget is Like a Household Budget and Should Be 'Balanced'

As economic contrarian Stephanie Kelton explains in her book *The Deficit Myth*, there is no more pernicious fiction than that the government should run the country like the Joneses' household. Governments have power to issue dollars (the Joneses don't), governments do not need to earn dollars before they spend (the Joneses normally do), and government can never go broke (the Joneses can).[22] When governments try to be like the Joneses they miss out on the opportunity to harness the power of their sovereign currencies to substantially improve life for their people.[23]

The supposedly self-evident notion that 'we can't live beyond our means' is a misreading of what occurs in the economy. Kelton gives the example of a government spending $100 but collecting only $90 in taxation. That is a government deficit of $10. Surely, that must be bad? No, she insists. That deficit is matched by a surplus of $10 somewhere else in the economy which creates growth and wealth. In any case, there is a correction on deficits. If they become too large, inflation will signal that spending must be reduced. She argues that deficits have been too *small* rather than too large, meaning that spending on such things as health, welfare, and education has been unnecessarily curtailed, to the detriment of the poor and struggling workers.[24] It has been posited, for example, that the austerity measures imposed by the Cameron government in Britain between 2010 and 2019 were so thoroughly nasty—with some £540 billion being cut from budgets over that period—that the Brexit option became all the more appealing for disgruntled voters.[25] There was a close correlation between the regions that suffered most from budget cuts, and support for the Leave vote, with voters (falsely) believing they would be better off economically under Brexit.[26] The Leavers used immigration as a scapegoat for the growing disadvantages experienced by Brits when, all along, it was the economic severities imposed by the conservatives in their pursuit of neoliberalism.[27] Migrants were a convenient 'political weapon' for the right-wing parliamentarians and press.[28]

Following the GFC governments in the US, UK and EU found it necessary to introduce 'quantitative easing'. They simply printed more money—trillions of dollars, pounds, and euros, to reduce the risks faced by financial institutions and to ensure money would be available for continuing investment and consumption. As one analyst observed:

> The money was created with keystrokes on a computer which simply credit the accounts that … financial institutions hold with the Federal Reserve. There has been no runaway inflationary impact of this 'printing' of trillions of dollars.[29]

He continues

> the need for balanced federal budgets is a myth. Like many myths, it does have some factual historical origins. Back when currencies were backed by gold it was possible for governments to go broke. Because modern currencies are not backed by anything material, sovereign governments can never run out of money and can never be insolvent in their own currency.[30]

The reasons politicians endlessly repeat the myth have more to do about justifying cuts to public services than following some immutable financial logic. The 'household analogy has been weaponised for purely political ends'.[31] Meanwhile, 2,153 billionaires own more wealth than 60% of the world's population—some 4.6 billion people.[32] Oxfam has calculated that if the richest 1% of people paid just 0.5% extra in taxation, some 117 million jobs could be funded, worldwide, to help improve outcomes in areas like education, health, childcare, and services for the elderly. A global tax of 1.5% on the wealth of billionaires would pay for the schooling of every child on the planet.[33]

Other mistaken ideas relate to the budget deficit and debt. Budget deficits, we are told, will punish the next generation. In contrast, debt helps build economies by providing services and infrastructure that improves standards of living for people for decades to come. What about government spending, in general? Doesn't it crowd out private investment, stopping entrepreneurs from being entrepreneurial? Stephanie Kelton argues this idea is based on the faulty assumption that, to finance its deficits, governments are competing for scarce funds—funds that would normally be available to private investors. Her research indicates that fiscal deficits in fact stimulate private savings and investment, improving overall economic growth. Then there's the notion that social security, health benefits, and other entitlements will eventually bankrupt the state. But money can always be found—it just might mean reprioritising policies and expenditure. Should tax cuts (that increase the deficit) be placed in the hands of billionaires? Foregoing a few nuclear missiles might help reduce the number of kids in poverty (in the US one in five children is in poverty).[34] Kelton pointedly states, in relation to the US,

The real crises we are facing have nothing to do with the federal deficit or entitlements … The fact that our infrastructure is graded at a D+ is a real crisis. The fact that inequality today stands at levels last seen during America's Gilded Age [1850–1890] is a crisis. The fact that the typical American worker has seen virtually no real wage growth since the 1970s is a crisis. The fact that forty-four million Americans are saddled with $1.7 trillion in student loan debt is a crisis. And the fact that we ultimately won't be able to "afford' anything at all if we end up exacerbating climate change and destroying life on this planet is perhaps the biggest crisis of them all … These are real crises. The national deficit is not a crisis.[35]

Myth 6: Economics Is a Science

One definition of economics is that it is the 'study of the ownership, use and exchange of scarce resources', that is, the science of scarcity.[36] A similar definition holds that economics is 'a science concerned with the process or system by which goods and services are produced, sold, and bought'.[37] Yet another calls it 'the science of studying human behaviour as a relationship between ends and scarce means that have alternative uses'.[38] Common to all is the claim that the discipline of economics is a 'science'. Economists insist they are building a science which is rigorous, based on objective facts, and is untainted by values or opinions. This is not the case. One perceptive cartoon features a professor giving the first lecture to a class of university students studying Economics 101. He points to the board where he has written in large capital letters 'THIS IS THE BEST OF ALL POSSIBLE WORLDS'.[39] That's all the students really need to know. Clearly, the professor has a sanguine view of life—one that fosters belief in the merits of the status quo. Why change when the wheels of the economy turn for the benefit of all? Unfortunately, his *un*real world does not include those who fall victim to racism, sexism, poverty, unemployment, or any number of other socio-economic disadvantages or who live with the 'externalities' of air pollution, toxic run-off, overgrazing, overfishing, and anthropogenic climate change. The professor seems to have forgotten the Great Depression, the GFC, and a host of other glitches.

Rather than being 'scientific', much of orthodox economics is ideological, helping to protect and financially advantage certain groups in society.[40] While being advanced as an objective understanding of the rules of commerce, it presents a particular version of the way things *should* work. As soon as the *should* enters the equation we are on a slippery slope; should work for whom? For those who are rich and powerful the (unsurprising) answer is 'for the rich and powerful'. It is no wonder that only 50% of the UK public trust economists—a figure plunging to 25% in the US.[41] Some reasons? The profession **lacks reflexivity** (there is little recognition of how ideas are generated and reproduced in society, and how the profession is influenced by them). Most economists appearing in the media are from banks, management firms, and think tanks. They have a serious **conflict of interest** in proposing 'objective' economic options. The profession's focus on **efficiency over equity** continually skews policy advice to governments. And economists like to profess certitude in a world of inherent uncertainty. They are known for **arrogance and overconfidence** rather than for reflection and humility.[42] It seems they believe in a new social Darwinism where only the 'strong and worthy' deserve to survive in a competitive market economy.[43]

The liberal economic model described in this chapter assumes that capitalism is a stable system of economic supply and demand which provides optimal outcomes for society. In contrast, it has been argued that:

> mainstream economics is not primarily a description or an explanation of the economy, but a *de facto* defence of capitalism, by discrediting any form of socialisation or any intervention by the state in the economy … This is the reason that neoclassical economics is practically devoid of any predictive and explanatory capacity. As an ideology, its social function is not to explain reality or predict events, but to preserve the capitalist system.[44]

Orthodox economics is an ideology because it is an instrument of deception, of social control and rule, and a weapon in the struggle for power.[45] It is a form of 'black magic'.[46] Yet, it is reproduced in academic and government circles 'by a socialisation process comparable to that of a fundamentalist religious sect'.[47] It serves the political function of distorting what is really happening and helps disguise the mechanisms at play in the creation of wealth and of poverty.[48] It carefully separates the economy—as an object of study—from politics, from culture, and from history, preventing its adherents from understanding the intimate connections between all four areas. It provides justification for a 'free market' where some are doing quite nicely, thank you, and the rest can sink or swim with the tide. It fosters an individualism that encourages avarice and discourages beneficence. But never think of changing what we have because, after all, we live in the best of all possible worlds.

Capitalism: The 'System We Know and Love'?

Capitalism did not spring from the eighteenth century as some intact, coherent, and societally-accepted form of organised economic life. Its genesis goes way back to slave times—a very early form of the exploitation of the sort found in today's world. In Roman and Greek times slaves were captured following wars, raids, and piracy where the spoils—in this case human beings—went to the victor. The owning of slaves was a sign of prosperity and it was not uncommon for a Greek household to own three or four slaves. They laboured in households, agriculture, mines, on roads, and in the construction of public buildings. It was not a happy time for those captured. Their food, clothing, and rest times were rationed, and they were regularly flogged, branded, and treated less like kindred spirits, more like domestic animals. They could be sold or rented. They could be killed for minor misdemeanours, with no repercussions for the owner. Many slaves attempted to escape—surprise, surprise! Indeed, slave rebellions against the Romans were part of the Servile Wars (think Spartacus in 71 BC).[49] Slaves, it appears, didn't much like their lot. Individually, they would abscond, in haste, at the first chance of freedom or join with others to try to defeat the military that was keeping the system of slavery in place.

The point here is there was an obvious struggle between owner and slave—the coercion used by the former to get the latter to labour, and to do so at minimal cost. It was an antagonistic relationship largely held together by a legal system that disenfranchised the slaves, along with a powerful military doing the bidding for the slave owners.

Fast forward to the feudal world of Europe in the Middle Ages. Serfs work on plots of land on the estate of a Lord of the Manor. In return, they are forced to pay rent for that land, or to give up either their time (to work on the Lord's land) or their produce (often up to half of what they have harvested from their own plot) to the Lord. The Lord is effectively extracting labour from the serf—it is forced labour (after all, the serfs would be better off keeping all their output). But the serf receives military protection from the Lord. Is this not mutually beneficial? No, at its heart it is an antagonistic relationship where surplus is created by the serf and appropriated by the Lord. A serf could not change occupation or marry or move off the land without the Lord's permission. Their lives were spent in servitude and poverty, while providing the propertied classes with the wealth to keep armies and live a life of privilege and ease. Attempts by the serfs to escape from their circumstances included many revolts and rebellions. Ultimately, the system faltered because of the volatility of serf/Lord relations, new forms of farming, the enclosure of lands by Lords for the grazing of sheep, and population growth.[50] The serfs forced from the land sought work as paid agricultural labourers and workers—that is, if they were not caught for vagabondage, whereupon they could be put in stocks, whipped, have a V branded on their forehead, an ear cut off, or be hanged.[51] Finding paid work was a definite priority.

The move from feudalism to capitalism is a long and complicated story. Here is the essence. With the demise of feudalism in the 1400s and 1500s a merchant class began to emerge, becoming quite powerful through land speculation, colonial plunder, extortionate moneylending, and by utilising the cheap labour of those abandoning the failing feudal economy. The merchant class grew tired of, and confronted, the rules and laws that had kept feudalism alive. The beheading of England's King Charles in 1649 can be interpreted as part of a rebellion by 'new money' over the monarchy and feudal laws, while the French revolution of 1789 was a revolt over an entrenched clergy and the feudal landed aristocracy.[52] The marketplace at the time was filled with products from small-scale artisans and farmers but, as a result of technical innovation, factories began to appear. These were owned and controlled by those with financial capital, who employed others who did not have financial capital but, instead, possessed a capacity to labour.

A beautiful synergy emerged which seemed fair to all. Labour was 'free' to offer itself to the highest bidder. Capital was 'free' to hire the workers most suited to the tasks at hand. This freedom was forever to disguise a very special relation. For it was the capitalists who controlled all aspects of production (what to make, what technologies to employ, how to organise the labour required, and so forth)—allowing them to control the productivity of those employed. Their property was private, protected by the law. The workers possessed the ability to labour—to expend labour power. Labour was treated as a commodity, like any other in the marketplace. If they wanted to survive, workers had to sell their labour power to gain an income to purchase food, clothing, and shelter. So, their relationship with the owners of capital was reciprocal? Unfortunately, no. If capitalists paid workers the full value of all the goods produced, how would the capitalist survive? There would be nothing left over—no profits—and the capitalist would go out of business.

So, here is the secret of the capitalist system—the worker is paid less, in wages, than the total value of the goods and services that the worker creates. The rest is captured by capitalists in the form of interest, rent, and profit.[53] Workers quickly recognised this. They understood that their labour was being exploited and formed unions to represent their interests. The violent history of capitalism is replete with stories of bosses undermining the conditions of their employees, workers withdrawing their labour, and the state bringing in the troopers to calm tensions (often shooting striking workers).[54] There is antagonism between those owning capital and those working for a wage. The former want to get as much value out of the workers as possible; the workers want to obtain a wage representing the real value of their work. There is a constant battle being fought over the conditions of work and the share of the pie going to capitalists and to the working class. What looks like 'freedom' in the workplace is really a relation of coercion and inequality. Capitalism provides us with just the latest example of the class conflict that was present when slaves confronted slave owners and serfs confronted Lords. In our time it is the workers taking on the owners of the means of production. We live in a world of exploitation and conflict. Car workers in the US, meatpackers in Brazil, textile workers in Bangladesh, and miners in South Africa all have good reason to oppose their employers—and do so on a regular basis.

Chicago Boys

How can the continuation of an economic system that alienates its workers, creates massive poverty in the face of record profits for capital, generates ill-health among its populations, pollutes the earth, and continues to produce climate-changing greenhouse gas emissions. be 'justified'? Part of the answer is by looking at the world through the rose-coloured glasses of a cohort of ideologues whose economic theories, and political followers, have celebrated and facilitated the expansion of capitalism.

Ludwig von Mises was born in 1881 and migrated to the US in 1940. He was a strong believer in the ideas embraced by classical liberalism and wrote and lectured on how a free market was the most rational way of allocating scarce resources. His central argument was that government laws and regulations to assist workers, or protect the environment, or to intervene in any way in the economy, would result in a misalignment of profit incentives. He considered that those with anti-capitalist leanings were simply jealous of others who had prospered through hard work and perseverance.[55] His unswerving approval of capitalism duly influenced a number of his students, among them Frederick von Hayek. Hayek understood that a free market was the best way to encourage entrepreneurship and technical progress. Governments could provide a safety net for the poor and vulnerable and fund agencies fighting crime but should refrain from interfering in wider economic life. Progress, he believed, was generated by a small number of highly talented and motivated innovators who were entitled to a disproportionate share of society's wealth. Inequality was inevitable in a world where some worked harder, and produced better societal outcomes, than others. During the 1940s he became involved with economists at the University of Chicago, taking his bag of ideas with him. It was with open arms that Milton

Friedman grasped the thoughts of Hayek and wove them into his own theories and prognostications. Here are some tastes of Milton's morality:

> Well first of all, tell me: Is there some society you know that doesn't run on greed? You think Russia doesn't run on greed? You think China doesn't run on greed? What is greed? Of course, none of us [is] greedy, it's only the other fellow who's greedy.
>
> A free market … is the most effective system we have discovered to enable people who hate one another to deal with one another and help one another.
>
> I am in favor of cutting taxes under any circumstances and for any excuse, for any reason, whenever it's possible.
>
> Many people want the government to protect the consumer. A much more urgent problem is to protect the consumer from the government.[56]

The latter sentiment was expressed neatly by Ronald Reagan when he told the American public that the nine most terrifying words they would ever hear were 'I'm from the government and I'm here to help'.[57]

Milton was a *laissez-faire* evangelist—one of the so-called Chicago School boys who believed corporations had no greater responsibility than to make money for their shareholders irrespective of the societal consequences, who argued vehemently that economic growth should not be hampered by environmental concerns, and who believed unfettered economic competition was beneficial despite its negative impacts upon workers' rights and rising economic inequalities.[58] Who should deal with any negative externalities? Paradoxically, Friedman argues it is the role of government to fix them. So, there you have it. You let the free-market system deliver benefits to capitalists and you demand the government clean up the mess they leave. You privatise the gains and socialise the losses.[59] Sound, judgement-free, economics apparently underpins this logic.

Not surprisingly, supported by the right-wing media and numerous think tanks across the US, Friedman's ideas were pursued with a vengeance. Why would they not be? They were a prescription for very hefty payments to CEOs, financiers, and assorted billionaires. Unsurprisingly, the field of management theory was developed largely to provide ideological justification for domination of workers by their bosses along with the high pay received by those doing the dominating.[60] Corporations have flourished, employing global legal systems to advance their power and to accrue profits. Their presence is felt in most of the 3,500 'special economic zones' scattered across the globe. In these zones—which employ more than 66 million low paid workers—unions are banned and governments police activities, ensuring the corporations make huge and uninterrupted profits from these global sweatshops.[61]

The deregulation of the finance sector has increased the mobility of capital, with global corporations having become one of the most important non-state actors on a global scale (but followed closely by religious actors and transnational criminal organisations).[62] As US law professor Peter Spiro has written:

> Developed countries are no longer well positioned to regulate multinational[s] … Corporations have offshore production facilities … As capital grows more mobile, firms exploit regulatory competition to lower production costs. States must balance the risk of capital flight against the desirability of higher regulatory standards.[63]

The growth of the corporate sector since the 1970s has been nothing short of a 'silent coup', according to investigative journalists Claire Provost and Matt Kennard—a coup which has consolidated the wealth of big business while undermining both democracy and the power of sovereign governments.[64] In 2024 Oxfam reported that billionaires run seven out of ten of the world's largest corporations and that the world's wealthiest 1% own some 43% of all the world's global assets. We live in a 'new age of billionaire supremacy, controlled by monopolists and financiers (one where) corporate power exploits and magnifies inequalities of gender and race, as well as economic inequality'.[65] Meanwhile, the Big Tech companies dominate economies, massaging the information we receive, selectively promoting what we can—or cannot—buy, and attempting to control our behaviour through algorithmic programming.[66]

Some Boats Rising, Most Boats Sinking

Friedman asserts that the individual's freedom is sacrosanct. And our freedom increases the less we experience government meddling. Of course, this assertion denies the possibility that government interventions and regulations can actually assist us to become more 'free' by constraining bad behaviour on the part of business. A second paradox, given Friedman's dislike of government, is that the monetary theory he developed relies heavily on the actions of those very governments he wants out of the way. They are needed to hold a tight rein on monetary supply. Friedman is fine with a state using monetary policy to enact stringent austerity measures on workers as a way of controlling inflation.

The capitalist world was losing its way in the 1970s. Economic growth was slowing, unemployment levels were rising, and inflation levels were soaring—resulting in 'stagflation'. Governments around the world were desperate to find a solution. Milton Friedman and his followers' time had arrived. Their argument was that government policies in the 'long boom' after the Second World War had led to excessive spending by the state, and expansionary monetary policy was driving inflation. The solution was obvious—reduce the activities of the state to prevent the 'crowding out' of private business activities. Government belt-tightening should reduce inflation and stimulate investment spending. Despite the dubious claims made by the monetarists,[67] political leaders around the world embraced the idea that tightened budgets would be the cure for stagflation. In the US, President Reagan reduced federal government spending, cut government ('red tape') regulation, tightened money supply, and reduced federal income tax and capital gains tax—all in line with Friedman's monetarist theory.

This was the birth of neoliberalism and many countries followed suit plunging, like so many lemmings, off the cliffs of insanity. In Britain, Thatcher's Conservative government adopted the fundamentals of monetarism but added some important new elements. State-owned assets were privatised, the finance industry was deregulated, there were reductions in income taxes (to favour the wealthy), workers' wages were constrained, and labour unions were attacked—all with the aim of controlling inflation. Inflation was controlled, but unemployment remained high and there was a decline in traditional manufacturing. Public assets were sold *en masse*, with the consequence, for England's water supply, that pipes, treatment plants, and reservoirs are now owned by a Malaysian corporation, a Norwegian bank, and US-based JP Morgan Asset Management. Dividends to shareholders of these entities increased dramatically, while infrastructure—once in the hands of local councils—has become grossly run down in private hands. 'Almost nothing seems to be working in Britain ... the country is "creaking"'. Sewage, which should head straight for a treatment plant, is being released into waterways so as to cut costs for the privately-owned plants. This widespread practice even boasts an innocuous name - 'flow trimming'.[68] Neoliberalism and planning co-exist in a very uneven way. In fact, they are incompatible—why try to plan when the free market is the best allocator of resources?[69] In an assessment of the 'Thatcher legacy' Kevin Albertson of Manchester Metropolitan University and co-writer Paul Stepney of Tampere University, Finland, have written in the *Cambridge Journal of Economics*:

> Thatcher claimed that she had improved the economic prospects of the UK and all its citizens through the application of neo-liberal policies ... The evidence, however, does not support the claim ... Economic growth was weaker under Thatcher than under preceding governments ... The costs of this lack of economic growth were disproportionately borne by the poor ... Nor were Thatcher's policies for creating democratic capitalism ... effective. An increasing proportion of the UK's productive assets and housing stock is now in the hands of foreign capitalists, while British households run up increasing debt to compensate for stagnant incomes.
>
> As Thatcher herself argued 'Those who think they know, but are mistaken, and act upon their mistakes, are the most dangerous people to have in charge'.
>
> On this, at least, we can all agree![70]

Perhaps her problems started with her briefcase—apparently the Iron Lady kept a copy of Hayek's *The Constitution of Liberty* handy at all times in case one of her ministers dared deviate from her free-market extremism.[71] Under neoliberalism, a rising tide of economic development was supposed to lift all boats. Everyone in the economy would benefit from policies designed to strengthen capitalism. The tidal analogy was joined by another slippery idea—that of 'trickle down'. It was claimed that reducing taxes on the wealthy would improve the overall health of the economy because increasing the wealth of the already-rich would stimulate their investment in job-creating industries, helping all.

This inegalitarian notion was buttressed by US economist Arthur Laffer. He pointed out that some of the most economically prosperous states in the US did not have income or estate taxes. Success would therefore come through the widespread abandonment of those taxes. The so-called Laffer curve (we should indeed laugh, if it were not so cruel) purports to show that as taxes are increased on the wealthy, revenues to government decline. Another paradox? Apparently not for neoliberal economists. When taxes become too high the wealthy decide that they no longer wish to invest in productive enterprises. *Ipso facto*, reducing taxes for the rich will bring about more investment in those enterprises, creating jobs and stimulating economic growth. This is all part and parcel of 'supply-side' economics. Businesses 'supply' the economy and the more they can supply the better. Therefore, businesses need to be caressed and stimulated with a reduction in taxes, less regulation, and lower rates of interest.[72]

The jury's verdict is in, and it is now clear that the tides and trickles should go the way of the baby's bathwater. Hundreds of billions in tax cuts to the wealthy in the US in Reagan's time resulted in less revenue for the state, limited job growth, and a general lack of investment in economic pursuits. Instead, economic inequalities began to increase in a dramatic way. Under Reagan the top income tax rate dropped precipitously from 70% to 28%.[73] As John McMurtry of the University of Guelph has argued in his book *Unequal Freedoms: The Global Market System as an Ethical System*, the theories of economists and actions of politicians who believe they are building a truly free and democratic society actually undermine those very ideals. In relation to the 'trickle-down' proposition he notes:

> Rich corporations and private beneficiaries of tax cuts never have to sign contracts with the rest of society to make good on their promises of social benefits to all … The rich's money-property increases from tax reductions come with no ties. The money-property will be invested where it

maximises money returns. It will assuredly not trickle down to the poor of the society. To project this beneficial outcome is a form of wishful thinking, whose source is market theology.[74]

McMurtry made this claim in 1998. Yet the same prescriptions have been rolled out, and the same outcomes have been evident, for the past two decades. Trump called tax cuts the 'rocket fuel' of the economy and slashed the rate to 21% in 2017. In 2022, Liz Truss's first act as Prime Minister was to hand tax cuts to Britain's rich. A study of tax cuts in 18 developed nations showed that they overwhelmingly favour the wealthy, while having little positive effect on economic growth and employment.[75] It is now firmly recognised that:

> Growing inequality is associated with less efficient economies, flourishing rent seeking and non-ethical behaviour, a loss of social trust and erosion of the law, lower public investment and 'the evisceration of democracy'.[76]

In 2014 Thomas Piketty, a professor at the Paris School of Economics, produced a 696-page tome *Capital in the Twenty-First Century* which carefully details how neoliberal policies have created manifest economic inequality. It is not only that the eight wealthiest billionaires own as much as half the world's population, but also that the gap between the wealthy and the rest is growing.[77]

Piketty argues that in today's economy, where the average return on capital is greater than the overall rate of economic growth, those with inherited wealth will see their fortunes growing at a greater rate than those receiving income from wages. With the ratio of wealth to income rising in all developed countries, Piketty sees the resultant inequality eventually undermining the foundations of democracy—unless government intervention via taxation reform can lead to wealth redistribution.[78] In complete opposition to the right-wing trope of make-the-rich-more-wealthy-and-we'll-all-be-better-off, Piketty believes capitalism is producing levels of inequality that are leading us back to nineteenth-century Dickensian times. It is producing levels of income disparity that are incompatible with democracy, leading to violence and crime and helping to turn America from the land of the free to the home of the jailed.[79]

As one analyst has claimed:

> It is scarcely an exaggeration to say that the modern gurus of libertarian economics – Friedman, Mises, Hayek, and their followers – were and are basically intellectual McCarthyites, motivated by a visceral hatred of communism and, by association, of all forms of socialism ... It is time for us to recognise that Friedman's libertarian capitalism is ... contrary to the best interests of most people. And that it is also incompatible with sustainable long-term economic strategy.[80]

In a pithier vein, 'I have a joke about trickle-down economics. But 99% of you won't get it'.[81]

Financing the Future

In 2013, I was interviewing New York bankers as part of a research project into the financialisation of the global economy. One steamy summer morning in June I entered a ritzy banking establishment in Madison Avenue and was ushered through some very tight security. I was greeted by the Head of Commodities Trading and took a lift to the twelfth floor. We walked past six rows of long tables with about 20 people seated at each table working multiple computer screens. 'These are our commodity traders', he gestured, 'all are millionaires in their own right'. (It took me a while to realise I'd just brushed passed US$120 million worth of human capital. This was only five years after the biggest financial meltdown in the US since the Great Depression.) We entered his well-appointed office and began the interview. 'What have been some of the effects of the financialisation of the US economy' I asked. 'I don't believe in "financialisation"' he replied 'it is a fiction of the left – there is a severe analytic problem with the use of this term'. That wasn't such a brilliant start. 'Do you think speculation is driving commodity prices at the moment' was my second question. 'No', he said 'we need all kinds of investors to help us discover the real prices of commodities. Take food. Futures traders actually help reduce food price volatility by producing reliable benchmark prices'. Stock answers—as one might have expected. What about large-scale acquisition of farmlands around the globe, or so-called land grabbing? He paused and said 'if you look at just the pure mathematics of the portfolios, they're wonderful investments; they're counter cyclical and if you have patient capital and you have that ability to save through time and it produces a public good. You can actually make more food for the world.' Sanguine responses from a well-heeled survivor of the GFC. He was candid and friendly and I was genuinely grateful he could give me 45 minutes of his (very) valuable time.

That afternoon, across town, I grabbed a takeaway coffee with a financial journalist and author of a best-selling book on commodity trading. A different story emerged. A detailed analysis of private equity (PE) firms in the US revealed their crucial role in the financialisation of the economy. Their *modus operandi* is pretty straightforward, he said—identify companies that might be struggling, repackage them or split them, reduce labour costs—all in the hope they will become more profitable—then sell them off and pocket the takings (think corporate raider Edward Lewis—played by Richard Gere—in *Pretty Woman*). 'Or, they'll buy a company, let the company go bankrupt and take the assets and sell them from under'. The journalist claimed 'PE is destroying businesses and jobs throughout this nation while billions of dollars are being made by these firms whose only rationale is to make as much money in as short a time as possible'. 'When businesses owned by PE are squeezed their workers suffer and their customers get inferior goods and services. This is now going on all over the world. It's one of the main features of financialisation.'

Just What Is Financialisation?

The deregulatory thrust that has accompanied neoliberalism has freed up capital markets, providing new opportunities for money lending and for the repackaging of debt. Since the 1980s we have seen the spectacular expansion in the size of financial markets, the growing significance of finance-based activities in the economy, and the application of new techniques to speed up flows of finance. This is financialisation—the increasing presence and influence of finance in the economy and in the lives of individuals and societies. It has three key components. The first is the presence of new players in the field. We all recognise that banks and investment houses have been around for generations. But not so sovereign wealth funds, PE, and hedge funds. These have been influential in the world of finance only since the 1990s.[82] The second component is the creation, and extension, of financial 'products' with names such as derivatives, junk bonds, options, credit default swaps, and collateralised debt obligations—all developed via the clever financial alchemy of banks and Wall Street traders for the purpose of making money. The third component of financialisation is the change in focus of business activity. Financialisation has helped to create what some call 'casino capitalism' where a company is judged by its share performance on the stock market rather than its contribution to the economy's material prosperity, where speculation is rife, where there are 'profits without production', and where money spins through the global economy at astonishing speed.[83]

According to British author and journalist Nicholas Shaxson we have all been financially cursed:

> The concept of the financial curse is simple: it's the idea that once a financial sector grows above an optimal size and beyond its useful roles, it begins to harm the country that hosts it … It also becomes politically powerful, shaping laws and rules and even society to suit it. The results include lower economic growth, steeper inequality, inefficient markets, damage to public services, worse corruption, the hollowing-out of alternative economic sectors, and widespread damage to democracy and society.[84]

At the international level the financial system is increasingly volatile, generating unpredictability and eventual 'contagion' (when, for example, the fragile debt-ridden US market of 2008 led to a series of financial shocks that heralded the GFC). We are living with a financial curse in which most of the complex financial instruments are scams.[85]

Let's look at the GFC in a little more detail. Before the GFC banks were happily financing house purchases. They did not want to keep these mortgages on their books, however, for fear of eventual default by their many customers. Mortgages are an illiquid asset.[86] To ease their financial risks they created Special Purpose Vehicles which allowed other banks and traders to purchase their mortgages. Debts (the money owed by customers) were packaged as securities and traded on the market. For what purpose? For the banks, the loans they had originally made to home buyers were paid back to them by those purchasing the security. For those purchasing the security—investment bankers, smaller banks and hedge funds—the mortgages they had bought from the big banks delivered monthly repayments from the home buyers. Furthermore, with less risk on their books the banks could offer even more loans. Neat? Yes, to a point. With available credit splashing around, the banks started lending money to people who had little chance of paying back their mortgage. As people began defaulting on their loans those financial entities that had purchased the securities were sitting on assets that were no longer in demand. They certainly didn't want to purchase any more mortgages from the bigger banks. With that stream of income defunct, there were major bankruptcies which, in turn, caused investors throughout the economy to lose confidence. The downward spiral was only halted by governments, around the world, pumping taxpayer money into their economies helping to keep afloat bankers and insurers deemed 'too big to fail'. (Another option would have been to nationalise the lot but, for some reason, that did not appear on the radar.)

Was subprime mortgage lending the cause of the meltdown? Superficially, it looks to be so. But if we dig a little deeper we can identify the role played by derivatives. These are the securities mentioned above. Their value is derived from an underlying asset or index, and they are best represented as future contracts, forwards, options, and swaps.[87] Importantly, many derivatives are not traded on exchanges; they are not in the public arena. Instead, they are used by institutions to hedge against risk and to speculate on the future price of an underlying asset.[88] They can hedge against risk by giving the buyer an opportunity to purchase a contract for an underlying asset that moves in a different direction from another asset owned by the investor. Here, the hedge is a sensible and mostly beneficial investment—profit in one asset can offset the losses in another.

But what about speculation? Derivatives can be volatile and high risk. The actual design of the contracts is often opaque—it is difficult to ascertain what has been bundled together in a contract (for example, I came across one contract combining gold and pigs) making it difficult for investors to predict its performance.[89]

Cambridge political economist Ha-Joon Chang has summed this up best:

> [F]inancial innovations created mortgage-backed securities (MBSs) which bundle together up to several thousand mortgages. In turn, these MBSs, sometimes as many as 150 of them, were packed into a collateralized debt obligation (CDO). Then CDOs-squared were created by using other CDOs as collateral. And then CDOs-cubed were created by combining CDOs and CDOs-squared. Even higher-powered CDOs were created. Credit default swaps (CDSs) were created to protect you from default on the CDOs. And there are many more financial derivatives that make up the alphabet soup that is modern finance.[90]

Importantly, many derivatives are traded over-the-counter (OTC). This means contracts are written outside of a stock exchange—where the latter normally provides transparency and reveals current market prices. Trading in an unregulated market means that the connection between the derivative and an underlying asset has been severed, with the contract owner betting—at high stakes—on particular market outcomes. It is a bit like cryptocurrencies—they have no fundamental value. They are 'a game of pass-the-parcel, in which speculators try to sell them to someone else before the price collapses'.[91] Just prior the GFC trillions of dollars had been invested in volatile and sometimes dodgy OTC derivative-based contracts that were complex and interdependent, meaning that if anything were to go wrong, the effects would be experienced throughout the entire financial system. Thus, as analysts of this historic episode have said, it became clear in 2008 that OTC derivatives increased the magnitude of financial system instability and probability of failure due to the complexity and lack of transparency of the contracts, disproportionate leverage exposure and dependencies on other markets vulnerable to disruptive forces.[92]

The 2008 financial crisis was primarily caused by derivatives in the mortgage market. The issues with derivatives arise when investors hold too many, being overleveraged, and are not able to meet margin calls if the value of the derivative moves against them.[93]

Some might think this has now all gone away? We have learnt our lesson, paid the high price for speculation, and have regulated our financial industries? Well, not so, it appears. Rather:

> Derivative contracts, more than 10 times the world GDP ... hang over the financial world like the sword of Damocles, but to the average investor the derivatives bubble is invisible ... [while] the true cause of what became known as the credit crisis continues unabated, outside the purview of the central banks and government.[94]

The very products developed through 'securitisation'—repackaging of assets into interest-bearing securities—to create financial growth and economic benefit were the Achilles heel of the financial system, leading to its collapse in 2008 and wringing trillions of dollars of loss from stocks and shares. Astute US investor Warren Buffet has described derivatives as 'financial weapons' that could destroy the world economy[95]—he would be one of the people best placed to know. According to Canadian researcher Max Haiven:

> Between the practices of high-frequency trading, inter-market arbitrage, the securitization of new synthetic financial assets ... and the internecine and corrupt entanglements of major banks, hedge funds and shadowy para-financial firms, it is no longer simple to trace any clear line between the financial imaginarium and the so-called 'real economy'.[96]

Those who created the sophisticated financial products of doom were too clever for their own good. But some unlikely financiers have benefited from securitisation. In 1997 that Goblin King from *Labyrinth*, David Bowie, began issuing bonds—so-called Bowie Bonds—to raise money for the purchase of recordings of his music held by his former manager. Investors in the bonds would, in turn, receive income from his previously released albums. It represented the first securitisation of the intellectual property of a pop star. The securities were buoyed by online music sales, providing investors with regular returns on their investment. When the bonds were redeemed in 2007, the rights to his 25 albums reverted to Bowie.[97] A win–win as some like to say.

But new concerns are arising in the world of high finance. Enter the algorithm. As discussed in Chapter 1, algorithms are math-based instructions programmed into computers to solve a problem or accomplish a desired outcome. They appear neutral—apolitical, amoral, and free from prejudice. But, according to a number of authors, they are central to technochauvinism—the belief that technology is the solution to every problem. Algorithms are largely unregulated and unchallenged, yet their application can reinforce biases and promote discrimination, bigotry, and coercion.[98] They have become, according to US data analyst and author Cathy O'Neil, 'weapons of math destruction'.[99]

Just as with music, there is a certain mathematical beauty to the algorithm. Every time you search Google, algorithms behind the scenes sift through hundreds of thousands of entries, delivering your request in split seconds. Algorithms are employed by companies to select staff, to measure their productivity, and to send goods to customers. They are present in our iPhones, TVs, and computers. In a world of computer dating they readily predict who might best accompany us to the bedroom.[100] They are everywhere and are indispensable for modern living. But in the hands of the finance sector their actions are never innocent. The high-frequency trading of stocks is known as HFT or algorithmic trading.[101] It entails algorithms identifying price discrepancies for a stock across different markets. They are then instructed to pounce. They will, almost instantaneously, purchase or sell that stock so as to make a profit—even a tiny profit—on the sale. It has cut out human influence—no person could do the mathematical calculations quickly enough to spot the small differences in market value and to make the trade. The algorithms undertake this task placing 'thousands of orders at blindingly fast speeds'.[102]

But things can go wrong. Just one suspect or faulty algorithm can result in the collapse of share prices, causing investor panic. Such market volatility can erode market confidence leading to flow on effects throughout the economy (examples include the so-called Flash Crash of 2010, the 'mini-crash' of Progress Energy in 2010, and the near-bankruptcy of Knight Capital in 2012).[103] After years of careful and detailed investigation the authors of a British government report posed the question 'Can high frequency trading lead to crashes?' Their answer was unequivocal—'it has in the past, and it can be expected to do so more and more in the future … financial instabilities can be expected to flourish in a world dominated by HFT'.[104]

Welcome to the casino—please place your bets wisely.

Are We Are All Neolibs Now?

Hollywood has a fascination with Wall Street. You might have a movie favourite. Was it the comedy *Trading Places* (1983)? Or *Boiler Room* (2000), a high-octane film about a dropout who becomes a stockbroker using 'pump and dump'[105] tactics to make a fortune? Maybe you cringed at the narcissistic, self-obsessed behaviour of Wall Street yuppie Patrick Bateman (Christian Bale) in *American Psycho* (2000)? Was it *Margin Call* (2011) about the 2008 financial meltdown and desperate attempts to dispose of toxic assets? For many it was *Wall Street*, the 1987 movie directed by Oliver Stone and starring Michael Douglas and Charlie Sheen. Douglas plays Gordon Gekko, a corporate psychopath who makes his money from insider trading and who lives by the motto 'greed is good.' My personal favourites are *The Wolf of Wall Street* (2013) and *The Big Short* (2015). Leonardo DiCaprio is the *Wolf* in a stunning performance about the rise of a small-time stockbroker who, consistent with his whatever-it-takes attitude, becomes one of New York's richest traders. He does so by defrauding investors while at the same time indulging in a lifestyle replete with drugs, prostitutes, yachts, and expensive cars. His character is viewed by many as the quintessential Wall Street trader—brash, unethical, self-serving, debauched, a clean-scrubbed gangster with a computer screen rather than a gun.[106] There is audience fascination here for the clever con-man which forms part of 'America's addiction to capitalist excess', according to film critic Matt Zoller Seitz.[107] The Wolf was, of course, male. These traders (85% of whom are male) are 'working in an insane elite world that institutionalizes competitive, power-oriented masculinity, and … doing whatever it takes'.[108] *The Big Short* looks at stock trading in the years leading up to the 2008 market crash. Several players—adept at using the new banking products created the decade before—were quick to recognise the instability of subprime mortgages. The traders and hedge fund managers who pulled off the big short[109] made millions by betting against the housing market in the US. They were greedy and opportunistic, but they could not have succeeded without the banking world's creation of 'deliberately concocted Byzantine financial tools whose main function was to help the rich get richer and screw over the little guy.'[110] (These tools still exist today.)[111]

If there is a common theme to these films it is that financial manipulation—ethical or unethical—can, in an unstable marketplace, create fortunes for the astute and/or lucky. Furthermore, their windfall is deserved. They have played their hand (even if it is an underhand) and won. It has been suggested that US workers 'see themselves not as an exploited proletariat but as temporarily embarrassed millionaires'.[112] Of course, such a perception is fuel for the fire of even more greed, competition and ruthless behaviour by the finance sector.

It is possible to identify, in a less theatrical and more sociological way, the culture that permeates Wall Street. In a revealing ethnographic study, anthropologist Karen Ho interviewed Wall Street investment bankers in the heady times before the 2008 GFC to identify their values and practices. The image they have of themselves is hardworking, efficient, competitive, globally-focused, and smart. Especially, smart. They believe they deserve the high incomes they receive because of the pressures they are under and the hours they work—all under a constant threat of dismissal if there's any hint of an economic glitch. They are 'liquid employees' making the big bucks while they can. In this high risk/high reward world where everyone works hard, there is an attitude that the 'lazy' and 'unaccountable' workers outside Wall Street should be made to raise their performance if they seek to achieve the American dream. The traders are part of, and embrace, the highly volatile conditions imposed by finance capital. They believe that increased liquidity in the marketplace is highly desirable, no matter what this might mean in terms of corporate failures, stock market meltdowns, and even their own jobs. They imagine themselves as warriors for capitalism. Competitive individualism runs rife among the white elite males pulling the strings. Importantly, Ho suggests, the ideologies and strategies of Wall Street brokers have spilled over into the entire global economy, helping to normalise marketplace brutality.[113]

Other important books have also revealed the excesses of Wall Street and the corporate world which it partners.[114] *Barbarians at the Gate* details the leveraged buyout, in 1988, of RJR Nabisco. The CEO, F. Ross Johnson, decided to turn the conglomerate into a private company, potentially making millions on the side. He was enjoying a huge salary and perks but wanted more. Corporate raider Kohlberg Kravis & Roberts (KKR) entered the scene, outbidding others and taking control of the company, subsequently spinning off divisions and cutting jobs. It was a lesson in corporate kleptocracy—the actions of a greedy CEO and of a hungry private equity firm (the barbarian waiting at the gate) leading to the destruction of one of America's most respected companies.[115] For his outstanding contribution to corporate greed, Johnson was blessed with a US$30 million payout and 'entered semi-retirement, laughing at the whole affair'.[116]

Published in 2018, *Black Edge* tracks the firm SAC Capital as it accumulates billions of dollars from extensive insider trading. It was founded by 'star' investor Steve Cohen whose illegal activity was given the euphemism of 'earnings intelligence'—the 'edge' was inside knowledge about companies that allowed SAC Capital to outplay the competition. The firm's culture was toxic and 'everyone was expendable, including partners and mentors. Cohen couldn't tolerate anyone making money before he did'.[117] His life was one of excess, living in a mansion in Greenwich, flying to his office by helicopter, and assembling one of the world's largest private art collections.[118] He was eventually pursued and caught by the FBI and his company was fined some US$2 billion. While the company pleaded guilty, Cohen kept his US$10 billion fortune. He walked away a free man, demonstrating to those outside the corporate world that Wall Street's key players can choose to live above the law.[119] He remains a hedge fund manager, owns the New York Mets baseball team, has a fortune of some US$13 billion, has an art collection worth US$1 billion, and donated US$1 million to Trump's inauguration. He has emerged a winner after one of the biggest criminal cases against a hedge fund in US history.[120]

In the 2023 masterpiece *Chaos Kings: How Wall Street Traders Make Billions in the New Age of Crisis*, financial journalist Scott Patterson describes how raw masculinity drives Wall St traders to outplay each other in exploiting market volatility.[121] They try to identify the next 'black swan' event—a pandemic, a cyberattack, national rivalries, climate change-induced devastation, and so on—and then adopt risky, counter-intuitive, trades on the stock exchange. Their money is made from identifying, and exploiting, future crises. In his review of Patterson's book, Carl Rhodes, a professor of organisation studies, has written

> *Chaos Kings* is not so much about the rapacious 'greed is good' mentality of the 1980s … the prevailing attitude [is] more like 'greed is amoral', technical even. As the profits flowed from the COVID disaster, there was little hint of ethical quandary. All stops were taken out in the pursuit of profit from pain … These [traders] are 'crisis hunters' who hide behind cold computer screens, playing with other people's lives as if they were meaningless pieces in a parlour game for the wealthy elite.

Read it and weep.[122]

The personalities and actions of F. Ross Johnson and Steve Cohen—like the traders in *Chaos Kings*—have been moulded through family values (or lack thereof), educational influences, peer group pressures, business norms, hyped-up masculinity, and aspects of popular culture, along with the free-market ideologies that jump out from the pages of the *Wall Street Journal*. They have been shaped, as people, through the process of socialisation. From the beginning of the neoliberal era in the 1970s and 1980s particular ideas have gained prominence. We exist as competitive, self-serving individuals. Personal advancement will come through self-improvement. We must become entrepreneurs of the self.[123] Hedonism has its place here—we can justify most things we do if it gives us pleasure. It is good to be cool, and therefore to know what to eat, watch, wear, read, and drive (we are 'acutely brand aware').[124] We need to be flexible and adaptable to survive in a fast-moving world. We believe in meritocracy; if people are enterprising, determined, and resilient they should achieve outcomes well beyond those of people who are indolent and uninformed. It is no wonder that we praise the successful entrepreneurs—they have achieved success through their individual talents. Wealth, privilege, and power are to be celebrated as evidence of the hard work and clever market positioning of 'the self'. We adopt the language of the marketers—we self-actualise, doing a lot of blue-sky thinking and imagineering. We want to incentivise those on our radar and go for the low-hanging fruit. We deep-dive with friends in the tent—always going forward.[125] We recognise that opportunism brings its own rewards, while collective ideals like 'community' and 'solidarity' belong to an older era and have little value in a robust competitive economy.

Like Ross Johnson and Steve Cohen, we have all been thoroughly programmed to take our places on the trading floor of the great stock exchange of life.

Or have we? As we will see in Chapter 8, normalising and legitimising market rule might be the desired way to turn us all into zombie supporters of capitalism, but the process is never complete. There is resistance. And there are contradictions in the system of capitalist production that—once exposed—reveal the true nature of its exploitative ways, together with its vulnerabilities. One thing seems for certain. Under capitalism, where bigger is always better and more is never enough, we are all living a 'twisted dream'.[126]

Notes

1. Most of the things sociologists are interested in are, in this way, 'reduced to error factors on … economist's regression equations.' See quote by Howard Newby in Lawrence, G. (1987) *Capitalism*

and the *Countryside: The Rural Crisis in Australia*, Pluto Press, Sydney, p. 307.
2. Fortunately, we have an alternative way to think about economics—political economy, an interdisciplinary approach which embeds the economy in a social context and which makes explicit the value judgements which underpin its reasoning. See Stilwell, F. (2002) *Political Economy: The Contest of Economic Ideas*, Oxford University Press, Victoria, p. 36. This will be discussed in Chapter 8.
3. Lawson, T. (2017) What is wrong with modern economics, and why does it stay wrong? *Journal of Australian Political Economy* 80: 26–42.
4. Smith, A. (1954) *The Wealth of Nations*, Volume 1, Dent and Sons, London, p. 13.
5. The concept of 'utility' is central to the argument, here. The individual gains satisfaction or 'marginal utility' from the sale or purchase of an additional unit of any item. Sociologist Max Weber demonstrated that this assumption was quite silly—the 'needs' of actors are socially constructed, and businesses regularly operate outside rationalities of marginal utility. See Weber, M. (1978) *Economy and Society: An Outline of Interpretive Sociology*, University of California Press, Berkeley.
6. The Editors. (2018) The cooperative human, *Nature Human Behaviour* 2(7): 427–428. There are many articles about human cooperation in this volume.
7. Ariely, D. (2009) The end of rational economics, https://hbr.org/2009/07/the-end-of-rational-economics.
8. See Tepper, J. and Hearn, D. (2019) *The Myth of Capitalism: Monopolies and the Death of Competition*, Wiley, New Jersey; Howard, P. (2016) *Concentration and Power in the Food System: Who Controls What We Eat?* Bloomsbury, London.
9. Keen, S. (2001) *Debunking Economics: The Naked Emperor of the Social Sciences*, Pluto Press, Australia; Diesendorf, M. and Taylor, R. (2023) *The Path to a Sustainable Civilization: Technological, Socioeconomic and Political Change*, Palgrave Macmillan, Singapore, pp. 162–169.

10. Stilwell, F. (1976) Liberal economic ideology and policy issues, in E. Wheelwright and F. Stilwell (eds) *Readings in Political Economy*, Volume 1, Australia and New Zealand Book Company, Sydney, p. 138.
11. See for more detail Dow, G. (2002) Anti-rationalism in political economy, *Journal of Australian Political Economy* 50: 72–81.
12. Bebchuk, L. (2012) Executive pay and the financial crisis, https://blogs.worldbank.org/allaboutfinance/executive-pay-and-the-financial-crisis.
13. Hess, A. (2021) In 2020, top CEOs earned 351 times more than the typical worker, https://www.cnbc.com/2021/09/15/in-2020-top-ceos-earned-351-times-more-than-the-typical-worker.html.
14. Hess, In 2020, top CEOs earned 351 times more than the typical worker.
15. Furhmann, R. and Kvilhaug, S. (2021) 5 CEOs with the biggest payouts during the Global Financial Crisis bailouts, https://www.investopedia.com/investing/5-ceos-biggest-payouts-during-global-financial-crisis-bailouts/. See also Yang, A. (2018) *The War on Normal People: The Truth About America's Disappearing Jobs and Why Universal Basic Income Is Our Future*, Hachette Books, New York, pp. 208–209.
16. New Economics Foundation. (2009) A bit rich: Calculating the real value to society of different professions, https://neweconomics.org/2009/12/a-bit-rich.
17. This section is drawn from: Mander, J. and Goldsmith, E. (eds) (1996) *The Case Against the Global Economy, and For a Turn Toward the Local*, Sierra Club Books, San Francisco; Nader, R. et al., (1993) *The Case Against Free Trade: GATT, NAFTA, and the Globalization of Corporate Power*, Earth Island Press, San Francisco; Stilwell, F. (2002) *Political Economy: The Contest of Economic Ideas*, Oxford, Melbourne; Fletcher, I. (2011) Why the theory of comparative advantage is wrong, *International Journal of Pluralism and Economics Education* 2(4): 421–429.
18. Daly, H. (1996) Free trade: The perils of deregulation, in J. Mander and E. Goldsmith (eds) *The Case Against the Global*

Economy, and For a Turn Toward the Local, Sierra Club Books, San Francisco, pp. 229–238.
19. Chang, H.-J. (2007) *Bad Samaritans: The Guilty Secrets of the Rich Nations and the Threat to Global Prosperity*, Random House, London; Coke-Hamilton, P. (2019) We must help developing countries escape commodity dependence, https://www.weforum.org/agenda/2019/05/why-commodity-dependence-is-bad-news-for-all-of-us/.
20. Masch, V. (2011) The myth of comparative advantage, https://www.huffpost.com/entry/the-myth-of-comparative-a_b_581814.
21. Masch, The myth of comparative advantage.
22. Kelton, S. (2021) *The Deficit Myth: Modern Monetary Theory and How to Build a Better Economy*, John Murray, UK, pp. 8–9.
23. Kelton, *The Deficit Myth*, p. 8.
24. Kelton, *The Deficit Myth*, p. 9.
25. Elliott, L. (2023) Tory austerity 'has cost UK half a trillion pounds of public spending since 2010', https://www.theguardian.com/business/2023/mar/03/tory-austerity-has-cost-uk-half-a-trillion-pounds-of-public-spending-since-2010.
26. Morris, N. (2018) David Cameron's austerity measures 'led to vote for Brexit', https://inews.co.uk/news/brexit/david-camerons-austerity-measures-led-to-vote-for-brexit-182802.
27. Wren-Lewis, S. (2019) The three big lies we were told that led to Brexit, the most damaging lie of all, https://www.independent.co.uk/voices/brexit-lies-austerity-conservatives-immigration-financial-crisis-racism-neoliberalism-a8929986.html.
28. Wren-Lewis, S. (2018) *The Lies We Were Told: Politics, Economics, Austerity and Brexit*, Bristol University Press, Bristol, UK.
29. Smith, W. (2014) Why the federal budget is not like a household budget, https://theconversation.com/why-the-federal-budget-is-not-like-a-household-budget-35498.
30. Smith, Why the federal budget is not like a household budget.

31. Van Lerven, F. and Jackson, A. (2018) Claims of ending austerity ring hollow, until we do away with the 'household fallacy', https://neweconomics.org/2018/10/a-government-is-not-a-household.
32. Oxfam. (2020) World's billionaires have more wealth than 4.6 billion people, https://www.oxfam.org/en/press-releases/worlds-billionaires-have-more-wealth-46-billion-people.
33. Oxfam. (2018) Reward work, not wealth, https://www.oxfam.org/en/research/reward-work-not-wealth.
34. Kelton, *The Deficit Myth*, p. 11.
35. Kelton, *The Deficit Myth*, pp. 11–12.
36. Economicsonline. (2021) The nature of economics, https://www.economicsonline.co.uk/Competitive_markets/What_is_economics.html.
37. Merriam-Webster. (2021) Essential meaning of economics, https://www.merriam-webster.com/dictionary/economics.
38. *The Economist*. (2021) Austrian economics, https://www.economist.com/economics-a-to-z#node-21529492.
39. This is featured on the cover of Edwards, R., Reich, M. and Weisskopf, T. (1986) *The Capitalist System: A Radical Analysis of American Society*, Prentice-Hall, New Jersey.
40. Edwards, L. (2007) *How to Argue with an Economist*, Second Edition, Cambridge University Press, Cambridge.
41. Quoted in Morgan, B. (2019) Why nobody trusts economists, https://harris.uchicago.edu/news-events/news/why-nobody-trusts-economists; see also Ipsos. (2020) Ipsos Veracity Index 2020, https://www.ipsos.com/en-uk/ipsos-veracity-index-2020-trust-in-professions.
42. These and other criticisms are found in Siminski, P. (2023) 6 reasons Australians don't trust economists, and how we could do better, https://theconversation.com/6-reasons-australians-dont-trust-economists-and-how-we-could-do-better-208833.
43. See Britannica Money. (2024) Neoliberal globalization, https://www.britannica.com/money/neoliberal-globalization.

44. Blanco, A. (2017) Reflections on neoclassical theory and the philosophy of science, *Journal of Australian Political Economy* 80: 43–64.
45. Samuels, W. (1992) *Essays on the Methodology and Discourse of Economics*, Macmillan, London.
46. Miller, N. (2023) *Economic Myths and Magic: Debunking the Illusions of Conventional Economic Thinking*, Cheltenham, UK.
47. Jones, E. (2002) The ascendancy of an idealist economics in Australia, *Journal of Australian Political Economy* 50: 69.
48. See Galbraith, J. (1976) Economics as a system of belief, in E. Wheelwright and F. Stilwell (eds) *Readings in Political Economy*, Volume 2, Australia and New Zealand Book Company, Sydney, p. 32.
49. Wikipedia. (2021) Third Servile War, https://en.wikipedia.org/wiki/Third_Servile_War.
50. Gurley, J. (1979) The critique of capitalism, in R. Quinney (ed.) *Capitalist Society: Readings for a Critical Sociology*, The Dorsey Press, Illinois, pp. 10–24; Edwards, Reich and Weisskopf, *The Capitalist System*; Stilwell, *Political Economy*.
51. London Lives. (2021) Vagrancy, https://www.londonlives.org/static/Vagrancy.jsp.
52. Edwards, Reich and Weisskopf, *The Capitalist System*, p. 10.
53. Edwards, Reich and Weisskopf, *The Capitalist System*, p. 12.
54. Some classic US confrontations are described in American Experience. (2021) Labor wars in the US, https://www.pbs.org/wgbh/americanexperience/features/theminewars-labor-wars-us/.
55. Wikipedia. (2021) Ludwig von Mises, https://en.wikipedia.org/wiki/Ludwig_von_Mises; New Economics Foundation. (2018) How markets became masters: The neoliberal roots of deregulation, https://neweconomics.org/2018/09/markets-became-masters.
56. Goodreads. (2021) Milton Friedman, https://www.goodreads.com/author/quotes/5001.Milton_Friedman.
57. Reagan.com. (2018) Ronald Reagan on Big Government | most terrifying words, https://www.reagan.com/ronald-reagan-on-big-government-most-terrifying-words.

58. Sibley, A. (2020) What's wrong with Milton Friedman's economics? https://www.researchgate.net/publication/340923828_What's_wrong_with_Milton_Friedman's_economics/citation/download.
59. Chomsky, N. (2006) *Failed States: The Abuse of Power and the Assault on Democracy*, Metropolitan Books, New York.
60. See Camgoz, S. and Ekmekci, O. (eds) (2021) *Destructive Leadership and Management Hypocrisy: Advances in Theory and Practice*, Emerald Publishing, Bingley.
61. See Provost, C. and Kennard, M. (2023) *Silent Coup: How Corporations Overthrew Democracy*, Bloomsbury Academic, London.
62. Spiro, P. (2013) Constraining global corporate power: A short introduction, *Vanderbilt Journal of Transnational* Law 46: 1101–1118.
63. Spiro, Constraining global corporate power, p. 1104.
64. Provost and Kennard, *Silent Coup*.
65. Oxfam International. (2024) *Inequality Inc: How Corporate Power Divides our World and the Need for a new era of Public Action*, Oxfam International, Oxford, UK.
66. See arguments in Varoufakis, Y. (2023) *Technofeudalism: What Killed Capitalism*, Penguin Random House, London.
67. For example, that expansionary fiscal policies (additional government expenditures) are 'bad' for economies (see Stilwell, *Political Economy*, p. 294).
68. Monbiot, G. (2024) How the overseas owners of England's water companies clean up by polluting our rivers, theguardian.com/commentisfree/2024/apr/26/england-water-companies-shareholders-dividends-river-sea; Harris, J. (2022) Britain has been avoiding its biggest problems for decades. Now we're paying the price, https://www.theguardian.com/commentisfree/2022/aug/16/britain-has-been-avoiding-its-biggest-problems-for-decades-now-were-paying-the-price.
69. Williams, B. (1976) Socialism and freedom, in Wheelwright and Stilwell, *Readings in Political Economy*, Volume 1, p. 104.

70. Albertson, K. and Stepney, P. (2020) 1979 and all that: A 40-year reassessment of Margaret Thatcher's legacy on her own terms, *Cambridge Journal of Economics* 44(2): 319–342.
71. Ranelagh, J. (1992) *Thatcher's People: An Insider's Account of the Politics, the Power, and the Personalities*, Fontana, Great Britain.
72. Liberto, D. (2023) 5 reasons why supply-side economics does not work: Many of the claims made by supply-siders have been disproven over the years, https://www.investopedia.com/supply-side-economics-6755346.
73. Ingraham, C. (2020) 'Trickle-down' tax cuts make the rich richer but are of no value to overall economy, study finds, https://www.washingtonpost.com/business/2020/12/23/tax-cuts-rich-trickle-down/.
74. McMurtry, J. (1998) *Unequal Freedoms: The Global Market as an Ethical System*, Garamond, Toronto, pp. 107–108. A similar argument was made by Ha-Joon Chang (2011) in his provocative international bestseller *23 Things They Don't Tell You about Capitalism*, Penguin, London.
75. Tooze, A. (2018) *Crashed: How a Decade of Financial Crises Changed the World*, Penguin, UK; Ingraham, 'Trickle-down' tax cuts make the rich richer but are of no value to overall economy, study finds.
76. This is a quote about the findings of Nobel prize-winning economist Joseph Stiglitz from Gough, I. (2017) *Heat, Greed and Human Need: Climate Change, Capitalism, and Sustainable, Wellbeing*, Edward Elgar, Cheltenham, UK, p. 117.
77. Oxfam. (2017) An economy for the 99%, https://www.oxfam.org/en/research/economy-99.
78. Piketty, T. (2014) *Capital in the Twenty-First Century*, The Belknap Press of Harvard University Press, Cambridge Massachusetts; see also Robeyns, I. (2024) *Limitarianism: The Case Against Extreme Wealth*, Allen Lane, London.
79. Paraphrased from Edelman, M. (2001) *The Politics of Misinformation*, Cambridge University Press, Cambridge, p. 124.
80. Sibley, What's wrong with Milton Friedman's economics?

81. Upjoke. (2021) Trickle down economics jokes, https://upjoke.com/trickle-down-economics-jokes.
82. Epstein, G. (2005) Introduction: Financialization and the world economy, in G. Epstein (ed.) *Financialization of the World Economy*, Edward Elgar, Cheltenham, pp. 3–16; Lawrence, G. and Smith, K. (2018) The concept of 'financialization': Criticisms and insights, in H. Bjorkhaug, A. Magnan and G. Lawrence (eds) *The Financialization of Agri-food Systems: Contested Transformations*, Routledge, London, pp. 23–41.
83. Stilwell, *Political Economy*, p. 28.
84. Shaxson, N. (2018) *The Finance Curse: How Global Finance Is Making Us All Poorer*, Vintage, London.
85. Shaxson, *The Finance Curse*; Graeber, D. (2018) *Bullshit Jobs: The Rise of Pointless Work and What We Can Do About It*, Penguin, UK.
86. Liquidity refers to the ease with which something will sell. Shares in some of the high-performing companies like Apple, Microsoft, Amazon, and Samsung will sell readily. They are easily turned into cash on short notice. An illiquid asset will not do as well because it generally lacks buyer interest. If you are looking to sell it is likely you will do so only by accepting a lower-than-market value. Houses, cars, antiques, televisions, and jewellery fall into the 'illiquid' category—they are 'fixed' assets. Because banks hold mortgages for houses, which are an illiquid asset, they were looking for ways to take this off their books: They did so by packaging houses into a security, which is liquid and sold easily in the marketplace.
87. Futures and forwards are financial contracts obliging the buyer of the contract to purchase an asset for an agreed-upon price, at some specified time in the future. Options give the buyers of contract the right (but not the obligation) to sell an underlying asset at a predetermined price. Swaps are yet another form of derivative, allowing cash flow exchange between two parties. Interest rate swaps and currency swaps are examples, here. See Corporate Finance Institute. (2021)

Derivatives, https://corporatefinanceinstitute.com/resources/knowledge/trading-investing/derivatives/.
88. Fernando, J. (2021) Derivative, https://www.investopedia.com/terms/d/derivative.asp.
89. Fernando, Derivative; Schmidt, T. (2016) *The Political Economy of Food and Finance*, Routledge, London.
90. Chang, *23 Things They Don't Tell You About Capitalism*, p. 238. See also Ferguson, N. (2008) *The Ascent of Money: A Financial History of the World*, Penguin, UK.
91. Hawkins, J. (2022) The spectacular collapse of a $30 billion crypto exchange should come as no surprise, https://theconversation.com/the-spectacular-collapse-of-a-30-billion-crypto-exchange-should-come-as-no-surprise-194442.
92. HeraMay, R. (2010) Forget about housing, the real cause of the crisis was OTC derivatives, https://www.businessinsider.com/bubble-derivatives-otc-2010-5.
93. Kenton, W. (2020) Derivatives time bomb: Definition and Warren Buffett's warnings, https://www.investopedia.com/terms/d/derivativestimebomb.asp.
94. HeraMay, Forget about housing, the real cause of the crisis was OTC derivatives.
95. Quoted in Kenton, Derivatives time bomb.
96. Haiven, M. (2014) *Cultures of Financialization: Fictitious Capital in Popular Culture and Everyday Life*, Palgrave Macmillan, London, p. 2.
97. Cheng, J. (2022) Bowie Bond: Definition, how it worked, history, https://www.investopedia.com/terms/b/bowie-bond.asp.
98. See Smith, R. (2019) *Rage Inside the Machine: The Prejudice of Algorithms and How to Stop the Internet Making Bigots of us All*, Bloomsbury Business, London; O'Neil, C. (2016) *Weapons of Math Destruction: How Big Data Increases Inequality and Threatens Democracy*, Crown Publishers, New York; Noble, S. (2018) *Algorithms and Oppression: How Search Engines Reinforce Racism*, NYU Press, New York; Shafer, M and van Es, K. (eds) (2017) *The Datafied Society: Studying Culture through Data*, Amsterdam University Press, Amsterdam.

99. O'Neil, *Weapons of Math Destruction*.
100. Slater, D. (2013) *Love in the Time of Algorithms: What Technology Does for Meeting and Dating*, Penguin Putnam, US.
101. Picardo, E. (2021) 4 big risks of high-frequency trading, https://www.investopedia.com/articles/markets/012716/four-big-risks-algorithmic-highfrequency-trading.asp.
102. Picardo, 4 big risks of high-frequency trading.
103. Picardo, 4 big risks of high-frequency trading; Sornette, D. and von der Becke, S. (2011) Crashes and high frequency trading: An evaluation of risks posed by high-speed algorithmic trading, Swiss Finance Institute Research Paper No. 11-63, http://dx.doi.org/10.2139/ssrn.1976249.
104. Sornette and von der Becke, Crashes and high-frequency trading.
105. 'Pump and dump' refers to the fraudulent tactic of selecting a poorly performing stock, encouraging investment by pumping in money to artificially inflate its value, then selling one's shares for a big profit while the price is high. The aftermath is that the value of shares invariably drops, with those who had invested on the expectation of continuous growth in the stock, losing their money. You win, they lose.
106. Seitz, M. (2013) *The Wolf of Wall Street*, https://www.rogerebert.com/reviews/the-wolf-of-wall-street-2013.
107. Seitz, *The Wolf of Wall Street*.
108. Connell, R. (2017) Foreword: Masculinities in the Sociocene, in S. MacGregor and N. Seymour (eds) *Men and Nature: Hegemonic Masculinities and Environmental Change*, RCC Perspectives, https://www.jstor.org/stable/26241448, pp. 5–7; CNBC. (2018) Wall Street wants more female traders, but old perceptions die hard, https://www.cnbc.com/2018/06/14/wall-street-wants-more-female-traders-but-old-perceptions-die-hard.html.
109. 'When you short something—usually a financial security, like a stock—it means you borrow it and sell it on the open market, with the aim of buying it back later at a lower price and pocketing the difference as a profit. Traders and investors sell short when they think that a security will decline in value. It's a bet that prices will fall'. See Baldwin, J. (2021) 'The

Big Short' explained, https://www.investopedia.com/articles/investing/020115/big-short-explained.asp.
110. Kenny, G. (2015) *The Big Short*, https://www.rogerebert.com/reviews/the-big-short-2015.
111. Yes, I mean both the instruments and the people using them.
112. The quote has been attributed to John Steinbeck, but no one seems to be able to trace it to any of his writings! See: http://quodid.com/our-words/citation-investigation/john-stienbeck-socialism-never-took-root-in-america/.
113. Ho, K. (2009) *Liquidated: An Ethnography of Wall Street*, Duke University Press, Durham, NC; Weeks, S. (2012) Review of Liquidated: An Ethnography of Wall Street, *Anthropology of Work Review* 32(2): 130–131; Maggio, R. (2017) *An analysis of Karen Z. Ho's Liquidated: An Ethnography of Wall Street*, Macat Library.
114. Of course, some of the movies mentioned above were also books.
115. Burrough, B. and Helyar, J. (1989) *Barbarians at the Gate: The Fall of RJR Nabisco*, Harper and Row, New York; Beattie, A. (2021) Corporate kleptocracy at RJR Nabisco, https://www.investopedia.com/articles/stocks/09/corporate-kleptocracy-rjr-nabisco.asp.
116. High Income Source. (2021) *Barbarians at the Gate* summary: Key insights, https://highincomesource.com/barbarians-at-the-gate-summary/; Beattie, Corporate kleptocracy at RJR Nabisco.
117. Senior, J. (2017) Review: 'Black Edge,' an account of a hedge fund magnate and insider trading, https://www.nytimes.com/2017/02/01/books/review-black-edge-an-account-of-a-hedge-fund-magnate-and-insider-trading.html.
118. Kolhatkar, S. (2018) *Black Edge: Inside Information, Dirty Money, and the Quest to Bring Down the Most Wanted Man on Wall Street*, Random House, New York.
119. Kolhatkar, *Black Edge*.
120. Wikipedia. (2021) Steve Cohen (businessman), https://en.wikipedia.org/wiki/Steve_Cohen_(businessman).
121. Patterson, S. (2023) *Chaos Kings: How Wall Street Traders Make Billions in the New Age of Crisis*, Simon and Schuster, New York.

122. Rhodes, C. (2023) 'Greed is amoral': How Wall Street supermen cashed in on pandemic misery and chaos, https://theconversation.com/greed-is-amoral-how-wall-street-supermen-cashed-in-on-pandemic-misery-and-chaos-207311.
123. Foucault, M. (1994) Technologies of the self, in P. Rabinow (ed.) *Michel Foucault: Ethics—Essential Works of Foucault 1954–1984*, Penguin, London, pp. 223–251.
124. McGuigan, J. (2016) *Neoliberal Culture*, Palgrave Macmillan, London; Hardy, J. (2021) The myth of the 'neoliberal self', http://isj.org.uk/neoliberal-self/.
125. Spicer, A. (2017) From inboxing to thought showers: How business bullshit took over, https://www.theguardian.com/news/2017/nov/23/from-inboxing-to-thought-showers-how-business-bullshit-took-over.
126. See Dowd, D. (1977) *The Twisted Dream: Capitalist Development in the United States Since 1776*, Winthrop Publishing, Massachusetts.

3

From Seedling to Supermarket: Farming, Fast Food, and the Fabrication of Trust

Today's world is one of media saturation by the advertising industry. A consistent stream of ads appears on smartphones, tablets, and in newspapers. And let us not forget billboards, radio, television, shopping malls, trains, taxis, gas stations, and sporting arenas. Many ads are intrusive, repetitious, and annoying. They invade our privacy and often lead us to eschew the very products the advertisers insist will improve our lives. Ads work best when they are targeted, persuasive, and welcomed.[1] Enter the world of McDonald's.

The after-school television hours for children growing up in the 1980s and 1990s would be filled with the exploits of the Hamburglar, Evil Grimace, and Captain Crook—all out to illegally procure items like a fillet-o-fish or a beef burger, but ultimately stymied by that loveable clown, Ronald McDonald. This was McDonaldland. Mayor McCheese was once there as well—that is, up until he was deposed from office. (He was found to have been plagiarised from the eponymous character in the 1960s children's show H.R. Pufnstuf and disappeared after a protracted lawsuit with his creators.)[2] McDonaldland characters were displayed at restaurants, were incorporated into children's outdoor play areas, became toys sold in their stores—or given away with Happy Meal boxes—and appeared in the in-house children's magazine *McDonaldland Fun Times*, and in the animated film, *The Adventures of Ronald McDonald*. For those wanting to be pen pals there was even a stationery set featuring coloured images of all the favourite characters.[3] Today, there are life-size effigies of Ronald sitting on park benches around the world—a perfect photo opportunity for the kids.

McDonald's has always known what it is doing. Many studies have shown that children develop emotional ties to brand mascots and that they find it difficult to tell the difference between advertising and factual information. Voilà! Have the children identify strongly with the brand characters, market them food and drinks high in calories but low in nutrients, add in a few toy giveaways (McDonald's is the largest distributor of toys in the world), and you have created a perfect setting for industry profit, and for developing cravings that last into adulthood, reproducing fast-food addiction in each new generation of consumers.[4]

If the cartoon character hook is so successful, why is it not used by others in the food industry? It is, in two ways. The first is the creation and deployment of fictional characters like Tony the Tiger (Kelloggs), Buzz Bee and Lucky the Leprechaun (General Mills), Chester Cheetah (PepsiCo), Cheesasaurus Rex (Kraft Foods), and the M&M chocolate buttons (Mars, Inc). The second is the licencing, to food companies, of characters owned by the media giants: Shrek (Dreamworks) is found on Twinkies, Nesquik, Cheetos, Gushers, and McDonald's burgers; Dora the Explorer (Nickelodeon/Viacom) advertises Nabisco's sugary fruit snacks; SpongeBob SquarePants (Nickelodeon/Viacom) and Scooby-Doo (Warner Brothers) advertise Burger King products; while Spider Man (Disney) has a major longing for Doritos. (According to one food scientist 'nacho cheese Doritos are the archetype of addictive processed foods. They've been engineered so you never feel like you've had enough'.)[5]

Then there are the advertising 'tricks' to make products on TV look much more desirable than they would be in real life. Newly picked strawberries often have a white-green base. Red lipstick changes all that. Brown food dye mixed whipped in with mashed potato makes a splendid chocolate fudge. White glue is an excellent substitute for cream on cakes and muffins. Shaken liquid soap gives coffee an incredibly frothy head.

And dissolving a seltzer in champagne keeps it bubbling forever in front of the eyes of viewers. These, and more, tricks are detailed in the Twitter/X visual 'How Things Work'.[6]

It is useful to consider the background to the rise of the fast-food industry before returning, later in the chapter, to explore its propensity to play with food.

All Farmed Out

If you are a farmer working two hectares of arable land in rural Peru, Kenya, or Thailand you and your family know where food comes from—directly from your field or bartered or purchased in small village markets. The food is fresh and is normally unadulterated. Globally, there are some 600 million family-based farms producing approximately 80% of the world's food—with farms of less than two hectares (totalling 500 million of the 600 million farms) responsible for providing 35% of all food, by value.[7] In these small-scale, peasant-based, and subsistence *traditional* food systems the technology employed is low level and staples are produced for direct consumption. Think here of countries like Bangladesh, Bhutan, Cambodia, and Mozambique. In contrast, in what we might term *modernising* food systems (for example, China, Brazil, India, and Mexico) we see food being distributed nationally, with wholesalers and retailers playing an increasingly important role in food movement and sale. Farming is semi-intensive—with some specialisation—and manufactured (processed) foods are available. In *industrialised* food systems—epitomised by the UK, US, Canada, Australia, and many EU nations—processed foods become widespread, supermarkets control most of the food sales to customers, there is extensive consumption of fast foods, and there are specialised, large-scale family farms and corporate farms producing much of the value of agriculture and selling it via national and international markets.[8] The process of financialisation, discussed in the previous chapter, drives agricultural intensification while at the same time marginalising the 'family farm' sector.[9]

Each of the three systems co-exists globally, and often in the same country. Each system has its virtues, and each its problems. In *traditional* food systems a drought or flood can have devastating consequences for food supply, with starvation and malnutrition direct outcomes. War and conflict add another level of uncertainty in the securing of adequate food calories. In *modernising* food systems weather events can also wreak havoc, while the growing intensification of farming and poor governance structures can mean that the environment is under constant threat. *Industrial* food systems also face challenges. Agri-chemicals[10] are a major source of pollution; farmworkers and food industry workers are exploited and face significant health issues; the treatment of animals in feedlots and other intensive production units is often poor; food chains can be disrupted, creating food shortages; and higher-value processed food diets produce poor health outcomes. But the key issue for the food system, *in toto*, is food security. There is enough food being produced to feed the world's population—one and a half times over.[11] The real problem is the ability of people to access that food—having the money and wherewithal to purchase necessary supplies. But it is the seeming need to grow ever more quantities of food, rather than to redistribute it, that has been deliberately evoked by Western governments and the agribusiness sector to justify the continuation of 'high-tech', corporate, solutions to food provision.

For those of us old enough to remember, the so-called Green Revolution was the great food success story of the 1960s and beyond. During my school and university years it was hammered home that commercial farming must, if it were to feed the world, improve both its efficiency (the most effective use of resources in producing output) and its productivity (increases in output per unit of input). In this regard there was nothing more brilliant than the achievement of plant scientist Norman Borlaug. He had combined dwarf (hybrid) varieties of wheat (and later, rice and corn), with modern agri-chemicals and reliable irrigation. Hey presto, crop yields boomed and it was predicted that the Green Revolution would make famine and starvation things of the past. For his efforts Borlaug received a Nobel Peace Prize in 1970. Yet, in 2023 there were an estimated 735 million people in the world going hungry, up some 122 million from 2019.[12] Today, nearly one in ten of the world's population suffers hunger, and this is forecast to worsen.[13]

What went wrong? While it is undeniable that food production increased from the application of Green Revolution technologies, those same technologies created numerous problems.[14] The so-called hybrid vigour that resulted from crossing plants with different genetic bases produced seeds that were generally sterile. Farmers who wished to keep using the 'miracle' seeds had to purchase them every year—a major financial burden for small-scale producers in traditional and modernising farming systems. Also, using the hybrid seed/chemical/irrigation formula placed farmers in a cycle of dependency which often meant fields were neither rested nor rotated with other crops, leading to soil nutrient deficiency and erosion. The chemicals deployed destroyed beneficial soil microbes, while the run-off of fertilisers and agri-chemicals entered local waterways, poisoning drinking water, destroying fish stock, and causing birth defects in human populations. Pesticides killed birds and insects and damaged entire ecosystems. Rice, one of the most 'successful' Green Revolution crops, shifted diets in poorer nations away from millets, barley, pulses, and lentils, reducing diversity of food intake.[15] Importantly, traditional cropping methods were abandoned and the knowledge base that accompanied those older methods was diminished, making it increasingly difficult for farmers to 'go back'. An unsustainable system of farming had largely been imposed on many nations of the Global South for the benefit of the corporations of the Global North that provided seeds, fertilisers, pesticides, and farm machinery.[16] Meanwhile, we were continually being told that American know-how and new technologies would save the world from hunger. We were being fooled.

From Green Revolution to Gene Revolution

The same efficiency/productivity drive at the heart of the Green Revolution has been uppermost in the minds of the agricultural scientists and agribusinesses in the Global North as they seek to perfect industrial agriculture. Just like the alienated production-line worker in Charlie Chaplin's *Modern Times*, the workers in beef, chicken, and pork processing factories are subject to time-and-motion studies designed to speed up throughput in these *dis*assembly lines. Farmers are being told to apply the latest technologies, increase the size of their holdings, improve their yields, and use varieties of crops with shorter growing periods. Chickens, once slaughtered at 15 weeks, are now ready for the knife at just six (and, through selective breeding, they are four times heavier today than they were in the 1950s).[17] Cattle which once roamed grassy fields are raised, in the last months of their lives, in Concentrated Animal Feeding Operations (CAFOs)—high density, industrial scale, animal houses—where an otherwise unfamiliar grain-based diet guarantees maximum weight gain before slaughter. It doesn't matter that CAFOs create toxic lakes of animal waste, require cattle to be fed a concoction of powerful antibiotics to keep them healthy, or that they produce ever-growing volumes of methane—a greenhouse gas that is some 25 times more potent than carbon dioxide. What matters is that they represent an efficient means of producing meat. Or so we have been told. When the true costs of production and the 'externalities' like pollution are added in, CAFOs are shown to be an *in*efficient and unsustainable way of producing meat protein.[18]

For example, Spain's desire to increase its industrial pork production has led to some major environmental problems, including the death of marine life in Mar Menor lagoon, one of the largest and most iconic saltwater lagoons in Europe. The cause was the run-off of nitrate-laden pig manure from farms from the Murcia region of south-eastern Spain. The run-off caused the growth of algal blooms which sucked oxygen from the lagoon, suffocating the fish population. As the mayor of another of Spain's regional provinces lamented 'we're being invaded by pigs'.[19] The promise was jobs and growth; the reality has been the constant stench of manure and the destruction of local roads by the endless presence of heavy vehicles servicing the farms. Nitrate levels have escalated in groundwater and citizens are now being told to avoid drinking water from local springs. Rather than creating population growth through new jobs, the industrialised form of pig farming is pushing people out of towns resulting, in some regions, in depopulation of up to 40%.[20] Tourist dollars are no longer arriving in the small, once-beautiful, villages that decided their future was in pigs. Spain's national reputation is also taking a hammering. The country's newfound label is that of the 'toilet of Europe'.[21] Yet, the proliferation of industrial farming appears unstoppable. Globally, CAFOs produce some 72% of poultry meat, 55% of pork production, and 42% of all eggs.[22] In the US—the most 'advanced' model for intensive animal production—some 70% of cows, 98% of pigs, and 99% of chickens and turkeys are housed in CAFOs.[23]

The drive for profit in food production has 'demanded' greater productivity. Enter biotechnology. In the 1990s geneticists were convinced that by manipulating genes, biological limits to production could be overcome. By inserting a gene from a fish into a tomato it was reasoned that the tomato would have better flavour and longer shelf-life. By selecting a gene from a chicken and placing it in a potato, the potato would be offered protection from disease. A pig was genetically engineered with genes derived from human DNA so that it might grow more quickly and produce leaner meat. Unfortunately, as it grew, its skin turned orange, blisters appeared, it developed arthritis, and it was promptly despatched.[24] That hasn't stopped the biotechnologists. In 2020 the US Food and Drug Administration (FDA) approved the genetic manipulation of pigs which lack a molecule called alpha-gal sugar. The so-called GalSafe pigs will be used to produce drugs, provide organs for transplantation, and produce meat for human consumption. The FDA has already approved the genetic modification of goats to produce an anti-blood-clotting agent in their milk and chickens to produce pharmaceutical drugs in their eggs. It has also approved for human consumption the AquAdvantage salmon containing DNA from the Atlantic salmon, the Chinook salmon, and the ocean pout (an eel-like fish with anti-freeze proteins in its blood). What is the 'AquAdvantage'? The salmon grow twice as fast as other farmed Atlantic salmon and do so by consuming 25% less food.[25]

While the proponents of genetic engineering consider their new products will provide more nutritious and tastier foods, increase food supply, impart disease resistance, and use fewer pesticides—all while cleaning up the environment—there are others who are less sanguine, pointing to development of food/chemical 'packages' that will boost the profits of multinational chemical, pharmaceutical, and agribusiness organisations which are 'going pharming'.[26] One of the latest ideas is to employ gene-editing[27] to improve the photosynthetic performance of crops, increasing biomass and drawing more carbon from the atmosphere, thereby addressing climate change. Genetic engineers are lobbying governments to provide them with more funding and to reduce regulation on the biotech industry. In many nations the GE agenda is being pushed not only by bio-scientists and agribusinesses, but also by publicly funded universities, research institutions, and government bodies. Some do so surreptitiously:

> Asian governments are cleverly embellishing [the] new GMOs in abstract language like 'new breeding techniques', 'nature equivalent', 'similar as conventional', 'natural' or 'nature friendly', so that these products can be exempt from key regulatory safeguards.[28]

The public is being deceived. We should always remember

> The pipeline for salvation technology is long and the benefit is hypothetical ... Technology solutions rarely lead to sustainable solutions [and] they may exacerbate harm. [We are] lulled into complacency by 'technological imaginaries' ...[29]

There is nothing intrinsically problematic about seeking to improve efficiency and productivity in agri-food systems. It is what farmers have sought, and have achieved, over millennia. Recall Swift's important insight from Gulliver's voyage to Brobdingnag:

> Whosoever could make two ears of corn or two blades of grass to grow upon a spot of ground where only one grew before, would deserve better of [human]kind, and do more essential service to [one's] country, than the whole race of politicians put together.[30]

Yes, for sure. But the issue is whether efficiency and productivity through genetic manipulation take precedence over other desirable outcomes such as enhanced sustainability, improved population health, better animal welfare, and planetary survival. And, of course, we should always be asking the question 'who is making the money?'

Is the world being deceived by the rosy promises of genetically-engineered future for agriculture? There would seem to be substance to this claim. First, GE crops are not designed to end hunger. Most of those around today—GE soybeans, corn, and canola—are for animal feed, biofuels, or industrial oils. Their increased presence in paddocks around the world is often at the expense of small-scale farming (thereby reducing local food availability), and of natural vegetation, including rainforests. Second, GE crops are no more productive than conventional plants.[31] Third, it was predicted that agri-chemicals could be eliminated or reduced through the use of GE crops. Wrong. GE crops lose their resistance and have to be treated with increased doses of potent pesticides. Fourth, it is said to be up to farmers to choose their own methods of production and that GE can happily co-exist with conventional forms of farming. But, GE pollen spreads into conventional and organic crops, compromising their integrity. For organic farmers the presence of GE means they cannot sell their products as 'GMO-free', thereby reducing their profits and undermining their livelihoods.[32] Fifth, national regulators allow releases of GMOs if they meet the criterion of 'safe enough'—something shown to be way below public expectations for transparency and trustworthiness.[33]

As political ecologist Erica Borg and critical theorist Amedeo Policante have written in their revealing book *Mutant Ecologies*:

> Technotriuphalism reigned supreme in the final decade of the twentieth century: genetically modified crops were touted as spelling the end of poverty and hunger. [Instead] they exacerbated unequal access to food, expanded colonial land relations, and generated unpredicted ecological problems ... [Yet, today] bioengineering represents a central element in [an] emerging political vision, offering novel means to redesign the biosphere and terraform the Earth.[34]

And for what purpose? To manipulate nature and create novel life-forms as a basis for continued capital accumulation. Borg and Policante argue that the drive for profits is responsible for the on-going mutation of biology, 'spinning new synthetic threads into the web of life'.[35] As the UN has stated, the goal of farming should be to improve human nutrition rather than simply to increase production. Agriculture must become:

> a central feature in the management of healthy ecosystems ... as we evolve beyond just 'yield per hectare' to broader working definitions of 'productivity' in agricultural landscapes that encompass valued ecosystem services such as water infiltration, carbon sequestration, and conservation of biodiversity.[36]

Learning Our ABCDs

A number of journalists and academics have depicted today's food system as an hourglass.[37] Food is produced at the top by millions of farmers, worldwide. Much of it is then funnelled through a very narrow neck, eventually finding its way to millions of consumers below, sitting at the bottom of the hourglass. It is the 'neck' of the hourglass that proves to be of great interest. This is where the food corporations reside. The neck is narrow because there are only a small number of very powerful food corporations occupying this space. To fully appreciate the shape and power of today's food industry it is useful to examine the corporations that procure and distribute foods and food inputs for the global population. These are the commodity traders.

The names Archer Daniels Midland (A), Bunge (B), Cargill (C), and Louis Dreyfus (D) may not be known to those outside farming circles but, together, the ABCDs form one of the most powerful and concentrated sectors in global agri-food chains. Archer Daniel Midlands, which had a revenue of US$97 billion in 2023, is a publicly traded company based in the US. It specialises in the processing of wheat, corn, oilseeds, and cocoa along with the production of animal feed, food ingredients, and chemical products. According to Jonathan Tapper and Denise Hearn, authors of *The Myth of Capitalism*:

ADM never met a price it did not want to fix. [It is] like a Mob family … In documents that came to light in court, an ADM executive wrote 'Our competitors are our friends. Our customers are our enemy'.[38]

Bunge, with a revenue of US$61 billion in 2023, is founded in the Netherlands but, since 2000, has located its headquarters in the US. It trades grains, oilseeds, and sugar and is the largest soybean oil processors globally. It also manufactures biofuels from sugar cane.

Since its creation some 156 years ago, Cargill has been family owned. It is highly profitable, boasting some 14 billionaires among its family members and directors. Its interests are widespread—vegetable oils, sugar, cotton, corn, biofuels, pharmaceuticals, and animal meat among them. The company's CEO, David MacLennan's gamble on surging demand for animal protein has paid off with the company delivering a record revenue of US$177 billion in 2023. Finally, Louis Dreyfus, a privately-owned company based in Paris, is a grain, oilseed, and coffee merchant. It generated a revenue of US$60 billion. The company's very colourful and attractive website also shows it has interests in bio-energy, beverages, pharmaceuticals, textiles, and shipping—and of course sustainability. Each of the ABCDs websites provides detailed information on how they are purportedly promoting sustainability throughout the food chain. It is not an exaggeration to say that the ABCDs—along with emerging rivals, the Asian-based NOW group, and China's COSCO—are in control of food trade globally (with the big four controlling close to 90% of all grains traded internationally).[39]

These corporate giants are recognising profits can be made in arenas outside agribusiness—pharmaceuticals, shipping, and biofuels have already been mentioned. They have also become adroit at using the finance system to their advantage through agricultural derivative markets and via financial subsidiaries that specialise in futures trading. They engage in speculation and have also found ways of limiting their tax liabilities, with Bunge incorporated in the tax haven of Bermuda, ADM in the US tax haven of Delaware, and Louis Dreyfus trading out of Switzerland. They are all known for secrecy in their dealings with the two privately-owned companies not required to disclose their financial details. In many ways, it is difficult to distinguish between the commodity traders and investment banks. They have become a central component in the process of 'financialisation' (discussed in Chapter 2) where financial actors, products, and logics insinuate themselves into every nook and cranny of economic and social life.[40]

The commodity traders are not the only ones in the narrow neck of the agri-food hourglass. There are now just four major firms involved in the provision of agri-chemicals—Corteva (a merger between Dow and DuPont), ChemChina (which acquired Switzerland's Syngenta), Bayer (which purchased Monsanto), and BASF. Together they are responsible for over 50% of market sales globally. But this level of market concentration is also the same for seeds, animal pharmaceuticals, animal genetics, and farm machinery. Each of these crucial farm-input industries is, in other words, operating in a distorted, oligopolistic, market, where—because of their power—a small number of companies can, and do, collude, inflate market prices, and limit the participation of new entrants (potentially narrowing innovation in the industry). Acquisitions and mergers in the agri-food industries help to improve the financial performance of firms. But the short-term monetary benefits provided to shareholders must be considered against the need for firms to create long-term, sustainable, options in the food system. The question needs to be asked:

> Rather than the world becoming too big to feed, have firms become too big to feed humanity equally, fairly, and sustainably?[41]

Other impacts of concentration in agri-food include the squeezing of farm incomes, information control through new data-control mechanisms, increased environmental and public health costs, labour abuses, and the consolidation of industrial agriculture.[42] The use of power to influence political decisions is another feature. In Brazil, for example, some 50 agribusinesses—including Cargill, Bayer, Syngenta, JBS, Nestle, and Bunge—joined forces in 2011 to create the Pensar Agro Institute (IPA). It is a right-wing think tank whose primary purpose is to ensure that any legislation passed by the government furthers the interests of the large corporations. Since 2022 such legislation has led to environmental destruction of the Amazon, the chemical poisoning of land and waterways, and the removal of indigenous peoples from their lands.[43] In the US the Farm Bureau, representing large-scale farmers, lobbies to ensure that farm bills favour the wealthy. It has fostered alliances with the fossil fuel industry and other conservative groups to deny that climate change is occurring. It also opposes legislation aimed at addressing climate change.[44]

Super-Marketed

When the top four or five firms in any industry control around 40% of the market that market is deemed to be 'highly concentrated'. When that percentage rises above 60, the market is considered to be 'significantly distorted'. When it is revealed that the five of the major supermarket chains in the US control 60% of market share, eyebrows are raised. But when it rises to 71% in France, 91 in Sweden, and 99 in Australia, the level of 'distortion' soars way above what economists would deem fair competition. This level of industry concentration has significant impacts upon consumers (who are subject to higher pricing) and suppliers (who are often victims of the procurement policies and practices of the supermarkets).[45] With concentration comes power and we should not be surprised to learn that supermarkets engage in profiteering, job slashing, anti-competitive practices, and a host of other dubious activities. They are no longer fit for purpose. Their capacity to continue to deliver food in a secure, predictable, manner has also been challenged. For Andrew Sims, British political economist and author of *Tescopoly*:

> The 'house of food' sits on shaky foundations. It is palpably unsafe for a future full of worsening ... climate and energy shocks.[46]

During the early 1950s my parents owned and operated a small grocery store in the inner Sydney suburb of Five Dock. It had the layout and look (and musty smell) of most other grocery stores at the time. Customers would walk through a rather narrow front door, stand in front of the counter, and request items that were stacked on shelves behind the counter. My parents would dutifully select the requested items and place them in paper bags. Money would be exchanged and the old black till with its round well-spaced keys would open and shut with regularity. But with not nearly enough regularity as it turns out—my parents left the business after several years to return to paid employment. The supermarket revolution—something which had originally begun in the US many decades earlier—had torn my parents' petty bourgeois dreams asunder.

Supermarkets are different from the grocery stores of old. They are much larger in size and offer a wide variety of items (up to 30,000 in the biggest stores). Consumers select items from goods displayed immediately in front of them, place them in a trolley or plastic basket, and head for the 'checkout'. Much like the first prototypical supermarket—Clarence Saunders' Piggly Wiggly store in Memphis in 1916—the novelties were free movement through the store, tightly-packed shelves full of colourfully-boxed and canned items, direct customer inspection of products on sale, and a final point of payment. Customers seemed to like the format, and the retailers sought to capitalise on its success by introducing other 'innovations'. It was found, for example, that if regularly-consumed items like milk and bread were placed at the back of the store, customers would be compelled to walk down the supermarket aisles to reach them—hopefully browsing and selecting other items along the way. Today, there are other tricks. The size of the supermarket trolley has grown. A bigger cart equals a bigger shop. Large boxes of goods ready for shelving crowd the aisles to slow people's movement. The ends of the aisles are usually reserved for 'special deals' like two-for-ones and weekly specials, designed to let shoppers know they are bagging-a-bargain (end-of-aisle displays are responsible for some 30% of supermarket sales—with soda pop being a favourite).[47] Aldi even boasts a famous middle isle with a

> rapidly rotating assortment of ultra-discounted oddities … You might find yourself walking into Aldi for coffee, pasta and milk and walking out with a discount welding helmet, an inflatable watermelon or a blanket for a horse (even though you don't own a horse).[48]

Aldi's middle aisle—which apparently 'inspires devotion' among British customers[49]—is known affectionately by many names:

> 'the WTF isle', 'treasure aisle-land' ... 'the Aisle of Wonder' and the 'Aile of Shite'.[50]

US-owned Costco has gone one step further. While buying diapers you might feel the desire to order a coffin? It will be delivered to your chosen address within eight working days. And, their sale of wedding rings would seem to give new meaning to the phrase 'walking down the aisle'.

In nearly all supermarkets selected brands are placed at adult eye level to improve purchase (the food manufacturers often pay a premium to have their items displayed in this way, at the so-called bull's eye zone). The wafting barbecued chicken smell induces a hunger craving that predisposes customers to purchase more food items. In some large supermarkets space is allocated to ye olde baker, the friendly fishmonger, or the portly butcher in his navy and white striped apron, taking many older customers back to an era of familiarity and trust. For the kids there's dancing bananas, singing celery sticks, mooing cash registers. This is truly a Disney-sequel.[51]

It doesn't end there. Constant but largely unseen surveillance ensures supermarket workers 'perform' their tasks in an efficient and genial manner. This is not unlike Foucault's panopticon effect where prisoners discipline their own behaviour for fear someone in authority might be watching from the tower.[52] Then there's music. Pleasant music is essential in the manipulation of behaviour—in this case of the consumer. A well-chosen music list holds a very important place in sales promotion. Researchers have shown that a supermarket playing classical music will increase the sales of higher priced items, while country music increases the sale of utilities. French music increases sales of French wine while German music inspires the purchasing of German wines.[53] 'Hidden persuaders', indeed. According to *Soundtrack your brand* a leading firm supplying supermarkets with playlists:

> Customers walk into your grocery store and hear music that immediately puts them in a good mood. They planned on breezing through the store

and only getting items on the list, but the music relaxes them and subtly causes them to take their time as they browse the aisles and end up buying more … And employees are happier with great music in the background that doesn't repeat.[54]

The checkout—where time is spent waiting for items to be scanned and packed—hosts a tempting variety of chocolates, sweets, soft drinks, and magazines. Sometimes these items are at children's eye level and reach, something especially annoying for already beleaguered parents. Still, little Oliver, Seth, Charlotte, or Isla have been very good of late and are fittingly rewarded with what has become a weekly *chupa chup*. (Salvador Dali is no doubt smiling from his grave as little children grasp for his artwork.)[55]

Recall This

Food is easily compromised. The air that surrounds it is replete with bacteria, fungi, and a host of flying nasties that like to lay eggs. And, while it has always been thus, there are some features of the industrial food production and distribution system that create contemporary concerns. Millions of people are affected by food poisoning every year.

Various food scares are occurring in the supermarkets on an uncomfortably regular basis. *Salmonella* in eggs, *E. Coli* in milk, *listeria* in Christmas leg hams, glass fragments in mayonnaise and in apple pies, mycotoxin contamination of apple juice, tomato paste with metal fragments, gingerbread men containing a mysterious 'undisclosed' ingredient, ice cream with rubber tracings, and organic tea with pesticide residues. There are nut allergens (along with cadmium and lead) in chocolate, exploding chilli sauce bottles, and button batteries in hot cross buns—the list goes on.[56]

Apart from these recent examples, history brims with stories of death and illness caused through food poisoning. A disease of the Middle Ages, St Anthony's fire, originated from fungus fermentation of rye grain. It is still around (now termed erysipelas) and produces gangrene, convulsions, hallucinations, 'crawling' skin, and for many, death. In the 1960s Canadians enjoyed a beer produced by Dow Ale. The beer was 'stabilised' with cobalt sulphate, producing cardiomyopathy in drinkers. Some 16 Quebecois citizens were killed and over 70 poisoned, with Dow Ale denying any responsibility. In 2023 sales of the popular Chinese beer Tsingtao took a dive in South Korea when a video emerged on social media of a worker urinating into a large vat of the beer at the company's Shandong brewery.[57] Wait for the PR industry to turn this to the company's advantage. 'Get on the piss with Tsingtao' could be the new catchy motto?

In 1971 a large shipment of grain was delivered to Basra, Iraq. It was for planting by local farmers and was doused with the toxic chemical methylmercury to protect it from fungus. Much of it never reached the farmers. The warning label was printed in English and Spanish, creating confusion among the locals who spoke neither language. But many were hungry and snaffled the seed. Its ingestion—largely by poor rural dwellers—resulted in 6,000 hospitalisations and close to 500 deaths. Then there was the 1981 tragedy in Spain when people purportedly swallowed industrial-use canola oil instead of olive oil—killing 600 people. I say purportedly because some excellent investigative journalism by *The Guardian's* Bob Woffinden discovered that fruits and vegetables available at the time had been heavily polluted by toxic agri-chemicals, and that the canola oil theory was a cover up. It is estimated that some 1,000 people died and approximately 25,000 people were seriously injured or disabled by the agri-chemicals—one of the biggest food poisoning disasters in modern Europe.[58]

We know that it can be a dog-eat-dog world, but few of us could imagine a cow-eat-cow world. Mad Cow Disease or *Bovine Spongiform Encephalopathy* occurs when cattle eat other cattle. Components of cattle not destined for human consumption are cooked, dried, powdered, and added to the feed supplements given to cows. If the powdered cow parts contain an abnormal protein (prion) the cow ingesting it can develop a condition which leads to a 'spongy' brain, incoordination, and death. If humans eat these infected cows (the disease might not show itself in cattle for five or six years in the cow's life) they will develop Creutzfeldt-Jakob disease, a brain disorder for which there is no cure. Approximately 230 people, largely British subjects, have died from the disease, along with nearly 200,000 cattle (with an additional 4.4 million killed as a precaution). Never undercook a beef patty. In 1993, in one of the biggest food poisonings in US history, people fell ill from eating Jack in the Box hamburgers bursting with *E. coli*. Of the over 700 affected four children died, with another 200 people becoming seriously ill, some developing permanent kidney and brain damage.[59]

So hungry you could eat a horse? Don't worry, you most likely have. 'Horsegate'—as it was invariably going to be dubbed—was a major food scandal which broke in 2013. In 2012 the Irish Food Standards Agency tested a number of frozen meat foods that had entered the country. DNA testing showed that over 30% of the products contained horsemeat. Of particular concern was the French food manufacturer, Comigel, which produced frozen beef favourites lasagne and spag bol for Tesco, Aldi, and Findus. The meat in these products was measured at close to 100% horsemeat. We realise the French have a certain penchant for eating horse flesh (and snails, frog legs, calf heads, ox tongues and pigeons). But the idea that their processed food could be fraudulently mislabelled and sent on to unsuspecting customers abroad was too much to bear. Strides had to be taken to find the culprit. What had happened? The simple answer is that the agri-food supply chain for beef had become so complex ('long') that adulteration could occur with relative ease, while allowing cost savings and increased profits for food fraudsters.[60]

Comigel was being supplied with beef from the Spanghero company which, in turn, purchased beef from a Cyprus-based Dutch trading company called Draap. For those with an intimate knowledge of the Dutch language, it might be noticed that 'draap' is 'paard' spelled backwards. And *paard* means horse. The Draap company had been importing horse meat from Mexico, South America, and Romania, had been labelling it as beef, and had been supplying it to Comigel since 2007.[61] Meat was seized, people arrested, and a cynical public reacted by turning away from frozen meat products—sales of frozen hamburgers in the EU dropped by over 40% within two months of the story breaking. EU officials acted quickly to contain the scandal. Traceability became the focus. Then a problem emerged. Tracing confirmed that the factories illegally processing horsemeat had been accredited by legitimate auditing schemes. The issue, in other words, was that regulation was a furphy. Long supply chains can have up to 450 critical points at which the integrity of the chain can be compromised. The public could simply not trust the industry players, governments, or regulatory bodies to monitor and prevent meat laundering.[62]

Fabricating Trust

Given consumer concerns over food safety and authenticity, retailers in the food industry are very keen to convince consumers of quality and provenance. To do so, they use various methods to fabricate trust. The first is private regulation. By developing their own auditing systems supermarkets can 'force' their suppliers to conform to the standards set down by those supermarkets. Retailer-defined standards cover food hygiene, non-GMs, package labelling, storage conditions, and much more (some farmers have complained that the compliance material they receive is thicker than a telephone book). GlobalGAP (for 'Good Agricultural Practice') is a form of international food governance developed to reassure consumers that anything produced under its banner is safely produced, safely handled, and is unadulterated. Food academic Bill Vorley has argued that GlobalGAP is, in reality

> a 'firewall' response to legislation – a mechanism to demonstrate proof of due diligence, safeguard reputation, and reduce legal liability for own-brand retailers. [It] is also a means to reduce governance costs for lead firms in value chains and to transfer costs of compliance further upstream.[63]

'Upstream' means farmers and processors. It is they who have to absorb the costs of compliance and who are 'squeezed' by the downstream food retailers. Outcome? The retailers are delivered a reputational advantage while dumping compliance costs on their suppliers.

Trust can also be fabricated through a regime of international standards. In Great Britain the Red Tractor logo on foods ranging from meat to cheese to fruit to vegetables is a guarantee of safe and healthy food that meets prescribed animal welfare standards (although it has come to light that Red Tractor pigs can be kept on concrete floors rather than straw and can have their tails removed without anaesthetics, and

Red Tractor chickens can be crammed 20 per square metre and often reach a size where their legs are no longer able to bear their fattened bodies).[64] The EU boasts Protected Designation of Origin and Protected Geographical Indication logos to cover food, wines and a variety of other agricultural products. In the Nordic nations the Keyhole is used to assist consumers in their choice of high-fibre, low-sugar, low-fat food alternatives. Argentina has an 'FS Certification' with its logo sporting a large green tick. France has a multi-coloured ABCDE 'Nutri-score' which has been praised for its clarity and simplicity. And so on. While each is an attempt to better inform consumers about the foods they are purchasing, the real beneficiaries are the food retailers who gain credibility through the presence, on their shelves, of these 'objective' food quality standards. The consumer-helpful labels appear to hide as much as they reveal.

The fabrication of trust also comes in the form of food manufacturers' and supermarkets' own branding and promotion. In an attempt to make the foods they sell more authentic, dairy manufacturers will put the face of a farmer (or better a farmer and family) on the front of their milk cartons. Packaged vegetables often come with a photo of a farmer and a statement of quality. Here are some other examples. Abbots advertises its 'village bakery' where loaves of bread 'graze' in an idyllic scene that could have been painted by Constable. The caption is 'We'd never force-feed our bread artificial colours and flavours'. Whole Foods, 'America's healthiest grocery store', shows a farmer walking through rows of healthy green vegetables along with the claim 'the highest standards weren't available to us. So we created them'. In Organic Valley's emerald-green farm paddock, farmer Jana McClelland strokes a rather large black and white Friesen cow with the brand Organic Valley claiming it is 'not just the where behind your food. But the who and the why'.[65] Food brands attempt to build consumer trust through farm-to-table images and metaphors. They do this to assure the consumer that the food is authentic, healthy, and animal-friendly even in cases where the image and words bear little resemblance to reality. Dairylea is a soft cheese manufacturer and the Bernard Matthews company a turkey producer:

> Both companies depict 'happy' animals on their product packaging; cows on a green field under a blue sky with plenty of room to roam are shown

on Dairylea Cheese Triangles, and on the packaging for its turkey nuggets and pieces, Bernard Matthews depicts a similar image with field gates and tractors.

According to Bronwen Reinhardt, a campaign manager for Compassion in World Farming, both images are false—'In reality the livestock are crammed into barren cages, kept indoors all their lives or kept in such close confinement that they are unable to express their natural behaviour'.[66]

Other bucolic tropes are tractors, wagons, barns, and hay bales, along with words that evoke simplicity and caring—'natural', 'handpicked', 'local', and 'pure'. It has been noted that for a society overly concerned with the risks and hazards of industrial foods such images and words

> reinsert human agency and traditional values back into food … seeking to make connections between the purchaser and the [origin] of the food item, [creating a] fragile version of 'trust' through claims of provenance, tradition and authenticity which in reality are underpinned by long and anonymous food supply chains and a pool of corporate employees.[67]

Rather than altering a sick food production and distribution system, the aim is to convince consumers that that system provides them with clean, green, and nutritious foods. We are being deceived.

Another significant 'player' in the fabrication of trust by the food retailers is the celebrity chef. Hired by the supermarkets to provide advice on food ingredients, meal preparation, and nutrition, their faces appear throughout the stores, they pop up in food magazines, and they make regular appearances in television ads and on talk shows. On the surface many take on the role of promoting healthy eating on limited family budgets; below the surface they are spruikers for the industrial food system and represent the smooth face of commerce. Sociologist Jane Dixon was one of the first to identify the importance of celebrity chefs, arguing that they use their charisma and influence to shape the food tastes of entire generations of consumers. They are among the most persuasive 'influencers' discussed in Chapter 1. Their role, according to

Dixon, is to 'compete with nutrition educators and other food knowledge producers, advertisers, scientists and government bureaucrats in creating a pecking order of foods, such that consumers change their diets regularly'.[68]

Those diets will well-suit the supermarkets if customers purchase own-brands and meal ingredients sourced exclusively from those retailers. It is the job of the celebrity chef to promote the foods of their employer while bringing to the table, as it were, their own 'take' on foods. Some, like Jamie Oliver, are advocates for home cooking and the ethical sourcing of animals. Sainsbury successfully used Oliver to promote quality over price, in an effort to distinguish its stores from Tesco and Asda. Others, like US/Australian Curtis Stone, promote product freshness and the supermarket's direct connection with farmers. Both trade on authenticity and trustworthiness. Communication researchers Tania Lewis and Alison Huber have summed it up nicely:

> Across the world, celebrity chefs have become unlikely cultural icons, offering consumers 'expert' guidance through the maze of food 'choice' we are presented with today, while at the same time reconnecting food to questions of pleasure, conviviality and sensory engagement in a globalized and often alienating food culture.[69]

In the process, supermarkets have positioned themselves as food authorities, employing symbolic capital to demonstrate they are good corporate citizens while, at the same time, engaging in unfair trading, abuses of market power, and pricing practices that undermine farmer viability. They are responsible for significant food waste, for marketing strategies that encourage impulse buying, for labour exploitation, and for stocking low-nutrient foods that cause obesity.[70] No wonder they need the wholly-believable Jamies of this world.

Fun with Fast Food

Ray Kroc was as astute as he was money hungry. His job in the 1950s was selling milkshake making machines to food outlets. At 52 years of age he could have become another Willy Loman in Miller's *Death of a Salesman*, but when he walked into the McDonald brothers' San Bernardino store to sell some of his machines he had his eureka moment. What he observed was not so much a hamburger joint but a food assembly line that would have made Henry Ford proud. The burgers were all of a standard size, they all had the same sauce and the same buns, and they were delivered at speed. There were no plates to wash. There was no need for tables and chairs because customers received their burgers within minutes and happily departed. The place was spick and span and the toilets 'sparkled'.[71] And there was no pinball machine, jukebox, or cigarette dispenser in the corner to attract troublesome teenagers or sundry ne'er-do-wells. Customers flocked beneath the great yellow arches. The 1950s was a time of growing affluence in the US and the motor car became the symbol of freedom and prosperity. San Bernardino happened to be at the end of Route 66—a freeway running through two-thirds of the US and made famous in the eponymous song (a rhythm and blues number written by Bobby Troup and performed by a host of singers including Nat King Cole in 1946, Chuck Berry in 1961, and the Rolling Stones in 1964). The McDonald brothers' golden arches attracted newcomers and the store, itself, was brightly lit—you couldn't miss it.

People were on the move and it was Ray's genius that identified a commercial opportunity. If customers were travelling they would crave the familiarity and reliability of a restaurant that served an affordable and well-known takeaway dish. It had to appeal to the whole family, especially the children who, in 60 to 80% of the time, influence where the family would eat.[72] And children liked savourless food, nothing too hot and spicy. So, here was the perfect combination—a familiar fast-food outlet serving familiar inexpensive bland food, in clean well-lit surroundings. Of course, the chain he had established could not bear his name—he'd recognised that a string of 'Kroc' outlets might not convey the right food message. So, he not only purchased the McDonalds store, but also used its name. Ray Kroc presented to the world the basic ethos of McDonald's—the famous QSCV (Quality, Service, Cleanliness, and Value). Another possible option is MCUS (Mass production, Cheap labour, Uniformity, and Standardisation)—'a frightening example of free enterprise gone wild'.[73] But it was not just hamburgers that were being 'sold'. According to a McDonald's executive:

> The message we're trying to get across is that going to McDonald's can be a fun experience for an American family. For a housewife, it's a mini-break in the day's routine. For Dad it's an opportunity to be a hero to the kids, but in a way which won't cost much money. For the children it's plain fun.[74]

Ray Kroc not only noticed the new highways being built across the US, but also the growing road networks across the US's sprawling suburbia. As his money accumulated he'd fly in his Cessna on school-spotting missions. He had a thing for roadways and schools, the conjunction of which was often the perfect place to locate the next McDonald's. Hospitals, too. There are over 20 outlets in hospitals in the US alone—what better endorsement for the McDonald's healthy lifestyle?

From one original store founded by the McDonald brothers in 1940, today McDonald's operates and franchises more than 39,000 restaurants in over 100 countries. It is the most valuable fast-food company in the world, with a brand value of US$130 billion. It serves around 69 million people each day.[75] It does so by

> providing customers with a uniformly pleasant 'McDonald's experience' [of] mass-produce[d] friendliness, deference, diligence, and good cheer through a variety of socialization and social control mechanisms.[76]

And the menus have become varied to cater for national food preferences. You can buy a McFalafel and McKebab in Israel, McRice burger in Singapore, Indonesia, and the Philippines, and a McAloo Tikki burger and Pizza McPuff in India. Canada boasts the McLobster roll while Italy has the Baci Perugina McFluffy, Australia the KitKat McFluffy, and Uruguay the Oreo McShake.[77]

But don't try getting on to the bandwagon and naming your own store with the Mc prefix. McCoffee (San Francisco), McBagels (New York), McMunchies (Scotland), and MacJoy (Philippines) were all taken to court by McDonald's for trademark infringement and were forced to change their names. All these outlets sold foodstuffs, so confusion with McDonald's was possible. Would McDonald's insist upon exclusive ownership of the Mc even when the Mc was not associated with food? Yes. When Quality Inn's McSleep hotel chain was about to be opened, McDonald's was on the move again with the court finding that 'Mc' had become so embedded in the public's mind as being associated with McDonald's that McSleep infringed McDonald's internationally recognised trademark. The chain was forced to alter its name to Sleep Inn. As Ray Kroc once announced, 'if any of my competitors were drowning, I'd stick a hose in their mouth and turn on the water.'[78]

According to behind-the-golden-arches investigators Max Boas and Steve Chain, while McDonald's can be rightly criticised for its overprocessed food offerings, its labour practices, and its advertising saturation,

> Ray Kroc's achievements are not to be underestimated. His optimism and faith had nurtured a giant complex. He had taken meat and potatoes and created a mass menu to fit the pace of highly industrialized life. He could claim his place among America's mass merchandizers who had revolutionised the methods of distribution.[79]

The Golden Arches symbol is now the most recognised in the world (ahead of the cross), and even the King of England owns a McDonald's franchise[80]—something must be right.

I must confess I have never eaten a McDonald's hamburger, but have visited their premises a number of times. Their toilets sparkle.

Feeding the Lie

The phrase 'Der Mensch ist, was er ißt' (man is what he eats) was first uttered by the nineteenth-century German philosopher Ludwig Feuerbach. He was greatly concerned about poverty in his nation and the inability of many of the poor to secure an adequate diet. Weakened minds and bodies were the consequences, leading to the inability of the nation to win wars.[81] Since Feuerbach's time, studies have discovered that the foods, liquids, and other substances we ingest (or fail to ingest) have significant impacts upon our physical and mental well-being. Deficiencies in micronutrients, such as iron, magnesium, and zinc, can result in growth retardation, while eating chocolate and high calorie foods releases 'pleasure' hormones such as dopamine which make us feel good. High protein foods improve our concentration and motivation. Carbonated drinks can induce agitation.[82]

In 2003 film maker Morgan Spurlock embarked upon a rather strange endeavour: For a month he ate three meals a day, seven days a week, at McDonald's. When the counter attendant asked if he'd like to 'supersize' the order, he would say 'yes'. At the end of the 'experiment' he had gained 11 kilograms, lost his sex drive, had heart palpitations, liver problems, and had experienced depression, headaches, and tiredness. Conclusion—a McDonald's fast-food diet is bad for you. Unfortunately for Spurlock, critics exposed his ploy. He was being disingenuous—he had eaten in four weeks as many McDonald's meals as a normal consumer would eat in eight years; he gorged himself on them; and he limited his exercise. He said he'd only consumed beverages from McDonald's, with one of his examining doctors concluding that fast food was 'pickling his liver'. This was largely dismissed in 2017 when Spurling confessed 'I've consistently been drinking since the age of 13 … I haven't been sober for more than a week in 30 years'.[83]

Finally, a science teacher from Des Moine, Iowa, ate nothing but McDonald's for three months, and lost 17 kilos. He had chosen varied items from the menu—oatmeal for breakfast, a salad for lunch, a hamburger for dinner—and exercised for 45 minutes each day.[84] Leaving aside the hype and sensationalism of Spurlock's *Super Size Me* (which grossed over US$22 million), the real point that can be made is that fast foods—whether from McDonald's, KFC, Pizza Hut, or any on our favourite downtown takeaway list—should be eaten in moderation or avoided if possible. They are loaded with fat, laden with salt, and are often supplemented by sugary drinks. Higher fat levels encourage overeating, salt drives up blood pressure, and sugary drinks can result in weight gain, diabetes, and cardiovascular disease. We know these things, so why are we continually drawn to poor health options?

Coaxing the Kiddies

The problem is that the advertising industry behind the Golden Arches and other fast-food chains has a bagful of tricks to make us buy. Food marketing is aimed, in particular, at young children and youths with the aim of fostering brand awareness and brand loyalty. As suggested at the beginning of the chapter, the marketing channels are the obvious ones of TV, the internet, supermarkets, schools, transport hubs, parks, playgrounds, kids' clubs, and sporting arenas. But there are also new players—Facebook/Meta, Instagram, Snapchat, and other social media where young users see newsfeeds with the 'likes' of their peers. Colourful adverts on social networking sites grab attention prompting users to click on linked pages that send them to corporate websites. Those sites create positive images of fast food, enticing the young viewers to try the fare. Such 'behavioural advertising' is well known in the marketing industry. Nutrition researchers Mary Story and Simone French have written that there are strong similarities between the marketing of unhealthy food and tobacco advertising:

> at one time tobacco companies were providing schools with free sports programs, scoreboards, and book covers featuring school logos on the front and cigarette ads on the back. Young children were targeted with the sale of candy and bubble gum in packages that resembled those of actual cigarette brands ... Use of the cartoon character Joe Camel to promote Camel cigarettes showed that 30% of 3-year olds and 80% of 6-year olds could make the association between Joe Camel and a pack of cigarettes. In the three years after the introduction of the cartoon camel character, preference for Camel cigarettes increased from 0.5 to 32% among adolescent smokers.[85]

It is important to recognise that children under eight years do not have the cognitive development to discern the intent of advertisements, treating their content as largely factual. For Story and French 'the intense marketing of high fat, high sugar foods to young children can be viewed as exploitation because they do not understand that commercials are designed to sell products and do not have the ability to comprehend or evaluate advertising'.[86]

Similarly, a University of Michigan researcher has reported:

> When teenagers are seeing fast food commercials, it really seems to be activating reward centers of the brain more effectively than other types of advertisements ... The teenagers that are showing this greatest reward activation of the brain seem to be at greater risk in gaining weight over time. It's hard for people to defend against because it's not a conscious process ... That whole system is primed for you to be motivated to seek out ultra-processed foods.[87]

It has been revealed that over 80% of food promotion ads viewed by children promote foods high in saturated fats, trans fats, salt, and sugar, with the food and beverage industries in the US spending close to US$1.8 billion each year to target children (often as young as two years of age).[88]

Today, two-thirds of food corporations, fast-food chains, and major media outlets, have no policies in place to restrict the marketing of junk food to kids. In most countries there is a reliance upon complex systems of voluntary codes of practice—yet another example of the failure of self-regulation under neoliberal globalisation.[89]

Globesity[90]

In his provocative book *The Industrial Diet* Canadian academic Tony Winson argues that human society has moved from a Paleolithic diet in early times to an industrial diet that had its roots in the seventy-year period up to the Second World War. This was followed by an 'intensified' industrial diet that was a product of the post-war years. The 1980s saw the advent of the globalized industrial diet with which we live today. For Winson, this has not been progress but rather a downhill journey. In Paleolithic times people ate a diversity of plants including nuts, berries, fruits, insects along with seafood, and wild animals. Grain intake was limited, and nothing was processed. The beginnings of the industrial diet coincided with technological breakthroughs such as the industrial milling of grain, the canning of fruits and vegetables, and the refrigeration of meat. It was dominated by large, horizontally-integrated firms producing low-cost, standardised, food products. Mass marketing helped to normalise and promote the industrial diet.

After the Second World War three basic processes were introduced that further sullied industrial foods—the simplification of whole foods, the shortening of time in the production of food (such as the intensive farming of animals), and the application of macro-adulterants (salts, sugars, and fats). The result was the creation of 'pseudo-foods' (junk foods), made palatable by the addition of chemicals with names like amyl acetate, ethyl methylphenylglycidate, 4-methylacetophenone, and neryl isobutyrate. From the 1980s the industrial diet has gone global resulting in 'spatial colonisation' by supermarkets and the fast-food industry. The result has been widespread nutritional degradation and the creation of overweight and obese bodies—contributing to a major crisis in public health.[91]

Have you ever heard of High Fructose Corn Syrup (HFCS)? You should have. If you live in the US you are consuming about 37 pounds (17 kilograms) of HFCS every year in products as diverse as soft drinks, snack foods, baked beans, canned fruits, barbeque sauce, salad dressings, and ice cream.[92] In the US, HFCS has emerged out of a curious interaction between agricultural subsidies, global geopolitics, and American ingenuity. In 1984 Coca-Cola used HFCSs rather than sugar to save on production costs. Corn producers had been heavily subsidised by the US government resulting in corn becoming cheaper than cane sugar. But geopolitics came knocking as well. Earlier, in the early 1970s, the Soviet Union was facing a famine and immediately began importing American corn. Corn prices skyrocketed and US farmers responded by planting as much as they could. The resultant overproduction of corn inevitably resulted in price falls.

Grain giants like ADM had a problem to solve—what would they do with the excessive volumes of the cheap excess corn they were processing? The answer was simple—create new markets. This is where ingenuity played its part. Scientists were engaged to extract starch from the corn. In one process, the starch was fermented to create ethanol, a new product for the fuel industry. In another process an enzyme was added that converted the starch's glucose into fructose, a substitute for cane sugar. All went well until cheap imported cane sugar drove down the price of HCFS. ADM had difficulty competing until one of its managers, Dwayne Andreas, came up with a brilliant idea. Why not stop the importation of cane sugar by imposing quotas? He approached sugarcane growers in Florida telling them that their future was being undermined by cheap imports. The growers lobbied Congress and found a willing ally in that free-marketer, Ronald Reagan, who set quotas so high that the price of Florida-grown sugar soared to double that of international producers. With domestic sugar prices reaching new heights, HCFS again became price competitive. Coke and Pepsi both jumped at the cheaper product, and the rest is history.[93]

Why should we have concerns about HFCS? After all, corn is a natural product. The problems are in its chemical structure (the liver must convert it to glucose, glycogen, or fat before it is available as energy) and its ubiquity. Small amounts of fructose, such as are found in fruits, can be readily processed by the body. But the Western diet is swamped with HFCS. In the US some 40% of sweeteners added to food and drinks are from HFCS, with high intake of such products leading to accumulation of fats in the liver. This can herald fatty liver disease and, in the longer term, type 2 diabetes.[94] Ingesting excess glucose triggers the brain to say 'stop', and appetite is thereby controlled. Not so for fructose, which increases the appetite—we continue to eat and drink even after we are full. The result? Visceral fat—the most harmful form of body fat—is accumulated around internal organs. This is the fat most commonly associated with diabetes, heart disease, stroke, artery disease, and various cancers. HFCS also promotes weight gain more than does glucose, with scientists concluding 'over consumption of HFCS could very well be a major factor in the "obesity epidemic," which correlates with the upsurge in the use of HFCS'.[95] It has been calculated that for a person drinking just one HFCS-laden soft drink each day a weight gain of some 15 pounds (7 kg) is likely to occur over a year.[96]

In his book *Fast Food Genocide*, medical practitioner Joel Fuhrman reveals the impact of the fast-food diet on Americans. The low-cost, low-nutrition, 'Frankenfoods' produce scientifically-proven effects including diminished concentration and intelligence, along with an increase in autism, childhood cancers, hyperactivity, mood swings, and diabetes. They negatively affect emotional well-being, creativity, and memory. Consumption of a fast-food diet produces anger and violence, and less self-control. As fast foods are addictive they reduce the ability to control food intake, while also negatively impacting human interactions and producing anti-social behaviour in children. Fast foods and processed foods contain an array of:

> artificial colors, artificial flavours, preservatives, pesticides, anti-foaming agents, emulsifiers, stabilizers, and thickeners … Fast foods are toxic; they accelerate death through these added toxins but also by supplying concentrated calories without substantial fiber or the micronutrients humans need to sustain a normal life.[97]

Americans will be particularly upset to learn that eating one hot dog can shorten one's life by some 36 minutes.[98] Hot dogs, like many other processed meat products, contain ingredients such as muscle trimming, head meat, animal skin, animal feet, fatty tissue, gristle, blood, and offal. Rectal tissue is another permissible inclusion.[99] Oh, and then there's sodium nitrate, sodium diacetate, sodium phosphate, maltodextrin, beef stock, potassium lactate, and corn syrup—all combined and cooked at high temperature to produce a 'meat emulsion'.[100] Air is then removed from the meat puree which is then pumped into casings—usually cleaned and processed animal intestines. The dogs are hung, sprayed with water, and are then 'bun ready'. Each year consumers in the US consume some 20 billion hot dogs.[101] There's no such thing as too many. In 2021 Joey Chestnut had his fourteenth win as US hot dog eating champion, devouring 76 hot dogs and buns in 10 minutes, way ahead of the women's champion Michelle Lesco who could only manage 30.[102] In 2023 Joey fell short of his record, only downing 62 dogs in the allotted time. 'What a roller coaster emotionally' he said after his win, 'I'm just happy. It's the Fourth of July and I got to eat some hot dogs and get a win'.[103] And a new women's champ emerged—Miki Sudo—who managed to consume 39.5 hot dogs in 10 minutes in front of an estimated 35,000 spectators.[104]

There is a problem. Hot dogs—along with instant noodles, low-protein breads, savoury packaged snacks, and other 'junk food' concoctions—fall into the category of ultra-processed foods (UPFs). UPFs not only lead to obesity, but also increase the risk of dementia, cardiovascular disease, and colon cancer.[105] UPFs are 'nutritionally empty mush', high in fats, salt, and sugar but low in protein and fibre. That does not seem to be affecting their popularity, with consumers in the US and UK deriving at least 50% of their calorific intake from UPFs.[106] We have become, in the words of infectious disease doctor and author Chris van Tulleken, 'ultra-processed people'.[107] Foods that have become 'mush' have had their cellular structure altered. Bodies react to these foods by viewing them as they would an infection—they create inflammation (people hooked on UPFs exhibit higher than normal white blood cell counts). Changes to the microbiome (microorganisms in the gut) also increase inflammation. There's even a new term for this—'fast-food fever'. The longer that bodies are inflamed, the more likely that chronic diseases will emerge.[108] Importantly,

> as ultra-processed foods become cheaper and other foods, such as vegetables and fish, become more expensive, the UPFs are taking up a bigger volume of children's diets. What's more, the pleasurable textures and aggressive marketing of these foods makes them 'appealing and aspirational' both to children and parents.[109]

They are also engineered to be addictive, with some 14% of the world's adult population and 12% of children experiencing 'substance disorder'. Like those on drugs, the behaviour of people hooked on UPFs includes extreme cravings, withdrawal symptoms, and an inability to limit intake.[110] Ironically, it is those with less money in their pockets—those facing food insecurity—who are eating increasing amounts of UPFs, and who are showing symptoms of addiction.[111]

In the early 2020s the world was focused upon halting the spread of COVID-19, with some 7 million deaths having been recorded up to the beginning of 2024.[112] During this same four-year period an estimated 11.2 million people died from overweight and obesity.[113] There are four overweight and obese people for every person who is malnourished,[114] with obesity being declared one of the major global crises of our time. But are the supermarkets and fast-food industries to blame? As one Republican member of US congress argued, eating is a matter of 'common sense and personal responsibility'.[115] After all, at least in the adult world, we are the ones who place food into our mouths. If we have become addicted to the industrial diet, surely it is our individual responsibility to face up to the consequences and wean ourselves off its tempting treats.

This is true, to a point. When we think of convenience food, we are talking about food we can grab, eat, and move on. We are busy people. If we are eating this food in the car we are 'dashboard dining'. In the US, one in four people eats fast food every day, consumes 30% more packaged food than fresh food, spends 10% of their disposable income on fast foods every year, and eats 20% of all meals in the car.[116] That is one in five meals in the car. While 'car cuisine' seems like an oxymoron it has nevertheless become a strange twenty-first century reality. How did it come to this? How did the dashboard become the dining table?

A fast-food outlet must grab your attention, as an encouragement for you to stop and purchase its products. Most of the signs for fast-food outlets have red signage (red says 'stop') and other 'warm' colours in their logos (which activate hunger). The smell of food is usually apparent when hitting the drive-through or when alighting from the vehicle.[117] Marketing teams in the fast-food industry style their products so they fit comfortably into car cupholders (for example, Chobani Yogurt and the Go Cup from KFC). The top of McDonald's wraps can be ripped open to allow a driver to eat with one hand while steering with the other. Most burger companies wrap buns so they will not dribble onto you while you are driving. Taco Bell developed the Crunchwrap Supreme, packaged in a hexagon shape for easy, no drip, eating (at over 500 calories it represents a third of an adult's daily calorie intake). 'Good to go' says the accompanying advert. Two new inventions are the French fry holder and the dip clip. (These innovations aside, the most popular choice of takeaway food for the car is the sugar-laden candy bar.)[118] US-based food writer Michael Pollan doesn't recognise the food packaged for the car as real foods, preferring to call them 'edible food-like substances'[119] that might be convenient for motorists but are nevertheless an adulterated, highly processed, simulacrum.

The problem is:

> Dashboard dining is universal. It includes all three key meals and snacks any time of day. It occurs year-round and nationwide. It is not limited to a specific gender or ethnicity. Heightened dashboard dining can occur around holidays or vacation time as families head out on road trips. Late-night drive-through windows cater to audiences that dig into their meals as they head home from a night on the town. Hurried parents use the convenience of these meals as they shuttle from one activity to another after school and on the weekends.[120]

The importance of Tony Winson's book, and books of a similar vein (Michael Carolan's *The Real Cost of Cheap Food*, Jennifer Clapp's *Food*, Delpeuch et al.'s *Globesity*, Holt-Gimenez' *A Foodies Guide to Capitalism*, Raj Patel's *Stuffed and Starved*, and Chris Rosin et al.'s *Food System Failure*)[121] is that they identify structural forces at work in creating and perpetuating the industrial diet. It is not only income inequalities that have grown with the expansion of capitalism, but food inequalities as well. It is the poor who are drawn to, or find it impossible to avoid, cheap but nutritionally empty processed foods, and it is they who gain the weight associated with the overconsumption of fats, sugars, and salts. It is a 'bitter paradox … the heaviest people are the ones with the lightest wallets'.[122] Neoliberal globalisation has fostered the growth and influence of the food and agribusiness corporations, and it is they who benefit from the global expansion of the industrial diet—even though this may not be obvious to all. There is, in Raj Patel's words, a behind-the-scenes 'hidden battle' for control of the world's food system,[123] a battle being won by the ultra-processed food manufacturing sector.[124]

The food industry has a systemic problem. It is not any one single fast-food company that is creating a global food environment that is impacting negatively on people and the globe. It is the entirety of the food production system—from the seeds farmers purchase, to the chemicals they use, to the environmentally unsustainable practices they engage in, to the animal feedlots, to the traders and processors of grains and meats, to the supermarkets that retail those products, to the advertisers who create tempting lies to keep us McHappy, to the consumers who have been trained to eat processed foods, and to the governments promoting the system through neoliberal options like industry self-regulation. But maybe there's some hope for change? When floods wiped out the entire lettuce crop in Queensland in 2022, KFC came up with a brilliant solution. It substituted its lettuce with cabbage, immediately increasing the nutritional content of its products while giving new meaning to the 'C' in KFC.

An unlikely saviour from obesity might just be on the way—shrinkflation. I know, a terrible word. Food and grocery manufacturers, coping with input cost inflation (estimated to be at a 40 year high),[125] are reducing the size of their products, while keeping prices at the same level. Consumers receive less of the product for the same price. In 2014 Coca-Cola decreased the size of its large bottle from 2 to 1.75 litres. Kraft Heinz, owner of Cottee's, cleverly altered the size of its glass jam jars from 500 grams to 375 grams. A 25% decline in size was matched by a 7% decline in price.[126] In 2016 Toblerone reduced the weight of its chocolate bars by 20 grams—by expanding the gaps between the chocolate triangles. A box of McVities Jaffa cakes decreased from 12 to 10, a packet of Doritos has been reduced by 10% in volume, a box of Coco Pops once 800 grams is now 720 grams, and so on.[127] And if you are eating less food, you probably don't need as much toilet paper—the Charmin company's 'mega' roll has gone from 264 double-ply sheets to 244 and its 'super mega' decreased from 396 sheets to 366. Cottonelle single-ply sheets have gone from 340 to 312. While over 2,500 products have been subject to shrinkflation,[128] it is not considered fraud because the product's weight, volume, and quantity are printed on the packaging. It is up to the consumer to detect the trickery.

In Chapter 8 we will explore some options for changing the dynamics and course of food production and procurement. In the meantime, it is instructive to recall food writer Michael Pollan's tips for a healthy diet:

1. Don't eat anything your great grandmother wouldn't consider to be food.
2. Don't eat anything with more than five ingredients, or ingredients that can't be pronounced.
3. Shop on the perimeter of the supermarket where the fresh foods reside.
4. Don't eat anything that won't eventually rot—with honey as one of few exceptions.
5. Don't fill to the brim—when you leave the table always be a bit hungry.
6. Don't eat between meals and when mealtime arrives, eat from a table, preferably with company.
7. Don't purchase food after you fuel your car—resist 'dashboard dining'.[129]

Unfortunately, for most of us, such a recipe will remain a difficult one to follow.

Notes

1. Rayport, J. (2013) Advertising's new medium: Human experience, https://hbr.org/2013/03/advertisings-new-medium-human-experience.
2. McDonald's settled for US$1 million for its indiscretion—see Behr, F. (2001) The real reason McDonald's got rid Of Mayor McCheese, https://www.mashed.com/395928/the-real-reason-mcdonalds-got-rid-of-mayor-mccheese/.
3. Bellomo, M. (2016) The weird history of McDonaldland toys, https://www.mentalfloss.com/article/69989/brief-history-mcdonaldland-and-toys-and-lawsuit-it-spawned.

4. Kraak, V. and Story, M. (2016) *The Use of Brand Mascots and Media Characters: Opportunities for Food Marketing to Children*, Healthy Eating Research, Robert Wood Johnson Foundation, Durham, NC; Chen, D. (2021) 75 of the craziest facts about McDonald's, https://www.rd.com/list/mcdonalds-facts-trivia/. Over 1.5 billion toys are given away with Happy Meals each year.
5. News.com.au. (2013) Why Doritos are so darned addictive, https://nypost.com/2013/10/03/why-doritos-are-as-addictive-as-crack/.
6. Twitter. (2022) How things work, https://twitter.com/fastworkers6/status/1594434377169403904?t=KgUUADEobO9Q9cnO3ozkXw&s=03.
7. FAO. (2021) Small family farmers produce a third of the world's food, http://www.fao.org/news/story/en/item/1395127/icode/.
8. Lawrence, G. (2017) Re-evaluating food systems and food security: A global perspective, *Journal of Sociology* 53(4): 774–796.
9. Stephens, P., Clapp, J. and Isakson, R. (2022) Financialisation and sustainable diets, in K. Kevany and P. Prosperi (eds) *Routledge Handbook of Sustainable Diets*, Routledge, London, Chapter 37.
10. Agri-chemicals and agro-chemicals are terms used interchangeably by scientists, farm businesses, and reporters, and they are used interchangeably in this chapter and throughout the book. They are shortened forms of 'agricultural chemical'. These chemicals include herbicides, fungicides, and insecticides, along with industrial produced fertilisers and growth agents for plants and animals.
11. Action Against Hunger. (2021) World hunger: Key facts and statistics 2021, https://www.actionagainsthunger.org/world-hunger-facts-statistics; FAO, IFAD, UNICEF, WFP and WHO. (2020) In brief to the state of food security and nutrition in the world 2021. Transforming food systems for food security, improved nutrition, and affordable healthy diets for all, FAO, Rome; Holt-Giminez, E. (2017) *A Foodie's Guide to Capitalism:*

Understanding the Political Economy of What we Eat, Monthly Review Press, New York.
12. Hunger, for the UN, is severe food insecurity where people might not have access to food for days on end. People suffer food deprivation—are undernourished—if they consume less than 1,800 calories per day. See FAO, IFAD, UNICEF, WFP and WHO, In brief to the state of food security and nutrition in the world 2021; see also WHO. (2023) 122 million more people pushed into hunger since 2019 due to multiple crises, reveals UN report, https://www.who.int/news/item/12-07-2023-122-million-more-people-pushed-into-hunger-since-2019-due-to-multiple-crises--reveals-un-report.
13. Action Against Hunger. (2023) World hunger facts, https://www.actionagainsthunger.org/the-hunger-crisis/world-hunger-facts/.
14. India, for example, was able to move from being dependent upon grain imports to become self-sufficient in grains—see Daisy, J. and Babu, G. (2021) Lessons from the aftermaths of Green Revolution on food system and health, Frontiers in Sustainable Food Systems, https://www.frontiersin.org/articles/10.3389/fsufs.2021.644559/full.
15. Clapp, J. (2016) *Food*, Second Edition, Polity Press, UK, p. 42.
16. Daisy and Babu, Lessons from the aftermaths of Green Revolution on food system and health.
17. CBC News. (2014) Chickens are 4 times bigger today than in 1950s, https://www.cbc.ca/news/canada/calgary/chickens-are-4-times-bigger-today-than-in-1950s-1.2792628.
18. See Weis, T. (2013) *The Ecological Hoofprint: The Global Burden of Industrial Livestock*, Zed Books, London; Johnston, J. and Weiler, A. (2020) Eating our way to a sustainable future? in K. Legun, J. Keller, M. Carolan and M. Bell (eds) *The Cambridge Handbook of Environmental Sociology*, Volume 2, Cambridge University Press, Cambridge, pp. 390–410; Bittman, M. (2021) *Animal, Vegetable, Junk: A History of Food from Sustainable to Suicidal*, Houghton Mifflin Harcourt, Boston; Winders, B. and

Ransom, E. (eds) (2019) *Global Meat: Social and Environmental Consequences of the Expanding Meat Industry*, MIT Press, Cambridge Massachusetts.
19. Kassam, A. (2023) 'We're being invaded by pigs': Spain's pork revolution faces backlash, https://www.theguardian.com/environment/2023/feb/06/pigs-spain-pork-revolution-backlash; Hekman, L., Rojas, Dominquez, D. and Kassam, A. (2021) 'Toilet of Europe': Spain's pig farms blamed for mass fish die-offs, https://www.theguardian.com/environment/2021/oct/13/toilet-of-europe-spains-pig-farms-blamed-for-mass-fish-die-offs.
20. Kassam, 'We're being invaded by pigs'.
21. Hekman, Rojas, Dominquez, and Kassam, 'Toilet of Europe'.
22. Harvey, F., Wasley, A., Davies, M. and Child, D. (2017) Rise of mega farms: How the US model of intensive farming is invading the world, https://www.theguardian.com/environment/2017/jul/18/rise-of-mega-farms-how-the-us-model-of-intensive-farming-is-invading-the-world.
23. FoodIndustry. (2022) What is a CAFO? https://www.foodindustry.com/articles/what-is-a-cafo/; Smith, K. (2021) 99% of all animal products in the US come from factory farms, https://www.livekindly.co/99-animal-products-factory-farms/.
24. It was sent to the abattoirs in breach of bio-safety rules at the time.
25. Schaufler, K., Floyd-Lapp, C., Parent, R. and Schofhauser, A. (2021) The world's first GMO salmon is coming to America, https://www.nongmoproject.org/blog/the-worlds-first-gmo-salmon-is-coming-to-america-2/; Sanchez, K. (2020) FDA approves genetically engineered pigs, https://www.theverge.com/2020/12/14/22175060/fda-approval-genetically-engineered-pigs.
26. Lawrence, G. and Grice, J. (2008) Agribusiness, genetic engineering and the corporatisation of food. In J. Germov and L. Williams (eds) *A Sociology of Food and Nutrition: The Social Appetite*, Third Edition, Oxford University Press, Melbourne, pp. 78–99.

27. In creating GMOs, a piece of foreign genetic material is placed within a host organism; with gene editing changes are made to an organism's genome *without* the insertion of foreign material.
28. GRAIN. (2022) GMOs in Asia: What's happening and who's fighting back? https://grain.org/en/article/6863-gmos-in-asia-what-s-happening-and-who-s-fighting-back.
29. Hiscox, T. and Heinemann, J. (2022) Chasing future biotech solutions to climate change risks delaying action in the present—It may even make things worse, https://theconversation.com/chasing-future-biotech-solutions-to-climate-change-risks-delaying-action-in-the-present-it-may-even-make-things-worse-194147.
30. Wikiquote. (2023) Jonathan Swift, https://en.wikiquote.org/wiki/Jonathan_Swift.
31. GRAIN. (2013) GMOs: Fooling—er, "feeding"—the world for 20 years, https://grain.org/article/entries/4720-gmos-fooling-er-feeding-the-world-for-20-years. 'In the most extensive and rigorous study, the Union of Concerned Scientists analyzed twenty years of GE crops [in the US] and concluded that genetically engineered herbicide-tolerant soybeans and corn are no more productive than conventional plants and methods. Furthermore, 86% of the corn productivity increases obtained in the past twenty years have been due to conventional methods and practices. Other studies have found GE productivity to be lower than conventional.'
32. GRAIN. (2016) *The Great Climate Robbery: How the Food System Drives Climate Change and What We Can Do About It*, GRAIN, Barcelona, pp. 165–170.
33. Kjeldaas, S., Dassler, T., Antonsen, T., Wikmark, O. and Myhr, A. (2022) With great power comes great responsibility: Why 'safe enough' is not good enough in debates on new gene technologies, *Agriculture and Human Values* 40: 533–545.
34. Borg, E. and Policante, A. (2022) *Mutant Ecologies: Manufacturing Life in the Age of Genomic Capital*, Pluto Press, London, pp. 6–8.
35. Borg and Policante, *Mutant Ecologies*, p. 1.

36. UN Department of Economic and Social Affairs, Division for Sustainable Development. (2012) *Food and Agriculture: The Future of Sustainability*, United Nations, New York.
37. See, for example, Patel, R. (2007) *Stuffed and Starved: Markets, Power and the Hidden Battle for the Food System*, Black Inc, Australia, pp. 12–13.
38. Tapper, J. and Hearn, D. (2018) *The Myth of Capitalism: Monopolies and the Death of Competition*, Wiley, New Jersey, p. 22.
39. For revenue figures see the following sites: For ADM, https://www.macrotrends.net/stocks/charts/ADM/archer-daniels-midland/revenue; For Bunge, https://www.macrotrends.net/stocks/charts/BG/bunge-global-sa/revenue; for Cargill, https://www.reuters.com/markets/commodities/cargill-fiscal-2023-revenue-rises-7-record-177-billion-2023-08-03/; for Louis Dreyfus, https://www.comunicaffe.com/louis-dreyfus-company-reports-2022-financial-results-and-announces-scope-1-2-emissions-reduction-target/. The Louis Dreyfus figure is for 2022. For additional information see also Blas, J. (2021) Crop giant Cargill reports biggest profit in 156 year history, https://www.bloombergquint.com/onweb/crop-giant-cargill-reports-biggest-profit-in-156-year-history; Louis Dreyfus Company. (2021) Guided by our purpose, https://www.ldc.com/; Murphy, S., Burch, D. and Clapp, J. (2012) *Cereal Secrets: The World's Largest Grain Traders and Global Agriculture*, Oxfam, https://www.oxfam.org/en/research/cereal-secrets-worlds-largest-grain-traders-and-global-agriculture; iPES Food. (2017) *Too Big to Feed*, http://www.ipes-food.org/_img/upload/files/Concentration_FullReport.pdf; Clapp, J. and Isakson, S. R. (2018) *Speculative Harvests: Financialization, Food and Agriculture*, Fernwood Publishing, Canada.
40. Lawrence, F. (2011) The global food crisis: ABCD of food—how the multinationals dominate trade, https://www.theguardian.com/global-development/poverty-matters/2011/jun/02/abcd-food-giants-dominate-trade, Clapp and Isakson, *Speculative Harvests*; Lawrence, Re-evaluating food systems and food security.

41. Keenan, L., Monteath, T. and Wojcik, D. (2023) Hungry for power: Financialization and the concentration of corporate control in the global food system, *Geoforum* 147, https://doi.org/10.1016/j.geoforum.2023.103909.
42. iPES, *Too Big to Feed*; Hendrickson, M., Howard, P., Miller, E. and Constance, D. (2020) The food system: Concentration and impacts, https://doi.org/10.13140/RG.2.2.35433.52326.
43. De Olho Nos Ruralistas. (2022) The financiers of destruction, https://deolhonosruralistas.com.br/wp-content/uploads/2022/08/Financiers-of-Destruction-2022-EN.pdf.
44. Wikipedia. (2023) American Farm Bureau Federation, https://en.wikipedia.org/wiki/American_Farm_Bureau_Federation.
45. This section draws from the following sources: Burch, D. and Lawrence, G. (eds) (2007) *Supermarkets and Agri-food Supply Chains: Transformations in the Production and Consumption of Food*, Edward Elgar, Cheltenham, UK; Carolan, M. (2013) *Reclaiming Food Security*, Routledge, London; Dixon, J. and Banwell, C. (2016) Supermarketisation and rural society futures, in M. Shucksmith and D. Brown (eds) *Routledge International Handbook of Rural Studies*, Routledge, London, pp. 227–239; Jolly, W. (2021) The supermarket tricks to get you spending more—and how to avoid them, https://www.comparethemarket.com.au/news/supermarket-tricks-and-how-to-avoid-them/; Lawrence, F. (2004) *Not on the Label: What Really Goes into the Food on Your Plate*, Penguin, Victoria; Lawrence, G. and Dixon, J. (2015) The political economy of agri-food: Supermarkets, in A. Bonanno and L. Busch (eds) *Handbook of the International Political Economy of Agriculture and Food*, Edward Elgar, Cheltenham, UK, pp. 213–231; Richards, C., Lawrence, G. and Burch, D. (2011) Supermarkets and Agro-industrial foods: The strategic manufacturing of consumer trust, *Food, Culture and Society* 14(1): 29–47.
46. Simms, A. (2023) Britain's 'house of food' sits on shaky foundations. To fix it, curb the big supermarkets, The Guardian, https://www.theguardian.com/commentisfree/2023/aug/15/britain-food-big-supermarkets-profits-jobs-suppliers. Also see

Simms, A. (2007) *Tescopoly: How One Shop Came Out on Top and Why it Matters*, Constable, London; and Burch and Lawrence, *Supermarkets and Agri-food Supply Chains*.
47. Cohen, D. (2015) Supermarkets are the problem, https://www.rand.org/blog/2015/02/supermarkets-are-the-problem.html.
48. Rice, X. (2019) The Aldi effect: How one discount supermarket transformed the way Britain shops, https://www.theguardian.com/business/2019/mar/05/long-read-aldi-discount-supermarket-changed-britain-shopping.
49. Rice, The Aldi effect.
50. Rice, The Aldi effect.
51. Ritzer, G. (2004) *The McDonaldization of Society*, Revised New Century Edition, Pine Forge, California; Burch and Lawrence, *Supermarkets and Agri-food Supply Chains*.
52. See, for a discussion on Whole Food workers, Lorr, B. (2021) *The Secret Life of Groceries: The Dark Miracle of the American Supermarket*, Avery, New York. As one Australian author has noted, surveillance measures, including ceiling cameras, 'treat every customer as a potential thief'. See Kelly, L. (2024) The secret sauce of Coles' and Woolworths' profits: High-tech surveillance and control, https://www.theconversation.com/the-secret-sauce-of-coles-and-woolworths-profits-high-tech-surveillance-and-control-224076.
53. Tait, M. (2021) Bread, wine, mind control: Supermarkets could be using music to change our shopping habits, The Guardian, https://www.theguardian.com/business/2021/dec/05/bread-wine-mind-control-supermarkets-could-be-using-music-to-change-our-shopping-habits.
54. *Soundtrack your brand.* (2021) Music that works for your grocery store, https://www.soundtrackyourbrand.com/music-for-grocery-stores/.
55. Smithfield, B. (2017) Salvador Dalí designed the logo for the famous lollipop company 'Chupa Chups', https://www.thevintagenews.com/2017/05/19/salvador-dali-designed-the-logo-for-the-famous-lollipop-company-chupa-chups/?edg-c=1.

56. Channel 9 News. (2021) Food recall, https://www.9news.com.au/food-recall; Doering, C. (2023) Chocolate contains 'concerning' amounts of lead and cadmium, Consumer Reports finds, https://www.fooddive.com/news/chocolate-contains-concerning-amounts-of-lead-and-cadmium-consumer-repor/697963/.
57. McCurry, J. (2023) Tsingtao beer loses its fizz in South Korea after video of worker appearing to urinate in tank, https://www.theguardian.com/world/2023/oct/25/tsingtao-beer-loses-its-fizz-in-south-korea-after-video-of-worker-appearing-to-urinate-into-tank.
58. Woffinden, B. (2001) Cover up, https://www.theguardian.com/education/2001/aug/25/research.highereducation.
59. Australian Institute of Food Safety. (2016) 5 infamous food poisoning cases in history, https://www.foodsafety.com.au/blog/5-infamous-food-poisoning-cases-in-history; Satore, M. (2020) 11 food related catastrophes in history that made us say 'really'? https://www.ranker.com/list/food-related-catastrophes-history/melissa-sartore; US Food and Drug Administration. (2020) All about BSE (Mad Cow Disease), https://www.fda.gov/animal-veterinary/animal-health-literacy/all-about-bse-mad-cow-disease.
60. As Felicity Lawrence has written, in long supply chains 'Networks of brokers, cold stores operators and subcontracted meat cutting plants have emerged to supply rapidly fluctuating orders "just in time". Management consultants KPMG estimate there are around 450 points at which the integrity of the chain can break down.' See Lawrence, F. (2013) Horsemeat scandal: The essential guide, https://www.theguardian.com/uk/2013/feb/15/horsemeat-scandal-the-essential-guide.
61. Lawrence, Horsemeat scandal.
62. Lawrence, Horsemeat scandal; Wikipedia. (2023) 2013 horsemeat scandal, https://en.wikipedia.org/wiki/2013_horse_meat_scandal; Taylor, S. (2019) What did we learn from the horsemeat scandal and should we still be worried? https://www.highspeedtraining.co.uk/hub/horsemeat-scandal-facts-and-effects/.

63. Vorley, B. (2007) Supermarkets and agri-food supply chains in Europe: Partnership and protest, in D. Burch and G. Lawrence (eds) *Supermarkets and Agri-food Supply Chains: Transformations in the Production and Consumption of Foods*, Edward Elgar, Cheltenham, UK, pp. 243–67.
64. Hickman, M. (2011) Consuming issues: What that tiny tractor logo on meat means, https://www.independent.co.uk/money/spend-save/consuming-issues-what-tiny-red-tractor-logo-meat-means-2034111.html. They probably don't need legs anyway, when they can prop themselves up on the other 19 birds.
65. May, T. (2016) 6 great uses of farm-to-table imagery in branding, https://www.creativebloq.com/features/6-great-uses-of-farm-to-table-imagery-in-branding.
66. Pointing, C. (2021) Happy farm animal images on meat and dairy labels said to mislead consumers, https://www.livekindly.co/happy-farm-animal-images-meat-dairy-labels-mislead-consumers/.
67. Richards, Lawrence and Burch, Supermarkets and agro-industrial foods, pp. 40–41.
68. Dixon, J. (2002) *The Changing Chicken: Chooks, Cooks and Culinary Culture*, UNSW Press, Sydney, p. 8.
69. Lewis, T. and Huber, A. (2015) A revolution in an eggcup? *Food, Culture and Society* 18(2): 301.
70. Cohen, Supermarkets are the problem; Burch and Lawrence, *Supermarkets and Agri-food Supply Chains*.
71. Boas, M. and Chain, S. (1976) *Big Mac: The Unauthorised Story of McDonald's*, New American Library, New York.
72. Szybillo, G. and Sosanie, A. (1977) Family decision making: Husband, wife and children, in W. Perreault (ed.) *Advances in Consumer Research*, Volume IV, Atlanta, Association for Consumer Research, pp. 46–49.
73. Sokolov, R. (1976) Big Mac, https://www.nytimes.com/1976/04/04/archives/big-mac.html; Leidner, R. (1993) *Fast Food, Fast Talk: Service Work and the Routinization of Everyday Life*, University of California Press, Berkeley.
74. Boas and Chain, *Big Mac*, p. 110.

75. It falls behind Subway in terms of numbers. Subway has some 40,000 outlets in 112 countries. See Rosenberg, M. (2020) Number of McDonald's restaurants worldwide, https://www.thoughtco.com/number-of-mcdonalds-restaurants-worldwide-1435174; Lock, S. (2021) Number of McDonald's restaurants, https://www.statista.com/statistics/219454/mcdonalds-restaurants-worldwide/.
76. Leidner, *Fast Food, Fast Talk*, p. 46.
77. Cardoza, R. and de Maria, M. (2021) 35 bizarre McDonald's items from around the world, https://www.eatthis.com/mcdonalds-food-around-the-world/.
78. Nicholson, A. (2017) 'The Founder' is a capitalist happy meal with a vanilla shake, http://www.mtv.com/news/2973377/the-founder-is-a-capitalist-happy-meal-with-a-vanilla-shake/; Wikipedia. (2021) McDonald's legal cases, https://en.wikipedia.org/wiki/McDonald%27s_legal_cases.
79. Boas and Chain, *Big Mac*, p. 27.
80. Maloney, M. (2017) Queen Elizabeth apparently owns a McDonald's in England, https://www.townandcountrymag.com/society/tradition/a13098382/queen-elizabeth-owns-mcdonalds-in-uk/. It is located some 80 miles from London in the Banbury Gateway Shopping Park and forms part of what has become, after the death of Queen Elizabeth, the King's Crown Estate.
81. Cherno, M. (1963) Feuerbach's 'Man is what he Eats': A rectification, *Journal of the History of Ideas* 24(3): 397–406. Feuerbach is quoted as saying 'Being is the same as Eating. Being means Eating. The empty concept of Being is fulfilled only in Eating', quoted in Cherno, p. 400.
82. Sawhney, V. (2021) Weirdly true: We are what we eat, https://hbr.org/2021/08/weirdly-true-we-are-what-we-eat.
83. Super Size Me. (2004) Plot, https://www.imdb.com/title/tt0390521/plotsummary; Center for Consumer Freedom Team. (2008) Is Super Size Me a big fat lie? https://www.consumerfreedom.com/2018/05/is-super-size-me-a-big-fat-lie/. Spurlock died from cancer complications in May 2024 after having released *Super*

Size Me 2: Holy Chicken in 2017. The latter exposed attempts by fast food chains to convince their customers that the chicken they were eating was healthy.
84. Pomeroy, S. (2014) Super Size Me? Science teacher loses 37 lbs. eating at McDonald's, https://www.forbes.com/sites/rosspomeroy/2014/01/07/super-size-me-science-teacher-loses-37-lbs-eating-at-mcdonalds/?sh=659f32d977cf.
85. Story, M. and French, S. (2004) Food advertising and marketing directed at children and adolescents in the US, *International Journal of Behavioural and Nutrition*, https://www.ncbi.nlm.nih.gov/pmc/articles/PMC416565/.
86. Story and French, Food advertising and marketing directed at children and adolescents in the US.
87. Pirnia, G. (2019) How fast food advertisements get under your skin, whether you like it or not, https://www.huffpost.com/entry/fast-food-marketing_l_5c890150e4b038892f493653.
88. Healthy Food America. (2021) Limits on marketing to kids, https://www.healthyfoodamerica.org/limits_on_marketing_to_kids.
89. Healthy Food America, Limits on marketing to kids; Obesity Policy Coalition, Food advertising to children, https://www.opc.org.au/downloads/policy-briefs/food-advertising-to-children.pdf.
90. See Delpeuch, F., Maire, B., Monnier, E. and Holdsworth, M. (2009) *Globesity: A Planet Out of Control*, Earthscan, London, p. 1.
91. Winson, A. (2013) *The Industrial Diet: The Degradation of Food and the Struggle for Healthy Eating*, New York University Press, New York.
92. Philpott, T. (2019) The secret history of why soda companies switched from sugar to high-fructose corn syrup, https://www.motherjones.com/food/2019/07/the-secret-history-of-why-soda-companies-switched-from-sugar-to-high-fructose-corn-syrup/; HRF. (2022) 19 notable high fructose corn syrup statistics, https://healthresearchfunding.org/19-notable-high-fructose-corn-syrup-statistics/; Healthline. (2021) 12 common foods

with high fructose corn syrup, https://www.healthline.com/nutrition/foods-with-high-fructose-corn-syrup.
93. Philpott, The secret history of why soda companies switched from sugar to high-fructose corn syrup; and see, for an in-depth account, Manning, R. (2005) *Against the Grain: How Agriculture Has Hijacked Civilization*, North Point Press, California.
94. Healthline. (2019a) 6 reasons why high-fructose corn syrup is bad for you, https://www.healthline.com/nutrition/why-high-fructose-corn-syrup-is-bad.
95. Bocarsly, M., Powell, E., Avena, N. and Hoebel, B. (2010) High-fructose corn syrup causes characteristics of obesity in rats: Increased body weight, body fat and triglyceride levels, *Pharmacol Biochem Behav* 97(1): 101–106; Healthline. (2019b) Types of body fat: Benefits, dangers, and more, https://www.healthline.com/health/types-of-body-fat#brown; Cleveland Clinic. (2020) Avoid the hidden dangers of high fructose corn syrup, https://health.clevelandclinic.org/avoid-the-hidden-dangers-of-high-fructose-corn-syrup-video/.
96. HRF, 19 notable high fructose corn syrup statistics.
97. Fuhrman, J. (2017) *Fast Food Genocide: How Fast Food is Killing us and What we can do About it*, HarperCollins, New York, pp. 6, 7, 16, 42, 59, 139. The quote is from p. 16.
98. Hall, N. (2021) Study reveals every hot dog you eat shortens your life by 36 minutes, https://manofmany.com/lifestyle/food/hot-dogs-shorten-life-span-study.
99. Kretzer, M. (2021) 5 times you probably ate animal rectums and didn't know it, https://www.peta.org/blog/foods-made-animal-rectums/.
100. Blevins, M. (2017) What are hot dogs really made of? https://www.businessinsider.com/what-are-hot-dogs-really-made-of-2014-7; Benshosen, A. (2020) This is secretly what's in your hot dog, https://www.eatthis.com/whats-really-in-your-hot-dog/.
101. Clark, J. (2021) The ultimate hot dog consumption stats, https://www.thehotdog.org/ultimate-hot-dog-consumption/.

102. Sterling, W. (2021) Nathan's hot dog contest 2021: Joey Chestnut wins for the 14th time, https://edition.cnn.com/2021/07/04/us/nathans-hot-dog-contest-2021-winners-joey-chestnut-michelle-lesco/index.html.
103. Lamour, J. (2023) Joey Chestnut eats 62 hot dogs for 16th Nathan's hot dog eating contest title, while Miki Sudo named women's champion, CNN, https://edition.cnn.com/2023/07/04/us/nathans-hot-dog-eating-contest/index.html.
104. Lamour, Nathan's famous hot dog eating results.
105. Anthony, A. (2022) Fast food fever: How ultra-processed meals are unhealthier than you think, https://www.theguardian.com/science/2022/oct/16/ultra-processed-food-unhealthier-harder-to-avoid-than-you-thought.
106. Anthony, Fast food fever; Beck, J. (2016) More than half of what Americans eat is 'ultra-processed', https://www.theatlantic.com/health/archive/2016/03/more-than-half-of-what-americans-eat-is-ultra-processed/472791/.
107. Van Tulleken, C. (2024) *Ultra-Processed People: Why Do We All Eat Stuff That Isn't Food … and Why Can't We Stop?* Penguin, Australia.
108. Anthony, Fast food fever.
109. Wilson, B. (2020) How ultra-processed food took over your shopping basket, https://www.theguardian.com/food/2020/feb/13/how-ultra-processed-food-took-over-your-shopping-basket-brazil-carlos-monteiro.
110. Gregory, A. (2023) Addiction to ultra-processed foods affects 14% of adults globally, experts say, https://www.theguardian.com/science/2023/oct/10/addiction-to-ultra-processed-food-affects-14-of-adults-global-study-shows.
111. Reported in EurekAlert. (2023) International team of scientists say identifying some foods as addictive could shift attitudes, stimulate research, https://www.eurekalert.org/news-releases/1003987.

112. Wikipedia. (2024) COVID-19 pandemic deaths, https://en.wikipedia.org/wiki/COVID-19_pandemic_deaths.
113. The WHO estimates that some 2.8 million people die from overweight and obesity each year. In four years, this comes to a total of 11.2 million people. See WHO. (2021) Obesity, https://www.who.int/news-room/facts-in-pictures/detail/6-facts-on-obesity.
114. World Health Organisation. (2021) Obesity, https://www.who.int/news-room/facts-in-pictures/detail/6-facts-on-obesity; World Health Organisation. (2021) Key facts, https://www.who.int/news-room/fact-sheets/detail/malnutrition.
115. Delpeuch, Maire, Monnier and Holdsworth, *Globesity*, p. 1.
116. DoSomething.Org. (2021) 11 facts about American eating habits, https://www.dosomething.org/us/facts/11-facts-about-american-eating-habits.
117. Bratskier, K. (2014) The tricks the fast food companies use to lure you in, https://www.news.com.au/finance/business/retail/the-tricks-fast-food-companies-use-to-lure-you-in/news-story/4c7571df57d08738fc54fba2b30f7c37.
118. Emery, D. (2014) Dashboard dining: A permanent part of the American lifestyle, https://www.provisioneronline.com/articles/100950-dashboard-dining-a-permanent-part-of-the-american-lifestyle; The Hamilton Spectator. (2020) Part 1: Dashboard dining, https://www.thespec.com/news/2008/03/05/part-1-dashboard-dining.html.
119. Pollan, M. (2008) *In Defense of Food: An Eater's Manifesto*, Penguin, London.
120. Emery, Dashboard dining.
121. Carolan, M. (2011) *The Real Cost of Cheap Food*, Earthscan, London; Clapp, *Food*; Delpeuch, Maire, Monnier, and Holdsworth, *Globesity*; Holt-Gimenez, *A Foodies Guide to Capitalism*; Patel, *Stuffed and Starved*; Rosin, C., Stock, P. and Campbell, H. (eds) (2012) *Food Systems Failure: The Global Food Crisis and the Future of Agriculture*, Earthscan, London.
122. Delpeuch, Maire, Monnier and Holdsworth, *Globesity*, p. 15.
123. Patel, *Stuffed and Starved*.

124. Wood, B., Williams, O., Baker, P. and Sacks, G. (2023) Behind the 'creative destruction' of human diets: An analysis of the structure and market dynamics of the ultra-processed food manufacturing industry and implications for public health, *Journal of Agrarian Change*, https://doi.org/10.1111/joac.12545.
125. Arvedlund, E. (2022) How shrinkflation hurts us, from more expensive toilet paper to fewer Doritos in a bag, https://www.inquirer.com/business/shrinkflation-2022-rising-prices-inflation-profits-20220315.html.
126. Barrett, J. (2023) Shrinkflation: Don't want to upset the customer with price rises? Just make your product smaller, https://www.theguardian.com/australia-news/2023/jun/17/shrinkflation-price-rises-product-smaller.
127. Arvedlund, How shrinkflation hurts us, from more expensive toilet paper to fewer Doritos in a bag; Corporate Finance Institute. (2022) What is shrinkflation? https://corporatefinanceinstitute.com/resources/knowledge/economics/shrinkflation/; Oltermann, P. (2023) Matterhorn no more: Toblerone to change design under 'Swissness' rules, https://www.theguardian.com/world/2023/mar/05/matterhorn-mountain-toblerone-packaging-design-switzerland.
128. Milligan, B. (2017) More than 2,500 products subject to shrinkflation, says ONS, https://www.bbc.com/news/business-40703866; GoodtoKnow. (2019) Supermarket products that are shrinking … but staying the SAME price, https://www.goodto.com/food/products-shrinking-but-staying-the-same-price-291144.
129. Pollan, M. (2009) *Food Rules: An Eater's Manual*, Penguin, London.

4

Saving the Planet with Pesticides and Plastic: Corporate Profiteering and Planetary Destruction

Saving the Planet with Pesticides and Plastic is the deliberately provocative title of a book written by Dennis Avery of the Hudson Institute, a Washington-based think tank set up to challenge 'conventional thinking' and help manage 'strategic transitions to the future.'[1]

Avery's book is subtitled *The Environmental Triumph of High-Yield Farming* and, in 432 pages, he explains to the reader why corporate farming—the use of pesticides, insecticides, monocultures, genetic engineering, and the latest mechanical and electronic technology—is not only the most rational approach to feeding the world, but also has multiple beneficial outcomes for the planet. If the world uses high-yielding varieties of seeds, more grain will be produced per hectare, providing more food for an ever-expanding global population, while removing the need to bring additional land under the plough. This will result in the preservation of wildlife habitat—protecting endangered animal and bird species. Rainforests need no longer be cut down. And high-tech farming apparently uses water more efficiently, thereby conserving supplies of the planet's scarce freshwater resources.

Pesticides are absolutely crucial to the high-tech model. They are targeted to kill the bugs that want to eat our food—bugs that should be eliminated from farming systems to insure increased output and productivity. Bugs = bad, pesticides = good. Importantly, 'there are no known consumer health impacts from pesticide usage', 'no danger to humans has yet been identified' from DDT and, unless misused 'currently approved … pesticides don't threaten wildlife'. 'Pesticide risks to farmers and farm workers … are low – and declining'.[2] Plastics, like pesticides, are much maligned yet have an important role to play in advanced agriculture. Plastic sheeting (polyethylene) is used throughout farming as an artificial mulch. Laid on top of the soil it increases soil temperature, promoting plant development and raising yields. It cuts water evaporation while preventing weeds from appearing. It covers greenhouses the world over and is especially important in sustaining food production in cold climates. Plastic wrapping of hay bales protects silage from drying out. Plastics are especially useful in storing and transporting agricultural chemicals—farmers would not be able to obtain their pesticides without them. We are told that much of the plastic sheeting is biodegradable, broken down by microbes to become part of the soil.[3] How could one not view the potent combo of pesticides and plastic as a force for human progress?

Apparently, there are some who think otherwise, and Dennis is quick to show them the error of their ways. So, you want to go 'organic', he asks? Well, organic farming is inefficient (low-yielding) and there is no way it could feed a burgeoning world population. Food produced organically costs consumers more and, in any case, cannot be produced in commercial quantities. As for 'natural' biological control of pests much heralded by organic farmers, Avery argues that their application is too specific to give the 'broad, cost-effective pest control … currently provided by pesticides'. He adds that bio-controls (natural substances used by farmers) have had side effects, 'leading to the extinction of nearly 100 species worldwide'.[4] And as for those who see the meatification of the diet as a problem, 'to forgo the production of beef would be to waste the world's grass resources and crop residue' and, 'as long as we need to graze the grasslands, we might as well make use of the meat … Letting the wolves have it all doesn't seem to make sense when the world wants more protein'.[5]

Searching through Avery's arguments, it is possible to find support for some of his claims—chemical pesticides are more potent than 'natural' methods of control, plastic containers are essential for transporting of agri-chemicals, and plastic covering of hot-houses provides excellent protection of plants from the elements. But when put to the test, most of his claims and assertions appear to be at odds with the knowledge-base of science. According to Charles Baier, an environmental toxicologist from the University of Idaho:

> Avery spends much of his effort dispelling popular concerns about the environmental ramifications of our chemical-based way of life ... In so doing, he dismisses nearly the entire body of peer reviewed scientific literature and instead replaces it with his own speculations, theories, and selected statistics.[6]

Avery is seen to be suffering a 'lack of objectivity'. The book is a 'random collection of selected quotations, hearsay and statistics'. He is not 'a scientist or even a respected public voice' but a 'muckraker'.[7] Baier continues:

> All pesticides and herbicides are designed to disrupt biological processes and bring death to target plants and animals. Given that humans have many of the same biological processes of other life forms, it is naïve to even suggest that we can continue to use these chemicals with absolutely no chance of affecting ourselves in the process.[8]

So, what do we know about pesticides and why would Avery want to distort and muckrake?

Chemical Concoctions

Pesticides are toxic chemicals that are used extensively in large-scale industrial farming systems throughout the world to control vermin, weeds, and diseases in plants. They play an important role in curbing destruction of the world's food supply, but leach into soils and waterways affecting many other forms of life.[9] Adverse effects include the poisoning of water courses, causing the death of fish and other marine life. They have severe impacts on fauna and flora, killing wildflowers, birds, and non-target species of insects, particularly those which pollinate plants.[10] They produce resistance in pest populations, often requiring higher applications of even more toxic chemicals to control those pests. Farmers find themselves on a 'chemical treadmill' having to up the doses and/or strength of the doses of insecticides and weedicides—a financial cost for the farmer and delivering more potent chemical pollution to the environment.[11] But the *real* off-farm costs of using pesticides are never calculated. The harmful 'downstream' effects of toxic chemicals are never set against profits in pesticide producers' financial balance sheets. Rather, environmental harms are, as we saw in Chapter 2:

> negative externalities ... non-market effects [whose] costs are not part of market prices. Negative externalities are one of the classic causes of market failure, whereby the polluter does not pay the full costs of his/her action.[12]

Effects of pesticides on the reproductive systems of animals and humans are severe. Pesticides interfere with endocrine systems (responsible for reproduction, development, growth, and behaviour of organisms). Immediate ('acute') health effects often experienced by farmworkers include skin burning and itching, nausea, dizziness, diarrhoea, and breathing problems, with longer-term ('chronic') population-wide effects including birth defects, infertility, cancers, and damage to internal organs. As endocrine disrupters, pesticides can mimic or block hormones that regulate brain development, metabolic functioning, and reproduction in humans and animals.[13] And just remember, if you are trying to do the right thing by your body, eating up to five servings of fruit and vegetables each day, you will receive a special bonus gift from the farmer—about 14 different pesticides that will accumulate in your colon.[14]

It should be remembered that pesticide production is a highly profitable enterprise. During the 1960s and 1970s pesticide businesses grew at or above 10% per annum.[15] When profits began to level off, corporations merged and began creating 'synergies' between agriculture and pharmaceuticals. Chemical/seed packages were developed to allow the bioengineered seeds to grow unhindered by the pesticides that are sprayed on the paddock to fight insects and weeds. Here the farmer and society are locked in. Agriculture becomes an activity designed to be run under the proprietary ownership of major transnational agri-chemical corporations—Syngenta, Bayer Crop Science, BASF, and Dow Agro Sciences. The global agro-chemical industry was worth $US253 billion in 2024.[16] To put this in perspective the global market was $US32 billion at the turn of the twenty-first century.[17] As geographer and agri-food researcher Annie Shattuck has written:

> Despite the attention to sustainable and organic agriculture over the past 20 years, the world has moved rapidly in the opposite direction … agriculture is becoming even more dependent on pesticides, not less, especially in the Global South.[18]

Researchers David Weir and Mark Schapiro based at the Center for Investigative Reporting in Oakland, California, examined the pesticide industry in the early 1980s. They came up with some interesting findings, published in their book *Circle of Poison: Pesticides and People in a Hungry World*.[19] They discovered that highly toxic chemicals—many, like endosulfan, banned in the US—were being sold by US corporations to nations of the Global South, such as Mexico, Argentina, and India. The chemicals were applied to crops such as coffee, vegetables, and fruit trees, only to be harvested, packed, and sent back to (you guessed it) the US. As David Weir has noted:

> Any [chemical] that was banned or heavily regulated or restricted or unregistered in the US was being … encouraged to be sent overseas, almost as compensation for the companies for losing the US market.[20]

In this way, the US essentially exported the would-be negative health impacts of agri-chemicals to the Third World—but got it back in spades. The results of the so-called circle of poison were first, the availability of cheap out-of-season fruits and vegetables for US consumers and, second, cancers, epilepsy, limb deformities, cognitive disorders, and respiratory diseases for farmers, farm workers, and rural communities in the Global South.[21]

We just don't seem to be able to get chemicals out of our food systems. Industrial fertilisers have become necessary for large-scale food production—agrarian capitalism equates to chemical capitalism.[22] Yet, when broken down in the soil, the nitrous oxides released by artificial fertilisers are two hundred times more lethal to the atmosphere than carbon dioxide; fertilisers contribute some 40% of agriculturally produced greenhouse gases.[23] Eschewing artificial fertilisers, organic farmers in the US took a lead by using 'biosolids' from sewage systems as a natural fertiliser for their fields and crops. What a great way to recycle human waste?

Unfortunately, the biosolids were found to contain polyfluoroalkyls (PFAS). Known as the 'forever chemical' because of their inability to be biodegraded, PFAS has been implicated in cancers, thyroid and liver problems, birth defects, immunosuppression, and declining human sperm counts.[24] PFAS can be found in thousands of consumer products, rendering bio-waste reuse a no-go for farmers. Many of the organic producers who inadvertently poisoned the food grown on their properties with PFAS biosolids are facing financial ruin.[25] Some 97 percent of US citizens have PFAS in their bodies and they have been detected in over 17,000 sites in Europe and the UK. In Zwijndrecht, Flanders, for example, people living within a 15 kilometre range of the city have been advised to avoid eggs from the area, to abandon home-grown vegetables, and certainly not even think of eating fish and wildfowl from the region, so polluted is the soil and water.[26] While the European Union has plans to ban PFAS, industry lobby groups have spent millions of Euros in campaigns to dissuade government action. Some 12 PFAS producers have engaged over 70 lobbyists at a cost of some €21 million per annum to oppose regulatory actions by the EU. Worse still, in the US the Environmental Protection Agency fails to test or regulate most PFAS released into the environment, and industry does not have a duty to tell consumers they are using these chemicals in manufacturing processes. Chemsec, a chemical not-for-profit organisation, has estimated that it would cost around US$26 trillion a year to clean up the mess on a global scale - and this does not include addressing human health concerns and environmental damage.[27] Pesticides and other chemicals are a Janus-faced companion of farmers, consumers, and the planet.

What about plastics? Originating from petrochemicals, they are polymers composed of long chains of hydrogen and carbon atoms. Because they come from non-renewable sources, they are not sustainable. While they might be useful as ground cover in agriculture, plastic sheeting does not—as Avery claims—readily break down in the soil. Petroleum-based plastics are not 'natural' substances found in the environment and cannot be destroyed by microbial action. They can be broken down by ultraviolet radiation but in their resultant new physical and chemical forms, they have toxic effects on microbial life.[28] A plastic bag takes between 10 and 100 years to decompose, a plastic diaper about 250 years, and a sandwich bag up to 1,000 years. But only if they are exposed to ultraviolet light. If they reside in landfill, away from light, they will remain unchanged forever.[29] The petroleum industry has argued for decades that plastics can be readily recycled. They knew this was a lie but, instead

> engaged in fraudulent marketing and public education campaigns designed to mislead the public about the viability of plastic recycling … These efforts have effectively protected and expanded plastic markets, while stalling legislative or regulatory action that would meaningfully address plastic waste and pollution.[30]

It is not as if production of plastics is being wound back—just take a look inside your COVID-19 Rapid Antigen Test Kit. It would seem that these indestructible RATs intend to live forever among the world's garbage. Globally, plastic production will double by 2040 and, by 2050, one-fifth of the world's oil production will be used to manufacture plastics.[31] The food industry that has become a major culprit:

> As food has gone global, it has displaced … local food production, manufacturing and consumption. Major corporations have profited from this shift, which requires longer and more complex supply chains. And longer supply chains means more packaging to keep food saleable.[32]

Microplastics and plastic nanoparticles are present in the food chain and are posing major problems for human, animal, bird, and fish populations through high toxicity and bioaccumulation. Plastics are present in the gizzards of some 90% of sea birds and in the stomachs of over half the world's sea turtles, with predictions that by 2050 the mass of plastic in the ocean will be greater than the mass of its fish inhabitants.[33] Thousands of tonnes of microplastic, from sewage sludge, is being dumped each year on farmlands on which our food is grown. Microplastics are pathogen-carriers and the germs end up in our food and water systems. When ingested they cause damage to human cells. In March 2022 microplastics were, for the first time, detected in human blood; in October of the same year they were detected—again for the first time—in human breast milk.[34] In February 2024 microplastics were found in human embryos, with scientists concerned with the damage they may cause to human cells. The latest balls up? They also seem to have a special liking for testicles.[35] The microplastics humans ingest daily come from polyethylene, polypropylene, and polyvinyl chloride—all components of plastic packaging. They hitch a ride on membranes of red blood cells and can end up in organs such as the heart, lungs, and brains with many effects still unknown.[36] One effect *is* known—they disrupt metabolic processes in humans, contributing to obesity.[37] It is estimated that the average person ingests some 5 grams of plastic—equivalent to swallowing a credit card—every week.[38] Fortunately for the oesophagus, the plastic enters the body in tiny particles.

Chemicals used to make plastics, bisphenols, and phthalates (pronounced THA-layts), are widespread in food and cause health problems such as asthma, anxiety, depression, heart disease, cancer, and decreased fertility—even when ingested at very low levels.[39] Once thought to be linked to plastic packaging, it was revealed in 2024, that their supply-chain sources also include plastic tubing, vinyl gloves, conveyor belts, and the linings of food cans. Like PFAS, their widespread use places them in the category of 'forever' chemicals.[40] Can plastics be recycled? Yes, but toxicity increases with every recycle.[41] Can plastics be burnt? Yes, but the substances released are not benign and include toxic gases from dioxins, mercury, and furans (ethers found in agro-chemicals), along with polychlorinated biphenyls—all threatening human, animal, and plant life.[42] Living a plastic life is killing us.

Avery would not agree. He compares environmental author Rachel Carson—whose wake-up book *Silent Spring* led to the banning of DDT and the creation, in the US, of the Environmental Protection Agency (EPA)—to Adolf Hitler saying bans on DDT have led to the deaths of 'five times as many [people] Hitler killed in his concentration camps'.[43] Why? Because DDT kills the malaria mosquito and having it banned supposedly increased mosquito populations, causing human deaths. If only we'd been able to spread around more of the stuff!

He continues,

> Misguided opposition to biotechnology, fossil fuels and increased atmospheric carbon dioxide could very well condemn millions of people to malnutrition and starvation, and numerous wildlife species to extinction.[44]

The truth of the matter? Pesticides and plastics are contaminants. To achieve sustainability in future farming systems, it will be necessary to 'detox agriculture'.[45] Given the evidence, Avery's book should be renamed *Poisoning the Planet with Pesticides and Plastic*—a title with a nice ring about it for those of us fond of both accuracy and alliteration.

Financing the Furphy

How and why did Avery get to publish such bunkum? If we follow the money, it leads to the Hudson Institute, mentioned earlier in the chapter. Established in 1961 by former-RAND military strategist Herman Khan, government lawyer Max Singer, and advisor to New York's Governor Nelson Rockefeller, Oscar Ruebhausen, the Institute began its life as a conservative think tank. It has not departed from that very noble tradition. Early funding was used to research the uses of nuclear power for warfare and for electricity generation. Kahn was the main driver and made national contributions to nuclear deterrence theory, eventually winning funding from the US Office of Civil Defense.[46]

Not content to limit the Institute's mission to discussions of nuclear war, Khan began recruiting an array of scholars (including philosophers, and political and social scientists) to help the Institute move into scenario-building in areas such as geopolitics, economics, science, and technology. Close ties were forged between corporate leaders and conservative politicians both in the US and abroad. By the 1980s the Hudson Institute had become international in focus and location—with branches in Bonn, Paris, Brussels, Montreal, and Tokyo.[47] Upon Kahn's abrupt and unexpected death in 1983, the Institute was restructured with Mitch Daniels—a former Reagan aide—becoming CEO. When Daniels left in 1990 to join pharmaceutical firm Eli Lilly (whose reputation includes dishonest advertising of its products),[48] he was replaced by Leslie Lenkowsky, a former George W. Bush administrator. Lenkowsky was a small-government advocate who had 'a track record of working for hawkish right-wing organizations'.[49] In 2004 the Hudson Institute moved its headquarters to Washington, ostensibly to expand its lobbying powers. And, given the hype over the September bombings of the Twin Towers in New York three years earlier, it began focusing upon issues relating to Islam and the Middle East and other national security concerns. It later helped spawn The Gatestone Institute, a far-right Islamophobic think tank known for promulgating inaccuracies and falsehoods.[50] The Hudson Institute was supportive of Trump's presidency, and Mike Pompeo (who, as Secretary of State was investigated over two cases of corruption) joined the Institute in 2021.[51] It gives out yearly awards to the nation's most deserving people. Recipients include Henry Kissinger, Ronald Reagan, Rupert Murdoch, Dick Cheney, Mike Pence, and Mike Pompeo. It is a certain bet that Donald Trump will eventually join the rogues' gallery.

Where does the Hudson Institute's money come from you might be asking? The main donors have been:

- The Lynde and Harry Bradley Foundation (whose aims include dismantling unions and privatising state assets)[52]
- Smith Richardson Foundation (a staunch defender of neoliberal economics, limited government, and an advocate for increased defence spending)[53]

- Hertog Foundation (providing education for those who will learn to become 'influencers' in the civic life and politics in the US)[54]
- Sarah Scaife Foundation (supplying generous funding to right-wing, anti-immigration, and Islamophobic organisations).[55]

But other funding received by the Hudson Institute is 'dark money'—undisclosed donations fed by anonymous sources to non-profit organisations and used to influence election results, and to seek to alter public opinion on political, economic, environmental, and social issues.[56] According to the *Guardian*, monies from unknown US sources have been syphoned into two secretive organisations—the Donors Trust and Donors Capital Fund—which, in turn, distribute funds to think tanks and right-wing activist groups which deny climate change, support the coal and gas industries, and promote other activities protecting profits while destroying the planet.[57] The Hudson Institute has received some US$7.9 million from Donors Trust and has used the money as we might expect—fighting those advocating for a reduction in world greenhouse gas emissions and lobbying to defeat climate bills in Congress.[58] And why wouldn't they do both? After all, the Hudson Institute's champion, Dennis Avery, is on record for declaring that the world is more likely to face the danger of a 'little ice age' rather than the perils of an overheated planet.[59]

Classic Cover-Ups

Let's stay with pesticides for a moment. Glyphosate is a chemical that was invented by a Swiss scientist in 1950. Its immediate application, in the 1960s, was in removing mineral deposits in pipes. But by the early 1970s Monsanto tested it, with great success, as a herbicide on perennial weeds. It was patented in 1971 and three years later was manufactured and sold under the trade name 'Roundup'. Sales were initially sluggish—farmers found that it would kill not only the weeds, but also any plant in the field. Then, in 1996, came the genetic engineering breakthrough Monsanto had been hoping for. A partner company, Agracetus, developed a 'gene gun' that could successfully create new genetically engineered varieties of soybean, maize, canola, sugar beet, and cotton that were 'Roundup Ready'.[60] They could be sprayed with as much Roundup as the farmer needed, and their growth would not be harmed. In fact, many of these plants would not grow to their potential *without* a hefty dose of Roundup—a perfect package for profit-making for the agrochemical industry. A significant bonus was that they reduced the amount of time and labour required to weed paddocks. Today, glyphosate, sold under various brand names including Roundup, Rodeo, UltraMAX, Buccaneer, and Razor Pro, is the most widely used herbicide in the world.[61]

Could anything go wrong? As we have seen with other synthetic agro-chemicals, there are often one or two small downsides to their application. In 2012, some 16 years after Roundup Ready soybeans had been commercialised and sprayed with glyphosate, French molecular biologist Professor Gilles-Eric Seralini showed that rats fed Roundup-tolerant maize, along with water containing Roundup at the level deemed acceptable in the US, developed severe liver and kidney damage.[62] Additionally, weed resistance has been detected throughout the US, involving ryegrass, horseweed, ragweed, amaranth, and waterhemp and globally, including goosegrass, plantain, Johnsongrass, and wild poinsettia, with glyphosate-resistance 'increasing at an alarming rate'.[63]

In 2016 glyphosate was present in 93% of urine samples from citizens across the US. In 2016 glyphosate was found in many popular foods sold in the US including Cheerios, Corn Flakes, Raisin Bran, and Frosted Flakes, along with Doritos Cool Ranch corn chips, and Ritz Crackers.[64] In 2023 US government scientists confirmed that glyphosate was producing biomarkers in urine that were linked to various cancers including lymphoma, myeloma, and leukaemia.[65]

In 2018 Monsanto was ordered to pay US$78 million to a Californian school groundkeeper who had developed non-Hodgkin's lymphoma caused by exposure to Roundup.[66] With more people coming forward with claims against Monsanto, US courts began examining communications between Monsanto and the Environmental Protection Authority (EPA). It was revealed that for over 30 years Monsanto and the EPA had colluded to tone down health concerns relating to glyphosate and to question the research of Professor Seralini.[67] In 2013 the EPA, at Monsanto's behest, increased the level of glyphosate allowed in foods.[68] In the words of Carey Gillam, author of *Whitewash: The Story of a Weedkiller, Cancer, and the Corruption of Science*,

> Monsanto requested and received approvals for greater and greater tolerances to dovetail with the increasing amounts of its weed killer being used on food and livestock feed crops, setting up the potential for people and animals to consume higher and higher levels of weed killer in their diets … [T]he EPA's assurance of safety … was cited for years by other federal agencies as a reason why they skipped over glyphosate when conducting annual testing programs specifically designed to make sure pesticide residues on food were within legal limits. Glyphosate got a pass while other, less widely used pesticides did not.[69]

The EPA's 'flexible allowances' for glyphosate was key 'to Monsanto's future as an agricultural powerhouse'.[70] Monsanto knew the glyphosate was a probable carcinogen but chose to hide this information from public view. It would ghost-write scientific studies to show Roundup was safe to use, it pressured researchers to change their findings about the toxicity of the product and, as shown above, it was in cahoots with the EPA.[71] Profit-making was at the fore. We should never forget that Monsanto was one of two main suppliers of Agent Orange, a herbicide used to defoliate vegetation and expose the enemy in the Vietnam War (called the 'American War' by the Vietnamese). Agent Orange was later linked to birth defects including dwarfism, twisted limbs, no limbs, spinal deformities, missing eye sockets, cancers, and other health problems.[72] But the US forces on the ground wouldn't miss out either, coming back home to develop chronic B-cell leukaemia, Hodgkin's disease, prostate cancer, soft tissue sarcomas, Parkinson's disease, peripheral neuropathy, and multiple myeloma, among others.[73] Monsanto had been 'cooking the books'—falsifying test results—to show that dioxin (the main ingredient in Agent Orange) was not a carcinogen.[74] The company was also found guilty of poisoning the Alabama town of Anniston, where one of its chemical factories was based, and covering up the crime. The eventual conviction cost the company some US$700 million, with Monsanto being found guilty of 'negligence, wantonness, suppression of the truth, nuisance, trespass and outrage'.[75] What is 'outrage'? According to Alabama laws, outrage relates to conduct 'so outrageous in character and extreme in degree as to go beyond all possible bounds of decency so as to be regarded as atrocious and intolerable in civilized society'.[76] It's nice to know who we are dealing with.

Monsanto and other agro-chemical firms used various tactics to deflect criticism of their products. They would pay 'experts' from academia and industry to talk up the benefits of pesticides—often the same people receiving funds from those companies for their research. Professors were asked to write policy briefs about the dire consequences for a world that rejected high-tech agriculture. One Professor, Illinois-based Bruce Chassy, travelled the world as an independent authority, praising pesticides and biotechnologies. His independence was later revealed as a sham when his professional and financial connections with Monsanto were discovered.[77] More openly, the bio-companies would engage public relations firms to deny the claims of opponents of glyphosate and of the genetic engineering of plants, and have their lawyers attempt to tear down any legislation or regulatory barriers that were deemed unfavourable to business.[78] They also paid dieticians to assuage consumer concerns about the ingestion of herbicides.[79] Anna Lappé, from the Small Planet Institute, exposed the 'stealth marketing' used by Monsanto in targeting (and paying) mothers involved in blogging to come along to one of its information sessions extolling the virtues of its weedicides and genetically engineered seeds. The hope was that, as social influencers, the moms would spread the message of the importance and necessity of chemical agriculture:

> Big Ag is giving the age-old techniques of shaping public opinion a new, sneakier spin. Much of today's marketing happens behind the scenes … on the Web pages of blogs, on Twitter feeds and Facebook pages, through sponsored content and industry-funded webisodes and on the stages of big-ideas festivals.[80]

Lappé claims the fast-food industry has also been 'aggressively' wooing the mommy bloggers, convincing them of the nutritional value of their products and the benefits of high-tech farming.[81]

Monsanto was acquired by German chemical firm Bayer for US$63 billion in 2018. Within two years it settled close to 100,000 lawsuits in the US, costing the company some US$10.9 billion.[82] The purchase of Monsanto ensured its tainted name would be forever erased. Unfortunately, the Bayer brand remains. According to *The Ecologist*'s Mick Grant,

> Bayer's history is even darker than Monsanto's. During WWII, Bayer was part of IG Farben, which collaborated with the Nazis to produce chemical weapons such as chlorine gas. Bayer also used scores of death-camp inmates as slave labour in its factories.[83]

It would seem unwise to put one's trust in the agro-chemical industry to protect humanity and to save the planet. Instead, we should be aware of the various methods of duplicity and deception employed by the corporate sector to deflect attention from their products' poor health and environmental records.

Whatever the industry, the playbook requires repeated and relentless use of this set of strategies:

- Cast doubt on the science
- Fund research to produce desired results
- Offer gifts and consulting arrangements
- Use front groups
- Promote self-regulation
- Use the courts to challenge critics and unfavourable regulations.[84]

There is a very long history of corporate cockups and state negligence, including attempts to hide the extent of disasters from public view. Environmentalist and co-founder of 350.org Bill McKibben once described the cosy relationship between the US government and the fossil fuel industry as producing 'the most consequential cover-up in US history',[85] while over 700 companies—Amazon, Tesco, ExxonMobile, and Marks & Spencer among them—have systematically hidden the impact of their operations on forests, water resources, and the climate.[86] India's government was partly culpable for the 1984 Bhopal cyanide gas leak, overlooking public concern to allow the plant to encroach upon densely populated areas of the city. The Union Carbide company was never forced by the government to introduce cleaner technology, despite constant gas leaks and public protests.[87] The Deepwater oil spill in the Gulf of Mexico in 2010 was viewed by the US federal court as 'deliberate misconduct and gross negligence'. But what happened to BP, the company responsible for the disaster? Instead of insisting that oil drilling cease, and that all environmental remediation be paid for by BP, the Obama administration

> accepted BPs cosmetic solution – something that improved appearances – and silenced concerns. It was a cover-up, not a cleanup ... The government missed addressing — and, in fact, increased — a vast ecological harm. Contaminating water, creating dead zones and killing off wildlife in order to perpetuate an industry exemplifies a profound disorder in [the state's] priorities.[88]

Meltdown Mayhem

When Russia began its illegal occupation of Ukraine in early 2022, it did not take long for troops to reach the Chernobyl nuclear power plant. Russian trucks and tanks entered the Red Forest, a ten square kilometre zone surrounding the disabled and decommissioned reactor. The Red Forest is so-named because of the eerie, but colourful, orange-red hue that the once bottle-green pine trees took on following the world's largest nuclear explosion. Although the Red Forest is one of the most radioactive sites on the face of the earth, the Russian soldiers were not deterred, jumping from their vehicles to dig trenches, lay land mines, and build sundry fortifications. Without any anti-radiation clothing in an occupation lasting over a month, the soldiers would have received very high doses of radiation—enough to kill many. It was reported that the invading army had little knowledge of the site and that they'd literally been sent in on a suicide mission. Not surprisingly, busloads of soldiers exhibiting acute radiation poisoning were seen leaving the site to reach hospitals in Belarus. Corpses of soldiers were returned to Russia via Belarus at night to avoid detection.[89]

This obvious cover-up in Ukraine by the Russians amounts to little compared with what happened following the Chernobyl meltdown. When the nuclear power plant exploded on April 26, 1986, a cloud of radioactive gas some 400 times greater than that released after the bombing of Hiroshima, entered the atmosphere.[90] Throughout the 1980s the Soviet Union had experienced 'dozens' of accidents at military nuclear establishments—all kept secret.[91] In 1982 the Chernobyl plant experienced a minor release of radiation, but this was hidden by the KGB to 'prevent panic and provocative rumours'.[92] The Soviets knew the plant was unsafe for years before the accident. Following the Chernobyl explosion the Soviets sought to conceal the effects of the accident from the public's view, issuing secret instructions to its officials to classify all information, particularly health-related concerns.[93] They even swapped soil and water samples taken by the French after the explosion with fake ones.[94] When those cleaning up the site (the so-called liquidators) were exposed to radiation, the Ministry of Health and Ministry of Defence insisted that doctors avoid using the diagnosis of 'acute radiation syndrome', in an effort to play down the significance of the disaster on workers' health.[95] But after the explosion it was going to be difficult for authorities to disguise the scale of the disaster when 'sky high' levels of toxic radiation were being detected in locations as distant as the Scandinavian nations.[96]

Thousands of people were hospitalised following the accident, the number reaching 10,000 one month after the blast. Then something strange occurred—most of the 10,000 were discharged with a clean bill of health. The Soviets had, overnight, changed the level of exposure that would be deemed 'acceptable'—it was now set at 50 times less than originally. Instead of having to evacuate some 1.6 million children who had been exposed to radiation, the number dropped roughly tenfold to 166,000. As one analyst wrote, it had 'become a matter of economics: the USSR could not afford to resettle so many people. The truth about the health of the population had to be concealed from the population itself'.[97]

Statistics were also manipulated to attempt to reduce the impact of the meltdown. The Soviet government initially refused to release information about the death toll, with the 'official' figure later being given as 31—two killed by the explosion and 29 who had acute radiation poisoning.[98] The World Health Organisation put the number of cancer-related deaths at 5,000, while that of the International Atomic Energy Agency sits at 60,000. The best estimate, from a report commissioned by Greenpeace International, suggests as many as 93,000 have been killed.[99] It is expected that in the years up to 2065 a further 30,000 to 60,000 people will die of thyroid and other cancers as a direct result of exposure to radiation from Chernobyl. Oh, and the area around the plant will remain unsafe for human habitation for the next 20,000 years.[100]

There is a distinctive pattern for the reporting of nuclear accidents. The most important accidents to date have been Windscale in England where a reactor producing plutonium caught fire in 1957, Chernobyl in 1986 where the explosion exposed the nuclear core, and Fukushima in Japan in 2011 when a tsunami caused by an underwater earthquake hit the plant causing the meltdown of three of the plant's reactors. According to journalist Paul Brown, the reporting of each disaster exhibited three key elements. The first was the attempt to disguise the true scale of the accident, leaving people unnecessarily exposed to leaking radiation. The second was to dispute any long-term health impacts that might result from the accident, with governments and industry reluctant to discuss health implications. The third was to downscale the time and cost required for the clean-up—with people being told their removal from the sites of devastation would be temporary. The lies were created and spread by governments—in close collaboration with power plant owners and nuclear regulators.[101] And why would they not collude? Nuclear power plants can only survive from the injection of public funding. And the nuclear lobby—and the governments that invest in nuclear power—have a vested interest in ensuring nuclear is seen as clean and safe in the minds of citizens.[102] Even when acknowledging plant failures, spokespersons for government and industry use words like 'accident' and 'incident', preferring *not* to talk of a 'meltdown', 'disaster', or 'catastrophe'.[103] According to Fred Pearce, author of *Fallout: Disasters, Lies and the Legacy of the Nuclear Age*,

From the Windscale fire in the U.K. to the Chernobyl disaster, from Rocky Flats to Three Mile Island in the U.S., and from Mayak in the USSR to Fukushima ... compulsive secrecy, deviousness, and lack of accountability have persisted, even as the technology has morphed from military to civilian uses. Nuclear subterfuge has eroded public trust, debate, and decision making alike.[104]

Warming to Climate Change

Any visitor to Singapore must take a trip to the Gardens on the Bay. Featuring three indoor conservatories, the Gardens occupy over 100 hectares and feature three domes. The Flower Dome—the largest glass greenhouse in the world—exhibits plants and flowers that survive in a Mediterranean-style climate, including cacti, succulents, and olive and gum trees. Tulips and orchids—along with fuchsia, dahlia, and lilies—are on display. The colours are spectacular. Vegetation from five of the world's seven continents are represented. The Cloud Forest Dome, the second enclosed structure, creates conditions found in high altitude tropical regions and hosts trees and other vegetation living in conditions of warm days, cool nights, and very high humidity. There are no gorillas in the mist, but the air is wet and there is a huge waterfall helping to set the scene (and soak the occasional guest). The third dome, Floral Fantasy has been designed to locate plants in imaginary worlds which feature mossy caves, bubbling brooks, and a floating bed of flowers. If you were religiously inclined, you could be forgiven for thinking you were in the Garden of Eden—minus the two nudes and pesky serpent.

Leaving the domes, the first things in sight are huge, towering, metal tree-like structures. Up to 50 metres in height, they form a grove of 'supertrees'. They are vertical gardens, providing shade during the day while being the scene, at night, of a sound and light show—the Garden Rhapsody. If this all sounds a little corny, it probably is. We are living in a simulacrum where the nature on display is as colourfully contrived as any street in a Disney theme park. It's a small world, after all. But the Garden by the Bay does celebrate the environment, and there is a genuine attempt to educate visitors about the ecological fragility of the beauty they are experiencing.

One of the exhibits is a video about climate change. It is a visually rich, seven-minute, run-through of what will happen to the planet if temperatures keep rising above pre-industrial levels. It's been designed with kids in mind, so there's a little more drama than subtlety. But what it shows is graphic and frightening. Up to 1.5-degree increase leads to what we have already been experiencing—more prolonged droughts, more severe rain events, melting of the ice caps, and people forced from their homes through bushfires, floods, and rising sea levels. At 1.6 degrees there will be a loss of 24% of the tundra, 23% of conifer forests, and 21% of scrubland. A 1.9-degree increase sees the extermination of one in every five amphibian species, and one in every ten reptile, bird, and mammalian species. A 2.3 increase sees the loss of two in every three flowering plants species. The last arctic polar bear dies at 2.7, and by 2.9 half of all species that remain on the planet are doomed. At 4.8 there is total extinction of all endemic species (especially vulnerable because their food, water, and shelter are limited to specific geographic locations). At 5.0 we're kaput, a dying rock in space.[105]

It is a challenging scenario—all of this will happen within the next 80 years, a proverbial blink of the geological eye. Unless, that is, we can halt climate change. Is this possible? The Intergovernmental Panel on Climate Change (IPCC) has said 'deep cuts' in greenhouse gas emissions must occur 'urgently'.[106] It stated

> The cumulative scientific evidence is unequivocal: Climate change is a threat to human wellbeing and planetary health. Any further delay in concerted anticipatory global action on adaptation and mitigation will miss a brief and rapidly closing window of opportunity to secure a liveable and sustainable future for all.[107]

The northern hemisphere experienced an extraordinary summer in 2022. Extreme heatwaves occurred in Japan, the US and UK, with temperatures above 40°C breaking existing records. Some 660,000 hectares of European forests were destroyed by wildfires, the worst ever experienced—with Spain, Romania, and Portugal the hardest hit. The US,

China, and Western Europe experienced record-breaking droughts while, in Southern Europe, Italy's Po river flowed at 90% below its average. The popular tourist attraction, Lake Garda, was at its lowest level ever recorded. In Germany, the Rhine had so little water, the transportation of goods was threatened. Some 60,000 people died in the European heatwaves of 2022.[108] In the same year severe flooding occurred in South Korea and the US. (Hurricane Ian, which struck Florida and the Carolinas in September has been described as 'one of the fiercest storms in US history', causing tens of billions of dollars of damage.)[109] Pakistan experienced the biggest flooding calamity ever with one-third of the country under water. Over 1,000 people were killed and 33 million displaced—creating a humanitarian crisis.[110]

Then, in 2023, heatwave conditions in Canada led to thousands of forest fires, burning some 3.8 million hectares of trees, and forcing the evacuation of some 120,000 people. The massive plume of smoke drifted over the northern US, creating a health emergency in many states. Temperature records were shattered in Italy, Spain, Mexico, and China. July 2023 was the hottest month recorded in human history.[111] But then came August (the hottest August on record) and then September (the hottest September on record). Unsurprisingly, 2023 was revealed as being the hottest year in human history, a year which '"smashed" the record … by a huge margin'. Indeed, 2023 was the hottest year on the planet in 100,000 years.[112] According to one climate modeller, not usually given to hyperbole, global temperature rises were 'absolutely gobsmackingly bananas'.[113] In western US states people fainting from the heat, and falling onto pavements and roadways, were receiving third degree burns from exposure to the 80°C temperatures emanating from those surfaces.[114] Hawaii's historic town of Lahaina was totally destroyed by a giant firestorm, incinerating 100 people—the highest death toll from a wildfire in US history.[115] The UN acknowledged that global warming is turning landscapes into 'tinderboxes' and predicted that 'extreme fires' would increase by 50% by the end of the century.[116]

It is not only the land, its river systems, and the people they support that are feeling the impacts of climate change. The oceans are warming, hastening the melting of polar ice and threatening terrestrial and sea life. Oceans are the hottest they have been in 1,000 years and are heating rapidly.[117] Some 40% of Antarctica's ice shelves have disappeared over the last 25 years—releasing some 7.5 trillion tonnes of water. The continent is warming at twice the rate of other parts of the world, way faster than current predictions from climate change modelling.[118] Water circulation in the world's oceans is driven by Antarctic sea ice. With the continued melting of this ice, it is anticipated that circulation of deep ocean currents will slow or completely shut down.[119] The Atlantic Meridional Overturning Circulation, as the current flow is known, is at its weakest point in 1,600 years and is predicted to collapse by 2050 if drastic action is not taken to reduce carbon emissions.[120]

Other areas of the ocean area also being affected by climate change. There is a zone in the ocean between 200 meters and 1,000 meters in depth. Known as the 'twilight zone' it is rich in organisms and organic matter—but is especially vulnerable to heating. Scientists are predicting that life in the twilight zone will decrease by as much as 40% as a result of continuing climate change.[121] Not only are many fish species being pushed to extinction, but their size is diminishing. They are 'shrinking'—with fish becoming smaller as the waters they inhabit grow warmer.[122] In the atmosphere, upper-level fast-flowing jet streams are being altered which, in turn, is likely to intensify the impact of heatwaves, droughts, and rainfall—something which could threaten food production in the world's 'breadbasket' regions and negatively impact global food security.[123] According to Mami Mizutori, the UN secretary general's disaster risk reduction representative, 'drought is on the verge of becoming the next pandemic, and there is no vaccine to cure it'.[124]

Economic modelling has not been helpful. In fact, economists have grossly miscalculated the upheavals that will be caused to food supply from climate change. As we saw in Chapter 2, economic models are often incomplete and misleading. As one critic noted:

> Most economic models ... rely on a fundamental premise – that we can gain useful insights into future damage by looking at how economies have been hit by earlier weather shocks. But there is a fundamental limitation here. Historically weather shocks tended to be local or regional. Even if there's intense drought in, say, India, harvests will still be good elsewhere ... But climate change could indeed lead to crop failures across

multiple regions at once. If that happened, food prices would surge to unprecedented levels.[125]

The current models don't capture such possibilities. The financial damage from future climate change has been 'severely underestimated' by economists. Some scientists are beginning to employ the term 'climate breakdown', but a more realistic expression would be 'climate catastrophe'. For climate expert Joelle Gergis we are seeing nothing short of an 'intergenerational crime against humanity'.[126]

In 2022 the IPCC produced five scenarios for the future of the planet. It's so-called 'middle of the road' scenario has the planet warming to 2.7 degrees above pre-industrial levels. Please have a look back at the predictions of our Singaporean friends. This will not be pretty.

What Is Going On?

We know what is happening. The climate is warming because of the release of greenhouse gases—in particular, carbon dioxide, methane, and nitrous oxide. Once in the atmosphere these gases act in the same fashion as the air in a greenhouse. Sunlight can enter, with some of it remaining trapped, heating the surrounding space. The so-called greenhouse effect is a normal feature of life on earth—in fact we'd burn to a crisp without it. But things get tricky if there is too much carbon in the atmosphere and temperatures rise beyond 'acceptable' bio-limits. Human beings are the ones implicated in global heating because of our use of carboniferous fuels in the pursuit of economic progress—the so-called anthropogenic warming of the planet.

Who are the main carbon polluters? Companies and governments burning coal, oil, and gas for the generation of electricity, heat, and transportation are the main culprits. Some 73% of all greenhouse gases come from the creation of energy from fossil fuels.[127] Industrial and residential use is paramount here. But so is iron and steel production, chemical and petrochemical production, and road transport. A further 18% is from farming, forestry, and land use and we can add another 7% emerging from the refrigeration, processing, and packaging of food. All up 25% of greenhouse gas pollution is from the agri-food sector.[128] So, in total, it's largely residences, manufacturing industry, transportation, and agriculture that can be held largely accountable.

For family residences in the West, and increasingly around the world, air-conditioned comfort—along with TVs, computers, white goods, motor vehicles, airline flights—are viewed as essential to modern living. While such consumption remains the norm in the Global North, the products of modern industrialisation are now being consumed in bucketloads, in places like China, India, South America, and the Asian nations—all to meet growing demand, and all premised on greater expenditure of energy. Diets in these nations are also changing. The demand for meat products is of concern. Globally, the demand for meat has tripled in the last 50 years, with the figure now reaching 340 million tonnes each year.[129] That's some 80 billion animals and birds killed each year for human consumption.[130] And demand continues to grow as those in the Global South develop a taste for animal flesh—accounting for some 80% of all new meat consumption.[131] The demand from the Global South is insatiable, despite the global system of meat production being unsustainable. Things will get a lot worse (in terms of greenhouse gas emissions, forest destruction, freshwater pollution, and land degradation), over the coming decades. It would seem nigh impossible for a growing world population to consume more beef while at the same time reducing livestock's negative impacts upon the environment.

We must confront a fundamental problem that is often ignored: Consumers in the richer nations appear unwilling to 'downsize' their lifestyles to help address global warming and environmental destruction. People in the poorer nations want to emulate the lifestyles and food choices of those in the wealthier nations. 'Why' they say, 'should we not aspire to and embrace the development patterns of the wealthier nations'? In fact, that is the promise that the poorer nations have been given if they behave correctly and become active players in the global world order.[132] For these nations, economic development is key to improving the life chances of the poor. Economic growth, jobs, more food, better housing—rather than carbon emissions reduction—are their main priorities.[133] They have seen the future—and it looks a lot like California.

But there is more to the story than the lifestyle preferences of the earth's human inhabitants: It is the profit-making desires of those companies whose growth rests on the expansion of fossil fuel production and consumption. The corporations producing fossil fuels—the oil companies, petroleum producers, and gas generators, along with the companies with intimate ties to the fossil fuel producers such as the electricity generators, transport corporations, iron and steel producers, cement makers, and so on—all have a stake in continuing with the status quo. They need a continued supply of cheap energy and lots of it, and now. In fact, the shareholders in those firms demand that returns on their investments increase. While it might be clear that fossil fuels will need to be replaced by new, renewable, technologies, delaying the inevitable will continue to bring in much-needed revenue. Regulations that might constrain the continued growth of fossil fuel production and/or foster the growth of renewables must be challenged by these industries head on.[134] If there is one thing that corporations require, it is continuing profitability. If there's one thing shareholders demand, it is growing financial returns. If there are three things that governments want, they are profitable corporations, satisfied shareholders, and happy voters—premised upon economic growth and current consumption patterns. All of which is reliant—at this time in the world's history—upon fossil fuel extraction and usage. While the use of renewables will grow quickly over the next few decades, by 2040 some 77% of the world's energy will still come from oil, coal, and natural gas. (Petroleum and other liquid fuel usage will have increased from 95 million barrels per day in 2015 to 113 million by 2040.)[135] China—the world's largest emitter of greenhouse gasses—has pledged, under the Paris Agreement, that its carbon emissions will peak by 2030; instead, it has refused to limit methane emissions and is pumping out increasing volumes of carbon, associated with expanding energy, transport, industrial, and residential sectors.[136]

Synaesthesia is an interesting condition where people experience one of their senses through another. You might read the word 'Toyota' and taste lemons, or eat a marshmallow and hear a song by Ariana Grande or Justin Bieber—just as many Republicans hear the phrase 'climate change' and see red. During his time as US president, Trump did as much as he could to stifle progress in addressing climate change. He abandoned the Paris Agreement, ditched Obama's Clean Power Plan (requiring the energy sector to reduce emissions), lifted restrictions on emissions from coal plants, weakened regulations on air pollution, removed protections on rivers and wetlands, had 'climate change' deleted from government websites, and increased logging in federally controlled forests. Oh, and he approved oil and gas production in waters of the Arctic, opened public lands for mining operations, and limited the power of state legislatures to block oil and gas pipeline expansion. Just to show he could stick it to the environmental lobby he had the word 'science' removed from the EPA's mission statement![137] Since coming to office in 2020 Biden has mouthed many sincere and bold carbon reduction pledges. Unfortunately, they might be coming a little late. According to the Climate Action Tracker, if present policies of 32 of the world's most polluting nations remain unchanged, global temperatures will reach some 3.4 degrees above pre-industrial levels by 2100. But what if these countries adhere strictly to their carbon reduction pledges? Will we all be saved? No. The temperature will have risen by a mere 3.2 degrees.[138] Global carbon emissions will need to be reduced to zero by 2050 if we want to keep temperature rises to 1.5 degrees above pre-industrial times. The modelling at the moment sees this as pretty much an impossibility.[139]

According to environmental writers for the *Guardian*,

> there are 195 gigantic oil and gas projects underway around the world that would each result in at least one billion tonnes of carbon dioxide emissions over their lifetimes, in total around 18 years of current global emissions … If we are going to keep to a 'safe' global climate, not only will these nascent projects have to be scrapped, nearly half of existing fossil fuel production will have to be shut down.[140]

During the run up to the start of his presidency, Joe Biden said he would not allow the oil industry to undertake any further drilling. Once in office he has approved over 300 oil and gas drilling permits *each month*, some 40% greater than occurred in the Trump years.[141] Of particular concern was his approval of the controversial Willow oil drilling plan for Alaska. ConocoPhillips will produce over 600 million barrels of oil over the next 30 years. This will create emissions equivalent to the yearly pollution from 66 new coal-fired power stations.[142] Utilising the new oil reserves is likely to completely undermine the benefits of his ambitious and costly Inflation Reduction Act, which is subsidising the moves to green energy throughout the US. Among the world's largest polluters are BP, Shell, Total, ExxonMobil, Chevron, and Saudi Aramco—responsible, along with others—for racking up damages to the planet, by 2050, of an estimated $5.4 trillion in the form of rising sea levels, droughts, floods, extreme heat and wildfires.[143] The top polluters will need to pay reparations of at least $209 billion a year to compensate victims of climate change.[144] There appears to be some reluctance to do so. Instead, we see the top polluters manipulating politics and politicians via large donations and lobbying. *Guardian* journalist George Monbiot has identified a *pollution paradox:*

> The most damaging companies have the greatest incentive to invest money in politics (by making donations to political parties, funding lobbyists and junktanks, hiring troll farms and microtargeters and all the other overt and covert techniques). So politics, in our money-driven system, comes to be dominated by the most damaging companies.[145]

When Liz Truss became prime minister of England in September 2022, she did her neoliberal best to appease the ruling class. With a staunch enthusiasm for 'bootleg Thatcherism', her first step was to introduce unfunded tax cuts to help the rich. Her second was to rush through a bill eliminating over 500 environmental laws to which Britain was obliged to adhere, as a member of the EU. She then removed the ban on fracking and stated her intention to increase production of gas and oil drilling in the North Sea.[146] We should not be surprised at these Conservative Party measures: When Truss was environmental secretary she overlooked cases of gross environmental negligence, ignored scientific advice that would have placed a limit on farmer exploitation of land and water resources, and said it was appropriate that massive funding cuts be made to her own department. She told reporters if she became Conservative leader she would 'put climate change on the back-burner' and would freeze levies that helped to fund 'green' climate change initiatives.[147] Her policies have been described as 'the biggest attack on nature in a generation'.[148]

Truss's prime ministerial successor—billionaire Rishi Sunak—has consistently voted against policies aimed at stemming climate change. He has given tax relief to companies exploring for North Sea gas and has vowed to limit the number of UK onshore wind farms.[149] In 2023 he stated his aim was to 'max out' North Sea oil and gas extractions, stating it was good for the climate because Britain would not have to ship its energy from halfway around the planet, reducing the fossil fuels used in transportation. Of course, he was conveniently ignoring the carbon releases that would come from the 100 or more new North Sea wells.[150] The decision is incompatible with Britain's goal of achieving net zero emissions by 2050. 'Extracting more fossil fuels … will send a wrecking ball through the UK's climate commitments', according to Lyndsay Walsh, the climate policy advisor for Oxfam.[151] And, the Donald promised his supporters that, if elected president in 2024, two of his first acts would be to 'close the border' and to 'drill, drill, drill'. In his campaign for the White House he has requested US$1 billion in donations from the oil firms, with a commitment that he will reduce regulations, and provide new tax breaks for the industry if he wins.[152]

In the meantime, the major polluters employ greenwashing techniques to convince an increasingly sceptical consumer base of their company's worthiness. Researcher Guy Pearse, author of *Greenwash*, asks 'so how do the big brands get away with their carbon scams?' and answers:

> slogans and logos, a few green products advertised heavily but made in very small numbers; impressive-sounding emission intensity targets; … conspicuous renewable energy installations at company headquarters; vocal speeches by the CEO; a glossy sustainability report full of isolated instances of green success stories; … a voluntary carbon offset program for customers; switching off for Earth Hour.[153]

Such techniques delude us that progress is being made when, in reality, we are sustaining the unsustainable—and will be doing so for many decades to come.

The Denial Machine

There are many from the religious right who do not deny that climate change is occurring. Let's follow the logic here—God created the world, it is His to do with it what He wants. If He allows greenhouse gas emissions to increase and the planet to die, it is His will. Should we try to interpose to halt greenhouse gas emissions? As US Reverend John MacArthur succinctly put it in 2020.

> God intended us to use this planet, to fill this planet for the benefit of man. Never was it intended to be a permanent planet. It is a disposable planet. Christians ought to know that.[154]

A little strange, perhaps? One out of every 15 Americans believe that God is in control of the climate and that our species is not implicated in global warming,[155] with some Evangelical groups wondering if climate change heralds the arrival of Armageddon, the final battle between good and evil before the world ends.[156] Why question the mysterious workings of the Ultimate Being? If climate change is occurring, it must be the work of God.

Then we move on to denial. Climate change is, for deniers, a fabrication, a hoax. Climate change is a lie created by the greens and/or communists bent on destroying the very essence of capitalism and western democracy. As that self-described stable genius, Donald Trump has thoughtfully penned, global warming is 'very expensive … bullshit … created by and for the Chinese in order to make US manufacturing non-competitive'.[157] Conflating weather and climate, Trump still tweets that a cold spell in New York or Atlanta *shows* the climate is not warming. 'Snowing in Texas and Louisiana … Global warming is an expensive hoax'.[158] For the ex-President, 'climate change' and 'hoax' should always accompany one and other in the same sentence. The majority of congressional Republican Party representatives agree.[159] Apparently, tens of thousands of scientifically educated men and women are part of an elaborate plan to fool the world that the climate is warming.[160]

The Donald's conspiracy theory aside, climate denialists play a very important role in shaping public opinion in favour of business-as-usual.

Well before Trump, one of George W's strategists wrote a famous memo stating that climate change was still up for debate and encouraged Republicans to 'make the lack of scientific certainty a primary issue'.[161] In the UK the Global Warming Policy Foundation (GWPC) is a charitable organisation which hopes to provide 'reason, integrity and balance' to today's 'irrationally alarmist' discussions about climate change.[162] It is an apparent champion of the world's poor—it is they who will suffer if actions to limit climate change are implemented. Its charitable status means it does not need to disclose its donors. One of its UK funders, it has been revealed, is the climate change-denying Institute of Economic Affairs, whose funders include those from the fossil fuel industry. It also receives 'dark money' from sources such as Donors Trust which, in turn, receives funding from the infamous Koch Brothers (whose activities are discussed below). According to climate expert Bob Ward from the London School of Economics, GWPF has abused its status as a charitable organisation by 'persistently disseminating inaccurate and misleading information about climate change as part of its campaign against climate policies in the UK and overseas'.[163]

I've synthesised below the five-prong attack employed by the denialists. The first tactic is to **target the science**, to question the scientific integrity of climate science research. Scrutinising the assumptions of any climate change modelling is what every scientist would welcome. But the denialists—usually scientists with qualifications outside climate science, or powerful conservative politicians, or right-wing journalists—seek to show that climate predictions are untrustworthy. They question whether greenhouse gas emissions are increasing, whether the atmosphere is heating, whether sea levels are rising, and whether ice caps are melting. They talk of 'natural cycles' of the planet and say that any changes observed today fit with past geological patterns or with current sunspot activity. Virtually all their claims are spurious, but their main game is to cast doubt on climate change science and to rule out anthropogenic causes.[164]

The second tactic is to **target the scientists**. Some believe scientists are making up climate change to improve their influence and standing in policy-making circles. Or, that they are manipulating data and over-dramatising their findings—all in the hope of gaining higher levels of funding for future research.[165] The climate scientists are being alarmist and they can't be trusted.[166] Attacking the person, rather than a person's argument, is a logical fallacy—the so-called *ad hominem* device for diverting attention. It has been around a long time but occupies a special place today in the artillery of the deniers.[167] A third prong of attack is to **target the organisations** which are concerned about climate change. Environmental groups are the main focus. Their ideas are viewed as loopy, their members are eco-zealots, and their attempts to have renewables replace fossil fuels are seen as a pipe dream. They are excoriated for being anti-tech, at a time when more technology will be the key driver of human progress. And, they are often considered to be peddling a hidden leftist agenda in the guise of 'greening' the world.[168] Environmentalism is really communism, if only people would wake up![169] Green-leaning political parties are similarly smeared. Their attempts to close coal-fired power plants, to tax carbon polluters, to subside the purchase of electric vehicles, and to launch campaigns seeking to reduce human impact on the environment, are construed to be the anti-business actions of eco-nuts.

The fourth tactic of the deniers is to **attack the proposed policy solutions** put forward by scientists and governments. The arguments here are many and are rolled out in various ways. Travis Coan and his colleagues have neatly categorised them. Policies are viewed as *harmful to society*. They increase costs of doing business, they weaken economic security, and they constrain the freedoms of current generations while limiting the wealth and benefits that would otherwise be available to future generations. Policies are viewed as *ineffective*—markets are better than governments at allocating resources, 'green jobs' can never replace traditional work options, and we'll never be able to contain the polluting practices of other nations (read: China). So why bother? Why penalise our nation, its businesses, and its people? Next, policies are seen as *too hard and expensive* to implement—they just won't work in practice. Policies promoting green energy are doomed to fail because renewables are an expensive and unreliable source.

Finally, the deniers claim **the world needs more energy** and we already have it in the form of cheap fossil fuels and nuclear power. To turn our backs on existing sources is to reign in economic growth at a time when people around the world are trying to improve their living standards by demanding access to more resources.[170] And, in any case, how can we be sure that a move away from existing energy forms will be beneficial?

The deniers are bent upon swaying opinion in favour of capitalist/industrial expansion. The various tactics, above, are aimed at confusing the public, raising doubts about the science of climate change and the policies that are being proposed and implemented. In the words of authors Naomi Oreskes and Erik Conway, the contrarians—the climate change deniers—are 'merchants of doubt'.[171] Just as decades ago the tobacco lobby sought to hide the risks of smoking, today's assorted climate change denialists are cherry picking facts, using fake experts, creating deception, and lying, as part of deliberate misinformation and disinformation campaigns. Along with conspiracy theories, ideas that mislead the public have persuaded governments to drop, or postpone, commitments to address climate change—which of course is the raison d'être of the denialists.[172] Make people doubtful and they will be less ready to support actions to address the problem.[173] Problem? What problem? The deniers claim that the science of climate change has not been settled—in the face of overwhelming evidence that the planet is suffering. And in the face of the views of those active in climate science—some 97% of whom consider that activities of people are warming the planet.[174]

Carbon dioxide levels are currently at their highest level over the past two to three million years.[175] In 2019 every scientific agency in the US viewed climate change as real, and human-driven, with the overall global cost of climate change (displaced people, coastal inundation, food destroyed by floods and droughts, climate mitigation costs, and so on) estimated to be around US$23 trillion by 2050.[176]

The five largest oil and gas companies in the world spend around US$200 million annually in seeking to delay or block climate change legislation.[177] In the three years following the Paris Agreement they spent over US$1 billion on misleading the public about climate change, and in lobbying to undermine bills that would affect their profit line.[178] They have a strong interest in keeping us addicted to fossil fuels. But, as we would expect, there are yet others with similar intentions. (Re)enter the think tanks. Some 90% of materials denying climate change are associated with right-wing think tanks.[179] These bodies are mostly registered as charitable organisations and so receive tax breaks subsidised through the public purse. The public is literally underwriting payment for the production of false advice—advice which could seriously compromise humanity and the planet over the next eight decades, or sooner.

In the 1970s US-based conservative think tanks were a bulwark against the threat of communism but that changed following the demise of the Soviet Union. The red scare transmogrified into the green scare.[180] It was in the 1990s that the George C. Marshall Institute (now the CO_2 Coalition) began questioning legislation being proposed or enacted to address ozone depletion, acid rain, and, of course, climate change.[181] Also in the US, some 162 think tanks and tax-exempt institutions have joined forces under the banner of the State Policy Network to question the need for climate change regulation (and to attack unions, block health-care legislation, and to push for further privatisation of education).[182] The State Policy Network has been accused of being a 'front' group for America's billionaires.[183] And where does the Network's money come from? Funding has been traced to Facebook, Microsoft, AT&T, Time Warner Cable, and Verizon. But we should also include the Koch brothers.[184]

The Kochs occupy a special place in climate change denial. The brothers Charles and (the late) David Koch have made billions of dollars from oil refining, chemicals, minerals, fertilisers, ranching, and commodity trading. The Koch Industries carbon footprint is vast—equivalent to 300 million barrels of oil each year (amounting to some 5% of all US emissions).[185]

Charles Koch has a net worth of some US$58 billion and is listed as the 20th richest person in the world. Koch Industries is, by revenue, the largest privately held company in the US.[186] The brothers have been generous donors to a number of important right-wing think tanks—not only the State Policy Network, but also the American Legislative Exchange Council, Americans for Prosperity Foundation, the Cato Institute, and The Heritage Foundation—all part of the so-called Kochtopus.[187] They fund dissident scientists to foster contrarian views, 'proving' to the public that there is widespread disagreement about climate change within the scientific community.[188] One of their friendly professors, speaking at a Cato Institute function in the early 1990s, revealed there was 'very little evidence at all' for climate change. One of Koch Industries main lobbyists questioned, in 2014, whether climate 'fluctuations' were the product of human actions. The Koch-funded Americans for Prosperity act as an astroturfing organisation—so-called because it pretends to be a grassroots and community-based entity, sending out people to door knock about doubts over climate change, while all the time being a front for the fossil fuel polluters.[189] In a move as brash as it was silly, the Heartland Institute decided to attack the IPCC by creating an organisation called the Nongovernmental International Panel on Climate Change (or NIPCC). Its purpose?

> Because it is not a government agency, and because its members are not predisposed to believe climate change is caused by human greenhouse gas emissions, NIPCC is able to offer an independent "second opinion" of the evidence reviewed – or not reviewed – by the Intergovernmental Panel on Climate Change (IPCC) on the issue of global warming.[190]

Can you guess its main finding? 'The impact of man-made global warming is benign and even beneficial to mankind and the natural world'.[191] To drive its point home, in 2017 it mailed over 300,000 free copies of its book *Why Scientists Disagree About Global Warming: The NIPCC Report on Scientific Consensus* to over 300,000 high school and college teachers across the US.[192]

The Koch brothers were great fans, and supporters, of the Tea Party, and backed Trump's 2017 decision to remove the US from the Paris climate agreement. They oppose bills that promote renewable energy and have been keen to stop scrutiny of the fracking industry. They have sought to halt the surge towards solar power in the US.[193] In 2014 they were

> spending heavily to fight incentives for renewable energy, which have been adopted by most states. They particularly dislike state laws that allow homeowners with solar panels to sell power they don't need back to electric utilities. So they've been pushing legislatures to impose a surtax on

this increasingly popular practice, hoping to make installing solar panels on houses less attractive.[194]

Their refineries have negligently polluted waterways and they have been forced to pay millions in criminal fines and remediation costs.[195] They have been strong Republican supporters, spending millions of dollars in federal and state elections to have their chosen candidates elected.[196] But while the brothers were railing against government interference in the economy, Koch Industries happily accepted tax breaks and subsidies that supported their business activities.[197]

There's more to be added to the mix. Public relations firms have been active on a global scale since the early 1900s. The early theorising about the important role played by mass communication was undertaken by Eduard Bernays whose path-breaking book *Crystalizing Public Opinion* appeared in 1923. But it was in the 1960s, when a cynical public was beginning to learn more of poisonous industrial emissions, workplace accidents, and ecological damage, that PR firms were hired by firms to provide a 'greenwash'.[198] The aim was to create narratives that would promote the green credentials of firms, while deflecting attention from their day-to-day practices. The whole point of PR is to concoct news to

> turn out what are essentially advertisements into a form that fits news coverage and makes a journalist's job easier while at the same time promoting the interests of the client.[199]

The organisation GRAIN, an international body promoting community-based and biodiverse food systems, has developed a 'greenwashing glossary' to alert an unsuspecting public to the tricks used by agri-food corporations as they pedal their wares. 'Net zero' emissions are the aims of many companies. But what that means is that they'll continue to pollute while offsetting their carbon footprint by growing trees. An example? Nestle's 'net zero' involves increasing sales of dairy and meat products by two-thirds in the ten years to 2030. To offset this, they will plant some 4 million hectares of trees every year. That's the size of Switzerland every year. As GRAIN reports 'the numbers don't add up', yet 'Nestle is just one of hundreds of corporations' promising to plant trees to offset carbon emissions.[200] In 2024 scientists looked into the pledges made by polluting firms and found

> there aren't enough trees or arable land in the world to offset growing emissions, and there never will be … it would require the use of almost 1.2 billion hectares of land - almost the equivalent of the total global land area used for crops.[201]

It can't be done. In other words, carbon offsetting is a furphy. Furthermore,

> As the international carbon-credits market booms, estimates of its worth in coming years range into the many trillions. Every dollar spent pursuing it will be a dollar not spent on cutting emissions: and it will implicitly justify continued use of fossil fuels.[202]

Then there's 'regenerative agriculture' and 'climate smart agriculture'. Both include the use of agri-chemicals, monocultures, and factory farming. We'll return to this in Chapter 8. 'Green finance' sounds good—it is the use of financial instruments (loans, investments, and debt mechanisms) to improve environmental outcomes for the planet. It is a way of 'meeting the needs of environmentalism and capitalism simultaneously'.[203] Good luck with that one. The problem with 'green finance' entering food and farming industries is that most of it is being channelled into corporate agriculture for the purpose of expanding existing (polluting) forms of commodity production, albeit under the greenwash labels of 'regenerative' and 'climate smart' farming.[204]

Today, misinformation is peddled through paid media campaigns, through social media, and through local events like rallies and public gatherings.[205] In the 1980s the Global Climate Coalition (US-based industries opposing action on climate) hired PR guru E. Bruce Harrison to create and run an international campaign opposing action on climate change. The Global Climate Coalition's PR activities (along with vigorous lobbying by oil producers like ExxonMobil) played an important role in convincing the US not to sign the Kyoto Protocol.[206] PR firms have been complicit in the denial of climate change and, therefore, in the delays in the containment of greenhouse gases.

Other culprits are websites and newspapers. The highly influential Fox News is notorious for climate change denial. Its hosts, guests, and commentators provide false narratives and tell deliberate lies about climate change and have done so over many decades. For Fox's former prime-time presenter Tucker Carlson 'not even climate experts understand the climate', while for Laura Ingraham we are living through 'the big climate con'. Ingraham believes those wanting action on climate are leftists bent on 'taking more of our money and more of our liberty' and who 'hate America anyway'.[207] Regular guests include Marc Morano (a serial denier) and Bjorn Lomborg (who claims it would be an overreaction to spend scarce resources on tackling changing climate).[208] Sean Duffy, a contributor to Fox News, has claimed that climate change activists are infiltrating schools, scaring pupils, and telling them not to have children. For Duffy, the activists are part of a political movement, not one connected in any way to science.[209] In 2019, on the program *Fox and Friends*, climate sceptic Patrick Moore claimed the climate crisis 'is not only fake news, it's fake science'—a quip that Trump tweeted with glee to his followers.[210] We very much understand that when Fox News wheels out its 'experts' to give a balanced view of climate change much of their counter-evidence is flimsy, inaccurate, or simply made up. The disinformation is deliberate because:

> The purpose of Fox hosts' and contributors' climate denial is to maintain an air of doubt about the existence and reality of our dangerously changing climate to provide cover for Republicans, who work actively to do nothing to stop the climate crisis, and the Big Polluters that bankroll their campaigns.[211]

Media expert, Dennis Muller, has written of the Murdoch press:

> Th[e] abandonment of a fundamental news media obligation to truth-telling is by definition harmful to a democratic society. Not only does it rob the population of a bedrock of reliable news, it debases the entire discourse. It is also a fraud on the people by misrepresenting propaganda as news.[212]

Disinformation is spread through other websites, including Facebook/ Meta, which generates some 69% of the digital content denying climate change.[213] The far-right Breitbart (associated with Trump's strategist Steve Bannon), Newsmax (known for its election fraud conspiracies), Townhall Media (linked to the Heritage Foundation), and the Media Research Centre (receiving funding from Exxon) are among the worst. And let's not leave out the Russians. They host their very own denialists on websites RT.com and Sputnik News.[214]

According to US Senator Sheldon Whitehouse, the 'algorithm-driven Facebook ecosystem' quickly generates information from a number of small, but influential, websites:

> Facebook and other social media companies make money when they send users down rabbit holes of climate denial ... That's a very dangerous business model for the future of the planet.[215]

The Murdoch-owned newspapers have had a field day with climate change. An Australian-based study of News Corp's reporting on climate change for the year up to March 2020 revealed that, on average, some 45% of coverage 'either rejected, or cast doubt upon consensus scientific findings' rising to some 77% in its tabloids.[216] Opinion pieces were the most biased, with particular venom directed at the rallies of Extinction Rebellion and at Greta Thunberg that 'global warming saint' and 'Swedish international incineration infant'. How is it, they ask, that 'Greta Thunberg ... with a range of mental conditions ... is the world's greatest authority on global warming?'.[217]

Two discourses were apparent. The first presents scientists as authoritarians contriving to limit free speech of detractors and therefore undermining democratic debate. This has wide appeal to those believing in individualism, small government, and the free market.[218] The second attempts to challenge the authority of science by likening it to a religious faith. The language chosen by the journalists and opinion piece writers is inflammatory. Climate science is variously described as a 'moral panic', 'catastrophe mongering', 'cult hysteria', and 'crazed beliefs', while climate change activists are part of a 'global destruction movement', a 'global fascist climate crisis horror show' and are on an 'anti-industrial, anti-capitalist crusade'. They are a 'warmist mob', 'weeping, screaming, brawling and spitting hysterics' while mouthing the 'whacky policies of the Greens'. They are (if you can believe it) 'Bolshewokes'. The consistent themes in Murdoch's News Corp papers were:

- Climate science is not based on facts;
- Climate science is a fraud and deception;
- The journalists who have joined the 'movement' are biased and unethical;
- Scaremongering is a deliberate tactic of the climate change campaigners;
- Believers in climate change want to shut down debate, damaging democracy.[219]

The colourful language (insults, exaggerations, smears, and invective) of the deniers is deliberate, of course. Its purpose is to provoke an emotional reaction in readers, helping to shape and reinforce right-wing views in the absence of rational debate and factual information.

And then it seemed that Rupert had a 'lightbulb' moment, with his media outlets starting to go soft on decarbonisation, reporting that some decarbonising policies could herald a trillion-dollar economic windfall for companies. Might the Murdochs join Greta on stage to display their new green credentials? Unfortunately, no. What appeared to be a volte-face turned out to be business-as-usual—clean coal is important for future energy generation, gas will help to halve current emissions, carbon pricing has no role to play in fixing our problems, and we should be looking to nuclear power.[220] It's all about leopards and spots.

Vested interests are intent upon debunking and destroying climate science. Do we honestly believe that the world's billionaires and their political lackeys have the interests of wider humanity and the planet at heart? They are busy building bunkers in New Zealand and Hawaii and planning for their families to live on the Moon and Mars. As the bumper sticker says *Think globally, act locally, panic internally.*

Notes

1. Hudson Institute. (2022) Promoting American leadership and engagement for a secure, free, and prosperous future, https://www.hudson.org/about.
2. Avery, D. (1995) *Saving the Planet with Pesticides and Plastic: The Environmental Triumph of High-Yielding Farming*, Hudson Institute, Indianapolis, p. 96, p. 107, p. 140, p. 98.
3. Avery, *Saving the Planet with Pesticides and Plastic*, pp. 525–333.
4. Avery, *Saving the Planet with Pesticides and Plastic*, pp. 164–190.
5. Avery, *Saving the Planet with Pesticides and Plastic*, p. 335, p. 348.
6. Baier, C. (2000) *Saving the Planet with Pesticides and Plastic*: A critical review, https://www.webpages.uidaho.edu/etox/resources/book_reviews/Planet.pdf.
7. Baier, *Saving the Planet with Pesticides and Plastic*.
8. Baier, *Saving the Planet with Pesticides and Plastic*.
9. Sharma, A., Kumar, V., Shahzad, B., Tanveer, M., Sidhu, G., Handa, N., Kohli, S., Yadav, P., Bali, A., Parihar, R., Dar, O., Singh, K., Jasrotia, S., Bakshi, P., Ramakrishnan, M., Kumar, S., Bhardwaj, R. and Kumar, A. (2019) *SN Applied Sciences* 1(1446): https://doi.org/10.1007/s42452-019-1485-1.
10. Pretty, J. and Waibel, H. (2005) Paying the price: The full cost of pesticides, in J. Pretty (ed.) *The Pesticide Detox: Towards a More Sustainable Agriculture*, Earthscan, UK, pp. 39–45.
11. Carolan, M. (2012) *The Sociology of Food and Agriculture*, Routledge, London, pp. 18–21; Buttel, F. (2006) Sustaining the unsustainable: Agro-food systems and environment in the modern world, in P. Cloke, T. Marsden and P. Mooney (eds) *Handbook of Rural Studies*, Sage, London, pp. 213–229.
12. Pretty and Waibel, Paying the price.
13. Roberts, J. and Reigart, J. (2013) *Recognition and Management of Pesticide Poisonings, Sixth Edition*, United States Environmental Protection Agency, Washington. See http://www2.epa.gov/pesticide-worker-safety.

14. Everyday Health. (2022) 12 foods to buy organic, https://www.everydayhealth.com/diet-nutrition-pictures/dirty-dozen-fruits-and-vegetables.aspx.
15. Dinham, B. (2005) Corporations and pesticides, in J. Pretty (ed.) *The Pesticide Detox: Towards a More Sustainable Agriculture*, Earthscan, UK, pp. 55–69.
16. Mordor Intelligence. (2024) Agrochemical Industry Size & Share Analysis—Growth Trends & Forecasts (2024–2029), https://www.mordorintelligence.com/industry-reports/agrochemicals-market.
17. EPA. (2004) Pesticides industry sales and usage 2000 and 2001 market estimates, https://nepis.epa.gov/Exe/ZyPURL.cgi?Dockey=3000659P.txt.
18. Shattuck, A. (2021) Generic, growing, green?: The changing political economy of the global pesticide industry, *Journal of Peasant Studies* 48(2): 246–247.
19. Weir, D. and Schapiro, M. (1981) *Circle of Poison: Pesticides and People in a Hungry World*, Institute for Food and Development Policy, San Francisco.
20. Quoted in Aljazeera. (2016) Circle of Poison, https://www.aljazeera.com/program/featured-documentaries/2016/11/15/circle-of-poison.
21. Aljazeera, Circle of Poison. An hour-long documentary *Circle of Poison* was made in 2015, the trailer for which can be found on IMDB: https://www.imdb.com/title/tt4679022/.
22. Shattuck, Generic, growing, green?
23. GRAIN. (2012) *The Great Food Robbery: How Corporations Control Food, Grab Land and Destroy the Climate*, Pambazuka Press, Cape Town, p. 114.
24. For the latter see Fleming, A. (2023) 'They're in the air, drinking water, dust, food ...' How to reduce your exposure to microplastics, https://www.theguardian.com/lifeandstyle/2023/jul/10/air-drinking-water-dust-food-how-to-reduce-exposure-microplastics.

25. Perkins, T. (2022) 'I don't know how we'll survive': The farmers facing ruin in Maine's 'forever chemicals' crisis, https://www.theguardian.com/environment/2022/mar/22/i-dont-know-how-well-survive-the-farmers-facing-ruin-in-americas-forever-chemicals-crisis.
26. Saha, J. (2024) Can you actually avoid 'forever chemicals' in your diet? salon.com/2024/05/04/can-you-actually-avoid-forever-chemicals-in-your-diet/; Salvidge, R. and Hosea, L. (2023) Revealed: Scale of 'forever chemical' pollution across UK and Europe, https://www.theguardian.com/environment/2023/feb/23/revealed-scale-of-forever-chemical-pollution-across-uk-and-europe.
27. Nelsen, A. (2023) EU to drop ban of hazardous chemicals after industry pressure, https://www.inkl.com/news/eu-to-drop-ban-of-hazardous-chemicals-after-industry-pressure; Ginty, M. and Lindwall, C. (2024) 'Forever chemicals' called PFAS show up in your food, clothes, and home, nrdc.org/stories/forever-chemicals-called-pfas-show-up-in-your-food-clothes-and-home; Chemsec. (2023) The top 12 PFAS producers in the world and the staggering societal costs of PFAS pollution, chemsec.org/reports/the-top-12-PFAS-producers-in-the-word-and-the-staggering-societal-costs-of-PFAS-pollution/.
28. United Nations Environment Programme. (2021) Plastic planet: How tiny plastic particles are polluting our soil, https://www.unep.org/news-and-stories/story/plastic-planet-how-tiny-plastic-particles-are-polluting-our-soil.
29. Staughton, J. (2022) How do we know plastic will take so long to decompose? https://www.scienceabc.com/nature/how-do-we-know-plastic-will-take-so-long-to-decompose.html.
30. Center for Climate Integrity. (2024) *The Fraud of Plastic Recycling*, https://climateintegrity.org/uploads/media/Fraud-of-Plastic-Recycling-2024.pdf.
31. Chakori, S., Aziz, A., Friant, M. and Richards, R. (2022) If the UN wants to slash plastic waste, it must tackle soaring plastic

production—and why we use so much of it, https://theconversation.com/if-the-un-wants-to-slash-plastic-waste-it-must-tackle-soaring-plastic-production-and-why-we-use-so-much-of-it-179107; Carrington, D. (2022a) Microplastics found in human blood for first time, https://www.theguardian.com/environment/2022/mar/24/microplastics-found-in-human-blood-for-first-time; Carrington, D. (2022b) Microplastics found deep in lungs of living people for first time, https://www.theguardian.com/environment/2022/apr/06/microplastics-found-deep-in-lungs-of-living-people-for-first-time; Scientists are experimenting with bio-plastics in the hope that these will break down more quickly than petroleum based plastics. However, there remains confusion about their costs and benefits—see Laycock, B., Lant, P. and Pratt, S. (2022) Do you toss biodegradable plastics in the compost bin? Here's why it might not break down, https://theconversation.com/do-you-toss-biodegradable-plastic-in-the-compost-bin-heres-why-it-might-not-break-down-178542.

32. Chakori, Aziz, Friant and Richards, If the UN wants to slash plastic waste, it must tackle soaring plastic production – and why we use so much of it.
33. Forbes. (2018) Five ways that plastics harm the environment (and one way they may help), https://www.forbes.com/sites/grrlscientist/2018/04/23/five-ways-that-plastics-harm-the-environment-and-one-way-they-may-help/?sh=40c245567a04; United Nations Environment Program, Plastic planet.
34. Crist, C. (2022) Microplastics found in human breast milk, https://www.medscape.com/s/viewarticle/982185?form=fpf; Carrington, D. (2022c) Microplastics found in human breast milk for the first time, https://www.theguardian.com/environment/2022/oct/07/microplastics-human-breast-milk-first-time.
35. Carrington, D. (2024a) Microplastics found in every human placenta tested in study, https://www.theguardian.com/environment/2024/feb/27/microplastics-found-every-human-placenta-tested-study-health-impact; Carrington, D. (2024b) Microplastics found in every human testicle in study, theguardian.com/environment/article/2024/may/20/microplastics-human-testicles-study-sperm-counts.

36. Carrington, Microplastics found in human blood for first time.
37. Carrington, D. (2022d) Environmental toxins are worsening obesity pandemic, say scientists, https://www.theguardian.com/environment/2022/may/19/environmental-toxins-are-worsening-obesity-pandemic-say-scientists.
38. World Wide Fund for Nature. (2019) No plastic in nature: Assessing plastic ingestion from nature to people, http://awsassets.panda.org/downloads/plastic_ingestion_press_singles.pdf.
39. Friedman, L. (2024) The plastic chemicals hiding in your food, https://www.consumerreports.org/health/food-contaminants/the-plastic-chemicals-hiding-in-your-food-a7358224781; Green Science Policy Institute. (2024) Bisphenols & Phthalates, https://greensciencepolicy.org/harmful-chemicals/bisphenols-phthalates/.
40. Green Science Policy Institute, Bisphenols & Phthalates.
41. Gayle, D. (2023) Recycled plastic can be more toxic and is no fix for pollution, Greenpeace warns, https://www.theguardian.com/environment/2023/may/24/recycled-plastic-more-toxic-no-fix-pollution-greenpeace-warns.
42. United Nations Environment Programme. (2022) Plastic bag bans can help reduce toxic fumes, https://www.unep.org/news-and-stories/story/plastic-bag-bans-can-help-reduce-toxic-fumes.
43. DeSmog. (2012) Dennis Avery, https://www.desmog.com/dennis-avery/.
44. DeSmog. (2022) The Hudson Institute, https://www.desmog.com/hudson-institute/.
45. Pretty, *The Pesticide Detox*.
46. Wikipedia. (2022) Hudson Institute, https://en.wikipedia.org/wiki/Hudson_Institute.
47. Wikipedia, Hudson Institute.
48. CHOICE. (2008) Eli Lilly fined for dodgy spin on impotence pill, https://www.abc.net.au/mediawatch/transcripts/0821_cialisrelease2.pdf.
49. SourceWatch. (2022) Leslie Lenkowsky, https://www.sourcewatch.org/index.php/Leslie_Lenkowsky; Militarist Monitor.

(2016) Leslie Lenkowsky, https://militarist-monitor.org/profile/leslie-lenkowsky/.
50. Council on American-Islamic Relations. (2022) Monitoring and combating Islamophobia, https://islamophobia.org/; Wikipedia. (2022) Gatestone Institute, https://en.wikipedia.org/wiki/Gatestone_Institute. Its former chair was John Bolton, Trump's former US national security advisor and US ambassador to the United Nations.
51. Kaplan, F. (2020) The ultimate disgrace of Mike Pompeo, https://slate.com/news-and-politics/2020/05/pompeo-disgrace-inspector-general.html; Wikipedia, Hudson Institute.
52. Sourcewatch. (2022) Lynde and Harry Bradley Foundation, https://www.sourcewatch.org/index.php/Lynde_and_Harry_Bradley_Foundation.
53. Powerbase. (2022) Smith Richardson Foundation, https://powerbase.info/index.php/Smith_Richardson_Foundation.
54. Hertog Foundation. (2022) About, https://hertogfoundation.org/about.
55. Sourcewatch. (2022) Sarah Scaife Foundation, https://www.sourcewatch.org/index.php/Sarah_Scaife_Foundation.
56. Mayer, J. (2017) *Dark Money: The Hidden History of the Billionaires Behind the Rise of the Radical Right*, Anchor Books, New York; Briffault, R. (2019) What is dark money? 5 questions answered, https://www.law.columbia.edu/news/archive/what-dark-money-5-questions-answered.
57. Goldenberg, S. and Bengtsson, H. (2015) Secretive donors gave US climate denial groups $125 m over three years, https://www.theguardian.com/environment/2015/jun/09/secretive-donors-gave-us-climate-denial-groups-125m-over-three-years.
58. Goldenberg and Bengtsson, Secretive donors gave US climate denial groups $125 m over three years; Wikipedia, Hudson Institute.
59. DeSmog, The Hudson Institute.
60. Mesnage, R. and Antoniou, M. (2018) Roundup Ready! Glyphosate and the current controversy over the world's leading

herbicide, in D. Dellasala and M. Goldstein (eds) *Encyclopedia of the Anthropocene*, Volume 5, Contaminants, Elsevier, Amsterdam, pp. 149–153; MacDonald, J. (2019) Mergers in seeds and agricultural chemicals: What happened? https://www.ers.usda.gov/amber-waves/2019/february/mergers-in-seeds-and-agricultural-chemicals-what-happened/; Dinham, Corporations and pesticides; Details of corporations at Verified Market Research. (2021) World's top 10 agrochemical companies redefining agriculture by using latest technology, https://www.verifiedmarketresearch.com/blog/worlds-top-agrochemical-companies/.

61. Burke, I. and Bell, J. (2014) Plant health management: Herbicides, in N. van Alfen (ed.) *Encyclopedia of Agriculture and Food Systems*, Elsevier, Amsterdam, pp. 425–440.
62. The Natural Farmer (2022) A short history of glyphosate, https://thenaturalfarmer.org/article/a-short-history-of-glyphosate/.
63. Boerboom, C. and Owen, M. (2022) Facts about glyphosate-resistant weeds, Purdue Extension Education, Indiana, https://weedscience.missouri.edu/publications/gwc-1.pdf.
64. The Natural Farmer, A short history of glyphosate.
65. Gillam, C. (2023) People exposed to weedkiller chemical have cancer biomarkers in urine—Study, https://www.theguardian.com/us-news/2023/jan/20/glyphosate-weedkiller-cancer-biomarkers-urine-study.
66. Paradoxically, glyphosate has also been patented as an anti-cancer compound that inhibits the growth of tumours in mammals—see Mesnage and Antoniou, Roundup Ready!
67. The Natural Farmer, A short history of glyphosate.
68. Gillam, C. (2017) *Whitewash: The Story of a Weedkiller, Cancer, and the Corruption of Science*, Island Press, Washington, p. 5.
69. Gillam, *Whitewash*, p. 40.
70. Gillam, *Whitewash*, p. 40.
71. Gillam, C. (2021) *The Monsanto Papers: Deadly Secrets, Corporate Corruption, and One Man's Search for Justice*, Island Press, Washington; Hahn, J. (2021) Monsanto's big lie about Roundup and

the system that enabled it, https://www.sierraclub.org/sierra/monsanto-roundup-epa-corporate-political-influence.
72. Grant, M. (2016) First Agent Orange, now Roundup: What's Monsanto up to in Vietnam? Ecologist special investigation, https://theecologist.org/2016/oct/10/first-agent-orange-now-roundup-whats-monsanto-vietnam-ecologist-special-investigation.
73. Hill and Ponton PA. (2022) Agent Orange diseases and symptoms breakdown! https://www.hillandponton.com/agent-orange-and-your-body-symptoms/.
74. Smith, J. (2010) Monsanto: The world's poster child for corporate manipulation and deceit, https://www.huffpost.com/entry/monsanto-the-worlds-poste_b_427035.
75. Smith, Monsanto.
76. Lobbywatch.org. (2006) Monsanto on trial in France (20/9/2006), http://www.lobbywatch.org/archive2.asp?arcid=7048.
77. Gillam, *Whitewash*, p. 121.
78. Gillam, *Whitewash*, p. 114.
79. Gillam, *Whitewash*, p. 132.
80. Lappé, A. (2014) Big Food uses mommy bloggers to shape public opinion, http://america.aljazeera.com/opinions/2014/8/food-agriculturemonsantogmoadvertising.html; see also Gillam, *Whitewash*, p. 129.
81. Lappé, Big Food uses mommy bloggers to shape public opinion.
82. Cooper, L. (2024) Landmark class action seeks to determine if glyphosate is cancer-causing, but how important is it in Australia? https://www.msn.com/en-au/money/markets/landmark-class-action-seeks-to-determine-if-glyphosate-is-cancer-causing-but-how-important-is-it-in-australia/ar-AA1n8B49.
83. Grant, First Agent Orange, now Roundup.
84. Nestle, M. (2018) *Unsavory Truth: How Food Corporations Skew the Science of What we Eat*, Basic Books, New York.
85. Quoted in McGreal, C. (2021) Big oil and gas kept a dirty secret for decades. Now they may pay the price, https://www.theguardian.com/environment/2021/jun/30/climate-crimes-oil-and-gas-environment.

86. Ambrose, J. (2019) Major global firms accused of concealing their environmental impact, https://www.theguardian.com/environment/2019/jun/16/major-global-firms-accused-of-concealing-their-environmental-impact.
87. Broughton, E. (2005) The Bhopal disaster and its aftermath: A review, *Environmental Health* 4(6), https://doi.org/10.1186/1476-069X-4-6.
88. Government Accountability Project. (2020) Truth dig: The Deepwater Horizon oil spill was a cover-up, not a cleanup, https://whistleblower.org/in-the-news/truth-dig-the-deepwater-horizon-oil-spill-was-a-cover-up-not-a-cleanup/.
89. Davis, K. and *The Sun*. (2022) Russian soldiers in Chernobyl suffering from radiation poisoning, https://www.news.com.au/world/europe/russian-soldiers-in-chernobyl-suffering-from-radiation-poisoning/news-story/d98c53269a96028413314534 38c482dd; Bove, T. (2022) Chernobyl employees say Russian soldiers had no idea what the plant was and call their behaviour 'suicidal', https://finance.yahoo.com/news/chernobyl-employees-russian-soldiers-had-183704381.html.
90. Bukszpan, D. (2011) 11 nuclear meltdowns and disasters, https://www.cnbc.com/2011/03/16/11-Nuclear-Meltdowns-and-Disasters.html.
91. Yaroshinskaia, A. (2006) Chernobyl: The big lie, https://journals.sagepub.com/doi/pdf/10.1080/03064220600746623.
92. Reuters. (2021) Unsealed Soviet archives reveal cover-ups at Chernobyl plant before disaster, https://www.reuters.com/world/unsealed-soviet-archives-reveal-cover-ups-chernobyl-plant-before-disaster-2021-04-26/.
93. Yaroshinskaia, Chernobyl, p. 23.
94. Reuters, Unsealed Soviet archives reveal cover-ups at Chernobyl plant before disaster.
95. Yaroshinskaia, Chernobyl, p. 23.
96. Yaroshinskaia, Chernobyl, p. 23.
97. Yaroshinskaia, Chernobyl, p. 25.

98. Plokhy, S. (2018) The true cost of the Chernobyl disaster has been greater than it seems, https://time.com/5255663/chernobyl-disaster-book-anniversary/.
99. Plokhy, The true cost of the Chernobyl disaster has been greater than it seems; Green, J. (2014) Chernobyl—How many died? https://theecologist.org/2014/apr/26/chernobyl-how-many-died.
100. Machado, K. (2022) Chernobyl: Over 35 years on, is it actually safe to visit? https://time.com/5255663/chernobyl-disaster-book-anniversary/.
101. Brown, P. (2016) Legacy of lies and cover-ups leaves nuclear energy revival elusive, https://www.ecowatch.com/nuclear-energy-accidents-2165717823.html.
102. Iurshina, D., Karpov, N., Kirkegaad, M. and Semenov, E. (2019) Why nuclear power plants cost so much—and what can be done about it, https://thebulletin.org/2019/06/why-nuclear-power-plants-cost-so-much-and-what-can-be-done-about-it/.
103. Fairewinds Energy Education. (2021) Meltdowns and shakedowns: Our nuclear energy, https://www.fairewinds.org/meltdowns-shakedowns/our-nuclear-legacy.
104. Quoted in Pearce, F. (2018) How the 'compulsive secrecy' of the Atomic Age has changed the way we think, https://time.com/5285811/nuclear-history-excerpt/.
105. The video can be found at https://www.youtube.com/watch?v=i47h1b9c17g. A scientific evaluation can be found at: Song, H., Kemp, D., Tian, L., Song, H. and Xu, D. (2021) Thresholds of temperature change for mass extinctions, *Nature Communications* 12(4694), https://doi.org/10.1038/s41467-021-25019-2.
106. IPCC. (2022a) Climate change: A threat to human wellbeing and health of the planet, https://www.ipcc.ch/2022/02/28/pr-wgii-ar6/?msclkid=6ff16805c5cc11ec933185a9f69fff03.
107. IPCC. (2022b) Climate change 2022; Impacts, adaptation and vulnerability, summary for policymakers, https://report.ipcc.ch/ar6wg2/pdf/IPCC_AR6_WGII_SummaryForPolicymakers.pdf.
108. Reported in Carrington, D. (2023) Deadly global heatwaves undeniably result of climate crisis, scientists show, https://www.theguardian.com/science/2023/jul/25/deadly-global-heatwaves-undeniably-result-of-climate-crisis-scientists-attribution.

109. Brooks, B. and Drake, J. (2022) After Hurricane Ian's deadly wrath, Florida, Carolinas begin recovery, https://www.reuters.com/world/us/florida-carolinas-count-cost-one-worst-us-hurricanes-2022-10-01/.
110. DW. (2022) Europe set for record wildfire destruction in 2022, https://www.dw.com/en/europe-set-for-record-wildfire-destruction-in-2022/a-62802068; King, A. (2022) A climate scientist on the planet's simultaneous disasters, from Pakistan's horror floods to Europe's record drought, https://theconversation.com/a-climate-scientist-on-the-planets-simultaneous-disasters-from-pakistans-horror-floods-to-europes-record-drought-189626; Vidal, J. (2022) Floods, storms and heatwaves are a direct product of the climate crisis—that's a fact, so where is the action? https://www.theguardian.com/commentisfree/2022/aug/04/floods-storms-heatwaves-direct-product-climate-crisis.
111. Osborne, M. (2023) July was likely Earth's hottest month on record, https://www.msn.com/en-us/weather/topstories/july-was-likely-earths-hottest-month-on-record/ar-AA1eKQ24; Livingston, I. (2023) These places baked most during Earth's hottest month on record, https://www.washingtonpost.com/weather/2023/08/02/july-hottest-month-global-temperatures/.
112. Carrington, D. (2024) 2023 smashes record for world's hottest year by huge margin, https://www.theguardian.com/environment/2024/jan/09/2023-record-world-hottest-climate-fossil-fuel. The previous record was set in 2016. Temperatures in 2023 were 0.17 degrees above this.
113. This is a quote from Zeke Hausfather from the Berkeley Earth climate data project. See Carrington, D. (2023) 'Gobsmackingly bananas': Scientists stunned by planet's record September heat, https://www.theguardian.com/environment/2023/oct/05/gobsmackingly-bananas-scientists-stunned-by-planets-record-september-heat. Berkeley Earth's mission is to 'to provide the most accurate, independent, and reliable record of climate change for the global climate science and policymaker communities'. See https://berkeleyearth.org/berkeley-earths-high-resolution-dataset-announcement/.

114. Salam, E. (2023) Severe burns cases on rise in US south-west as extreme heatwave takes toll, https://www.theguardian.com/us-news/2023/jul/21/burns-cases-excessive-heat-arizona-nevada; Cabral, S. and Matza, M. (2023) US heatwave leads to rising number of burns, medics say, https://www.bbc.com/news/world-us-canada-66275785.
115. Valerio, M. and Sumpter, A. (2023) 100 days after the Maui fires, 4 names remain on the missing list. These are the people trying to find them, https://edition.cnn.com/2023/11/18/us/maui-fires-100-days/index.html.
116. Tidman, Z. (2022) Global warming 'turning landscapes into tinderboxes,' UN wildfires report warns, https://www.independent.co.uk/climate-change/news/global-warming-wildfires-un-report-b2020821.html.
117. Carrington, D. (2024) 'Astounding' ocean temperatures in 2023 intensified extreme weather, data shows, https://www.theguardian.com/environment/2024/jan/11/ocean-warming-temperatures-2023-extreme-weather-data.
118. Badshah, N. (2023) Antarctica has lost 7.5tn tonnes of ice since 1997, https://www.theguardian.com/world/2023/oct/12/antarctica-has-lost-7-5tn-tonnes-of-ice-since-1997-scientists-find.
119. Fraser, A., Weldrick, C., Dalman, L., Corkill, M. and Wongpan, P. (2023) Fractured foundations: How Antarctica's 'landfast' ice is dwindling and why it is bad news, https://www.nationaltribune.com.au/fractured-foundations-how-antarctica-s-landfast-ice-is-dwindling-and-why-that-s-bad-news.
120. Carrington, D. (2023) Gulf Stream could collapse as early as 2025, study suggests, https://www.theguardian.com/environment/2023/jul/25/gulf-stream-could-collapse-as-early-as-2025-study-suggests.
121. Harvey, F. (2023) Why are ocean temperatures warmer than ever? Even experts are scratching their heads, https://www.theguardian.com/environment/2023/apr/26/accelerating-ocean-warming-earth-temperatures-climate-crisis.

122. Clark, T. (2023) The world's fish are shrinking as the climate warms: We are trying to figure out why, https://phys.org/news/2023-06-world-fish-climate-figure.html.
123. Kornhuber, K., Lesk, C., Schleussner, C., Jagermeyr, J., Pfleiderer, P. and Horton, R. (2023) Risks of synchronised low yields are underestimated in crop model projections, *Nature Communications* 14(3528), https://doi.org/10.1038/s41467-023-38906-7.
124. Quoted in Smedley, T. (2023) Drought is on the verge of becoming the next pandemic, https://www.theguardian.com/news/2023/jun/15/drought-is-on-the-verge-of-becoming-the-next-pandemic.
125. Neal, T. (2023) Have some economists severely underestimated the financial hit from climate change? Recent evidence suggests yes, https://theconversation.com/have-some-economists-severely-underestimated-the-financial-hit-from-climate-change-recent-evidence-suggests-yes-214579.
126. Neal, Have some economists severely underestimated the financial hit from climate change?; Welz, A. (2024) *The End of Eden: Wild Nature in the Age of Climate Breakdown*, Bloomsbury, UK; Gergis, J. (2024) 'An intergenerational crime against humanity': What will it take for political leaders to start taking climate change seriously? https://theconversation.com/an-intergenerational-crime-against-humanity-what-will-it-take-for-political-leaders-to-start-taking-climate-change-seriously-231383.
127. Richie, H. (2020) Sector by sector: Where do global greenhouse gas emissions come from? https://ourworldindata.org/ghg-emissions-by-sector.
128. Richie, Sector by sector.
129. Richie, H. and Roser, M. (2019) Meat and dairy production, https://ourworldindata.org/meat-production.
130. Richie and Roser, Meat and dairy production.
131. Leiva, M. (2022) Meat consumption is unsustainable, so why is it still increasing? https://www.investmentmonitor.ai/sectors/agribusiness/meat-consumption-is-unsustainable-so-why-is-it-still-increasing.

132. Chang, H. (2008) *Bad Samaritans: The Guilty Secrets of Rich Nations and the Threat to Global Prosperity*, Random House, London.
133. Reddy, B. and Assenza, G. (2009) Climate change—A developing country perspective, *Current Science* 97(1): 50–62.
134. Businesses in the US have joined forces in powerful lobby groups to oppose legislation to reduce greenhouse gasses and to oppose the Kyoto and Paris agreements. See Wikipedia. (2022) Climate change denial, https://en.wikipedia.org/wiki/Climate_change_denial.
135. Jezard, A. (2017) Fossil fuels will still dominate energy in 20 years despite green power rising, https://www.weforum.org/agenda/2017/10/fossil-fuels-will-dominate-energy-in-2040/.
136. Stern, D. and Ahmed, K. (2023) China is pumping out carbon emissions as if COVID never happened. That's bad news for the climate crisis, https://theconversation.com/china-is-pumping-out-carbon-emissions-as-if-covid-never-happened-thats-bad-news-for-the-climate-crisis-207933.
137. Street, P. (2019) Russiagate trumps environmental catastrophe for the dismal Democrats, *Red Flag*, 4 June, p. 18.
138. Climate Action Tracker. (2022) Climate Action Tracker, https://climateanalytics.org/what-we-do/climate-action-tracker/.
139. Evans, M. (2019) Racing towards a climate catastrophe, *NTEU Advocate* 26(2): 26.
140. Carrington, D. and Taylor, M. (2021) Revealed: The 'carbon bombs' set to trigger catastrophic climate breakdown, https://www.theguardian.com/environment/ng-interactive/2022/may/11/fossil-fuel-carbon-bombs-climate-breakdown-oil-gas.
141. Conley, J. (2021) Will Biden continue drilling boom on public lands despite campaign pledge? https://www.laprogressive.com/climate-change-2/drilling-boom-on-public-lands.
142. Newburger, E. (2023) Biden Interior approves controversial Alaskan oil drilling project, https://www.cnbc.com/2023/03/13/biden-interior-approves-controversial-alaska-oil-drilling-project.html.

143. Lakhani, N. (2023) Fossil fuel firms owe climate reparations of $209bn a year, says study, https://www.theguardian.com/environment/2023/may/19/fossil-fuel-firms-owe-climate-reparations-of-209bn-a-year-says-study.
144. Lakhani, Fossil fuel firms owe climate reparations of $209bn a year, says study.
145. Monbiot, G. (2023) Here's the truth about Sunak's plans for the North Sea: he will sell out the planet to the dirtiest bidders, https://www.theguardian.com/commentisfree/2023/aug/01/rishi-sunak-north-sea-planet-climate-crisis-plutocrats.
146. Monbiot, G. (2022) Environmental destruction is part of Liz Truss's plan, https://www.theguardian.com/commentisfree/2022/sep/30/environmental-destruction-is-part-of-liz-trusss-plan.
147. Erdem, S. (2022) Slasher Truss scares the Greens with her climate illiteracy, https://www.theneweuropean.co.uk/liz-truss-environment-policies-suna-erdem/.
148. Smith, S. (2022) End to EU laws, mini-budget and farming review an 'attack on nature', https://www.independent.co.uk/climate-change/news/environmentalists-citizens-assembly-rspb-national-trust-wwf-b2178748.html.
149. Smith, S. (2022) What will Rishi Sunak as prime minister mean for the climate? https://news.yahoo.com/rishi-sunak-prime-minister-mean-095851946.html.
150. Stickings, T. (2023) Rishi Sunak aiming to 'max out' North Sea oil and gas developments, https://www.independent.co.uk/news/uk/politics/rishi-sunak-net-zero-2050-b2384753.html.
151. Walker, P. (2023) New North Sea oil and gas licences will send 'wrecking ball' through climate commitments, https://www.theguardian.com/environment/2023/jul/31/rishi-sunak-approval-100-new-north-sea-oil-and-gas-licences-fossil-fuel-climate-crisis.
152. Bradner, E. (2023) Trump sidesteps question when asked if he plans to abuse power if reelected, https://edition.cnn.com/2023/12/05/politics/trump-2024-fox-town-hall/index.html; Stone, P. (2024) Trump's $1bn pitch to oil bosses 'the definition of corruption', top Democrat says, http://newsrounds.econaiplus.com/top-democrat-says-Trump-ibn-pitch-to-oil-bosses-the-definition-of-corruption/.

153. Pearse, G. (2012) *Greenwash: Big Brands and Carbon Scams*, Black Inc., Victoria, p. 241.
154. Quoted in Braterman, P. (2020) 'God intended it as a disposable planet': Meet the US pastor preaching climate change denial, https://theconversation.com/god-intended-it-as-a-disposable-planet-meet-the-us-pastor-preaching-climate-change-denial-147712.
155. Roser-Renouf, C., Maibach, E., Leiserowitz, A. and Rosenthal, S. (2016) Global warming, God and the "end times", https://climatecommunication.yale.edu/publications/global-warming-god-end-times/.
156. Geselbracht, D. (2021) For some evangelical Christians, climate action is a God-given mandate, https://fore.yale.edu/news/For-some-evangelical-Christians-climate-action-is-a-God-given-mandate; Wikipedia, Climate change denial.
157. Phillips, T. (2016) Climate change a Chinese hoax? Beijing gives Donald Trump a lesson in history, https://www.theguardian.com/us-news/2016/nov/17/climate-change-a-chinese-plot-beijing-gives-donald-trump-a-history-lesson.
158. Cunanan, P. (2018) 5 key tactics climate change deniers use and how to counter climate change denial, https://ecowarriorprincess.net/2018/03/key-tactics-climate-change-deniers-use-how-counter-climate-denial/.
159. Wikipedia, Climate change denial.
160. Nuccitelli, D. (2015) Fiddling with global warming conspiracy theories while Rome burns, https://www.theguardian.com/environment/climate-consensus-97-per-cent/2015/feb/11/fiddling-with-global-warming-conspiracies-while-rome-burns.
161. Geselbracht, For some evangelical Christians, climate action is a God-given mandate.
162. Wikipedia. (2023) The Global Warming Policy Foundation, https://en.wikipedia.org/wiki/The_Global_Warming_Policy_Foundation.
163. Quoted in Wikipedia, The Global Warming Policy Foundation, and also see Shenker, J. (2021) Meet the 'inactivists', tangling up the climate crisis in culture wars, https://www.theguardian.com/environment/2021/nov/11/inactivists-tangling-up-the-climate-crisis-in-culture-wars-manston-airport-kent.

164. Coan, T., Boussalis, C., Cook, J. and Nanko, M. (2021) Computer-assisted classification of contrarian claims about climate change, *Scientific Reports* 11(22320), https://doi.org/10.1038/s41598-021-01714-4; Cook, J., Ellerton, P. and Kinkead, D. (2018) Deconstructing climate misinformation to identify reasoning errors, *Environmental Research Letters* 13(2): 024018. https://doi.org/10.1088/1748-9326/aaa49f.
165. Douglas, K. and Sutton, R. (2015) Climate change: Why the conspiracy theories are dangerous, *Bulletin of Atomic Scientists* 71(2): 98–106; Uscinski, J., Douglas, K. and Lewandowsky, S. (2017) Climate change conspiracy theories, *Climate Science*, https://doi.org/10.1093/acrefore/9780190228620.013.328.
166. Yoder, K. (2021) Climate change deniers are over attacking the science. Now they attack the solutions, https://grist.org/politics/study-charts-show-rising-attacks-on-clean-energy-and-climate-policy/.
167. Gleick, P. (2020) Book review: Bad science and bad arguments about in 'Apocalypse Never' by Michael Shellenberger, https://yaleclimateconnections.org/2020/07/review-bad-science-and-bad-arguments-abound-in-apocalypse-never/.
168. The so-called 'watermelon' allusion—environmentalists are green on the outside but red in the middle. See also Hornsey, M., Harris, E. and Fielding, K. (2018) Relationships among conspiratorial beliefs, conservatism and climate scepticism across nations, *Nature Climate Change* 8: 614–620.
169. Oreskes, N. and Conway, E. (2010) *Merchants of Doubt: How a Handful of Scientists Obscured the Truth on Issues from Tobacco Smoke to Global Warming*, Bloomsbury, New York.
170. Coan, Boussalis, Cook and Nanko, Computer-assisted classification of contrarian claims about climate change.
171. Oreskes and Conway, *Merchants of Doubt*.
172. Uscinski, Douglas and Lewandowsky, Climate change conspiracy theories; Beder, S. (1997) *Global Spin: The Corporate Assault on Environmentalism*, Scribe, Melbourne, pp. 91–115.
173. Douglas and Sutton, Climate change.

174. Cook, Ellerton, and Kinkead, Deconstructing climate misinformation to identify reasoning errors.
175. Quoted in Uscinski, Douglas and Lewandowsky, Climate change conspiracy theories.
176. Meyer, R. (2019) There's snow on TV, so Trump's tweeting about climate change, https://www.theatlantic.com/science/archive/2019/01/its-cold-so-trump-is-doubting-climate-change/580885/; Rainforest Alliance. (2021) 6 claims made by climate change skeptics—and how to respond, https://www.rainforest-alliance.org/everyday-actions/6-claims-made-by-climate-change-skeptics-and-how-to-respond/.
177. Maslin, M. (2019) The five corrupt pillars of climate change denial, https://theconversation.com/the-five-corrupt-pillars-of-climate-change-denial-122893.
178. The Climate Reality Project. (2019) The climate denial machine: How the fossil fuel industry blocks climate action, https://www.climaterealityproject.org/blog/climate-denial-machine-how-fossil-fuel-industry-blocks-climate-action.
179. Wikipedia, Climate change denial.
180. Wikipedia, Climate change denial.
181. DeSmog. (2022) George C. Marshall Institute, https://www.desmog.com/george-c-marshall-institute/.
182. SourceWatch. (2022) State Policy Network, https://www.sourcewatch.org/index.php?title=State_Policy_Network.
183. Robbins, D. (2014) Myths and facts about the Koch brothers, https://www.mediamatters.org/washington-post/myths-and-facts-about-koch-brothers.
184. Pilkington, E. (2013) Facebook and Microsoft help fund rightwing lobby network, report finds, https://www.theguardian.com/world/2013/nov/14/facebook-microsoft-rightwing-lobby-network-spn.
185. Robbins, Myths and facts about the Koch brothers.
186. Wikipedia. (2022) Charles Koch, https://en.wikipedia.org/wiki/Charles_Koch.

187. Kopan, T. (2013) Report: Think tanks tied to Kochs, https://www.politico.com/story/2013/11/koch-brothers-think-tank-report-099791.
188. Beder, *Global Spin*, p. 92; Wikipedia has reported in 2022 that Charles now considers human activities are having some impact upon global warming. However, he firmly believes any government action to improve things will be doomed to failure. It is all-American know how and technology that are the keys—see Wikipedia, Charles Koch.
189. The Climate Reality Project, The climate denial machine.
190. The Heartland Institute. (2022) NIPCC, http://climatechangereconsidered.org/about-the-nipcc/.
191. The Heartland Institute, NIPCC.
192. The Heartland Institute, NIPCC.
193. Robbins, Myths and facts about the Koch brothers.
194. Robbins, Myths and facts about the Koch brothers.
195. Robbins, Myths and facts about the Koch brothers.
196. Robbins, Myths and facts about the Koch brothers.
197. Leonard, C. (2019) *Kochland: The Secret History of Koch Industries and Corporate Power in America*, Simon and Schuster, London, pp. 400–413.
198. Beder, *Global Spin*, pp. 107–121.
199. Beder, *Global Spin*, p. 113.
200. GRAIN. (2022) An agribusiness greenwashing glossary, https://grain.org/en/article/6877-an-agribusiness-greenwashing-glossary.
201. Feik, N. (2024) Climate change policy, *Journal of Australian Political Economy* 92: 226.
202. Feik, Climate change policy, p. 226.
203. World Economic Forum. (2020) What is green finance and why is it important? https://www.weforum.org/agenda/2020/11/what-is-green-finance/.
204. GRAIN, An agribusiness greenwashing glossary.
205. Brulle, R. and Werthman, C. (2021) The role of public relations firms in climate change politics, *Climate Change* 169(1–2), https://doi.org/10.1007/s10584-021-03244-4.

206. DeSmog. (2022) Global Climate Coalition, https://www.desmog.com/global-climate-coalition/.
207. Fisher, A. (2021) In 2021 Fox News is still spreading dangerous climate denial, https://www.mediamatters.org/fox-news/2021-fox-news-still-spreading-dangerous-climate-denial.
208. Fisher, In 2021 Fox News is still spreading dangerous climate denial; Stiglitz, J. (2020) Are we overreacting on climate change? https://www.nytimes.com/2020/07/16/books/review/bjorn-lomborg-false-alarm-joseph-stiglitz.html.
209. Reported in Fisher, In 2021 Fox News is still spreading dangerous climate denial.
210. Reported in Fisher, In 2021 Fox News is still spreading dangerous climate denial.
211. See Fisher, In 2021 Fox News is still spreading dangerous climate denial.
212. Muller, D. (2022) As News Corp goes 'rogue' on election coverage, what price will Australian democracy pay? https://theconversation.com/as-news-corp-goes-rogue-on-election-coverage-what-price-will-australian-democracy-pay-181599.
213. Paul, K. (2021) 'Super polluters': The top 10 publishers denying the climate change crisis on Facebook, https://www.theguardian.com/technology/2021/nov/02/super-polluters-the-top-10-publishers-denying-the-climate-crisis-on-facebook.
214. Paul, 'Super polluters'.
215. Quoted in Paul, 'Super polluters'.
216. Bacon, W. and Jegan, A. (2020) Sceptical Climate: Lies, Debates, and Silences—How News Corp produces climate scepticism in Australia, https://climate-report.wendybacon.com/part-3/.
217. Bacon and Jegan, Sceptical climate.
218. Hornsey, M. (2021) The role of worldviews in shaping how people appraise climate change, *Current Opinion in Behavioural Sciences* 42: 36–41.
219. Bacon and Jegan, Sceptical climate.
220. Mocatta, G. (2021) What's behind News Corp's new spin on climate change? https://theconversation.com/whats-behind-news-corps-new-spin-on-climate-change-169733.

5

The Power to Lie: Propaganda and Post-truth Politics

President George W. Bush, the 43rd President of the United States of America, was at his enigmatic best when he said of his nation:

> We'll be a land where the fabric is made up of groups and loving centers.

But he was much more forthcoming in his pronouncement that

> Intelligence gathered by this and other governments leaves no doubt that the Iraq regime continues to possess and conceal some of the most lethal weapons ever devised ... weapons of mass destruction.[1]

Don't be discouraged if you cannot decipher the first quote—I imagine the former President, himself, would struggle to clarify its meaning. It was one of his famous 'Bushisms'—one of his incoherent, but largely innocent, bumblings that occurred throughout his time in office.[2] As my Aussie compatriots would certainly have conjectured at the time—was there a kangaroo loose in the top paddock?

But the second was a much clearer and more profound statement. It was a lie that cost the lives of an estimated 2.4 million Iraqis, 189,000 US soldiers, and resulted in the dislocation of some 9 million Iraqi citizens who were displaced or who currently reside in refugee camps outside the country. It cost the American taxpayers US$2 trillion.[3] It was not only the lie about Saddam Hussein's possession of WMDs but about the very purpose of the war. It appears the war was *not* about destroying the WMDs. As former assistant secretary of the British civil service, John Chapman, explained:

> There were only two credible reasons for invading Iraq: control over oil and preservation of the dollar as the world's reserve currency ... By invading Iraq, Bush [took] over the Iraqi oil fields, and persuaded the UN to lift production limits imposed after the Kuwait war.[4]

The US was looking for a decisive victory in Iraq that would frighten any oil-producing nation from erring away from a position that challenged US hegemony. It didn't get the decisive victory, but it did get Saddam Hussein. Before the invasion the then Secretary of Defense, Donald Rumsfeld, stated that removing Saddam Hussein would 'enhance US credibility and influence throughout the region', thereby demonstrating 'what US policy is all about'.[5] We now all clearly know what US policy is about.

The US seems to enjoy a good dust-up. Since its formation in 1776 the US has been involved in some 225 internal and external conflicts—and this excludes the 'war on drugs' and the 'war on terror'. That is 225 of its 243-year existence, a very handsome average of 93% of its history.[6] If the ruling class of the US were to open a shopfront in some downtown mall, it would surely carry the name 'Wars-R-Us'.

And, in relation to the issue of societal deception, two-thirds of US interventions have been clandestine operations involving deployments to such nations as—in alphabetical order—Albania, Brazil, Bulgaria, El Salvador, Greece, Guatemala, Haiti, Iran, Israel, Italy, Malta, the Philippines, Romania, and Slovakia.[7] What has the US been doing in these places? Some of the activities include rigging elections, supporting parties that align with American values and, more sinisterly, overthrowing sitting governments. Between 1947 and 1989 some 72 US interventions were undertaken to remove 'undesirable' regimes.[8]

Propaganda has played an important role.

Perfecting Propaganda

Every picture tells a story, and the poster is one of the richest of storytellers. There are some classics from war. The modern trend surely had its beginning in the painting *Memento Marengo* which shows a flowing red-caped Napoleon astride his dashing white horse as he rides into battle. Unfortunately, war didn't turn out well for Napoleon, or for his horse. Marengo was captured at the Battle of Waterloo in 1815 and brought to an English stud. Somehow unable—or reluctant—to breed with English horses, he died at 38 and his skeleton was put on display at the National Army Museum in Chelsea, where it remains without two of its hooves. One hoof became an English snuff box, the other a silver inkwell.[9] But the trend was established—stir up nationalistic sentiments through colourful imagery and patriotic messaging.

One of the best-known posters is the 1914 image of Britain's Lord Kitchener with military cap, handlebar moustache, and stern gaze, his finger pointed directly at the viewer. 'Join your country's army. God save the King'. Kitchener was viewed as masculinity personified—a figure of strength and of 'absolute will and power'.[10] In one of the silliest wars ever waged,[11] over 2.4 million men voluntarily joined the British army between 1914 and 1915, with the Kitchener poster being seen as key in inspiring recruitment.[12] Encouraged by the direct appeal approach, the US launched its own famous poster in 1916, a year before it entered the Great War. This featured a silver-haired, serious looking, Uncle Sam, with a 'white goatee on a chiselled face … bushy eyebrows over burning eyes' in a star-decorated top hat pointing a bony index finger and demanding 'I want You for the U.S. Army'.[13] What red-blooded American male could resist?

Other posters come to mind. One issued during World War II featured a mix of white, black, and brown British patriots marching forward as one to protect the country. We're all in it together—no worries about class or ethnicity. An American Red Cross poster from the same era invited women to knit socks for the boys at war. Carrying the provocative 'Our boys need SOX', it was a great hit with the public. The Russians created a 'Build Tanks' poster with a young couple staring upwards into an unknown world. The aim was to question whether they'd have any future at all if the Nazis prevailed.

Canada produced the curiously ambiguous 'Lick them over there!' poster in 1939 showing a giant soldier, with gun in hand, straddling the ocean between Canada and Europe.[14] American artist Norman Rockwell created the iconic Rosie the Riveter painting in 1943 to praise the work of women in US munitions factories and in other war-effort endeavours. Featured on the cover of the *Saturday Evening Post*, it showed Rosie in faded blue denim, sitting eating her lunch, large rivet gun on lap, with the stars and stripes as a flowing backdrop. Beneath her right shoe was a copy of Hitler's *Mein Kampf*.[15] During the Second World War

> words, posters, and films waged a constant battle for the hearts and minds of the American citizenry ... The Government launched an aggressive propaganda campaign ... Persuading the American public became a wartime industry, almost as important as the manufacturing of bullets and planes.[16]

Writing in 1935 US propaganda analyst O. W. Riegal summed this up nicely:

> The function of the war poster is to make coherent and acceptable a basically incoherent and irrational ordeal of killing, suffering and destruction that violates every accepted principle of morality and decent living.[17]

In pre-World War II Germany, Joseph Goebbels' wonderfully named Ministry of Public Enlightenment and Propaganda controlled the content of newspapers, film, radio, and the theatre throughout the country before and during the Second World War. (Goebbels recognised the word 'propaganda' had negative connotations and wanted it removed from the title. Hitler, who knew exactly what he was doing, would have none of it.) As early as 1933 the Nazi Party ensured only racially pure (Aryan) editors and journalists could publish in the press. In *Mein Kampf* Hitler argued that effective propaganda must always appeal to the 'primitive sentiments of the broad masses' and be limited to 'a few bare essentials' and 'stereotyped formulas', 'always emphasiz[ing] the

5 The Power to Lie: Propaganda and Post-truth Politics

same conclusion'.[18] And what conclusion might he have had in mind? That Jews could not be trusted, were parasitic, subhuman, and must be exterminated. His anti-Semitic message was reproduced in textbooks, film, newsreels, music, the press, and even in children's books. Snow White's father made his mark in film as the leader of an army conquering an 'eastern' enemy. The film appeared one month after Germany invaded Poland.[19] The tale of *Cinderella* was reworked to show how a very perceptive prince knew there was 'alien' blood in the stepmother's daughters and recognised the racial purity of the Nordic young maiden with the slender foot. Little Red Riding Hood sported a cloak emblazoned with swastikas and was saved not by her woodcutter father, but by a soldier in an SS uniform with an uncanny resemblance to Hitler.[20] Grimm, indeed.

Then there were the German posters

> Poster art was a mainstay of the Nazi propaganda effort, aimed both at Germany itself and occupied territories. It had several advantages. The visual effect, being striking, would reach the viewer easily. Posters were also, unlike other forms of propaganda, difficult to avoid.[21]

They were everywhere. A favourite was of young Aryan children looking upward to a bright future—in front of the large image of a steely eyed and determined Führer. Strong white men with laurel crowns featured on 1936 Olympic posters. A sepia-coloured poster features a young German farm worker, with cupped hands to mouth, yelling to the viewer to join Hitler's Youth Landdienst, or agricultural workforce. And for a very good reason—another poster features a different farm worker booting a Jewish man off the land with the title 'German export: Out of our German country with the slimy Jewish band'. They needed more youths for the Youth Landdienst. Disease—and the need to 'cleanse'—were also prominent themes. One, featuring a Jew in the form of a crazed crab-like lunatic, bore the caption 'Tuberculose Syphilis Cancer are curable … It is necessary to finish the biggest curse: The Jew!' Music was not off limits. Black American saxophonists were depicted as monkeys (jazz was deemed a degenerate form of musical expression).[22] Anyway, who needs jazz when free copies of *Mein Kampf* were readily available and given away freely to all soldiers and newlyweds (something that the latter would have gladly poured over on their wedding night).[23]

Through propaganda the Nazis sought to convince the 'white' German population—children, youth, adults, the elderly—that Jews were not only the cause of Germany's (and the world's) problems, but that their annihilation was crucial to German prosperity. This was brainwashing at its best (worst). Jews were demonised and removed from positions of authority and influence in public and professional life. They were viewed as undeserving leeches and treated as such. Propaganda justified the creation of concentration camps, leading to the the subsequent deaths of millions of human beings.

Oh, Those Russians

Totalitarian states are particularly adept at propaganda. By emphasising the absolute power of the leader and the infallibility of the system, a state-controlled media can spread unambiguous messages, without fear of contradiction. Following the October 1917 revolution, a famous poster of Lenin was created showing him sitting atop the world with broom in hand, sweeping emperors, a cleric, and a banker off the globe. 'Comrade Lenin cleanses the earth of filth' was the title, and demonstrated the regime's sincere dislike of the monarchy, religion, and the bourgeois class.[24] Created by the Department of Agitation and Propaganda, the poster was one of hundreds that delivered simple messages to a largely illiterate population. But the purpose was always the same—to convince them they'd been liberated from serfdom by the Bolsheviks.

The creation of *The New Soviet Man* (sic) was the intention of much of the propaganda. The *Man* was hard working, cooperative, selfless, and believed in equality and sacrifice. One ideal was a collective, community, approach to life (as distinct from the petty-bourgeois family unit). Children were taken from families and 'nationalised', including re-socialisation in the school system.[25] The fighting skills of heroes and patriots were lauded but after Stalin took the helm, there emerged a distinctive personality cult around the great man. The state-run press, including *Pravda* (meaning Truth), began labelling him as an inspirational genius, beloved and wise. He was compared to the indomitable twelfth-century Roman emperor Augustus—a powerful leader who could do no wrong. Poets, writers, and artists were enrolled to promote his image. Posters showed him with smiling children, consistent with his newfound status as Father to the nation. Statues appeared throughout Russia. Households dedicated spaces ('Stalin rooms') to hang his portrait.[26] In keeping with this image,

> every event, every celebration, every tradition and every holiday was infused with something recognizable from the past along with Stalin's image. The desired result was always to hold Stalin up and repress everything else.[27]

At 5'5" inches (165 cm) in height, he was a towering figure.

One aim of the Bolsheviks was to create a classless society, with much of the propaganda in posters, the press, and newsreels portraying Soviet workers as the luckiest human beings alive. If they didn't consider themselves lucky—or sought to question Stalinist orthodoxy—they might find themselves, like Solzhenitsyn's Ivan Denisovich, shivering and starving in a Siberian gulag, regretting the errors of their ways. Capitalism was depicted as 'a dead herring—shining as it rotted'.[28] By the time of Khrushchev, a 1960s Socialist Utopia had been fashioned around technological advancement, especially the Soviets' leading performance in the space race. The Soviet Union's propaganda activities abroad had helped to spread conspiracy theories about the assassination of JFK and the death of Hitler, tried to provoke racial tensions in the US by sending phony messages to US citizens from the Ku Klux Klan, and sought to position Martin Luther King Jr. as a fraud who secretly received government payments.[29]

Before its invasion of Ukraine in February 2022, Russia launched a disinformation campaign to persuade its citizens that Ukraine was a failed state, and that Ukraine—in concert with NATO—had plans to attack and destroy Russia. The film *Solntsepyok* ('Sunbaked' in English) appearing in 2021 contained many of the same misleading messages. Ukrainians are depicted as criminal skinheads involved in the senseless murdering and rape of villagers and crying out for the removal of all

Russians. A US general, in league with the Ukrainians, promises to assist. The Ukraine army begins (for no apparent reason) to start dropping bombs on its own people. The main character, the Russian Vlad, has no choice but to pick up a gun and join Ukraine's pro-Russian militia. It is, as film critic Greg Dolgopolov acknowledges, 'a textbook example of propaganda [priming] the Russian audience for the future war'.[30]

At the beginning of the war Russian citizens could tune in to the highly popular *Zvezda* ('The Star') television and radio outlets owned by Russia's Ministry of Defence. Operating 24 hours a day, seven days a week, the concerned populace could learn that the Ukraine was supporting Middle Eastern terrorists, that it was manufacturing chemical and biological weapons, that Europe had intentions to make Ukraine a 'gay colony' and that, due to their poorly run economy, Ukrainians were stealing crumbs from pigeons in order to survive. Oh, and that the Ukraine army was full of Nazi zombies.[31] That well-known dictatorial kleptocrat Vladimir Putin—who has amassed billions of dollars during his presidency[32]—compared himself to Peter the Great who, 300 years earlier, conquered foreign territories, taking back what was 'rightfully' Russia's. It was only reasonable that the new tsar would seek to restore balance. But, in a caring manner, he ordered not a full-scale, bloody, and brutal invasion of Ukraine. Rather it was pitched as a 'special military operation' designed to bring the wayward nation back into the loving arms of the Soviet state.[33] The invasion was based on the lie that Ukraine posed a serious threat to Russia. Putin's real intention was to sure up the security of his regime, and to protect his own position, while promoting the ideology of Russia's cultural greatness, the benefits of nationalist statism, and the nation's on-going struggle against western forces.[34]

Chinese Checkers

You haven't really lived until you have thumbed through a copy of Chairman Mao Zedong's *Little Red Book* (currently available on Amazon for under US$10). Replete with such gems as 'To read too many books is harmful', 'war can only be abolished through war', 'communism is not love. Communism is a hammer', 'a revolution is not a dinner party', and

5 The Power to Lie: Propaganda and Post-truth Politics

'if you want to know the taste of a pear, you must change the pear by eating it yourself' (WTF?), the book is the second biggest seller of all time (after the *Bible*, and just before *The Quran*, *The Lord of the Rings*, and *Harry Potter and the Philosopher's Stone*). It has sold over one billion copies.[35]

A compilation of quotations drawn from Mao's 40 years as a revolutionary and national leader, the book was made small enough to be placed in the pocket of a shirt, close to the beating Chinese heart. Like *Mein Kampf*, the *Little Red Book* was foisted on unsuspecting comrades at the slightest opportunity. Quotations were studied and repeated in schools, factories and in military bunkers. Readings were held on buses, while Chinese air hostesses found themselves preaching the words of Mao to captive audiences at 30,000 feet. Long-term imprisonment would befall anyone found to have damaged or destroyed the sacred text. The *Little Red Book* was expected to be carried by all Chinese during the Great Proletarian Cultural Revolution from 1966 to 1976. The Cultural Revolution aimed to purge enemies of the state and anyone with bourgeois inclinations, and Mao's Red Guards would regularly check to see if suspect citizens were carrying the book and if they could recite passages from it.[36] Mao wanted to reinvigorate his nation but, alas,

> the Cultural Revolution crippled the economy, ruined millions of lives and thrust China into 10 years of turmoil, bloodshed, hunger and stagnation.[37]

The aim of the book had been to indoctrinate the population—to have everyone, literally, 'reading from the same page'. It was an attempt at 'controlling information [to] control a whole culture'.[38] Yet, it was a major propaganda failure, seen today as a contributor to a decade of chaos in which up to two million Chinese were killed.[39] It was withdrawn from circulation in China in 1979 with over 100 million copies subsequently pulped—a major win for the recycling industry, rather than for the proliferation of Mao's idiosyncratic messages.

But the book was only one bullet in Mao's artillery. Film, print media, posters, cultural arts, the education curriculum, and work study groups, were all means of inculcating 'socialist' values. After Mao's death in 1976

Deng Xiaoping began his own propaganda campaign to convince people of the virtues of 'socialism with Chinese characteristics'. He abandoned many accepted doctrines of the Party and began liberalising sections of the economy, only to be told he'd gone too far following the protests and massacre at Tiananmen Square. Stronger propaganda would be required to contain protest.

By the 1990s mass communication was the tool-of-choice for those in power in China. Combining public relations ideas and techniques, social psychology, advertising, and state-based education, the Chinese state sought to convince its citizens of their progress under socialism. The 2008 summer Olympics allowed them to showcase their nation's economic and sporting prowess and, a year later they went global with a multi-billion dollar western-style news campaign to persuade the world of China's leading international role.[40] The Chinese government has tight control over all media content and regularly issues statements that attack democracy, delegitimise pro-independence movements in Tibet and Taiwan, and censor outside criticism of Chinese government policies. The state owned and run Xinhua News Agency has been described as 'the world's biggest propaganda agency', largely employing soft power to convince audiences at home and abroad of the government's peaceful intentions and pursuit of harmonious relations with competing powers.[41] In 2021 Xi Jinping's four volume set *Thought on Socialism with Chinese Characteristics for the New Era* was released for consumption by students from primary school to university, with teachers and instructors required to 'plant the seeds of loving the party, the country and socialism in young hearts'[42]—a TikTok hope for a media-savvy generation. With such inspiration from the leader, it is no wonder the Chinese Communist Party has deemed that Xi can rule forever.

Living the Dream

Fortunately, there is nothing like Soviet or Chinese propaganda in the Land of the Free and the Home of the Brave. *Un*fortunately, the US has its own style of propaganda and it is just as, or even more, effective than that employed in the socialist states. We learned earlier of the power of the Uncle Sam recruitment poster in the First World War. What is less well-known is that Woodrow Wilson's Committee on Public Information (CPI), formed by the president at the same time, produced and disseminated propaganda designed to cement and enhance the policies of Wilson's administration. Created without congressional approval the CPI released

> a gusher of tendentious handouts [including] pamphlets, books, syndicated articles, posters, advertisements, cartoons and films.[43]

Enlisted to disseminate messages were university professors, labour organisations, travelling salespersons, and members of the Boy Scouts. The aims were threefold—to generate nationalistic fervour, to mobilise public opinion behind America's entry into the Great War, and to denigrate Germans and Germany. The CPI created a carefully crafted image of America designed to inspire patriotism. Americans were positioned as civic citizens, placing public duties and responsibilities before all else. They believed in equality of opportunity, the family unit, community obligation, and an 'utter belief in principles of American democracy'.[44] (This was all before neoliberalism, of course, justifying and lauding personal greed.)

The US was home to millions of first- and second-generation Germans and Irish. Many Germans supported their mother country. Most of the Irish despised Britain. Others in the US were pacifists. None wanted US troops fighting alongside Britain and against Germany. So, government-produced anti-German posters did the rounds. One showed a German soldier as a wild-eyed ape with flashing teeth, bloodied club in hand, holding a helpless young maiden. The top caption was 'Destroy this mad brute' and the lower caption 'Enlist'. Other showed 'Huns' as 'kidnappers and frightening giants' and battlegrounds 'strewn with molested women, set against the backdrops of burning cities—all aimed to stir emotion rather than any rational judgement'.[45] As with much propaganda, the state was crafting and controlling knowledge.

During the Second World War, the propaganda tool-of-choice of the Roosevelt government was the quasi-independent Writers' War Board

(WWB). Just as in First World War there were many in the US who did not favour intervention, so the WWB's main task was to convince them otherwise. A monthly report was prepared and sent to thousands of journalists, writers, and broadcasters throughout the US, detailing the stories they should focus upon in their writings and talks. The WWB sent draft editorials to newspapers, presenting the war effort in a positive light. 'War scripts' were sent to schools and radio stations, prepared speeches were delivered to politicians, and drafts of cartoons were sent to artists for later publication in newspapers and magazines. Because the WWB presented stories from many different writers using many different angles, its work was 'not easily identifiable as a concerted effort to influence public opinion'.[46] The WWB became, at the time, 'the greatest propaganda machine in history'.[47]

During the Cold War years beginning in the 1950s, the US government created propaganda to disparage the Soviet Union and its allies. It did this through outlets such as television, music, and literature. One famous video sent to schools across America was 'How to spot a Communist'. (It's not that easy, as some work 'silently'.)[48] Senator Joseph McCarthy of Wisconsin knew exactly how to spot one. He saw them in sleeper cells in important institutions such as government departments, the military, universities, and the film industry. At the height of McCarthyism in the early 1950s, thousands of people were accused of having communist sympathies, government workers were dismissed from their posts, and screenwriters, film producers and actors were either blacklisted or sent to gaol. Even the creator of Mickey Mouse and the B-grade actor who would later become President of the United States found themselves before investigating committees. School children were taught to dive under their desks to escape the enemy—in so-called duck and cover drills. In a somewhat bizarre form of propaganda, Mosinee, a small town in Wisconsin, was 'invaded' on May 1, 1950 by a group of returned US servicemen dressed in trench coats and pretending to be Soviet soldiers.

> The mock Reds heralded their arrival by arresting Mosinee's mayor and chief of police. These 'arrested' local officials were marched to the town's main intersection, renamed 'Red Square', and subjected to a mock

trial. Local priests were also arrested and detained behind barbed-wire. 'Communists' took over the town library, confiscating most of its books. They forced the local cinema to show Russian propaganda films. Local restaurants were ordered to take hamburgers and steaks off the menu and replace them with coarse black bread and potato soup.[49]

(They should have kept hamburgers on the menu: they actually had their beginnings in Russia and Mongolia.)[50] McCarthy found his 'sinister types' lurking throughout America; they had a particular penchant for hiding under beds. He and his cronies had tapped directly into America's fear of communism—something which had become a national paranoia. His only positive legacy was that, following the Cold War era, Hollywood started producing some clever, subtle, spoofs of the Red Scare, including the *Invasion of the Body Snatchers* (1978) and *The Thing* (1982).

In Vietnam during the 1960s, the US dropped billions of leaflets telling of the perils of possible communist domination. It also paid musicians and actors to go deep into the jungles to convince the locals of the virtues of democracy, as represented by the government in Saigon. But many Vietnamese recognised the government in Saigon as a puppet regime, and they viewed the US as just another colonial power, no better than the French who had dominated the region for over six decades. The French had justified their presence as a 'civilising mission', to bring the region out of its supposed backwardness and penury while, all the time, exacting profits, exploiting labour, and destroying local culture.[51] Although US propaganda failed to impress, that of local citizens did. The Vietnamese produced posters showing women in rice paddies firing on the US invaders, pictures of a smiling 'Uncle Ho' (Ho Chi Minh), and US planes being shot out of the sky. Cultural icons like the lotus flower and white doves symbolised the peace they wished for.[52] Meanwhile, a photograph of Vietnamese children running naked and scarred from blazing fires triggered by napalm dropped by American aircraft was not great publicity for the war, back home.[53] The Pulitzer Prize-winning photo of the 'Napalm Girl', published in 1973, is considered to have hastened the end of the war, with the US's humiliating withdrawal occurring later that year.[54] (In 2004 street artist Banksy produced a print showing the black-and-white photo of the Napalm Girl skipping somewhat unhappily between coloured images of Mickey Mouse and Ronald McDonald—juxtaposing the horrors of warfare with the joys of consumer capitalism.)

Iraq invaded Kuwait in 1990, yet again heralding Middle Eastern oil production instability that would affect Americans (spot oil prices rose from US$21 to US$40 a barrel in the three months following the invasion).[55] But the US needed reasons, other than self-interest, to become involved in the war. At home, in the US, a supposedly grassroots organisation known as Citizens for a Free Kuwait was formed. Funded by some US$11 million of Kuwaiti government money, the Citizens used their funds to hire the global marketing firm Hill+Knowlton, with the latter producing news releases, TV videos, 'Free Kuwait' T-shirts and bumper stickers, and paying speakers to visit college campuses. A delegation was also sent to Congress.[56] One woman from the Citizens told Congress of Iraqi soldiers entering Kuwaiti hospitals and throwing babies out of incubators onto the floor. It was unimaginable, unthinkable, that she might have been telling fibs. But alas. The woman turned out to be a member of Kuwait's Royal Family and the daughter of Kuwait's US Ambassador—she wasn't even in Kuwait at the time.[57] While Hill+Knowlton's 'baby-atrocity routine [had] won over the hearts', something else was needed for the sceptics, so the Pentagon employed other tactics:

> … [flooding] the major media outlets with reports of a top-secret satellite image that allegedly showed 250,000 Iraqi troops and 1,500 tanks amassed at the Iraqi-Saudi border. Once again, this was misinformation … Commercially available … shots of the exact same region, during the same time frame, revealed no Iraqi soldiers anywhere near the border.[58]

Hill+Knowlton had lied. The military had lied. But it was too late for a change of course. Convinced Senators approved the US involvement and troops were sent to the region in 1990. Hill+Knowlton—whose clients have included tobacco firm Philip Morris, the Church of Scientology, and the money-laundering Bank of Credit and Commerce International[59]—had done a splendid job in improving the (otherwise tainted) image of the Kuwaiti royals, and in depicting Saddam Hussein as a brutal murderer, one coming from the same mould as Adolf Hitler.

Saddam's demonisation would later become crucial in the American public's support for the war in Iraq.

The Iraq war commenced in 2003 after the US convinced some 50 nations to join its Coalition of the Willing. The Coalition was presented as multilateralism at its best. However, many of the 'willing' were victims of US bullying, bribery, and coercion. You want our development dollars? You do as we say.[60] The pretext for war was, as described earlier, that Saddam Hussein's regime possessed weapons of mass destruction—weapons that could be used by the dictator at any time against the US. But the motivation was deeper. The US had experienced a terrorist act of unbelievable devastation on the 11th of September 2001 when al-Qaeda-based extremists captured four passenger planes and flew two of them into the Twin Tower buildings of the World Trade Centre in New York. (A third plane hit the Pentagon and a fourth crashed in a field in Pennsylvania.) The death toll at all sites amounted to 2,977 (not including the 19 hijackers).[61] In response to the atrocity, the US administration under George W. Bush vowed to track down—and either capture or kill—al-Qaeda's leader Osama Bin Laden. Bush declared that Iraq (along with Iran and North Korea) formed an 'axis of evil' bent on poisoning their own citizens and developing nerve gas and nuclear weapons that would threaten the world order.

Saddam's regime had earlier been forced to comply with various UN resolutions to remove weapons of mass destruction, something Bush believed was not occurring. Bush claimed

> Iraq continues to flaunt its hostility toward America and to support terror ... This is a regime that has something to hide from the civilized world ... Saddam Hussein's regime is a grave and gathering danger.[62]

But the UN weapon inspectors who had carried out a detailed on-ground examination of Iraq's military sites concluded that the nation did not possess chemical, biological or, indeed, nuclear, weapons. In 2003 Bush announced that Saddam had sought to purchase uranium from Africa— a lie, as it turned out. But it was enough to push the Coalition of the Willing into war with Iraq. Baghdad fell in April 2003, a month after the invasion. The invasion violated international law, with the US failing to obtain support for its actions from the UN. But, in the US, the constant repetition of the phrases 'Iraq', '9/11', and 'war on terror' convinced the majority of Americans that Iraq was a terrorist nation.[63]

While the administration had controlled the language and had framed the argument for war, behind the scenes the neoconservative US think tank Project for a New American Century (PNAC) played a clandestine role,[64] feeding propaganda on Iraq to an amenable US press that would repeat, uncritically, various claims designed to put fear into the public and to soften them up for the forthcoming war:

> The PNAC was very influential in changing U.S. foreign policy as well as promoting favourable news coverage about going to war with Iraq … [Its] propaganda campaign … convince[d] the American people that attacking Iraq was tantamount to attacking 'terrorists' … The American people were not aware of the story behind this push.[65]

The invasion was a furphy, based on the weapons-of-mass-destruction lie, the falsehood Iraq was trying to procure uranium to manufacture nuclear weapons, and that the Iraqis were somehow linked to the destruction of the Twin Towers. These were fabrications, false pretences for war. As was suggested in the beginning of this chapter, the real purpose of war was to allow the US to reduce global oil vulnerabilities and price fluctuations by policing the Persian Gulf. The method to achieve this? Regime change in Iraq. But yet another—equally plausible—explanation also emerged at the time. George W. Bush simply hated Saddam and Iraq. He publicly stated at a US fundraiser that 'they tried to kill my daddy'.[66] After his capture in December 2003, the evil Saddam got his comeuppance. He was purportedly forced by US marines to watch—repeatedly—the South Park movie which depicts him as the gay boyfriend of Satan.[67]

It is estimated that between 4.5 and 4.6 million people have been killed by US and allied forces in Afghanistan, Iraq, Libya, Pakistan, Somalia, Syria, and Yemen since the post 9/11 attack, with another 3.7 million people having died indirectly from disease and squalor associated with war displacement.[68] And it is women and children who have suffered the most.[69]

Meanwhile, the propaganda has continued apace. Many of us know of the US military-industrial complex—the intricate entwining of the Pentagon and the commercial industries producing the weapons of war. The relationship is strengthened when ex-military officers take on jobs with defence contractors, when the CEOs from the giant companies (Boeing, Lockhead Martin, Northrop Grunman, and General Dynamics among them) cosy up to politicians, and when a warmongering media put fear into the hearts of citizens, helping governments to justify increased defence budgets and, ultimately, attacks on foreign territories. An 'iron triangle' between government officials, lawmakers, and the heads of various military manufacturers, ensures that the weapons (and company profits) just keep coming. And you, too, can get in on the act. Whether your preference is joint light tactical vehicles, hypersonic missiles, or nuclear-powered Virginia-class attack submarines, you can't go wrong with a share portfolio in war, according to *The New York Times*.[70] How could you not profit when the US government spends one-sixth of its yearly budget (some US$700 billion) on defence?[71] But a forgotten element in all of this is another 'complex', the so-called military-entertainment complex which produces the propaganda that justifies defence expenditure, and helps recruit personnel.[72]

It works like this. The US Department of Defense (DoD) seeks constantly to improve the image of the military in the eyes of the public. In doing so it works closely with the film and television industry to create the 'right' images for viewer consumption. In fact, many Hollywood productions are overseen by the Entertainment Media Unit set up within the Pentagon. How many productions? At least 800 in a recent count.[73] Notable entries include *The Green Berets* (1968), *Top Gun* (1986), *Last Action Hero* (1993), *Air Force One* (1997), *Black Hawk Down* (2001), and *Top Gun: Maverick* (2022). As US journalist Johnny Rico has asked

> Where can you rent the use of two B-2 bombers, two F-16 fighter jets, a National Airborne Operations Center, three Marine CH-53E helicopters, a UH-60 Army helicopter, four ground vehicles, 50 Marines, and oh, yes, an aircraft carrier for just one million dollars?
> Answer: The Pentagon[74]

The arsenal above was put together for the making of the 2002 movie *The Sum of All Fears*, an adaptation of the Tom Clancy novel and starring Ben Affleck as war hero Jack Ryan. Taxpayers' money was, and is, being spent to underwrite 'positive' images of the US militia. But, in terms of reciprocation, movies like *The Sum of All Fears* could not have afforded to be made *without* the generous support of the military. Other films did not receive subsidies—*The Deer Hunter* (1978) and *Platoon* (1986) among them. Why? Both films were explicitly anti-war. The DoD also provided equipment used in many of the Bond-franchise films (including *Licence to Kill* (1989), *GoldenEye* (1995), and *Tomorrow Never Dies* (1997)) and made changes to scripts where it was considered necessary.[75] The DoD states its main purposes in working with filmmakers are twofold—'to accurately depict military stories and make sure sensitive information isn't disclosed'.[76] But what did the Department hope to achieve, you might ask, when it put the public's resources to work in *Indiana Jones and the Last Crusade* (1989), *Batman and Robin* (1997), *King Kong* (2005), and *Wonder Woman 1984* (2020)? Why did the military allow Katy Perry to train with marine commandos at Pendleton's Camp Horno, use an M-16, and practise grappling moves, for her 2012 music video 'Part of Me'?[77] We could say 'who cares, it is better to make movies, not war'. But manipulations are often less than innocent. When the CIA secretly purchased the rights to the 1954 animated film *Animal Farm*, it clearly believed the story needed a makeover.

> As part of its cultural offensive against Godless Communism, the CIA … stipulated that any trace of heroism, intelligence, or sympathy be erased from the characters, lest the audience have too much affection for quasi-communists. As such, the ending of the film was radically altered from that of the book, with the cynical donkey Benjamin leading a revolt to retake Manor Farm - showing the triumph of the individual over collectivism.[78]

Pigs should never win. Orwell clearly got his own ending wrong.

Another feature of the military-entertainment complex is the use of computer software for war game simulation. The entertainment industry is replete with clever, life-like, computer games which are subsequently harnessed for military use. Real-time combat strategy games have been one creation; the flight simulator for the training of pilots has been another (which is, of course, an excellent idea). To assist in such developments, DoD funds went directly to entertainment firms to develop computer graphics and three-dimensional navigation in 'virtual' war-like environments. Mutual benefit extends from virtual reality to multimedia to multisensory extended realities.[79]

But does the Pentagon's use of public money to subsidise movies make a difference? It certainly does for recruiting. The original *Top Gun* was so successful with young audiences that the Air Force began running recruitment ads before the start of each screening. Navy recruitment stands were also located next to theatres.[80] The film's release resulted in a 500% increase in applications from would-be navy aviators.[81] The hugely popular film made US$344 million at the box office, helped to rehabilitate the military's tarnished Vietnam War reputation and, more importantly, gave a new generation of American movie-goers a reason to 'love war'.[82] When *Captain Marvel* was released in 2019 the US Air Force ran a parallel campaign to recruit females. It worked. Girls wanted to be Carol Danvers and do their bit for intergalactic peace. Following the film's release the Air Force received its highest number of female applicants in five years.[83] And, Katy Perry's combat-blackened face was viewed as excellent publicity for female recruitment into the marines. In his book *Operation Hollywood*, journalist David Robb explains how the Pentagon's modified movie scripts are designed to target children and youth—future recruits for the war effort.[84] The blockbusters 'deliberately reiterate the morality of the military and war' even though viewers are never told they are 'enjoying military-subsidized-and-sculpted productions'.[85] As independent journalist Jonathan Cook has written, Hollywood's war films contain

> carefully purposed propaganda, designed to force-feed aggressive western military intervention, dressed up as humanitarianism, to unsuspecting audiences ... Militarism, superior firepower, and an absolute belief in the justice of one's cause ... are the ways to save [humankind] from evildoers.[86]

A Web of Deceit

Social media have been a gamechanger for propagandists with some 70 nations worldwide having used websites that allow agents of the state to create and/or share mis- and dis-information.[87]

Brexit provides an excellent example of the role of social media in the creation and distribution of lies and deceit. A majority of UK citizens voted on June 23, 2016 for Britain to leave the European Union. Since that time, many political analysts have sought to understand how UK citizens concluded that leaving the EU would improve their futures. There were many lies circulating at the time—most originating from the Leave campaigners and politicians such as Boris Johnson and Nigel Farage. It was argued that immigration was a major problem, causing wages to fall and reducing people's access to public services. (The real cause of both were the austerity measures put in place by David Cameron's Conservative Party.) It was claimed money saved by Britain in leaving the EU would help improve the bottom line of the National Health Service. (There was no guarantee that any 'saved' money would make its way to the NHS.) There was concern Türkiye would join the EU and the UK would be 'invaded' by Muslims. (Türkiye has not joined the EU and, given its human rights violations, looks unlikely to do so for many decades.) Britons were told they were being 'ruled by Brussel bureaucrats'. (Ministers in the EU Council represent national governments that have been democratically elected and are accountable for their actions and voting.)[88] There was the promise of a 'green Brexit', with the Leavers claiming Brexit would deliver greater protection for the environment. (The progressive environmental policies of the EU are being wound back and there are new, 'draconian' laws to stop environmental protests.)[89] And so forth. According to one critic, Brexit was a 'complete disaster', a 'bunch of total lies'.[90] For another Brit 'no other topic in our nation's history has inspired so many untruths'.[91] So how did this happen? How were the lies disseminated?

This is where the media come in. The tabloid press and broadcast media were quick to repeat the claims of the Leave politicians about the Brussel bureaucrats and the threats of uncontrolled immigration. They reproduced simple, emotionally charged, messages—such as 'support democracy, support Brexit'.⁹² Social media was also crucial in pushing the Brexit cause. Their very architecture helped to polarise the debates between the Leavers and Remainers. Facebook/Meta provided 'filter bubbles' which allowed users to confirm their prejudices in 'ideologically segregated communities'.⁹³ Politicisation of Brexit was a function of social media platforms that allowed people to convey direct, emotion-laden, biased, messages quickly and spontaneously. Leave supporters on Twitter/X and Instagram provided engaging, lively, commentary in contrast to the Remain appeal to the logic of voters. In such a milieu, emotion won hands down.

More recently, in the war between Israel and Hamas, the news media in Australia, Canada, and the US have employed language in their coverage of the conflict that is pro-Israel.⁹⁴ And, social media have again demonstrated their willingness to spread lies and propaganda. Since the bombing of Israel by Hamas militants in October 2023, disinformation spread quickly on social media, with Facebook/Meta and Instagram revealing Hamas soldiers had beheaded babies and had raped Israeli women—both claims being without foundation.⁹⁵ A video of Hamas fighters paragliding into an Israeli music festival turned out to be Egyptian paratroopers skydiving over Cairo. A rocket fired from Gaza was an old clip from Syria. The 'lost girl' video showing a Palestinian man asking an abandoned child 'who are your parents?' was filmed a month before the attacks of October 2023. Viewers were even treated to conflict scenes taken from a fictional video game.⁹⁶ Nothing should surprise us. In 2021 Twitter/X posts purporting to be from the Israeli Defence Forces saying 'we just love killing' and 'just bombed some kids' were identified as fakes. A Hamas truck loaded with missiles travelling down a street in Gaza was a clip from the town of Abu Snan in Israel, recorded in 2018.⁹⁷ Importantly, only hours after Hamas attacked Israel in 2023, X owner, Elon Musk, used his position as the owner of the platform to spread misinformation about the conflict. He spread fake news about US funding destined for Israel and told his 150 million followers to visit a site of a known conspiracy theory promoter.⁹⁸ As ethicist, and Professor of Philosophy, Nir Eisikovits has argued, social media exist to drive engagement—'to show people what they will likely agree with or to show them content that will outrage and shock them'. But just as 'junk food harms your body', so too 'junk information and junk engagement hurt the body politic'.[99]

As we saw in Chapter 1, social networking allows for the near-instantaneous delivery of content throughout the world. Social media platforms are 'devilishly useful' in propagating 'an insidious, potent array of weaponised forms of information used to cajole, harass, hoodwink, and otherwise exploit publics'.[100] For example, YouTube has allowed North Korea to show its (fabricated) bombs striking a US aircraft carrier, while Twitter/X and Instagram's users have peddled strange and deadly 'cures' for COVID-19. Fake accounts (bots) contain information from people using various aliases (sock puppets). The fake accounts generate fake news—'news' that can saturate social media. Those producing and distributing this information come in three forms—'hecklers' (who actively discredit those whom they oppose), 'honey pots' (who employ sexual flirtation and flattery to have a reader click on to malware), and 'hackers' (who use malware to get into a user's account).[101]

This is the world of post-truth politics where rumours, speculation, lies, fake news, and political propaganda can be readily launched on social media, and a host of other sites without the audience knowing the truth or otherwise of the assertions being made. Post-truth politics eschews factual information appealing, instead, to voter emotion. A plethora of truth claims is confusing for audiences, while the lack of an authoritative gatekeeper means that false assertions go unchallenged. The goal is to influence, not to promote informed debate.

The main intentions of those producing and sending false information is to saturate a targeted audience with information that will damage a person or group's reputation, produce social discord, and undermine support for policies that are perceived not to be in the sender's interest. In a notorious intervention in US politics, the Russian government conducted aggressive multi-pronged cyberattacks before and during the 2016 US election contest between Hilary Clinton and Donald Trump. Russia's Vladimir Putin had long blamed Hilary Clinton, the then US Secretary of State, for provoking rioting in Moscow in 2011 during his bid for the Russian presidency. The Russian state-based Internet Research Agency created some 470 accounts delivering 80,000 Facebook entries attacking Clinton. Russian bots created a further 50,000 twitter accounts, producing close to four million tweets—the vast majority of which supported Trump and some of which accused Democrats of practising witchcraft. Approximately 20% of all tweets about the US presidential election came from Russia—enough to help undermine Hilary Clinton and raise the profile of The Donald.[102]

But Trump also employed his very own tactics on his way to, and during his time in, the White House. Tactics to control and influence the media included berating those who disagreed with him (the once-favoured CNN had become a 'network of liars'), blacklisting journalists from news outlets that were not favoured, threatening the media with libel actions, and bypassing the media completely—using tweets as a major form of contact with the public.[103] His personal style was also highly influential. Linguists believe that Trump's unfinished, fractured, sentences which move quickly from topic to topic, and are full of non sequiturs, comprise a conversational style that appeals to voters. He shrugs, raises his eyebrows, encouraging the audience to engage with him and to form their own conclusions—the conversational tics of a great salesperson.[104] But, of course, Trump was no ordinary president. He wanted fame to go with his riches, stating 'I have so many rich friends and nobody knows who they are'.[105] He once told *Playboy* magazine 'The show is "Trump" and it is sold-out performances everywhere'.[106] And his logic is impeccable. In the mid-term elections of 2022 Trump endorsed a number of candidates stating 'Well, I think if they win, I should get all the credit. If they lose, I should not be blamed at all'.[107] Most of them lost.

By the time of the 2020 US election Facebook and other social media had managed to dismantle most of the Russian botnets. But just before the election another Russian creation sprang into life. Called 'Peace Data' the site began spreading lies about both Biden and Trump with the purpose of creating uncertainty among American voters. According to one media scholar

> a fake news story travels six times faster on social media than a verified story ... Quantity is more important than the quality of the message conveyed, because one of the objectives is to drown the real news in a constant stream of fake news.[108]

Result? Voter confusion via lies and obfuscation. People simply don't know who, or what, to believe. Seeds of doubt have been sown. Will the fake news go away as social media outlets spot the bots and dismantle them (as Reddit did with some 1,000 Russian sites in 2018)?[109] Not likely. With all the frustration and futility of whack-a-mole, when one site is deactivated another pops up in its place. There is now an army of 'cyber troops' (citizen influencers and 'disinformation-for-hire-services') which are paid by governments to spread false news. The army of fake news generators includes 'strategic communication' firms currently operating in some 50 nations which use amplification strategies to promote the messages of their funders, resulting in the proliferation of 'misinformation on an industrial scale'.[110]

'Knowledge is power', as Englishman Sir Francis Bacon is purported to have muttered, seems to be a self-evident aphorism in a world of high-tech information flows. But knowledge is only powerful when it is put to use as a means of influencing and changing things. Here, the social media are at the fore:

> Social media platforms are some of the world's most powerful businesses – not least because they can collect massive amounts of data, and use algorithms to turn the data into actionable knowledge.[111]

As we have come to understand in relation to TikTok, personal data such as dates of birth, addresses, bank accounts, marital status, political affiliations, and images are harvested and sent to its parent company ByteDance—an organisation 'beholden to the Communist Party of China'.[112] Information is not only *not* secure but can be weaponised for perverse reasons—including the proliferation of mis- and dis-information. Those working for the Russian media outlet, *Zvezda*, have confessed as much arguing that 'false data' and 'destabilising propaganda' are perfectly sound vehicles to be employed in the battle for hearts and minds. In Russia, the media are just 'another type of armed force'.[113]

Propaganda undermines democracy. A major premise of representative democracy is that the voting public has access to reliable and truthful information. When foreign governments deliberately mislead voters, or when home governments blitz the public with fake media messages designed to sway public opinion towards an administration's policies—rather than reveal the truth—democracy is the loser.[114]

Empire Records

We have seen how cleverly designed posters can be harnessed to drive humanity to war. Flags serve much the same purpose, consolidating national identity, stimulating patriotic feelings, and helping justify one nation's decision to maul another. It was certainly appropriate for author Tim Marshall to name his 2017 best-seller *A Flag to Die For*.[115] Marshall argues that because a flag embodies a nation, its symbolic powers are enormous. While human societies have been drawing images and representations on cloth well before ancient Egyptian times, it is only relatively recently that flags have been flown. Older cotton cloth was just too heavy to fly on flagpoles. Chinese silk provided the breakthrough. Purchased by merchants along the Silk Road, the lightweight garment became the go-to fabric for the Crusaders, sundry armies, and eventually nation-states (every nation on earth is represented by a flag).[116] They come in many colours and styles and are used to rally loyal subjects, start (and end) motor races, cheer on teams from the bleachers, indicate surf conditions, (supposedly) show golfers where to aim, wave off trains from platforms, drape over coffins, and be torched at protest rallies. Today, flags are made of nylon or polyester—fabrics that are lightweight and which have the strength to remain intact during sandstorms, heatwaves, and blizzards. (Some are also fire-proof.)

So revered and sacred are the flapping symbols of nationhood that flag protocols are nearly as important as flags, themselves. Here's the advice for would-be flag fliers:

- Flags should always be handled and displayed respectfully.
- Flags should always be flown freely and as close as possible to the top of the flagpole.
- Two flags should not be flown from the same flagpole (one would be 'over' the other—a sign of disrespect).

- A flag should never be flown if it is damaged, faded, or dilapidated. When the material of a flag deteriorates, it should be destroyed privately and in a dignified way.
- The flag should not be flown upside down (something done in the past by wayward sea vessels as a sign of distress).
- The flag should not fall or lie on the ground or be used as a cover (a coffin is the exception).
- When multiple flags are flown together, they must all be the same size.[117]

Ceremonies for raising and lowering flags are also prescribed. A nation's flag must be raised briskly and lowered solemnly. It should not be raised before first light or lowered after dusk. When members of the public are present, they should be silent during its raising or lowering—with people in uniform being required to salute. Then there's the folding. After it is lowered the US flag is folded 13 times—one fold for each of the original colonies (represented by the stripes in the stars and stripes). Each fold has a meaning—the first, existing life; the second eternal life; the fourth represents belief in divine guidance; the sixth stands for one indivisible nation under God; … the thirteenth confirms the US motto 'in God we trust'.[118] Flag-folding is replete with religious meaning, despite the nation's secular pretensions.

Yet, while the US flag does not explicitly *display* religious symbols, others around the world do. In fact, some 64 of the world's 196 nations' flags display religious imagery. Of those, some 48% exhibit Christian symbols (mostly crosses), with another 33% showing Islamic religious symbols (mostly the crescent moon). Buddhist and Hindu symbols appear on five flags, the Star of David appears prominently on the Israeli flag, while golden suns on Uruguayan and Argentinian flags represent *Inti*—the Inca sun god. The rising sun on the Japanese flag has its roots in Shintoism.[119] By providing citizens with the icons and images that evoke deeply held cultural beliefs, flags both embrace a nation's past and give cause to protect its future.

Other flags have a more practical use. Maritime flags provide a means of communication over the waters. The flags and their meanings are found in the *International Code of Signals*. There are flags for each letter

5 The Power to Lie: Propaganda and Post-truth Politics

of the Latin alphabet, and pennants to represent numbers. If you are flying a yellow flag with a solid black circle, I know that you are altering your course to port. If you fly a flag with blue top and bottom stripes and a white stripe in the middle, you are on fire (and presumably the flag will not be flying for much longer). If I observe your ship flying a blue flag with yellow stripes at top and bottom, you are telling me 'keep clear - I am manoeuvring with great difficulty'. But if things get worse, and you have time on your hands, you can raise a companion white flag with a blue cross at centre, telling me not only is your manoeuvring awry, but that you are also sinking.[120] If you fly the Jolly Roger, you are either pretending to be Captain Jack Sparrow and/or have disreputable and mischievous intentions.

The colours of flags are saturated with meaning. White is associated with peace and harmony. Red conjures up strength, power, and war (red for blood). Blue signifies determination and liberation. Green is for fertility and prosperity. Gold symbolises wealth and energy. Orange represents courage and sacrifice. Black symbolises vengeance—the death of enemies (but can also represent a black population, such as in the modern flags of African nations). Of course, when combined things can seem a little puzzling. The US flag of red, white, and blue must, at one and the same time, stand for power/war, peace/harmony, and determination/liberation. What? And, of course, while Americans claim these colours as their very own, they also appear on the flags of 28 other nations—including US soul mates Russia, Cuba, and North Korea.[121] A good majority of the world's population must be receiving the same confused messaging as their brethren in the US. No wonder the world's a mess.

But if flags are known for anything it is warfare and colonisation. In days of yore flags carried onto the battlefield would be dipped in the blood of the conquered warriors and be lifted high in the air for all to see—a definitive assertion of victory. During America's civil war flags assumed great importance. With vocal calls and bugles drowned out on the killing fields, flags showed the positions of regiments, and pointed the direction in which the troops must advance. Soldiers were taught, literally, to follow the flag. The flagbearer was obviously a key player. Yet

[a]s the regimental flags were so conspicuous in battle, they were often used [by the enemy] as a target for rifle and artillery fire. Of course, the mortality rate of color bearers was high.[122]

For the fighters who successfully returned to the safety of a camp, flags would be paraded in front of them—designed to remind them of forthcoming commitments, and as an attempt to boost morale. In recent times the famous Confederate flag—which stood for defiance and rebellion of the South in the Civil War—has been draped over the shoulders of would-be White House invaders. But its anti-black, racist, sentiments have not been lost on the Ku Klux Klan which has employed it as a recruitment tool.[123] (For all Ku Klux Klan members reading this, please note that there is only one 'human race'. Race is not a biologically recognised attribute, but a social construct invented to justify subjugation and oppression of others.) In 2020 Trump called the Confederate flag a 'source of pride' for people in the South.[124] This would, of course, include the 56% of people of colour who reside in that region of the US.

The colonial period is of special significance in understanding state power and expansion—along with the great lie of racial inferiority. While colonialism—the territorial and economic control by one power over a dependent area or people—had been practised since antiquity with empires such as the Greeks, Romans, and Egyptians expanding their borders, modern colonialism began in the fifteenth century, the so-called Age of Discovery, when the Portuguese began looking for sea-based trade routes and foreign wealth. This was the time that the flags of colonial nations were being firmly planted in conquered territories. Spain followed Portugal in its sea journey of conquest, raiding, and plundering Central and South America for its gold and silver. It was also on a mission to convert heathens to Christianity—a most worthy cause and a religion eagerly embraced by the locals—just ask Portugal's Prince Henry the Navigator whose southern nautical 'adventures' advanced Christianity while fuelling the African slave trade. Or maybe Deigo de Landa the Spanish Bishop of Yucatan who decided the best way to write an accurate account of the Maya was to burn thousands of that culture's sacred manuscripts.[125] It was for good reason that former anti-colonial activist, and later Kenyan Prime Minister, Jomo Kenyatta was to lament, some centuries later:

> When the Missionaries arrived [we] had the land and [they] had the Bible. They taught us how to pray with our eyes closed. When we opened them, they had the land and we had the Bible.[126]

Missionaries were agents of colonialism. Non-Christian ideas were inferior to Christian. Savages were to be 'tamed' and their superstitious and outdated beliefs obliterated. Their bodies needed to be cleansed, not only spiritually—but with soap, a wonderful western contribution to hygiene.[127] Cleanliness was, indeed, next to Godliness.

The Butcher's Apron

Might there have been 'good' colonisation? After all, soap does have beneficial uses. In 2017 political scientist Bruce Gilley caused something of a stir when his article 'The Case for Colonialism' was published in the reputable journal *Third World Quarterly*. Gillies argued that while colonialism might have a bad name, it produced many beneficial outcomes, improving the living conditions of 'most' Third World peoples, introducing 'effective governance', catalysing economic development, and enhancing human welfare.[128] Unfortunately for Gillies a petition with over 10,000 signatures was presented to the journal seeking retraction of the paper, and 15 members of the board resigned in protest over its publication. The article was later withdrawn after hefty criticism of the empirical 'facts' Gillies used, and the gross historical inaccuracies the paper contained. It was full of falsehoods and misinformation—the very opposite of the integrity, honesty, and factual accuracy demanded by the academy.[129] But Gillies was not the first, nor will he be the last, to praise the good work of the British imperialists. Eminent historian Niall Ferguson has argued that while the British might have been a touch overbearing, they improved the lives of the peoples over whom they ruled, while creating an efficient system of governance and trade—a prelude to a thriving world capitalism.[130] Who would dispute the benefits the British have brought to humanity?

So, how did the colonised experience colonisation? Forceful invasions by nations such as Germany, Belgium, France, and Britain were undertaken to exploit new regions of the world, financially enriching royalty and the ruling classes of the invading nations. Locals were brutalised, exploited, and enslaved to ensure the steady flow of wealth back to the home countries. Bloody battles ensued. In Central and South America the Spanish conquistadores spread Christianity (along with other diseases like influenza, smallpox, and syphilis) and killed those who resisted conversion to Catholicism. It is estimated that by 1600 CE some 56 million people had died from warfare, disease, and societal collapse. (The loss of so much life actually led to the cooling of the planet—the so-called little ice age.)[131] But colonialism was a profitable enterprise for some:

> The Spanish and Portuguese empires were built upon religious fanaticism and conquest, slavery, spices, gold, silver, emeralds and tobacco ... [They turned this wealth] into stone, building huge cathedrals, castles and fortresses.[132]

Then there was King Leopold II of Belgium. With his eye on ivory, timber, and rubber—the latter product of particular economic value with the development of tyres for motor vehicles—Leopold had his troops invade central Africa, creating the Congo Free State in 1885. His army used forced male labour in the forests, holding family members hostage until quotas were met. If men escaped, Leopold's militia would pursue them with vigour, cutting off hands and genitals and hanging severed heads in local villages.[133] This, apparently, was the best way to civilize the natives. Once word got out about the atrocities being committed, the Belgian government was forced to take responsibility for the colony. In 1908 the fledgling colony became the Belgian Congo. During Leopold's reign some 10 million Africans lost their lives.[134]

The French also saw it as their duty to civilize Africans and made every attempt to do so—from Cameroon to Senegal to Chad to Morocco and Rwanda. Today, some 29 African nations are awaiting return of the riches looted by the French during colonial times.[135] Algeria, in particular, could do nicely with the estimated US$180 billion in gold and silver

5 The Power to Lie: Propaganda and Post-truth Politics

taken from the colony during the 132-year of French occupation—a period in which between five and ten million Algerians were killed.[136] As Franz Fanon documented in *The Wretched of the Earth*, blacks were seen to be devoid of culture and were viewed as intellectually inferior to whites. They were treated with contempt and were subject to unspeakable violence, leading to social breakdown and psychological malaise. They were being conditioned to accept their role as slaves under colonial rule.[137] The Vietnamese also had the advantage of being 'civilised' by the French. The French seized land and collectivised it into rubber and rice plantations. Locals were then forced to work for as long as 15 hours each day, without adequate food and water supplies, and without breaks. When wages were paid they were 'pitifully small', with many receiving payment in rice.[138] Malaria, malnutrition, and dysentery were commonplace on plantations. The opium grown by the settlers was a profitable export but was also used to create addiction among the Vietnamese—a primary mechanism for social control. French culture and language were forced on locals and their temples, pagodas, and monuments destroyed. French names replaced traditional names of streets and towns. Men and women were 'increasingly dehumanised' in their encounter with the colonialists, with any form of dissent met with repression, imprisonment, or death.[139] Before French rule in 1883, some 80% of the Vietnamese population was 'functionally literate'. In 1939 it had dropped to 20%.[140]

The preferred civilizing practices of the Dutch in Indonesia were torture, rape, execution, the burning of villages, along with the theft of property and food supplies.[141] The Dutch termed this 'ethical imperialism'.[142] Predating the holocaust, Germany can proudly lay claim to the first genocide of the twentieth century. It occurred from 1904 to 1907 when ethnic extermination was practised on the Herero and Nama peoples of German South West Africa (now Namibia). The tribes had protested German occupation and, for their insubordination, were driven by the German armed forces into the desert. Without water most died from dehydration, but starvation was also a popular way to go. Up to 100,000 Herero and some 10,000 Nama lost their lives. Those who survived were captured and placed in concentration camps where they died from abuse, exhaustion, and disease.[143] As a result of its loss to the Allied powers in First World War, Germany's colonies were divided between Britain, France, Belgium, and Portugal. Before this, the German colonial record was remarkable like that of its victors. Following First World War, a summary of German colonists' practices included:

> expropriation of the tribal lands, seizure of sacrificial cattle, maladministration of justice, excessive … severity of treatment, invasion of native rights and customs, flogging of women, forced labour and recruiting of natives by means of forced levies, or a combination of all … in every case [native tribes] have been suppressed with a ruthless barbarity.[144]

There is one European nation that surpassed the brutality of its fellow colonisers: Great Britain. The Tudor conquest of Ireland was one significant infringement. Between 1536 and 1691 the Irish were to suffer at the hands of the English. King Henry VIII had had enough with Papal authority and decided it was he who would be God's representative on Earth. He needed to be obeyed. His predisposition was towards expansion—of waistlines as well as coastlines. New wealth would allow him to acquire some 50 palaces during his lifetime (with Hampton Court becoming his 'royal pleasure palace').[145] The Irish had been ruled by Anglo-Irish Lords for almost two centuries and Henry was concerned about their loyalty to him. He also desired some of their riches. He was declared King of Ireland and began centralising authority, imposing English law, culture, and language, confiscating monastic property, and replacing the Catholic church with the Protestant church of Ireland.[146] Bloody conflict and famine were responsible for between 60,000 and 100,000 Irish deaths following the Tudor invasion (about one-tenth of the Irish population).[147] Henry also fancied a slice of France, funding three invasions between 1512 and 1546. His invading armies used scorched-earth strategies, starving, and slaughtering any civilians who questioned Henry's right to rule.[148] In later centuries Britain would be known by the derogatory phrase 'perfidious Albion'—a reference to the lies, deceit, and betrayals British royalty and politicians employed in pursuit of personal and national self-interest.[149]

Then there's the terrifying triangle of slavery. On the first leg British merchant ships supplied manufactured goods to Africa and received spices, gold, ivory—and slaves—in return. In the second leg, the ships crossed the Atlantic where the slaves were sold to plantation owners and wealthy households. With the newly gained money, tobacco, sugar, rice, and cotton were purchased for the third leg back to Europe, where the cargo was sold, enriching the merchants, the Treasury, and royalty. The slave trade was also rather kind to British plantation owners in the Caribbean, with a steady supply of unpaid labour creating huge fortunes.

It was Elizabeth I who, in 1564, funded the early slave-trade exploits of English trader John Hawkins. In 1660 the Duke of York established the Royal African Company (RAC) which exported slaves to British colonies in the Americas. Many of the 187,000 captured slaves had their skins branded with the letters 'RAC' or 'DY'—for Duke of York.[150] From the 1500s to the 1800s some 12 million Africans were carried to the Americas by ships of the slave-trading nations, with Britain's tally put at 3.4 million.[151] (Portugal was the main offender transporting some 5 million slaves.)[152] Slaves were considered 'chattel', holding the same status as cattle. They were chained, starved, tortured, and fell victim to all manner of disease. Sharks regularly followed the slave ships, well-aware of the human bounty that would be tossed overboard during the journey. It is estimated that some 50% of African slaves died during their time on board ship, with African women subjected to 'the wanton and unrestrained licentiousness of the crew'.[153] They were summarily raped.

Meanwhile, Oliver Cromwell, at the behest of the English parliament, invaded Ireland in 1649, supposedly to avenge the Irish massacring of Protestant settlers some seven years earlier. His real mission? Well, to retake Ireland for Britain, and confiscate property held by Catholics, of course. But genocide was right up there, with the Irish population estimated to have dropped by over 40% during the time of his occupation.[154] Cromwell was the very model of a modern Major General. Indeed, the Lord Protector was known to have a funny side—which included clever puns, pillow fights, and practical jokes. For some he was the 'laughing Roundhead'.[155] The Irish just didn't seem to be in on the joke.

Did the British bloodshed stop after Cromwell's campaign ended in 1653? For some strange reason, many of the colonised seemed to resent, rather than embrace, the presence of the British. A little later, in the eighteenth and nineteenth centuries, the British aristocracy turned against their own people, appropriating common land available to the public for cropping and grazing. They fenced it and policed it, starving the locals and forcing them into the cities where their new role was to provide cheap labour for industrialists. Members of the new proletariat were not happy—crime, dissention, and rebellion were direct products of locational displacement and workplace exploitation. Disorder had to be quelled and it was, via a new blanket of legislation, designed to ensure compliance:

> The Riot Act banned public disorder; the Combination Act made trade unions illegal; the Workhouse Act forced the poor to work; the Vagrancy Act turned joblessness into a crime. Eventually, over 220 offences could attract capital punishment … or transportation.[156]

After the American War of Independence in the late 1770s, it was no longer possible to send those convicted of crimes in Britain to the shores of its former north American colonies. The British sought, instead, to establish a colony in Australia—an antipodean dumping ground for criminals and political dissenters. Unfortunately, the Aboriginal peoples took umbrage. But spears were no match for guns, with mass killings of First Nation peoples beginning in 1794 and continuing until 1928.[157] Some involved the use of native police, slaughtering fellow blacks, under the command of British officers.[158] Some 14,000 Aborigines died in genocidal massacres.[159] Across the Tasman, while seeking to retain their lands, over 2,000 New Zealand Māori died at the hands of British troops.[160] Previously unknown 'white' diseases such as smallpox, influenza, measles, tuberculosis, and syphilis ran rampant among native populations of Australia and New Zealand, causing widespread misery and death—a not-so humanitarian colonial legacy.[161]

The British conquest of India, which began in 1742, was not only about financial gain. It was to civilise the heathen—a cause that poet Rudyard Kipling would call, in a later century, 'the white man's burden'. Arrogance and racism were a neat match. When the British arrived, India was one of the richest places on earth—a major trader with a near monopoly in spices and high-quality textiles.[162] During the 1700s, India and Europe were on par in terms of economic wealth. By the 1900s, after two hundred years of British rule, India's share of the world economy had declined sixfold.[163] Through crippling taxation, trade restrictions, and conscious de-industrialisation foisted on the Indian economy, within two centuries India was impoverished. Staples such as rice were exported from India to other parts of the British Empire, and the food remaining was priced beyond the reach of many locals. Starvation and poverty were rife.[164] Indian economist Professor Utsa Patnaik has estimated that between 1765 and 1938, Britain extracted some US$45 trillion from India.[165]

During the rule of the British Raj (1872–1921), the life expectancy of the average Indian dropped by 20%.[166] Destitution resulted in death from starvation (some 10 million Bengalis died in the Great Bengal Famine [1769–1770], while up to 3.5 million suffered the same fate in the famine of 1943).[167] Christian missionaries, employing deception and coercion, sought to colonise the Indian mind—something which went hand in hand with the shaping of values, morals, and worldviews imposed by the British education system. Legal systems were imposed that would stimulate trade and financial flows, along with the creation of private property. The subjugation of India was not only at the hands of the British. Indian soldiers trained and armed by the British were as brutal as the colonisers. The Brits were particularly clever. The taxes they exacted from locals were used to purchase guns and munitions which, in turn, would be used on the very people who had paid the taxes—something no doubt seen as a virtuous circle.

The British fought the Opium Wars with China, hoping to keep the locals hooked and profits flowing. They took on the Boers in Africa, filling concentration camps with the men, women, and children they had captured. When Malayans began fighting for national liberation in 1948, the British launched attacks, burning houses, spraying food crops with defoliants, and moving people into 'new villages' (yet more concentration camps). They fought the Kenyans in the Mau Mau uprisings of the 1950s where they used beatings, sexual torture, and executions to dissuade the locals from embarking upon anti-colonial activities. They fought a covert war in Yemen from 1962, supplying fighter jets and other weapons to royalists.[168] The list goes on. As do the stories of resource exploitation, financial theft, cultural annihilation, malnutrition, poverty, political alienation, and genocide.[169] Colonisers captured territories already inhabited by people—people who resisted the invaders. Violence was the handmaiden of conquest.

With its strong slashes of red on a blue and white cloth, it is no wonder that the Union Jack is referred to in the colonies as 'the butcher's apron'.

Up for Grabs

Fortunately, colonialism is a thing of the past. Or is it?

Imagine being a small-holder farmer in Cambodia, Vietnam, Uganda, or Peru. You and your trusty ox are tilling the soil your forebears have worked for hundreds, if not thousands, of years. A truck pulls up and a government official instructs you immediately to vacate the land. You have never held a written, legal, title—you have a customary right to your fields. You are told it is now government land to be leased to a transnational company that plans to amalgamate properties in the region and grow palm oil for export. The heavily armed soldiers in the back of the truck provide a strong signal that any protest will be futile. You and your family have no choice but to leave. You receive no compensation and join—in some shanty town—the many other families whose land has been seized and whose livelihoods have been ruined.

The modern-day conquistadores are not looting and pillaging for gold. Their treasure is of a very different sort—it is scarce land, water, and natural resources. According to latest estimates some 68 million hectares of land have been expropriated by foreign investors since 2008.[170] Water-grabbing is on the rise, with pension funds and private equity firms purchasing scarce water resources for the production of water-intensive crops such as fruits and nuts. This is at a time when the UN has warned of a 'global water crisis' and has predicted mounting conflicts that will accompany struggles over access to water.[171] Finance is always looking for the next big thing. When dot.com bubbles and urban real estate bubbles burst, funds rush into other potentially profitable ventures. The global food crisis of 2008, sparked by the Global Financial Crisis (or 'great recession') convinced corporate and institutional investors that purchase of farmlands would be a good bet.[172] It would guarantee immediate income (from the sale of farm commodities) and generate future profits (from future commodity sales, as well as speculation in land prices). Agricultural property taxes are also often woefully low, and agriculture is highly subsidised by taxpayers—particularly in the US. Both are incentives for the super-rich to invest in farmland.[173] Biofuels can be grown and sold to an expanding market. And planting new forests in far-off African lands is an excellent way for polluting corporations to offset their carbon emissions.[174] This is, of course, a form of 'green colonialism', where the labour and lands of marginalised people in the Global South are exploited by those in the Global North. In this case, carbon offsets in the Global South are a colonial-style impost that allows polluting companies to continue with business-as-usual, while allowing citizens in the Global North to maintain their existing lifestyles and privileges.[175]

Food-poor but otherwise wealthy nations like Qatar, Saudi Arabia, and Singapore, consider it imperative to invest in farmlands to ensure food will be available for their growing populations.[176] Chinese cash is being splashed around the world via its 'belt and road' initiatives to shore up that nation's future food supply. China is capital-rich, but land-poor, and targets nations in the Global South for extraction and export of resources.[177] And, as was noted above, governments in financially poor nations eagerly welcomed the foreign dollars to assist in modernising their farming systems. Surely this must be good for the world—after all, global capital is finally being able to do something to develop 'underutilised' farmlands, forests, and rangelands in the Global South?[178]

Unfortunately, the large-scale land acquisitions that are occurring in some of the most poverty-stricken nations—Ethiopia, Sierra Leone, South Sudan, and the Congo among them—are not aimed at helping these nations feed their citizens but to export food and fibre internationally to expand corporate profit-making. The wealth management industry in the Global North—worth trillions of dollars—is offering investors access to a diversity of highly productive agricultural sites throughout the world. Many know little about agriculture or food production but do understand two things—arable land is scarce, globally, and food will become increasingly expensive via the impacts of climate change and population growth.[179] Could there be a better investment than farmland?

I was undertaking a series of interviews in New York in 2013 and was fortunate to speak with a senior development economist from the UN. I was interested in his take on 'land grabbing'. While asserting that nations in the Global South would benefit from financial investments that created 'backward and forward linkages' throughout their economies, he noted that where land purchase is for economic extraction alone

> you are evicting local farmers. You are taking available land from people who have been working it for centuries, for generations. For local people this is a question of losing their livelihood, this is a question of losing their existence ... You must recognise that land has a very emotional aspect. It is not like other foreign investment.

He then gave an example of the distortion foreign capital has wrought.

> In many countries what is happening is that the agricultural sector is producing commodities for export, producing food and fibre for consumers in the rest of the world, to the detriment of the nutrition and needs of the households of subsistence farmers.

What sits nicely with the theory of 'comparative advantage'—as outlined in Chapter 2—appears to be failing the poorest and most vulnerable members of the global community. Indeed, the need for the top-down 'modernisation' of small-scale and peasant agriculture rests on a lie. It is asserted by agri-business elites and land- and water-grabbers that only high-tech farming can deliver future prosperity and food security to nations struggling with malnutrition, hunger, and poverty. We need the latest technologies to feed the predicted 9 billion people who will inhabit the earth by 2050. What is conveniently forgotten is that peasant and small-scale agriculture, urban gardening, and hunting/gathering, currently feed some 70% of the world's population. These systems do so using only 30% of the world's land and water resources.[180] In contrast, large-scale commercial farming feeds 30% of the world while using 70% of resources.[181]

Peasant and small-scale farms produce a rich variety of foods for local consumption and trade. The farms are biodiverse, and the use of agrochemicals and fuel is quite limited, placing fewer demands on an already stressed environment.[182] Peasant farming contributes in a positive way to local food security, employment, economic development, and sustainability.[183] The problem is that traditional, peasant, farming presents a barrier to corporate expansion. The result? The small-scale farmers are denied support from their governments to stay on the land and create local, stable, and thriving food systems.[184]

Land- and water-grabs are taking place in circumstances where legal and procedural mechanisms over land leases and purchases are opaque or absent, leaving the small holders with little recourse to challenge their dispossession. There is a lack of transparency in negotiations, vaguely defined rules and procedures, gaps in legislation, and a failure to 'take account of local interests, livelihoods and welfare'.[185] Oxfam has shown that a good deal of activity is occurring in nations with poor governance, helping investors to profit while avoiding or minimising red tape.[186] Resource extraction is leaving in its trail soil degradation and pollution of air and waterways. And, it is not just the land that is appropriated. So too are the 'memories, histories, roots, and connections' of displaced peoples—along with resources, identities are being plundered.[187] Today, in Myanmar, the vast confiscations of land occurring in that country has been described as 'nothing less than gross and systematic violations of internationally recognised human rights and other legal norms [and] include crimes against humanity and war crimes'.[188]

Corruption is rife. In the Amazon where deforestation is proceeding at an unprecedented rate, many of the large land-grabbing investors belong to criminal syndicates which 'use the land for money laundering, tax evasion and illegal mining and logging'.[189] Huge swathes of rainforest are being cleared for cattle grazing and soybean production, with investors having lobbied Brazil's National Congress to soften laws that limit the purchase of public lands, and to approve laws that weaken environmental protections, and that lead to less surveillance.[190] It is estimated that

> about 30% of public forests (14 million ha) were illegally registered as private property in the National Rural Cadastre System (CAR) as of the

end of 2020. As the CAR is self-declaratory, land grabbers draw fictitious rural properties within public forests ... The case of digital land grabbing has stimulated subsequent cycles of deforestation and fires, which is necessary to appropriate and introduce the lands into the market.[191]

The growing process of digitising land and natural resources might seem to provide support for the small landholders, helping to verify traditional rights. But the opposite appears to be happening. The new mapping technologies, in the absence of strong state surveillance, are enabling lands and resources to be reclassified as private rather than communal. Titles can then be sold and resold in the financial marketplace, giving local and foreign investors legal ownership of public property. In Colombia, for example, aerial digital mapping of lands has resulted in some 48% of titles being redrawn—allowing the legal possession of lands which have, in effect, been illegally procured.[192]

In Laos' Champassak province 100 families were told to leave their properties to allow the construction of a cassava processing plant, with soldiers threatening that—were they to plant any new crops—they would be destroyed. (In this case compensation was offered but was about one-third of the value of properties.)[193] In Africa, land is being grabbed and then amalgamated, with the large farms creating jobs—but mainly for seasonal workers. Those previously working the land have lost lands and livelihoods. The large farms are growing non-food crops at lower productivity levels than the small farms they have displaced.[194] When production is for the global market, little consideration is given to local environmental, social, or economic impacts of investment.[195] Rather than improving the lives of locals in Africa, land acquisitions are

> depriving local communities of access to natural resources, such as land, forest, and water, increasing ... the risks of poverty for these populations.[196]

In Romania there have been 'massive' land acquisitions aimed at consolidating holdings in anticipation of the introduction of intensive agriculture.[197] Eastern and Central European nations are being targeted because of fertile soils and excellent water availability for irrigation. Features of appropriation include the illegitimate and fraudulent taking of land, expulsion of peasants, the demise of rural communities, and environmental vandalism.[198] In regard to the latter, the expansion of cattle grazing increases the amount of greenhouse gases in the atmosphere, contributing to global warming.

We are told by the right-wing media and think tanks, agribusiness, and international investors, that the world has no choice but to embrace high-tech farming—it is so efficient. On the face of it, that may seem so. But many studies have shown peasant systems use inputs more efficiently than high-tech farming and are highly productive (something sociologist Jan Douwe van der Ploeg has called 'the neglected truth').[199] And, when its 'externalities' are considered, high-tech farming is downright dangerous for people and the planet. What is rarely explained is that the land- and water-grabs are about profit generation for the wealthy rather than food security for the many. They represent territorial restructuring—colonising land and resources for capitalist development.[200] Forcing people off farmlands to export monocultural crops like palm oil (for industry) and soybeans (for cattle) reduces the quantity and diversity of food available for local consumption. It also has 'devastating human rights effects [while] encouraging vigilantist politics'.[201] What is heralded as agricultural 'progress' might be better described as resource theft and societal and environmental destruction—part and parcel of living in an era of 'rogue capitalism'.[202]

No national flags need flutter over the newly acquired lands. Global finance does not have a 'home'.

Notes

1. The first quote is from a speech by President George W. Bush in Kalamazoo, Michigan, on 27 March 2001, see https://www.govinfo.gov/content/pkg/PPP-2001-book1/pdf/PPP-2001-book1-doc-pg320.pdf; the second is from a transcript of the President's war ultimatum speech from the Cross Hall in the White House, 18 March 2003, see https://www.theguardian.com/world/2003/mar/18/usa.iraq.

2. Other famous utterings include 'I know how hard it is to put food on your family', 'More and more of our imports come from overseas', 'The most important job is not to be governor, or first lady in my case ...'. See Weisberg, J. (2001) *George W. Bushisms: The Slate Book of the Accidental Wit and Wisdom of our 43rd President*, Simon and Schuster, London.
3. Cachero, P. (2020) US taxpayers have reportedly paid an average of $8,000 each and over $2 trillion total for the Iraq war alone, https://www.businessinsider.com.au/us-taxpayers-spent-8000-each-2-trillion-iraq-war-study-2020-2?r=US&IR=T; Medea, B. and Davies, N. (2018) The staggering death toll in Iraq, https://www.salon.com/2018/03/19/the-staggering-death-toll-in-iraq_partner/; Washington Institute. (2021) Costs of war, https://watson.brown.edu/costsofwar/costs/human/refugees/iraqi.
4. Chapman, J. (2004) The real reasons Bush went to war, https://www.theguardian.com/world/2004/jul/28/iraq.usa.
5. Quoted in Butt, A. (2019) Why did Bush go to war in Iraq? The answer is more sinister than you think, https://www.commondreams.org/views/2019/03/20/why-did-bush-go-war-iraq-answer-more-sinister-you-think.
6. Shar, S. (2020) The US has been at war 225 out of 243 years since 1776, https://www.thenews.com.pk/print/595752-the-us-has-been-at-war-225-out-of-243-years-since-1776.
7. Shar, The US has been at war 225 out of 243 years since 1776.
8. Shar, The US has been at war 225 out of 243 years since 1776; see also McCoy, A. (2017) *In the Shadows of the American Century: The Rise and Decline of US Global Power*, Haymarket Books, Chicago, p. 55.
9. Wikipedia. (2022) Marengo (horse), https://en.wikipedia.org/wiki/Marengo_(horse).
10. Tynan, J. (2013). *British Army Uniform and the First World War: Men in Khaki*, Palgrave Macmillan, UK, p. 35.
11. White, H. (2022) If growing UW-China rivalry leads to 'the worst war ever', what should Australia do? https://theconversation.com/friday-essay-if-growing-us-china-rivalry-leads-to-the-worst-war-ever-what-should-australia-do-185294.

12. Wikipedia. (2022) Lord Kitchener wants you, https://en.wikipedia.org/wiki/Lord_Kitchener_Wants_You.
13. Andrews, T. (2017) The Uncle Sam 'I Want YOU' poster is 100 years old: Almost everything about it was borrowed, https://www.washingtonpost.com/news/morning-mix/wp/2017/04/03/the-uncle-sam-i-want-you-poster-is-100-years-old-almost-everything-about-it-was-borrowed/.
14. Canva. (2022) 50 powerful examples of visual propaganda and the meanings behind them, https://www.canva.com/learn/examples-of-propaganda/.
15. Norman Rockwell Museum. (2022) *Rosie the Riveter*—1943, https://www.nrm.org/rosie-the-riveter.
16. National Archives. (2022) Powers of persuasion, https://www.archives.gov/exhibits/powers-of-persuasion.
17. Holmstrom, D. (1994) World War II posters—pictures of persuasion, https://www.csmonitor.com/1994/0405/05101.html.
18. Brendon, P. (2016) Death of truth: When propaganda and 'alternative facts' first gripped the world, https://www.theguardian.com/media/2017/mar/11/death-truth-propaganda-alternative-facts-gripped-world; Wikipedia. (2022) Propaganda in Nazi Germany, https://en.wikipedia.org/wiki/Propaganda_in_Nazi_Germany.
19. History Network News. (2010) Nazi fairy tales paint Hitler as Little Red Riding Hood's saviour, https://historynewsnetwork.org/article/125576.
20. Wikipedia, Propaganda in Nazi Germany.
21. United States Holocaust Memorial Museum. (2022) Origins of Neo-Nazi and white supremacist terms and symbols, https://www.ushmm.org/antisemitism/what-is-antisemitism/origins-of-neo-nazi-and-white-supremacist-terms-and-symbols; Wikipedia, Propaganda in Nazi Germany.
22. DW. (2020) How the Nazis used poster art as propaganda, https://www.dw.com/en/how-the-nazis-used-poster-art-as-propaganda/a-55751640.

23. The book has been described as 'turgid, repetitious, wandering, illogical'. See Britannica. (2022) *Mein Kampf*, https://www.britannica.com/topic/Mein-Kampf.
24. Jowett, G. and O'Donnell, V. (2015) *Propaganda and Persuasion*, Sixth Edition, Sage, California.
25. Wikipedia. (2022) Propaganda in the Soviet Union, https://en.wikipedia.org/wiki/Propaganda_in_the_Soviet_Union.
26. Lamb, J. (2017) Joseph Stalin's cult of personality, https://historycollection.com/joseph-stalin-cult-personality/.
27. Lamb, Joseph Stalin's cult of personality.
28. This refers to the herring's bioluminescent properties. The quote is found in Service, R. (2003) *A History of Modern Russia, from Nicholas II to Putin*, Harvard University Press, Massachusetts, p. 405.
29. Wikipedia. (2022) Propaganda in the Soviet Union.
30. Dolgopolov, G. (2022) How Solntsepyok, a brutal 2021 propaganda film, primed Russians for war with Ukraine, https://theconversation.com/how-solntsepyok-a-brutal-2021-propaganda-film-primed-russians-for-war-with-ukraine-185701.
31. Pankieiev, O. (2022) How Russia's unanswered propaganda led to the war in Ukraine, https://theconversation.com/how-russias-unanswered-propaganda-led-to-the-war-in-ukraine-180202; see also StopFake. (2017) Dependent media—Russia's military TV Zvezda, https://www.stopfake.org/en/dependent-media-russia-s-military-tv-zvezda/.
32. Horvath, R. (2022) The banality of Putin's evil, https://www.lowyinstitute.org/the-interpreter/banality-putin-s-evil.
33. Pankieiev, How Russia's unanswered propaganda led to the war in Ukraine; Jackson, J. (2022) Putin warns against taking Russia's retreats as defeat, https://www.newsweek.com/vladimir-putin-russia-ukraine-retreat-warning-1714426.
34. Horvath, The banality of Putin's evil; Snegovaya, M., Kimmage, M. and McGlynn, J. (2023) The ideology of Putinism: Is it sustainable? https://csis.org/analysis/ideology-putinism-it-sustainable.

35. All Top Everything. (2022) Top 10 best-selling books of all time, https://www.alltopeverything.com/top-10-best-selling-books-of-all-time/.
36. BBC News. (2015) Who, what, why: What is the Little Red Book? https://www.bbc.com/news/magazine-34932800.
37. Phillips, T. (2016) The Cultural Revolution: All you need to know about China's political convulsion, https://www.theguardian.com/world/2016/may/11/the-cultural-revolution-50-years-on-all-you-need-to-know-about-chinas-political-convulsion.
38. University of Washington. (2012) Mao's Little Red Book, 1964, https://ischool.uw.edu/podcasts/dtctw/maos-little-red-book.
39. Phillips, The Cultural Revolution.
40. Wikipedia. (2022) Propaganda in China, https://en.wikipedia.org/wiki/Propaganda_in_China.
41. Wikipedia. (2022) Propaganda in China.
42. The Economic Times. (2021) China's kids get schooled in 'Xi Jinping thought', https://m.economictimes.com/news/international/world-news/chinas-kids-get-schooled-in-xi-jinping-thought/articleshow/85823160.cms.
43. Hamilton, J. and Kosar, K. (2020) Call it what it is: Propaganda, https://www.politico.com/news/magazine/2020/10/08/government-communication-propaganda-427290.
44. See Funk, C. (1994) The Committee on Public Information and the mobilization of public opinion in the United States during World War I: The effects on education and artists, *Journal of Social Theory in Art Education* 14: 120–147.
45. See Funk, The Committee on Public Information and the mobilization of public opinion in the United States during World War I; Neumann, C. (2009) Committee on Public Information, https://www.mtsu.edu/first-amendment/article/1179/committee-on-public-information.
46. Howell, T. (1997) The Writers' War Board: U.S. domestic propaganda in World War II, *The Historian* 59(4): 795–813. The quote is on p. 813.

47. Quoted in Howell, The Writers' War Board: U.S. domestic propaganda in World War II, p. 795.
48. See video at: https://www.youtube.com/watch?v=KQVXHl MvOoU.
49. Llewellyn, J. and Thompson, S. (2020) Reds under the bed, https://alphahistory.com/coldwar/reds-under-the-bed/.
50. Louise, C. (2021) Hamburger history hour: Where did hamburgers originate? https://eatwithme.net/hamburger-history-hour-where-did-hamburgers-originate/.
51. Llewellyn, J., Southey, J. and Thompson, S. (2019) French colonialism in Vietnam, https://alphahistory.com/vietnamwar/french-colonialism-in-vietnam/.
52. Irvine, D. (2017) Propaganda posters: Life during war in Vietnam, https://edition.cnn.com/travel/article/cnngo-travel-vietnam-propaganda-poster-art/index.html. See also Chandler, R. (1981) *War of Ideas: The U.S. Propaganda Campaign in Vietnam*, Routledge, New York.
53. Recker, J. (2022) Fifty years later, Kim Phuc Phan Thi is more than 'Napalm Girl', https://www.smithsonianmag.com/smart-news/Kim-Phuc-Phan-Thi-Napalm-Girl-180980227/.
54. Renkl, M. (2020) When a picture Is worth a thousand tears: Photos of suffering children have the power to soften sentiment toward the "other." Can that still happen in a polarized age? https://www.nytimes.com/2020/02/17/opinion/photojournalism-children-nick-ut.html.
55. Henderson, D. (2014) Who caused the August 1990 spike in oil prices? https://www.econlib.org/archives/2014/06/who_caused_the.html.
56. Wikipedia. (2022) Propaganda in the United States, https://en.wikipedia.org/wiki/Propaganda_in_the_United_States.
57. Wikipedia, Propaganda in the United States.
58. Quoted in Shah, A. (2003) Media, propaganda and Iraq, https://www.globalissues.org/article/400/media-propaganda-and-iraq.
59. Wikipedia. (2022) Hill+Knowlton strategies, https://en.wikipedia.org/wiki/Hill%2BKnowlton_Strategies.

60. Anderson, S., Bennis, P. and Cavanagh, J. (2003) Coalition of the willing or coalition of the coerced? https://ips-dc.org/wp-content/uploads/2003/02/COERCED.pdf.
61. Jackson, P. (2021) September 11 attacks: What happened? https://www.bbc.com/news/world-us-canada-57698668.
62. Quoted in Gwozdecky, M. (2005) Iraq WMD timeline: How the mystery unravelled, https://www.npr.org/2005/11/15/4996218/iraq-wmd-timeline-how-the-mystery-unraveled.
63. Pillar, P. (2011) The Iraq war and the power of propaganda, https://nationalinterest.org/node/1216; Gershkoff, A. and Kushner, S. (2005) Shaping public opinion: The 9/11-Iraq connection in the Bush Administration's rhetoric, *Perspectives on Politics* 3(3): 525–537.
64. Bourgois, P. (2020) Project for a New American Century, https://www.e-ir.info/2020/02/01/new-american-century-1997-2006-and-the-post-cold-war-neoconservative-moment/. PNAC commenced its activities in 1997 but was dissolved in 2006 after it had achieved its main goal of having the US substantially increase its military budget, and go to war in the Middle East.
65. Altheide, D. and Grimes, J. (2005) War programming: The propaganda project and the Iraq war, *The Sociological Quarterly* 46(4): 617–643; Taibbi, M. (2019) 16 years later, how the press that sold the Iraq war got a way with it, https://www.rollingstone.com/politics/politics-features/iraq-war-media-fail-matt-taibbi-812230/.
66. Al Jazeera. (2011) The connection between Iraq and 9/11, https://www.aljazeera.com/news/2011/9/7/the-connection-between-iraq-and-9.
67. Stuff. (2009) Saddam forced to watch South Park, https://www.stuff.co.nz/entertainment/tv-radio/2326680/Saddam-forced-to-watch-South-Park. The movie's title was *South Park: Bigger, Longer and Uncut*.
68. Savell, S. (2023) *How Death Outlives War: The Reverberating Impact of the Post-9/11 Wars on Human Health*, Watson Institute for International and Public Affairs, Brown University, Rhode

Island, p. 2. Available at: https://watson.brown.edu/costsofwar/files/cow/imce/papers/2023/Indirect%20Deaths.pdf.
69. Savell, *How Death Outlives War*, p. 2.
70. Gray, T. (2020) How to invest in the military-industrial complex, https://www.nytimes.com/2020/04/15/business/how-invest-military-industrial-complex.html.
71. Gray, How to invest in the military-industrial complex.
72. Stockwell, S. and Muir, A. (2003) The military-entertainment complex: A new facet of information warfare, https://one.fibreculturejournal.org/fcj-004-the-military-entertainment-complex-a-new-facet-of-information-warfare.
73. Spy Culture. (2022) 'Complete' list of DoD assisted movies, https://www.spyculture.com/complete-list-of-dod-assisted-movies/.
74. Rico, J. (2019) Hollywood films funded by the Pentagon, https://www.liveabout.com/pentagon-support-for-war-films-3438458.
75. Secker, T. and Alford, M. (2017) How Hollywood promotes war on behalf of the Pentagon, CIA and NSA, https://renegadeinc.com/how-hollywood-promotes-war-on-behalf-of-the-pentagon-cia-and-nsa/.
76. Department of Defense. (2018) How and why the DOD works with Hollywood, https://www.defense.gov/News/Inside-DOD/Blog/article/2062735/how-why-the-dod-works-with-hollywood/.
77. Ellis, L. (2018) Was Katy Perry in the military? https://celebanswers.com/was-katy-perry-in-the-military/.
78. Rothschild, M. (2021) Movies and TV shows sponsored by the US Government, https://www.ranker.com/list/movies-and-tv-shows-sponsored-by-the-government/mike-rothschild; Wikipedia. (2022) Military-entertainment complex, https://en.wikipedia.org/wiki/Military%E2%80%93entertainment_complex.
79. Stockwell and Muir, The military-entertainment complex; Wikipedia, Military-entertainment complex.

80. Zenou, T. (2022) 'Top Gun', brought to you by the U.S. military, https://www.washingtonpost.com/history/2022/05/27/top-gun-maverick-us-military/; Sirota, D. (2022) America's Top Gun problem, https://www.levernews.com/lever-time-americas-top-gun-problem-also-elisabeth-epps-vs-corporate-interests/.
81. Zenou, 'Top Gun', brought to you by the U.S. military.
82. Sirota, D. (2011) 25 years later, how 'Top Gun' made America love war, https://www.washingtonpost.com/opinions/25-years-later-remembering-how-top-gun-changed-americas-feelings-about-war/2011/08/15/gIQAU6qJgJ_story.html.
83. Saveliev, D. (2021) New Marvel film puts spotlight on Hollywood's military ties, https://responsiblestatecraft.org/2021/11/05/new-marvel-film-puts-spotlight-on-hollywoods-military-ties/.
84. Robb, D. (2004) *Operation Hollywood: How the Pentagon Shapes and Censors Movies*, Prometheus, New York.
85. Sirota, 25 years later, how 'Top Gun' made America love war.
86. Cook, J. (2017) Wonder Woman is a hero only the military-industrial complex could create, https://www.jonathan-cook.net/2017-07-07/wonder-woman-is-a-hero-only-the-military-industrial-complex-could-create/.
87. Robitzski, D. (2019) Dozens of countries are deploying propaganda on social media, https://futurism.com/the-byte/countries-sponsor-propaganda-social-media.
88. See for more details: Wren-Lewis, S. (2018) *The Lies We Were Told: Politics, Economics, Austerity and Brexit*, Bristol University Press, Bristol; Hutton, W. (2021) The case for Brexit was built on lies. Five years later, deceit is routine in our politics, https://www.theguardian.com/commentisfree/2021/jun/27/case-for-brexit-built-on-lies-five-years-later-deceit-is-routine-in-our-politics; Independent. (2018) Final say: The misinformation that was told about Brexit during and after the referendum, https://www.independent.co.uk/news/uk/politics/final-say-brexit-referendum-lies-boris-johnson-leave-campaign-remain-a8466751.html.

89. Laville, S. (2024) UN expert condemns UK crackdown on environmental protest, https://www.theguardian.com/environment/2024/jan/23/un-expert-condemns-uk-crackdown-on-environmental-protest.
90. Quoted in Kollewe, J. (2023) Brexit is a 'complete disaster' and 'total lies', says former Tory donor, https://www.theguardian.com/business/2023/jan/31/brexit-lies-tory-billionaire-guy-hands-uk-eu-economy.
91. Kelly, M. (2019) Here's an A to Z list of Brexit lies, https://www.gq-magazine.co.uk/article/list-of-brexit-lies.
92. Savage, M. (2019) How Brexit party won Euro elections on social media—simple, negative messages to older voters, https://www.theguardian.com/politics/2019/jun/29/how-brexit-party-won-euro-elections-on-social-media.
93. Brändle, V., Galpin, C. and Trenzc, H. (2021) Brexit as 'politics of division': Social media campaigning after the referendum, *Social Movement Studies* 21(1–2): 234–253.
94. Carland, S. (2024) Australian media's Instagram posts on Gaza war have and anti-Palestinian bias. That has real-world consequences, https://theconversation.com/australian-medias-instagram-posts-on-gaza-war-have-an-anti-palestine-bias-that-has-real-world-consequences-221609.
95. Spencer, S. and Gore, D. (2023) What we know about three widespread Israel-Hamas war claims, https://www.factcheck.org/2023/10/what-we-know-about-three-widespread-israel-hamas-war-claims/.
96. Kennedy, R. (2023) Israeli-Hamas war: Fact-checking online misinformation, https://www.reuters.com/world/middle-east/fact-checking-online-misinformation-israel-hamas-conflict-2023-10-09/; Ohlheiser, A. (2023) Don't believe everything you see and hear about Israel and Palestine, https://www.vox.com/technology/2023/10/12/23913472/misinformation-israel-hamas-war-social-media-literacy-palestine.
97. BBC. (2021) Israel-Palestinian conflict: False and misleading claims fact-checked, https://www.bbc.com/news/57111293.

98. Gilbert, D. (2023) Elon Musk Is shitposting his way through the Israel-Hamas war, https://www.wired.com/story/elon-musk-israel-hamas-war-disinformation-x/.
99. Eisikovits, N. (2023) War in Gaza: An ethicist explains why you shouldn't turn to social media for information about the conflict or to do something about it, https://theconversation.com/war-in-gaza-an-ethicist-explains-why-you-shouldnt-turn-to-social-media-for-information-about-the-conflict-or-to-do-something-about-it-218912.
100. Spry, D. (2019) Share, like, comment, attack: Social media as weapon and battlefield, https://www.lowyinstitute.org/the-interpreter/share-comment-attack-social-media-weapon-and-battlefield.
101. Watts, C. (2016) Hackers, hecklers & honeypots—Russia's 3 personas promoting Trump that undermine democracy, https://twitter.com/selectedwisdom/status/795252890860453888.
102. Marineau, S. (2020) Fact check US: What is the impact of Russian interference in the US presidential election? https://theconversation.com/fact-check-us-what-is-the-impact-of-russian-interference-in-the-us-presidential-election-146711.
103. Reich, R. (2016) Trump's seven techniques to control the media, https://robertreich.org/post/153748549760.
104. Golshan, T. (2016) Trump says the press mangles his 'beautiful flowing sentences'. We asked linguists to weigh in, https://www.vox.com/policy-and-politics/2016/12/14/13953528/trump-beautiful-sentences-linguists.
105. Cillizza, C. (2022) A very revealing Donald Trump quote about why he ran for president, https://edition.cnn.com/2022/09/26/politics/donald-trump-president-quote-maggie-haberman-book/index.html.
106. Quoted in McAdams, D. (2020) *The Strange Case of Donald Trump: A Psychological Reckoning*, Oxford University Press, New York, p. 118.
107. Gabbatt, A. (2022) Has 'Trumpty Dumpty' taken a great fall from Rupert Murdoch's grace? https://www.theguardian.com/us-news/2022/nov/10/rupert-murdoch-trump-desantis-ny-post.

108. Marineau, S. (2020) Fact check US: What is the impact of Russian interference in the US presidential election?
109. Marineau, S. (2020) Fact check US: What is the impact of Russian interference in the US presidential election?
110. University of Oxford. (2021) Social media manipulation by political actors an industrial scale problem—Oxford report, https://www.ox.ac.uk/news/2021-01-13-social-media-manipulation-political-actors-industrial-scale-problem-oxford-report.
111. Tuffley, D. (2022) Concerns over TikTok feeding user data to Beijing are back—and there's good evidence to support them, https://www.nzherald.co.nz/world/the-conversation-concerns-over-tiktok-feeding-user-data-to-beijing-are-back-and-theres-good-evidence-to-support-them/UGRH6UXHPSGJK25PY3ACNQMOXQ/.
112. Quoted in Tuffley, Concerns over TikTok feeding user data to Beijing are back—and there's good evidence to support them.
113. Quoted in StopFakeOrg. (2017) Dependent media—Russia's military TV Zvezda, https://www.stopfake.org/en/dependent-media-russia-s-military-tv-zvezda/.
114. Stanley, J. (2015) *How Propaganda Works*, Princeton University Press, Princeton.
115. Marshall, T. (2017) *A Flag to Die For: The Power and Politics of National Symbols*, Scribner, New York.
116. Marshall, *A Flag to Die For*, p. 5.
117. RACGP. (2022) Flag protocol—about the three flags, https://www.racgp.org.au/FSDEDEV/media/documents/Faculties/ATSI/NFATSIH-flag-protocal.pdf.
118. Ochman, P. (2021) The meaning behind traditional flag folding, https://www.chaptershealth.org/chapters-of-life-blog/patients/meaning-behind-traditional-flag-folding/.
119. Theodorou, A. (2014) 64 countries have religious symbols on their national flags, https://www.pewresearch.org/fact-tank/2014/11/25/64-countries-have-religious-symbols-on-their-national-flags/.
120. Wikipedia. (2022) International Code of Signals, https://en.wikipedia.org/wiki/International_Code_of_Signals.

121. WorldAtlas. (2022) Countries with red, white and blue flags, https://www.worldatlas.com/articles/countries-with-red-white-and-blue-flags.html.
122. NcNamara, R. (2018) Why were flags so important in the Civil War? https://www.thoughtco.com/flags-importance-in-the-civil-war-1773716.
123. Corbould, C. (2020) Why is the Confederate flag so offensive? https://theconversation.com/why-is-the-confederate-flag-so-offensive-143256.
124. Chiacu, D. (2020) Trump says Confederate flag proud symbol of U.S. South, https://www.reuters.com/article/us-usa-trump-confederate-idUSKCN24K0I0.
125. Wikipedia. (2022) Christianity and colonialism, https://en.wikipedia.org/wiki/Christianity_and_colonialism.
126. GoodReads. (2022) Jomo Kenyatta, https://www.goodreads.com/quotes/21275-when-the-missionaries-arrived-the-africans-had-the-land-and; see also McMichael, P. (2012) *Development and Social Change: A Global Perspective*, Sage, Los Angeles, p. 29.
127. Wikipedia, Christianity and colonialism.
128. Gilley, B. (2017) The case for colonialism, *Third World Quarterly*, https://doi.org/10.1080/01436597.2017.1369037.
129. Khan, S. (2017) The case against 'The case for colonialism', https://www.cato.org/commentary/case-against-case-colonialism.
130. See Ferguson, N. (2002) *Empire: The Rise and Demise of the British World Order and the Lessons for Global Power*, Penguin, London.
131. Milman, O. (2019) European colonization of Americas killed so many it cooled Earth's climate, https://www.theguardian.com/environment/2019/jan/31/european-colonization-of-americas-helped-cause-climate-change.
132. See discussion in Haynes, J. (2021) *Great Furphies of Australian History*, Allen and Unwin, Sydney, p. 52.
133. Sartore, M. (2021) The most devastating atrocities committed by every European colonial empire, https://www.ranker.com/list/worst-colonial-european-regimes/melissa-sartore.

134. Sartore, The most devastating atrocities committed by every European colonial empire; Mousseau, S. (2024) Colonialism revamped in the Democratic Republic of Congo, https://africanarguments.org/2024/04/colonialism-revamped-in-the-democratic-republic-of-congo/.
135. Bonny, A. (2020) Africa awaits closure of French colonial crimes, https://www.aa.com.tr/en/africa/africa-awaits-closure-of-french-colonial-crimes/2067938.
136. Bensaid, A. (2021) France's silence over colonial crimes ensures confrontation with Algeria, https://www.trtworld.com/magazine/france-s-silence-over-colonial-crimes-ensures-confrontation-with-algeria-50756.
137. Fanon, F. (1963) *The Wretched of the Earth*, Grove Press, New York.
138. Alpha History. (2022) French colonialism in Vietnam, https://alphahistory.com/vietnamwar/french-colonialism-in-vietnam/.
139. Rydstrom, H. (2015) Politics of colonial violence: Gendered atrocities in French occupied Vietnam, *European Journal of Women's Studies* 22(2): 191–207; Walsh, L. (2015) The crimes of French imperialism, https://redflag.org.au/article/crimes-french-imperialism; Alpha History, French colonialism in Vietnam.
140. Walsh, The crimes of French imperialism.
141. TRT World. (2022) Dutch army's notorious record in global conflicts from Indonesia to Bosnia, https://www.trtworld.com/magazine/dutch-army-s-notorious-record-in-global-conflicts-from-indonesia-to-bosnia-54982.
142. Luttikhuis, B. and Moses, D. (2012) Mass violence and the end of the Dutch colonial empire in Indonesia, *Journal of Genocide Research* 14(3–4): 257–276.
143. Wikipedia. (2022) Herero and Namaqua genocide, https://en.wikipedia.org/wiki/Herero_and_Namaqua_genocide.
144. Quoted in Library of Congress. (2022) Treatment of natives in German colonies, https://www.loc.gov/item/a22000971/.

145. Historic Royal Palaces. (2022) Henry VIII Renaissance prince or terrible Tudor? Who was the real Henry VIII? https://www.hrp.org.uk/hampton-court-palace/history-and-stories/henry-viii/#gs.ca1jju.
146. Wikipedia. (2022) Tudor conquest of Ireland, https://en.wikipedia.org/wiki/Tudor_conquest_of_Ireland.
147. Stack Exchange. (2022) What was the likely death toll of the Tudor invasion of Ireland? https://history.stackexchange.com/questions/56390/what-was-the-likely-death-toll-of-the-tudor-invasion-of-ireland.
148. Murphy, N. (2016) Violence, colonization and Henry VIII's conquest of France, 1544–1546, *Past & Present* 233(1): 13–51.
149. Wikipedia. (2023) Perfidious Albion, https://en.wikipedia.org/wiki/Perfidious_Albion.
150. Thomas, T. (2022) What are the British monarchy's historical links to slavery? https://www.theguardian.com/uk-news/2022/mar/23/british-royal-family-monarchy-historical-links-to-slavery.
151. Chew, C. (2020) Remembering Britain's leading role in the Atlantic slave trade, https://historiesofcolour.com/THE-BRITISH-SLAVE-TRADE.
152. Chew, Remembering Britain's leading role in the Atlantic slave trade.
153. Quoted in Chew, Remembering Britain's leading role in the Atlantic slave trade.
154. Griffin, N. (2008) How many died during Cromwell's campaign? https://www.historyireland.com/how-many-died-during-cromwells-campaign/.
155. Little, P. (2016) Oliver Cromwell, the laughing Roundhead, https://www.historytoday.com/archive/oliver-cromwell-laughing-roundhead.
156. Sparrow, J. (2022) Friday essay: A slave trade—how blackbirding in colonial Australia created a legacy of racism, https://theconversation.com/friday-essay-a-slave-state-how-blackbirding-in-colonial-australia-created-a-legacy-of-racism-187782.

157. Walquist, C. (2018) Evidence of 250 massacres of Indigenous Australians mapped, https://www.theguardian.com/australia-news/2018/jul/27/evidence-of-250-massacres-of-indigenous-australians-mapped.
158. Allam, L. and Evershed, N. (2019) The killing times: The massacres of Aboriginal people Australia must confront, https://www.theguardian.com/australia-news/2019/mar/04/the-killing-times-the-massacres-of-aboriginal-people-australia-must-confront.
159. Allam, L. and Evershed, N. (2022) Almost half the massacres of Aboriginal people were by police or other government forces, research finds, https://www.theguardian.com/australia-news/2022/mar/16/almost-half-the-massacres-of-aboriginal-people-were-by-police-research-finds.
160. Keenan, D. (2022) New Zealand wars, http://www.TeAra.govt.nz/en/new-zealand-wars; see also Campbell, H. (2021) *Farming Inside Invisible Worlds: Modernist Agriculture and its Consequences*, Bloomsbury, London.
161. See, for example, National Museum Australia. (2022) Smallpox epidemic, https://www.nma.gov.au/defining-moments/resources/smallpox-epidemic.
162. Rao, S. (2016) British colonization of India, https://www.indiafacts.org.in/british-colonization-india/.
163. Tharoor, S. (2017) *Inglorious Empire: What the British did to India*, Hurst, London.
164. Rao, British colonization of India.
165. Polya, G. (2019) Britain robbed India of $45 trillion & thence 1.8 billion Indians died from deprivation, https://mronline.org/2019/01/15/britain-robbed-india-of-45-trillion-thence-1-8-billion-indians-died-from-deprivation/.
166. McQuade, J. (2017) Colonialism was a disaster and the facts prove it, https://theconversation.com/colonialism-was-a-disaster-and-the-facts-prove-it-84496.
167. Sartore, The most devastating atrocities committed by every European colonial empire.

168. Sartore, The most devastating atrocities committed by every European colonial empire; Yee, A. (2022) Five of the British Empire's worst atrocities under Queen Elizabeth's reign, https://www.liberationnews.org/five-of-the-british-empires-worst-atrocities-under-queen-elizabeths-reign/.
169. Alexander, C. (2017) Colonialism in India was traumatic—including for some of the British officials who ruled the Raj, https://theconversation.com/colonialism-in-india-was-traumatic-including-for-some-of-the-british-officials-who-ruled-the-raj-77068; Getz, T. and Streets-Salter, H. (2010) *Modern Imperialism and Colonialism: A Global Perspective*, Prentice-Hall, New Jersey.
170. Yang, B. and He, J. (2021) Global land grabbing: A critical review of cases studies across the world, *Land* 10(3), https://www.mdpi.com/2073-445X/10/3/324.
171. GRAIN. (2023) Squeezing communities dry: Water grabbing by the global food industry, https://grain.org/en/article/7039-squeezing-communities-dry-water-grabbing-by-the-global-food-industry.
172. Smith, K. (2023) Land grabs, in M. Clarke and Z. Xinyu (eds) *Elgar Encyclopedia of Development*, Edward Elgar, Cheltenham, UK, pp. 403–407.
173. Scrimgeour, G. (2023) Agricultural land is becoming an investment vehicle for the rich, https://jacobin.com/2023/06/agriculture-property-tax-break-use-value-assessment-superrich-mark-zuckerberg-investment.
174. The Oakland Institute. (2023) *Green Colonialism 2.0: Tree Plantations and Carbon Offsets in Africa*, https://www.oaklandinstitute.org/green-colonialism-two-carbon-offsets-africa. As the authors of the report argue 'industrial tree plantations cause extensive harm to both the environment and communities – driving deforestation [of native species], land grabs, destruction of livelihoods, as well as toxic contamination of land and water' with carbon offset programs having a 'terrible track record, systematically failing to reduce carbon emissions'—see The Oaklands Institute, *Green Colonialism* 2.0, p. 5.

175. Earth.Org. (2021) What is green colonialism? https://earth.org/green-colonialism/; Tramel, S. (2024) Five things to know about the global land rush and how to stop it, https://www.commondreams.org/opinions/5-things-global-land-rush.
176. Lawrence, G., Sippel, S. and Burch, D. (2015) The financialisation of food and farming, in G. Robinson and D. Carson (eds) *Handbook on the Globalisation of Agriculture*, Edward Elgar, Cheltenham, pp. 328–349; Lawrence, G., Lyons, K. and Wallington, T. (eds) (2010) *Food Security, Nutrition and Sustainability*, Earthscan, London.
177. Yang and He, Global land grabbing.
178. Geisler, C. and Makki, F. (2014) People, power, and land: New enclosures on a global scale, *Rural Sociology* 79(1): 28–33.
179. Farmlandgrab.org. (2023) Wealth advisors gain access to global farmland investment from Nuveen via iCapital, https://www.farmlandgrab.org/post/view/31664-wealth-advisors-gain-access-to-global-farmland-investment-from-nuveen-via-icapital.
180. Oakland Institute. (2022) Peasants still feed the world, even if FAO claims otherwise, https://www.oaklandinstitute.org/peasants-still-feed-world-even-if-fao-claims-otherwise; ETC Group. (2022) Small-scale farmers and peasants still feed the world, https://www.etcgroup.org/content/backgrounder-small-scale-farmers-and-peasants-still-feed-world; GRAIN. (2014) Hungry for land: Small farmers feed the world with less than a quarter of all farmland, https://grain.org/article/entries/4929-hungry-for-land-small-farmers-feed-the-world-with-less-than-a-quarter-of-all-farmland.
181. Oakland Institute, Peasants still feed the world.
182. GRAIN. (2012) *The Great Food Robbery: How Corporations Control Food, Grab Land and Destroy the Environment*, Pambazuka Press, Cape Town.
183. GRAIN. (2012) *The Great Food Robbery*.
184. GRAIN. (2010) Global agribusiness: Two decades of plunder, https://grain.org/article/entries/4055-global-agribusiness-two-decades-of-plunder.

185. Cotula, L., Vermeulen, S., Leonard, R. and Keeley, J. (2009) *Land Grab or Development Opportunity? Agricultural Investment and International Land Deals in Africa*, IED/FAO/IFAD, London/Rome.
186. Global Agriculture. (2022) Land grabbing, https://www.global agriculture.org/report-topics/land-grabbing.html.
187. World Rainforest Movement. (2022) Water and land: Inseparable threads of life, https://www.wrm.org.uy/bulletin-articles/water-and-land-inseparable-threads-of-life; Smith, Land grabs.
188. Displacement Solutions. (2019) Land grabbing as an internationally wrongful act: A legal roadmap for ending land grabbing and housing, land and property rights abuses, crimes and impunity in Myanmar, https://reliefweb.int/sites/reliefweb.int/files/resources/DIS6171%20Land%20Grabbing%20as%20an%20Internationally%20Wrongful%20Act%20v4_1.pdf.
189. Carrero, G., Simmons, C., Walker, R. (2022) The great Amazon land grab—how Brazil's government is clearing the way for deforestation, https://theconversation.com/the-great-amazon-land-grab-how-brazils-government-is-clearing-the-way-for-deforestation-173416.
190. Carrero, Simmons, Walker, The great Amazon land grab; Friends of the Earth. (2022) Red Handed Deforestation and Bunge's Silent Conquest: How Land-Grabbers and Soy Speculators Enable the Destruction of Brazil's Cerrado, https://1bps6437gg8c169i0y1drtgz-wpengine.netdna-ssl.com/wp-content/uploads/2022/04/Red-Handed-Deforestation.pdf.
191. GRAIN. (2022) The digitalisation of land: More data, less land, https://grain.org/en/article/6832-the-digitalisation-of-land-more-data-less-land.
192. GRAIN, The digitalisation of land.
193. Gerin, R. (2022) Lao villagers told to vacate their farms by month's end, https://www.farmlandgrab.org/post/view/31112.
194. Loho, P. (2022) Large-scale land acquisitions in Africa: Is bigger really better? https://www.farmlandgrab.org/post/view/30872.
195. Tulone, A., Galati, A., Pecoraro, S., Carroccio, A., Siggia, D., Virzi, M. and Crescimanno, M. (2022) Main intrinsic

factors driving land grabbing in the African countries' agro-food industry, *Land Use Policy* 120(September): 1–9; Sullivan, J., Samii, C., Brown, D. and Agrawal, A. (2023) Large-scale land acquisitions exacerbate local farmland inequalities in Tanzania, *PNAS* 120(32): e2207398120, https://doi.org/10.1073/pnas.2207398120.
196. Tulone et al., Main intrinsic factors driving land grabbing in the African countries' agro-food industry.
197. Constantina, C., Luminita, C. and Vasileb, J. (2017) Land grabbing: A review of extent and possible consequences in Romania, *Land Use Policy* (62)March: 143–150; Tulone et al., Main intrinsic factors driving land grabbing in the African countries' agro-food industry.
198. Constantina, Luminita, and Vasileb, Land grabbing.
199. Larson, D., Otsuka, K., Matsumoto, T. and Kilic, T. (2012) Should African rural development strategies depend on smallholder farms? An exploration of the inverse productivity hypothesis, *Policy Research Working Paper 6190, The World Bank Development Research Group, Agriculture and Rural Development Team*, Worldbank, Washington, DC; van der Ploeg, J. (2017) The importance of peasant agriculture: The neglected truth, https://edepot.wur.nl/403213.
200. McMichael, P. (2023) Critical agrarian studies and crises of the world-historical present, *Journal of Peasant Studies*, https://doi.org/10.1080/03066150.2022.2163630; McMichael, P. (2014) Rethinking land grab ontology, *Rural Sociology* 79(1): 34–55; Holt-Giminez, E. (2017) *A Foodie's Guide to Capitalism: Understanding the Political Economy of What We Eat*, Monthly Review Press, New York, p. 104.
201. McMichael, Critical agrarian studies and crises of the world-historical present.
202. Seufert, P., Herre, R., Monsalve, S. and Guttal, S. (2020) *Rogue Capitalism and the Financialization of Territories and Nature*, FIAN International, Germany; GRAIN. (2012) *The Great Food Robbery*; McMichael, Rethinking the land grab ontology; Holt-Giminez, *A Foodie's Guide to Capitalism*.

6

Praying for Salvation: Forgeries and Fallacies of Religion

I was 14 years of age and living with my parents and sister in the not-so-salubrious suburb of Rydalmere, in Sydney's west. My mother was unwell, and I discussed her circumstances with the local minister of religion at a rectory located near the beautifully named Kissing Point Road. The conversation went something like this:

Geoff: My mother is ill and does not seem to be getting better.
Minister: Have you prayed for her?
Geoff: Yes.
Minister: If it is God's will then she will recover.
Geoff: What if she doesn't recover?
Minister: Then God has chosen to take her to heaven, for which you should thank him in prayer.

I'm sure I nodded and was appropriately deferential, but I smelled a rat. My mother either lives or dies, but God wins out both ways. And, of course, one must never question God's will. (Fortunately, my mother lived for another 16 years despite the lack of prayer from her son. Of course, if I'd prayed, she may have lived longer.)[1]

Let us consider one of the most prominent agencies of societal deception—the church. Why do people practise religion? There are many sane and sound reasons.[2] Most of the prominent religions—Christianity, Islam, Judaism, Hinduism, and Buddhism—provide comforting answers to four important questions; Why were we born? What is our purpose in life? Who is looking after us on earth? And, of course, where do we go when we die? For modern-day Christians, the usual answers are that we are born to serve God's will, to live a good and moral life, to bear the suffering that accompanies life's journey, and our life on earth is guided by the mighty hand of God. When it's all over our souls face judgement day. This is when God determines our destiny. If we've been good—or have been not-so-good but have asked for forgiveness—we can live on forever in God's sanctuary for the saintly. We will meet those we have known in the past and we will 'laugh, love and grow ethically, intellectually and spiritually'.[3] If we have egregiously sinned, we might experience endless suffering, burning in hell in the company of the Devil. Along life's Christian journey we might be pulled into the odd crusade, be invited to burn witches at the stake,[4] or take part in an exorcism to remove demonic spirits from a body possessed.

Muslims embrace Islam (literally 'submission') by incorporating religion into every facet of their daily lives. Muslims are born to serve the will of Allah and to spend their lives in ritual prayer, declaring faith to Allah, providing for the poor, fasting and, if at all possible, undertaking a pilgrimage to Mecca. Their lives are basically a test from Allah as they endure evil and suffering on Earth as preparation for elevation to the garden of Paradise. In death they face the day of judgement. Having been good on earth is an excellent guarantee of an afterlife of ecstasy—one accompanied by sensual pleasures including couches, wine, and (for the men) maidens with 'dark, wide eyes like hidden pearls'[5]; having been bad consigns them to an afterlife of hell, with its blazing flames in, presumably, a location shared by a large congregation of wayward Christians.

Jewish beliefs in an afterlife are varied. Some Jews believe heaven houses souls until they can be reunited with their bodies during resurrection—a time at which the Messiah will appear. Others believe that people live on through those they influence in their everyday lives. We nourish thought and behaviour in our fellow life travellers and we are part of them. Or, heaven might be a place, as one rabbi predicted in the third century, where there is

> no drinking, no mating, no trading, no jealousy, no hatred, and no enmity; the righteous sit with crowns on their heads and enjoy the splendour of the divine Presence.[6]

And there's no eating—no lox, no bagels.

Despite some small differences regarding heaven's culinary offerings, there is a lot in common for these three, large, monotheistic (one supreme God) religions.

What about the Hindu and Buddhist faiths? Hindus, like the Christians and Muslims, believe in a supreme being—in this case Brahman. Brahman is formless and immortal. Everything contains a little bit of Brahman. The soul resides in people, animals, plants—all living things—and is eternal. It can't be destroyed. The aim for humans is to achieve dharma by living a virtuous, moral, and sober life. By doing so, upon death, the soul (atman) will move into another human being. If life has not been lived honourably, you might become a warthog, a jellyfish, or blade of grass. But if you do live your various earthly lives morally—moving your way up the ladder of virtue—you will eventually reach moksha. Your soul will have been liberated from the previous cycle of birth and death and will unite with Brahman. You've achieved a state of perpetual bliss.

Buddhists share with Hindus a belief in reincarnation. For Buddhists the aim of existence is to discover the path to enlightenment while living a moral 'middle way'—one neither embracing wealth and luxury nor experiencing destitution. It is not permitted to take the life of another human being. The life of animals is also sacred—so forget the caveman diet and get used to the lacto-vegetarian option of milk products and plant-based foods. If a good life is lived and spiritual fulfilment attained, it is possible to reach the state of nirvana. No god is required to decide whether you are enlightened or not. People are born to experience suffering and will do so over many cycles of birth and death. Their hope is that nirvana—the state of enlightenment—will be reached through spiritual meditation and reflection.

Of course, the above summary greatly underplays the myriad tenets, assumptions, and practices of the world's main religions. 'Religion' itself is a debatable term. While it is convenient to see religion as a coherent body of knowledge about spiritual affairs, those involved in 'religion' range from genuflecting Anglicans, Lutherans, or Roman Catholics to those worshiping moon and sun gods. All up, over 10,000 'religions' are practised around the world—a multitude from which to choose.[7] And so it was in the past …

Back to the Future

In Ancient Greece or Rome worldly events could be explained by the contentment or exasperation of the gods. Consider the Romans. When personal or societal misfortune occurred, it was obviously caused by one or other divine power having been slighted. Beware the gods. Most families chose a favourite god to worship and constructed a small shrine at which to place items of value, garnering protection for the family. If calamity struck it was a sign of a god's anger. Blood sacrifices might then be required to appease the god or gods. Jupiter, the king of all gods was married to his sister Juno (the goddess of childbirth) and they ran a heavenly council. The council comprised various offspring of the couple, along with children from Jupiter's 14 other marriages—including the sons Mercury, Mars, Apollo, and sundry others. It also included Venus who arose from bloodied and testicle-ridden seafoam following the castration of Uranus by his son Saturn. Then, after Saturn died his three sons divided the world among themselves—Jupiter taking to the heavens, Neptune to the sea, and Pluto to the underworld. Cerberus, a three-headed dog, protected the underworld and presumably sported a very large collar.

The Greek and Roman gods were colourful characters with strange traits. The Romans sang the praises of Cardea, the goddess of door hinges. Terminus was the god of boundary lines, marked by stones. To move a stone was a mortal sin and if you were identified and located, you could be legally killed by the citizenry. Other cultures also exhibit some interesting beliefs. The Aztecs believed in Tlazolteotl who enjoyed feasting on excrement as well as anything in a state of decay, including the newly dead. The native American Innu worshipped Matshishkapeu, the spirit of flatulence. Marvellous things were revealed from the sounds of wind, Matshishkapeu having chosen this somewhat unusual means of speaking to his believers. The Vikings worshipped the Pig of Eternal Bacon, while the Yoruban of Africa had a god of smallpox. The Scandinavians believed in the malevolent Loki who transformed himself into a mare and mated with a stallion, resulting in the birth of an eight-legged spider-horse. When the Egyptian Osiris was killed by brother Set, his body parts were thrown across Egypt with his genitals cast into the sea and eaten by a fish (it was okay though, the goddess Isis put all the rest of his body back together and gave him a golden phallus which made up for the loss). The Greeks had the lecherous goat-like Pan who had an enormous sexual appetite and enjoyed the company of men, women, nymphs, and animals. He was one of the very few gods who died—possibly from over-action. I'm not sure if he ever met the Sumerian goddess of sex and fertility, Inanna, who was also known for her prolific liaisons. They would have been a perfect match. The Greeks also had an Unknown God who was responsible for anything that had been inadvertently left out of the assignments of the other gods.[8]

Could We Be so Silly?

Fast-forward a couple of millennia and we can observe some continuities. For example, if you believe, *inter alia*, that God is an extraterrestrial being living on a planet circling a star named Kolob, that people—looking and dressing very much like Quakers—are living on the moon, that the Garden of Eden was once in Missouri, and that the Holy Ghost goes to sleep each evening at the stroke of midnight, then you are clearly a modern-day member of Joseph Smith's Mormons.[9] In contrast, if you believe that Xenu once ruled the Galactic Confederacy of 76 planets, captured and froze his followers' souls, eventually sending them to earth where they were placed at the base of volcanoes, then 'nuke-ed' into oblivion, then you would be a member of the Church of Scientology (and a very senior member, as it turns out; the secrets are not divulged to the young and gullible).[10]

All this goes to show that people have a penchant for believing virtually anything. People construct meanings and pass them on through culture. People who believe in gods are not silly or stupid. But they have been misinformed and misled—deceived—by the 'sacred' teachings of the spiritual doyens in the societies in which they have lived. The ancient gods and spirits, for example, embodied the taboos, desires, hopes, and fears of people who were seeking meaning in a world dominated by an unstable mixture of pleasure, delight, hunger, disease, war, and death. The gods of the ancients looked and acted much like their followers on earth—they were gods but in human form and dress, displaying human-like emotions such as jealousy, anger, love, and caring. The perceptive Xenophanes, writing some 2,500 years ago, claimed in his poem *The Making of Gods*:

> The Ethiops say that their gods are flat-nosed and black, while the Thracians say that theirs have blue eyes and red hair. Yet if cattle or horses ... had hands and could draw, and could sculpt like men, then the horses would draw their gods like horses, and cattle like cattle; and each they would shape bodies of gods in the likeness, each kind, of their own.[11]

In ancient times belief in, and worship of, gods provided a societally constructed means of sanctioning behaviour while explaining the joys and pains of living. Modern religions do the same as their ancient counterparts—the Christians inculcate their children in the beliefs and values of Christianity, the Jews in Judaism, and the Muslims in Islam. The various claims in these systems of belief become irrefutable truths for their followers. What at all is wrong with this? The problem is that once written in stone, the various ideas become vehicles for religious bigotry and fanaticism. These religions promote falsehoods and lies such as the existence of angels, souls, spirits, heaven, hell, gods, and the Devil. There is no scientific evidence for any of this. And 'fate'—the notion that our lives are predetermined by a supernatural power—turns out to be just another four-letter word. Religions cajole or scare their followers into submitting to these fantasies—with the threat of eternal damnation for those who know well the consequences, yet remain silly enough not to conform. Or they can send in the morality police to ensure women are wearing the hijab, attending prayer sessions, and keeping well away from men. What virtually all religions do—ancient, modern, Christian, Islamic, or Judaist—is to act as agents of social control, approving or disapproving certain behaviours, and moulding society in ways that serve nicely the interests of the upper echelons of the church, of sundry monarchies, of the political elite, and of the well-to-do in civil society. Anthropologist Sir James George Frazer once proposed in his 1890's classic *The Golden Bough* that world cultures were moving from a belief in magic, to a belief in religion, to a recognition and acceptance of scientific explanation.[12] It seems the wheels of history are turning ever so slowly.

The Idea of 'Belief'

In late 2021 I received a request to mark a PhD thesis:

> Amiably stated for your kind consideration … I visited your web page and [was] keen enough to decide to send my dissertation for evaluation to your honour. Therefore, your Excellency is requested to accept my appeal for dissertation evaluation … Thanking you in anticipation.

I normally act positively upon requests such as these (especially ones that refer to me as 'your Excellency'), but in this case I was embroiled in some inane departmental politics and was unavailable. I emailed the student to let him know. He replied:

> Thank you for your response. May Almighty Allah give you more happiness and prosperity in this and after life. Amen

This was a very kind and generous response from someone who both didn't know me and had had his request rejected. Clearly, he was a man of faith, and I'm now secretly hoping I might be the recipient of greater happiness and prosperity.

What Makes Us Believe?

Maybe it is the awe of visiting one of Europe's large cathedrals or mosques. To walk through the ornate façades and stand within the walls of the Basilica di Santa Maria del Fiore in Florence, St. Peter's Basilica in Vatican City, or the Basilica di San Marco in Venice is to be mesmerised by the grandeur of the structures, to be astounded by the beauty of the stained-glass images of the Biblical favourites, and to ponder the many millions of faithful who have visited to burn candles, sing, and pray. A visit to the Sultan Ahmed Mosque (Blue Mosque) in Istanbul is no less inspiring given its stunning blue-tiled walls, its stained-glass windows (containing no images of people, which is in keeping with Muslim religious sensibilities), its famous fountain, domes, and minarets, indeed, its overall majesty. Notre Dame in Paris was another church of splendour—until it burnt down in what might have been a not-so-friendly Act of God in April 2019.[13] Because we can appreciate the sacred, does that mean we 'hard-wired' to believe in gods, as some neuroscientists suggest?[14]

Biologists have shown that religious practices increase serotonin levels in the brain—serotonin is the so-called happiness neurotransmitter.[15] Psychotropic medications affect neurotransmitters in the brain. I'm saying Marx recognised that religion was an opiate, which affected the brains of people. In other words, he was 'psychotropically correct' to say so.[16] It is hard to hold back—religious belief activates the very brain circuits which give us pleasure from sex, drugs, and rock and roll.[17] Given the right setting and stimuli we are putty in the hands of those who would inculcate us with chants, songs, mantras, psalms, and other religious propaganda. But religions have done something much more powerful—they have appropriated rituals. Rituals are performed at the time of birth, marriage, and death. They allow people to gather and to share their culture—its belief systems, language, songs, and dance. Virtually all Christian rituals have their roots in paganism, along with its various symbols—cupids, shepherds, fruit, robes, scrolls, holly, mistletoe, fir trees—even the halo.[18] The Catholic mass and Protestant communion—with their bread and wine—derives from the early worship of the sun gods Ba'al and Osiris (by eating bread, the sun was entering the worshipper's body). Easter was created from the celebration, by pagans, of the spring equinox, where eggs represented fertility—new life. Christmas day, the 25th December, was previously the day of birth of the sun-god Mithras. Our months, and days of the week, have names derived from Roman paganism, while many a famous Christian church was built upon the sites once used for pagan ceremonies. (Jesus' birthplace, the Church of Nativity in Bethlehem, had once been a shrine to the pagan god Adonis.) Pagan symbols—gargoyles and mermaids, for example—can be seen today gracing those very churches. In appropriating pagan rituals and iconography, the Christian church sought to 'convert' non-believers to the cause—something much more easily achieved by insinuating Christian ideologies into festivals and practices well-known and loved by the ancients.[19]

That religion is a so-called default setting for humans has been widely canvassed. But just because we have a brain that is susceptible to religious ideologies does not mean that we are genetically predisposed to god-worship. Not all societies have been religious—which would be the case if we were biologically programmed to 'believe'. Atheism was common in ancient Greece and Rome. Pre-Socratic Greek philosophers like Anaximander and Anaximenes sought to explain dramatic events such as thunder, lightning, and earthquakes as natural phenomena—not as punishment from angry gods. In his plays, Euripides pointed to the flaws in religious thinking.[20] Atheism has spread rapidly during the present century. In the US in the last two decades atheism grew from 6% to 23% of the adult population.[21] Nations where over 60% of the population identify as atheists include Japan, Sweden, Estonia, the Netherlands, Norway, Hong Kong, the UK, Germany, South Korea, Canada, Spain, Finland, Australia, and France, along with—no matter how strange it might seem—Spain, Israel, and Ireland. In China some 91% of the population are atheists—the highest figure for any nation.[22] Apart from the US, the wealthier the country the more irreligious its populace.[23] In today's world the more secular societies—such as those in

Scandinavia—are more equitable, peaceful, healthy, happy, law abiding, and contented than those fostering strong religious adherence.[24]

Sociologists have had some interesting 'takes' on belief. One approach has to do with social cohesion—religion functions to hold societies together by providing shared rules for living. A primary insight of sociology is that people belong to groups and through their interaction with group members they are socialised into sharing particular beliefs which are not unswervingly 'true' but which contribute to social reproduction. Beliefs give moral meanings to communities and, because of this, are often fiercely defended. They are viewed as common sense, normal, and natural. They reinforce traditional values, reaffirm group membership, and sanction behaviour. These are the so-called functionalist ideas promoted by nineteenth-century French social analyst (and atheist) Émile Durkheim. Religion functioned as a social glue, enhancing community well-being. An alternative, critical, approach views religion as false consciousness—a tool used by the powerful to subjugate the lower classes. Religion provides a justification for hard work and obedience in the here-and-now for the promise of glory in the afterlife. For Karl Marx, the moral codes of life don't descend from a tablet in the sky or appear as gold plates in some never-to-be-seen stone box. People create religions—and the religious beliefs therein—all bearing a strong connection to the material conditions in which those people live. But once people create religions they end up being controlled by them. Religions provide illusory happiness, foster servility, and side with society's oppressors. For Marx, religion needs to be abolished.

Finally, German sociologist Max Weber undertook an encyclopaedic examination of the world's great religions and came up with a theory that linked beliefs to economic behaviour. His main claim in *The Protestant Ethic and the Spirit of Capitalism* was that a belief in Calvinism actually 'drove' the formation of capitalism. Here's the logic: Calvinists in sixteenth-century Europe believed in predestination—some followers would be chosen by God to live with him in heaven. But nobody knew who would be chosen. The best way to get your foot in the door was to live a frugal and productive life for the glory of God. Idleness was sinful, and monies earned could not be spent in a carefree or profligate manner. That would be un-Godly. This set of beliefs (the Protestant

Ethic) produced a 'spirit of capitalism' which ensured monies accumulated during one's hard and sober working life would be reinvested in the economy. In this way, the religious ethos of the Calvinists contributed to the formation of capitalism—beliefs have material outcomes. (This is in contradistinction to Marx who, as it was suggested earlier, saw material conditions driving beliefs.) Yet, since Weber's time (he died in 1920), scholars have scrutinised his logic and found it wanting. Various elements of capitalism actually predate Protestantism; capitalism also flourished in Italian merchant states—under the influence of Catholicism, not Protestantism; Weber misunderstood the Calvinist meaning of a 'calling'; and, that it was Protestantism that actually embraced capitalism's risk-taking, profit-making, behaviour, not the other way around.[25] Yet, Weber had produced a very neat account—one which will forever have us debating the importance of ideas and ideologies in the creation and maintenance of economic systems.

Meanwhile, let us not ignore the prejudices—including those of race and gender—that are built into religion and continue to produce suffering and alienation. While women hold an elevated place in Eastern religions such as Hinduism, Buddhism, and Sikhism, many other religions have embedded within them gender stereotypes and biases which limit women's access to education, the labour market, leadership positions, and public life. Indeed, a patriarchal reading of the Christian bible reveals a divine male God who created the world for men to rule women, masters to rule slaves, and sovereigns and potentates to rule their subjects.[26] According to one analyst:

> Sexism and misogyny are explicitly woven into the dogma and traditions of mainstream religions. God is personified as male, and his representatives are male … Religious texts espouse notions of mental, moral, and spiritual inferiority of women, and religion is used to justify gross forms of gender inequality all around the world.[27]

Religions—particularly those of a one, all-knowing, god—demand obedience. The souls of heathens/infidels must be filled with the love of the one true god if they are to reach heaven. They must be taught the 'truth' and be delivered from evil and ignorance. Recently, one of my

Brisbane friends visited her letterbox to discover an invitation to a prayer meeting. An accompanying folded note suggested she shouldn't hesitate. Headed SIN INVOICE it read:

FROM:	God the Father
TO:	You, the Reader
FOR:	You were born a sinner
TOTAL OWING:	A sinless life
PENALTY:	Everlasting burning
DUE DATE:	Right now

The message inside the note said

> Dear Reader,
> You have been born a sinner. Even the good works you have done, currently do, or will do in the future, will not pay for one sin. Your good works are nothing but filthy rags in God's eyes (Isaiah 64: 6). You are now headed for the literal, everlasting and burning flames of hell.

Not a prospect one might look forward to. The note was composed by an organisation called Australian Bible Ministries, whose website confirms it as a creationist church bent on bludgeoning its brethren into taking Jesus as their saviour. Their note promised those attending its meetings would be brought 'peace, joy and satisfaction'—a much better prospect than the flames.

In earlier times, the crusades were steeped in much cruelty. The aim of the Christian crusades was to recapture territories lost to expansionist Muslim states—to bring people back into the fold of Christianity. In the quest for territory and souls approximately nine million people died, while others were tortured for entertainment, for practicing witchcraft, or for military intelligence.[28] Islam had a well-developed notion of holy wars well before Christianity's crusades of the eleventh century. In the 600s Muhammad had been clear about his intentions—to make war with those not following his teachings. His soldiers conducted jihads against those who would not accept Allah as the one God. Soldiers dying in a jihad would go straight to paradise and be greeted by 72 virgins. (Or is it raisins? According to the Koran, martyrs will receive 'hur' in heaven. In Aramaic hur means 'white'—most commonly referring to 'white grapes', or raisins. The martyrs may have been deceived.)[29]

Conquest of territories throughout time has been built upon notions of inferiority of the enemy. The Spanish were notorious for their callous and inhumane treatment of captives, but England, France, Holland, Belgium, and Portugal were not far behind. Racism is an ideology holding that some ethnic or racial group is inferior to one's own and deserves to be treated as such. With prejudice and discrimination rife, it is easy to justify the continued subjugation of the oppressed. The Christian bible contains many passages that command slaves to obey their masters. After all, didn't the Israelites of the Old Testament own slaves? And black Africans were seen to be descendants of Ham who was cursed in the book of Genesis—they deserve their fate as lowly slaves. Racism was further fuelled in the 1860s with some branches of science and white theology evoking (and misinterpreting) Darwin—proposing blacks were on an evolutionary scale more akin to apes than human beings.[30] Jews have been persecuted by Christians ever since Theodosius I proclaimed Christianity to be the official religion of the Roman state in 380 CE. For a thousand years Jews—blamed directly for Christ's crucifixion—were legally prevented from fully participating in society. Then they were sent to gas chambers. Today, anti-Semitism remains rife even in the most Christian of the love-thy-neighbour societies.

If helping fellow beings has not been a strong suit of the 'great' religions, how do they treat the environment? The short answer is—with contempt. There is a very strong line in Christian teachings that God created the earth for the benefit of human beings and it is there for the taking by the industrious. Here is *Genesis* 1: 28:

> And God blessed them and God said unto them, Be fruitful and multiply; and replenish the earth and subdue it; and have dominion over the fish of the sea, and over the fowl of the air, and over every living thing that moveth upon the earth.

It seems that for the last two thousand years, there's been a lot more subduing than replenishing—a great deal of domination. In his essay

'The Historical Roots of our Ecological Crisis' historian Lynn White argues that Christianity is anthropocentric in word and deed.[31] White argues that the Christian bible elevates the status of humans over all other creatures. Animals and crops must be attended to. But this is to ensure that they will be of continued benefit to humankind—a sentiment also at the heart of Islam.[32] There is a strong essentialist ideology permeating many religions, positioning nature as subservient to humankind. Animals were not seen to experience pain because they lacked a mind. This belief has legitimised an array of cruel and abhorrent practices against non-human species.[33] Recollect that Christianity replaced paganism, which revered nature. The animism of the pagans located the divine in rivers, lakes, forests, rocks, and soil. Taking spirits out of nature and locating them in a sky-based male god meant that rather than being part of nature, humans could become its exploiters.[34] Through the ages, and with the development of science, 'nature' could be worked upon to increase human benefit. 'Progress' is now dependent upon technologies that can extract more from the environment, increase profits for business, and expand consumption. An unsustainable form of economic growth is a consequence of the industrial revolution which, itself, rested upon the Promethean-Christian proposition that nature is God's gift to be appropriated for human benefit.

Miracles and Manipulation

Do you believe in miracles? If you live in the US, then for some 80% of your fellow citizens the answer is a resounding 'yes'. And for doctors in the US? Just a little below—at 74%.[35] If some three quarters of the scientifically trained medical profession believe in miracles, then who might argue with them? Maybe the doctors need to call upon miracles in their daily practice? A miracle is a truly remarkable occurrence that cannot be explained by natural or scientific laws—'an extraordinary event manifesting divine intervention in human affairs'.[36] It is god-inspired and god-enacted. It allows common folk to experience first-hand the glory of god. Eastern religions such as Buddhism and Hinduism consider that through the performance of mystical acts, miracles can occur. Muhammad cured the sick and blind and fed a thousand people on a baby goat. He also split the moon, to convince non-believers of his powers. For those following the Western religions of Christianity, Islam, and Judaism there is a personal god who intervenes in the world at his own choosing, delivering beneficial outcomes that would be otherwise inexplicable. In a huge nod to the health profession, God has ensured that some 95% of miracles have been healings of the physically ill.[37]

Have you ever tried ranking your favourite miracles from the Bible? Ira Gershwin and his co-writers of 'It ain't necessarily so', featured in the 1935 musical *Porgy and Bess*, were quite clear about theirs—the diminutive David's success over the six-cubits-and-a-span-high Goliath, Jonah's three days inside a whale, Moses' rescue from the bullrushes, and Methuselah's extended lifespan of 969 years. If you apply a 'scale of incredulity', others seem to also warrant attention. My list in descending order is: the virgin birth; the resurrection of Jesus; the former's walking-on-water episode; the five loaves and two fish feeding the multitudes; the raising of four-day-dead Lazarus; Jesus' spittle and mud eye-pack that allowed a blind man to see; and, the healing of a paralytic at Capernaum (the meaning of paralytic here was 'paralysis' rather than the present-day meaning of being three sheets to the wind. Indeed, Jesus seemed quite at ease with drinking, famously turning water into wine). Even those practising religion readily question its claims. In his novel *White Noise*, Don DeLillo's nun, Sister Hermann Marie, simply pretends to believe in the religion she follows:

> Do you think we are stupid? … Saved? What is saved? This is a dumb head, who would come in here to talk about angels. Show me an angel. Please. I want to see one … show me a saint. Give me one hair from the body of a saint.[38]

Or, as Woody Allen has pleaded:

> If only God would give me a clear sign! Like making a large deposit in my name in a Swiss bank …

He concludes:

Not only is there no God but try getting a plumber on weekends.[39]

The virgin Mary *is* one woman who holds a very special place in Christianity. She had not yet had sex with her husband before the Holy Spirit had his way with her, assisting her in conceiving the first of her children, Jesus. It was a miracle. It was also a miracle that Paul's letters and the gospels of John and Mark contain no hints of Mary's heavenly conception, or of the room in an inn, or the journey to Bethlehem.[40] To the great embarrassment of Christians, Mary appears in the Koran more than she does in the Bible.[41] According to Philip Almond, Emeritus Professor in the History of Religious Thought at the University of Queensland, we know five important things about Mary. First, she was an 'accidental virgin': an incorrect translation from Greek to Latin to English meant that 'almah' (young woman) was corrupted to 'virgin'. Second, once Mary had been recognised as virginal, it would not have been appropriate for the mother of God to be involved in any hanky-panky. So, despite her having four additional sons, the early Christian church deemed Mary a virgin in perpetuity. Third, while everyone (apart from Jesus—who lacked a human father and was born of a virgin) was tainted with original sin and was in need of redemption, God had ensured Mary was spared. In 1854 Pope Pius IX confirmed this—she is the only fully—human person who has been born without original sin, someone 'immaculately conceived'.[42] Fourth, she ascended into heaven—Pope Pius XII changed Catholic doctrine in 1950 to confirm the fact. Fifth, she became a goddess of the sky—she is known as the Queen of Heaven (along with Our Lady of the Lilies, and Periwinkles). She will occasionally descend from heaven to hear her followers' prayers and pass them on to God. She has appeared at least 21,000 times all over the world—although this is well below the 80,000 sightings of UFOs in the US alone.[43]

Jesus has been conspicuous as the subject of paintings, stained-glass images, TV and film portrayals, tattoos, and sculptures. In paintings he has been depicted as bearded with long hair or, in pastoral scenes, young and beardless with short hair to his shoulders and wearing a tunic.[44] Unfortunately, there are no physical accounts of Jesus in the Gospels—we don't know if he was short, tall, thin, fat, or dark, olive, or white skinned. By the fifth century he also came with a halo. Somehow, over time, a pale-skinned, long-haired, bearded, version emerged and prevailed. But in the 2001 British documentary, *Son of God*, he was shown in a very new way. Using skull shapes and other features from first-century Jewish men, forensic anthropologists were able to determine that Jesus would have had curly black hair and a short, black, cropped beard.[45] The image created was of a short-faced swarthy man looking slightly neanderthal.[46] So much for the blue-eyed Brad Pitt-like saviour above grandmother's fireplace.

The Shroud of Turin—the supposed burial cloth of Jesus—shows the face of a bearded long-faced Viking-like character. Unfortunately, radiocarbon dating reveals the cloth originated some 1300 years after Jesus' crucifixion,[47] so that's one image we can happily discard. But the face of Jesus continues to turn up. He appeared on a piece of naan bread in Surrey, on a three-cheese pizza in Brisbane, in the crease of a drying sock in Kent, on the side of a hill in San Francisco, on a drainpipe in Coventry, and was burnt onto the bottom of an electric iron in Massachusetts.[48] He has been photographed in clouds and has turned up numerous times on pieces of toast. One piece of toasted Jesus was available on eBay with bidding starting at US$25,000 (it is not known if it has been sold).[49] The 'Daily Bread' toaster produces an image of Jesus every time a slice of bread is inserted. It can be purchased for around US$40. The 'Grilled Cheeses Sandwich Press', providing an even clearer image of the messiah, is available from Amazon for US$45[50]—a great snack with a glass of full-bodied red.

There are close to 100 statues of Jesus, the most famous of which is Christ the Redeemer perched atop Corcovado Mountain in Rio. Built between 1926 and 1931, the statue is the largest Art Deco statue ever created, reaching a height of 30 metres—38 if you include the pedestal.[51] It is truly breathtaking. Other monsters are Christ the King figure in Poland, standing some 52 metres tall (the largest in the world) and the Christ of Peace statue of some 40 metres, in Cochabamba, Bolivia. One of the most famous—due to its sculptor rather than its height—is another Christ the Redeemer. Created by Michelangelo, the statue of just over two metres in height, is found in Rome in the church of Santa Maria Sopra Minerva. The King of Kings statue at the Solid Rock Church in

Ohio featured Jesus' torso from waist up, with hands raised to the sky. It was some 19 metres in height until struck by lightning, and destroyed by fire, in 2010. It was replaced by a new statue, *Lux Mundi*—or Light of the World—standing at 16 metres. With arms slightly curled towards the observer it is referred to as the 'Hug Me Jesus' statue.[52] But the one that gets the critics award is surely that of a baby Jesus housed in a church in the town of Guadalupe, Mexico. Standing at nearly seven metres and weighing 900 kilograms, its claim to fame is not only that it is one of the biggest baby Jesus statues in the world, but also that it bears an uncanny resemblance to 1970's and '80's pop artist Phil Collins.[53] It certainly gives his hit 'Take a Look at Me Now' contemporary relevance.

Did Jesus have a navel? We know that Adam and Eve didn't—neither developed inside a woman's womb. Adam was formed by God from dust, while Eve was formed from one of Adam's ribs. But what about Jesus? The question has puzzled theologians for millennia. If Mary were a normal woman, then her first-born son might have been expected to have a navel—after all he would have required nurturing from the placenta via an umbilical cord. After birth the cord would have been cut and tied, giving Jesus a navel. He would have shared Mary's blood. But Jesus' blood—as we are told many times throughout the New Testament—was 'precious' and pure blood, so perhaps it was not to have been tainted by Mary. It follows that if Jesus' blood was pure, he did not need to have an umbilical cord attached to his mother and therefore would have been born without a navel. It would have been yet another miracle. Today most Christians don't seem to have a problem with Jesus having a belly button. After all, Mary was conceived through an immaculate conception which means she was free from original sin. Her blood was pure and would have remained pure as she nourished her son in the womb—a normal birth with a tied umbilicus would be consistent with God's desire for a son of purity. A slight problem for the faithful is that Mary's Immaculate Conception finds no place in the scriptures. And as Thomas Aquinas (1225–1274) had argued, if Mary was free of original sin, she would not have needed redemption, rendering the birth of her son superfluous.[54] But if she did have original sin, her uterus would have been polluting her own progeny. I guess we'll never know whether Jesus was navel-less or not. But we know one thing for certain—he was not short of foreskins, with over 30 churches in Europe claiming to have had the holy prepuce in their possession.[55]

Bad Habits

It would not have been much fun being a nun in the Middle Ages. The brides of Christ were married to their maker and, although the Messiah rarely appeared in public, or in the bedroom, they had taken a vow of chastity. They lived in cold, dank, monasteries and dedicated their lives to meditation, prayer, and community service. It was gruelling:

> In the sixteenth and seventeenth centuries … a nun could generally stand about ten years of incarceration before it killed her. By the end of that time the lack of exercise and sunlight, the gloom, the damp walls, the loneliness, the monotony and the sheer boredom of a life without any hope of change had planted in her the tuberculosis, the dysentery or one of the various fevers that carried her off. Many of the poor creatures actually went mad.[56]

Poverty, chastity, and obedience to God were three strict rules that guided their behaviour. Or did they? Lustful Popes, Cardinals, and sundry monks abounded. With nunneries being places of sexual repression, it was not unheard of for nuns to be found in convulsions where they would arch the bodies thrusting their pudenda forward—as in coitus (the position is known as arc de cercle). In a nunnery in Cologne in 1565, so many nuns were found convulsing in this way that it was described as an 'epidemic'.[57] The nuns went to extraordinary lengths to show their faith in God. Nun Veronica Giuliani (1660–1727) believed so strongly that Jesus was the lamb of God that she took a young lamb to bed, kissing it and encouraging it to suckle upon her breasts. She was later beatified by Pius VII and canonized by Pope Gregory XVI in 1839.[58] Christina of St. Trond (1150–1224) appeared to enjoy lying in hot ovens, being racked on the wheel, and keeping the company of corpses. Upon her apparent death she was laid in a coffin and a funeral service held. Astonishingly (she is called Christina the Astonishing) she sprang out of the coffin ('arose full of vigour'), levitated up to the church rafters and told the congregation that, during her death, she had witnessed heaven, purgatory, and hell. She became the patron of people with mental health disorders.[59] Christina Ebner (1277–1356) joined a congregation of Dominican nuns just outside of Nuremberg. After falling gravely ill she began having visions which she began writing down. She combined her visions with those of her fellow nuns, compiling the *Book of Sisters*. After several years of self-torture she had a vision that Christ had visited her bed and that she had borne a child to him. So enthralled was she by her vision that she cut a two-dimensional cross shape on her chest, above her heart, and ripped off the flesh. Not to be outdone, Margaret Mary Alacoque (a famous French nun of the seventeenth century) wrote in her diary how, after one of her patients had vomited, she 'could not resist' licking it up with her tongue 'an action which seemed to cause her so much pleasure that she wished she could do it the same every day'.[60] She was beatified by Pope Pius IX in 1864 and canonized by Pope Benedict XV in 1920.

Chastity more-or-less guaranteed degenerate behaviour in the Middle Ages. Sadism and masochism were a feature of convent life, as were phantom pregnancies. Nuns would self-flagellate, wear hair shirts, and not wash. 'Lacerated by the devils they could feel in their bodies [they] danced, howled, writhed on the ground and shouted marvellously inventive obscenities to satisfy their audiences'.[61] Some gave up the pretence of being virtuous, enjoyed the company of the local priest, and bore children.

Repression was such that:

> Many Christian ascetics have described how they could never get rid of the thought of sex ... Some fasted in the hope that this would reduce their desire; others kept a [bucket] of water in their cell to stand in when the temptation became unendurable. In this unenviable state, men are quick to find sexual overtones in every object, every action of others. And it was just these men, restless, unhappy, obsessed, driven by the energies of their bottled-up libidos, who were apt to obtain positions of power in the Church and stamp it with their character.[62]

For the common folk, kissing, fornication, and involuntary nocturnal emissions were all deemed sins, as was masturbation. In the third century other small pleasures were equally condemned—'horse racing, the theatre, dancing ... and mutton chops were equally accursed'.[63] Sex was to be performed in one position with any evidence of 'more canino' (doggy fashion) requiring seven years of penance. As Gordon Rattray Taylor has noted, the Church went further, reducing the number of days that sex was allowed to occur:

> First, it was made illegal on Sundays, Wednesdays and Fridays, which effectively removed the equivalent of five months in the year. Then it was made illegal forty days before Easter and forty days before Christmas, and for three days before attending communion ... and was also forbidden from the time of conception to forty days after parturition.[64]

The Church's obsessive fear of sex was based upon myth (for example, menstruation was a punishment for women because of Eve's fall from grace) and upon magical beliefs about sex as 'contamination'—thus the need for purification ceremonies. It was not much fun at all for the laity. But the outcome was one that could be readily predicted. Possessing common carnal desires, members of the flock sinned on a regular basis. They would therefore need to confess their sins and be forgiven. They could do this in a church for payment—for penance. They also gave tithes of 10% of their earnings and paid for sacraments such as baptism and marriage. Vast areas of land were bequeathed to the Church from its loyal but dying subjects. It is unsurprising that the Catholic church grew rich and powerful through the Middle Ages—even if the cost was the sexual subjugation of its followers.

Europe in mediaeval times has been compared to a 'vast insane asylum' where

> the Church's code of repression produced ... over a period of four or five centuries, an outbreak of mass psychosis for which there are few parallels in history ... The medieval Church was obsessed with sex to a painful degree. Sexual issues dominated its thinking in a manner which we should regard as entirely pathological.[65]

Sex was for procreation, not for pleasure. Sex had to be rigidly contained. Thus, the invention of the *chemise cagoule*, or cowl shirt, a heavy nightshirt worn by Catholic men. It covered all areas of the torso to below the knees but contained a small opening at the centre to facilitate the impregnation of a man's wife. The Church believed that the ideal for every human was complete celibacy but clearly understood that sex, which was sinful, was necessary for the creation of new souls to worship God. St Jerome understood that sexual relations allowed for the creation of more virgins, which was a good thing. But he also understood that virgins were brides of Christ and that should a man 'take' a virgin he was actually committing adultery—against God. While a little convoluted, this thinking led the Church to one conclusion—that all forms of sexual activity apart from procreation must be banned.[66]

One of the Greats

On the way to visit our daughter and her family we head to Brisbane's southwest through the leafy suburb of Augustine Heights. It is an 'aspirational' suburb according to the real estate blurb. What it is aspiring to is never disclosed, but perhaps it has something to do with heaven. It is part of Australia's largest master planned community sitting within the greater area of Springfield (think Homer Jay Simpson territory—but without the nuke plant). Augustine Heights features streets with give-away names like 'Brigid Boulevard', 'Dominic Street', 'Francisca Drive', 'Hallow Crescent', and 'Patricius Place'. It hosts St Augustine College as well as a catholic primary school. Its churches include the Augustine Centre and the Chapel of St Monica (named after Augustine's mother). The suburb—with its white curbed and guttered concrete footpaths, underground electricity, landscaped gardens, and manicured lawns—honours one of the leading lights in the Catholic church. In fact, after Jesus and Paul, Augustine is said to have been third most influential person in Catholicism, shaping the doctrines of the Church up to and beyond the Protestant reformation.[67] In the race for spiritual recognition Jesus had clearly won gold, Paul silver—but the bronze is nothing to be sneezed at.

For it was St Augustine of Hippo (354–430 CE) who created the idea of original sin. In his early years Augustine had several mistresses, but eventually came to the view that chastity was preferable to marriage. Augustine identified Adam as the person who passed on sin, and therefore eventual death, to his children. The sin of Adam was the sin of all. We have been all irrevocably damaged because of Adam. That was insightful, but the problem was that Augustine was reading from a poor translation of Romans 5: 12 from the Latin. While Paul believed death came to all because all people sin, Augustine's 'take' was that all humanity was cursed to die by Adam's one act of disobedience—we are all responsible for what Adam did.[68] And Adam had tasted of the forbidden fruit (never named but some think it was an apple, grape, or etrog).[69] Adam's semen had been 'shackled by the bond of death' which has been transmitted through the human race. Every human, conceived from sperm that originated with Adam, was born contaminated with sin.[70] Except Jesus, of course, who was conceived without semen and who, apparently, lacked *libido*.[71] When Catholics see a newborn baby they readily recognise it has been cursed by sin. Baptism is needed as soon as possible for if a baby dies and is not baptised, it will go straight to hell. For Augustine babies were so infected with sin that, until baptised, they should be considered to be 'the very limbs of Satan'.[72] (The cruelty contained therein led eventually to the creation of 'limbo' where the souls of unbaptised babies were suspended indefinitely, neither in heaven nor in hell. Limbo was eventually discarded, with Pope Benedict XVI deciding in 2007 that unbaptised children would, indeed, go straight to heaven, whereupon millions of very grateful but unbaptised souls-in-suspension rushed to join the angels.)

Augustine knew a great deal about human sexuality. During his stay in Carthage, North Africa, and at the age of sixteen he wrote a 'frenzy gripped me and I surrendered myself entirely to lust'. His parents worried that he was 'floundering in the broiling sea of … fornication' and forcefully advised him to try to avoid other men's wives.[73] At university the eighteen-year-old Augustine 'revelled in promiscuity' but then settled down with his mistress.[74] He would pray to God and ask the Lord 'give me chastity, but not yet'.[75] When he was thirty his family decided he should be married and chose a ten-year-old to be his bride. (She had to wait two years to be of legal age but, in any case, the marriage was cancelled when Augustine became a priest. Thereafter he began his struggles with celibacy.)

Given his earlier lascivious proclivities—and predating Freud—he believed no person was capable of overcoming lust. He considered that 'at the core of each person was not an incorruptible divinity … but a putrid lust which continually contaminated the whole being'.[76] Free-will had gone out the window and, along with it, any semblance of a caring God. Bodies were no longer controlled by brains. Women were considered sexual predators, just as Eve had been in the garden. Christian men were implored to hate women for 'the corruptible and mortal conjugal connection, sexual intercourse and all that pertains to her as a wife'.[77] Women were subordinate to men and could not know God until they were married to a man. A woman had no rights over her body but must:

> Surrender her body to her husband on command, receiving from such use no personal pleasure, but allowing herself to be used solely as an instrument of procreation.[78]

Sexual desire for Augustine was proof that original sin had raised its ugly head and permeated the masses. We should be ashamed of those desires—'lust is a usurper, defying the power of the will, and tyrannizing the human sexual organs', he wrote.[79] If the Church could be criticised for its attitude to sex before Augustine's time, it was certainly opening itself up for a great deal more criticism as part of his legacy.[80]

But what about celibacy of the priesthood? The Church had not always condemned sexual relations of its leaders. Six centuries after Augustine's time priests in parishes were often married, and bishops often kept the company of mistresses. But, after Pope Gregory VII's inauguration in 1073, a strict edict was put in place: Priests must be celibate. (Gregory was, apparently, wanting priests to concentrate more upon heavenly matters and the welfare of their congregations, rather than lustful pleasures.)[81] So it came to pass that priests—and nuns—must be celibate. According to some experts this simply drove clerical sex underground. After all, we are not born to be celibate—it is not normal to deny the sexuality of humankind. Many priests agreed, leading to the discovery of the skeletons of newborns in unmarked graves in many Catholic churchyards. Today, the rape of nuns remains rampant.[82] And, as is well-known, children are also particularly vulnerable targets. One report on sexual abuse and paedophilia in the French Catholic church identified some 330,000 instances of child sexual abuse over the seventy-year period to 2020.[83] From 1940 to 2023 over 200,000 children were abused at the hands of clergy in Spain's Catholic Church.[84] Investigations in nations such as Australia, Chile, Germany, Ireland, Poland, and the US have revealed similar stories of abuse. As the *Guardian* concluded

> The theology of the male priesthood has allowed flawed human beings to believe themselves to be above the law; a corresponding culture of deference has too often made the church a safe space for abusers … an insular, arrogant culture, deeming itself outside the jurisdiction of secular morality, has routinely ignored the suffering of the abused while offering mercy, secrecy and escape routes to the abusers.[85]

In 2021 The Office of the High Commissioner for Human Rights openly criticised the Catholic church for its failure to cooperate with investigations and legal proceedings, largely to protect perpetrators and to limit the costs of compensation to the abused.[86] A recent investigation has accused Benedict XVI of misconduct when he was an archbishop in Germany in the 1970s and 1980s. He had always denied knowing of the sexual improprieties of priests during his time as archbishop. But he had lied at the time and had failed to act.[87]

The Church's deceit, along with its desire to cover up the wrongdoings of its most loyal practitioners, have real-world consequences in the destruction of young lives and the continued subjugation of women.

Cooking the Books

If you are going to evince suspicion best it be for those who have claimed to have gone into the desert, communicated directly with God, conveyed to others what God had said, and believe they have delivered unto the world the blueprint for eternal life. Deserts seem to breed delusion.

Emerging from the Middle East, the great books—the Torah (first part of the Jewish bible), the Christian's Holy Bible, and the Koran (dictated to Muhammad by the angel Gabriel) of the Muslims, are advanced as being direct interventions by God. The Torah and the Christian Bible's New Testament share the books of Genesis, Exodus, Leviticus, Numbers, and Deuteronomy. And, Islam recognises that God unveiled grand truths through various Jewish and Christian prophets. It recognises Noah, Abraham, Moses, and Jesus as true messengers of God. So what would all three monotheistic religions agree upon? What do we know about these prophets? The Bible, for one, notes that Noah managed to produce three sons—when he was 500 years of age; the daughters of Lot seduced their father after imbibing him with alcohol, just to ensure the family line was preserved; Moses did not drink or eat for forty days and forty nights; Balaam's donkey decided to speak to his owner 'Am I not your donkey, which you have always ridden, to this day?; in Deuteronomy males are forbidden to attend church if their testicles have been bruised by stones and their members severed; finally, in Exodus, God parts the sea with a blast from his nostrils. The New Testament doesn't fare much better. It is well known that the Gospels of Matthew, Mark, Luke, and John were not from the pens of Jesus' disciples but were written by anonymous authors between 40 and 80 years after Jesus' death. 'It now seems highly unlikely that any of the sayings attributed to Jesus in the Gospels were ever spoken by an historical figure'.[88] Furthermore:

> The teaching ascribed to Jesus is a farrago of plagiarisms from Jewish sources. The myth of a god who is put to death and rises again, the sacramental eating of the god, and many other features of the Gospel story, are common to the whole ancient world. Why suppose Jesus to be more historical than Osiris, Tammuz, Attis, Dionysus or Mithra?[89]

Gerd Rüdiger Puin, a German scholar specialising in Oriental studies, has described the Koran as a cocktail of ideas, many of which predate Muhammad. It contains numerous sentences that are either contradictory or make incomprehensible claims.[90] One in every five sentences, he asserts, makes no sense at all.[91] Many of God's supposed untainted words are, in fact, indiscernible. The authenticity of textual material has been questioned, with scholars identifying a multitude of historical errors, contradictions, and other assorted mumbo jumbo.[92] According to one scholar who has written on the totalitarian nature of Islam, the Koran is 'not worthy of a compassionate deity'.[93] But, like the Bible and Torah, the Koran is viewed by millions worldwide as a holy text—one whose messages cannot and should not be doubted. For Christians, Jews, and Muslims such unquestioning belief in their texts is central to faith.

But are the followers of these religions really reading 'God's' words? What if those words had been tampered with—and on a regular basis? It appears that over the centuries, many dedicated followers have sought to make the sacred texts a little more palatable. The Church 'repeatedly distorted and even falsified the Biblical record in order to produce justification for its laws'.[94] There were fights between Christian sects, between Christians and pagans, between Christians and Jews. How did you get the upper hand? By claiming that your 'reading' was the proper one. Fraudulent reworking of biblical material was totally justified where lying and deceit served the 'truth'. Machiavelli revisited. Humble peasants and fisherfolk—the apostles Peter, James, and John—have their names on elegantly composed Greek biblical texts when it was certain they had no knowledge of the language (it seems James could not even write).[95] Well-respected authority figures in the early church, Clement of Rome and Ignatius of Antioch were claimed to be authors of text composed by other people while 'letters written in the names of such stalwarts as Peter and Paul [were] produced by secretaries and coauthors, rather than the apostles themselves'.[96] As Bart Ehrman, author of the very revealing *Forgery and Counterforgery: The Use of Literary Deceit in Early Christian Polemics* has stated:

> Arguably the most distinctive feature of the early Christian literature is the degree to which it was forged … From the period of the New Testament, from which some thirty writings survive … only eight go under the name of their actual author, and seven of these derive from the pen of one man. To express the matter differently, only two authors named themselves correctly in the surviving literature of the first Christian century … Among the earliest surviving writings of the Christians – those that make up the New Testament – nearly half (13/27) are forged.[97]

The Gospels by Peter, Thomas, and Philip were forged, as was Paul's letter to the Alexandrians and Laodiceans, as was Jesus' message to Abgar. Ehrman discovered over 50 biblical forgeries in the first 400 years of Christianity.[98] But it seems that for every forgery there was a counter-forgery—written works that attempted to counter claims made in earlier forgeries! It's like *Mad* magazine's *Spy vs. Spy* but with more profound, other-worldly, implications. The ungainly term 'pseudepigrapha' (spuriously attributing authorship) is applied to works that are written in the name of a favourite biblical hero. The text makes its way into the bible and, over time, has the same holy status as other texts. It's a forgery. Or, is it a 'forgery' if it is composed under God's guidance? Should it hold a precious place because the authors honestly believed that they were writing under God's influence? Should the forged sections be discarded as poppycock? Good questions, indeed. What would the New Testament look like if deliberately manipulated text were removed? The additions (forgeries) served theological agendas of the day or were incorporated for polemical purposes.[99] Christian theologians openly deceived to serve what they interpreted as the greater good. They lied in the cause of a higher truth. Techniques employed included plagiarism, fabrication, falsification, and incorrect attribution. Examples include imitating the style of an early Gospel writer; adding a personal touch to impart authenticity; providing first-person narratives; warning the reader that earlier texts were false and should be dismissed; and, inserting tracts of forged material into already-existing texts.[100] All are mechanisms of societal deception and all are examples of the literary deceit that flourished in the early Christian church. Should we swear on the Bible, or swear at it, I wonder?

Pussies in Paradise

We all know how important a pet can be for companionship. In the US some two-thirds of households keep a pet and some 90% of those people consider the animal to be a family member. Married women are particularly fond of canine company, with some 40% of women dog-owners revealing that they obtain more emotional support from Fido than from their children or husband.[101] A separate study in the US found that humans are more empathetic to dogs than they are to other human beings.[102] Findings from a survey of Australians conducted in 2021 found that 37% of women and 26% of men would prefer to spend time with a pet than with a human being.[103] Because of such emotional ties an important question arises. When they die do cats and dogs go to heaven?

Unfortunately, the answer is not at all clear-cut. One line of reasoning is that in the Resurrection all of God's creatures will be restored to life. This would include field mice, orangutans, and presumably serpents. But these animals, just like dogs and cats, do not have souls—so the second, counter, argument is that they will miss out. A third line is that if animals are self-aware and display characteristics like affection and loyalty (soul-like qualities), as dogs do, they might find their way to heaven (Japanese scientists have found dogs separated from their owners produce tears of joy when reunited).[104] We can expect a great deal of barking and sobbing at the Pearly Gates. Even the Popes—who are infallible, incapable of error—appear not to know the fate of the four-legged. For Pope Paul VI and Pope Francis, the afterlife is open to all God's creatures but for Pope Benedict XVI animals are not 'called' to heaven, they just die.[105] Prophet Muhammad was certainly an animal lover. When his cat, Muezza, fell asleep upon the sleeve of his robe he took to the sleeve with a pair of scissors so that he might not disturb the sleeping animal. His single act of kindness aside it appears that, for Muslims,

> on the day of reckoning, all creatures will rise up and have justice for any wrong that was done to them, including animals. However, only humans and jinn [supernatural creatures] will be judged on their actions and go on to the afterlife.[106]

So, if you are Muslim and would like your pet to go to join you in paradise, you'll have a better chance if you convert to Christianity; but there are still no guarantees.[107] According to one Christian minister with robust anthropocentric certitude:

> Animals don't have the same hope [of deliverance] as humans do, because humans are distinct among all God's creations. We're made in God's image; animals (and angels) are not (Gen 1:26–27). Among living beings, we have a unique ability to reason (Ps. 32:9). Jesus came to save humans, not angels or animals.[108]

Here, here! In any case, many of us are allergic to cat and dog hair, and there is no guarantee we'll be able to purchase antihistamines or nasal corticosteroids in the Kingdom of Heaven.

Thank God for Darwin

It was St Paul who saw faith as 'the conviction of things not seen'. To those who 'believe in the unseen' was Muhammad's dedication of the Koran.[109] If we have faith, we believe in the certainty of unseen realities.[110] And, as Jesus was reported as saying to Doubting Thomas 'blessed are those who have not seen and yet have believed'.[111] This is belief for belief's sake—there is no rationality required. Blind faith, we might say. Freud called religious doctrines 'illusions ... so improbable [and] so incompatible with everything we have laboriously discovered about the reality of the world'.[112] Scientists also believe in things they cannot see—gravity, electric currents, sound waves, and Wi-Fi and Bluetooth signals, immediately come to mind. But scientists know they exist, and they can accurately measure them and predict their behaviour. They have been scientifically established as factual phenomena. Not so with the beliefs of the church. Indeed

> faith is religion's answer to the challenge of reason [but] its quicksilver essence can never be rationally pinned down: the harder you press, the faster it squirts out from under your finger. Like the alien monster in countless movies, faith only gets stronger every time you shoot at it.[113]

There exist major areas of disagreement between the church and science.[114] A trivial, but interesting one, is that of transubstantiation.[115] When you kneel in a Catholic church to take your bread and wine, you are not actually eating bread and drinking wine. It is quite literally Christ's body and blood. A rather macabre thought, really. However, the most important disagreement is about the creation of the universe. According to the Bible, God created the cosmos. For science, the cosmos was created in a Big Bang some 13.8 billion years ago. (Maybe God caused the Big Bang? But if he existed before the Big Bang, who created God?)[116]

Another disagreement is over the origins of life. The bible acknowledges God's instantaneous creation of Adam and Eve but scientists understand, from evolutionary theory, that all complex life evolved from small microorganisms about 3.7 billion years ago. Darwinism was attacked with unrelenting ferocity in the nineteenth century by those hoping to preserve a literal meaning of the Scriptures.[117] Creationists (those who *do* believe the Bible to be literally true) continue to perpetuate biblical myths completely dismissed by science. And they are doing so with great verve. Take, for example, the Creation Museum, a US$27 million structure covering 75,000 square feet located in Petersburg, Kentucky. It provides a visual treat for those believing in the book of Genesis. Half a million visitors each year learn about 'God's infallible Word'. You will be able to 'explore the idyllic Garden of Eden alongside Adam and Eve. You'll see Adam naming the animals, the creation of Eve, the tree of life, and the serpent cunningly coiled in the Tree of the Knowledge of Good and Evil'. You can meet Ebenezer a 'stunning full-size Allosaurus. He's a testament to the reality of the global Flood of Noah's day and the truth of God's Word'. (Remember, dinosaurs supposedly lived at the same time as humans—there were two of them on the Ark.) Other exhibits question Darwin's theory of evolution, and explain the evils of pornography, teen pregnancies, and abortion. You can participate in the 'Eden Animal Experience' where you'll see 'a variety of exotic and domestic animals [and] fall in love with our alpacas, coatis, wallabies, and more in our zoo!'[118]

But that's not all. Once the visit is over you can travel 70 kilometres down the highway to the address of 1 Ark Encounter, Williamstown, Kentucky where you will come upon—you guessed it—an Ark Encounter. It features a replica of Noah's Ark—built to specifications provided in the Bible. It is 155 metres long, 26 metres wide, and

16 metres high. The Ark, as we know, contained representatives of all animal species in the world at the time of the flood (some 7,000). Many of them pop up as you make your way through the Ark. We learn that Noah was 480 years old when God commanded him to build the Ark. It took him 100 years. After the waters receded, he busied himself for another 470 years, finally dying at 950. Unsurprisingly, perhaps, the Ark Encounter makes its workers sign a statement of faith as a condition of employment.[119] As a cynic once remarked 'Creationists have often made me question evolution. But probably not in the way they think'.[120]

Finally, the Devil. There are over 20 verses in the Bible that describe someone called Satan. Anthropologists and sociologists have argued that a characteristic of many cultures is to view a phenomenon in relation to its 'other'—sacred and profane, clean and unclean, right and wrong. If you are going to believe in God, it is helpful to construct the 'other'—in this case Diablo, the Prince of Darkness, Lucifer, Beelzebub, or Satan. For the ancients, if God was good then he could not be responsible for the evil that filled the world. A demonic force was clearly at work.[121] In early Zoroastrian scriptures Ormazd, the supreme deity, created both the virtuous and benevolent Spenta Mainyu and his destructive and nasty twin brother Ahriman. Likewise, Christians are told that the Devil was the serpent in Genesis. For Peter, he prowls around like a roaring lion waiting to devour unwary souls. In Corinthians Satan disguises himself as an angel of light. In Isaiah Satan—once an angel—falls from heaven because he was jealous of the accolades going to the Lord. He, along with a third of the angels he'd managed to brainwash, were cast from heaven. In Revelation 20:10 he is the beast who is thrown into a fiery lake. And what does he look like? In the fourteenth century illustrated biblical text the *Codex Gigas* ('giant book'), he appears as a two-tongued, green-faced, red-horned, razor-toothed monster. In Dante's poem *Inferno* (from his *Divine Comedy* of the fifteenth century), he was a featherless winged beast with a lizard-like tail. He's also been a flying goat, sported cloven hooves, been dressed in red tights for theatre fans—all the time holding a pitchfork.

For movie-goers Satan seems to be a favourite. The Devil has a baby with Rosemary in the eponymous *Rosemary's Baby*—a Roman Polanski film from 1968. A satanic cult convinces Guy to have his wife raped by the Devil, telling him it would improve his chances of making it as an actor. Who could resist such a deal? It was truly scary. (What was also scary is that it featured the Dakota building in the upper west side of Manhattan, where John Lennon would be killed.)[122] In *The Devil's Advocate* (1997) Al Paccino's devil was played with 'all the energy, zest, and gusto of a camp Tasmanian devil with a hardcore methamphetamine habit'.[123] In contrast, Sam Neill's devilish character, Damien Thorn is a 'devil who has watched too many James Bond movies'—a prim and proper Englishman with style and manners. The devil shows up as a female in the Mel Gibson-directed film *The Passion of the Christ* (2005). Rosalinda Celentano plays a 'simplistic but hugely effective Satan [with] no gimmicks or special powers just a terrible tenacity, alien otherness and overwhelming urge to do the wrong thing'. In *The Witches of Eastwick* (1987) Jack Nicholson plays Daryl Van Horne—'a devil for the modern age. He's a womanizer, a con man, a manipulator, and last but not least, a deadbeat dad'. Finally, child actor Juliette Carton is a small angel/devil in Martin Scorsese's *The Last Temptation of Christ*. She helps Jesus from the cross so he might enjoy the company and pleasures of Mary Magdalene.[124] The music score for the film, composed by Peter Gabriel, received widespread acclaim.[125] But it was not celebrated quite as much as Mike Oldfield's score for *The Exorcist* (1973). Every time I hear *Tubular Bells* my brain is filled with the image of a girl's head doing a 360 while regurgitating mushy peas. I'm certainly not the only one shivering—it is regarded as one of the scariest movies of all time.[126]

What is even more scary is that people actually do believe in Devil possession. Not only that but also that the Devil must be exorcised to free the spirit of the poor unfortunate he has possessed. Exorcism has 'boomed' in the US and in other nations where Pentecostalism (belief in the spirit world) is on the rise.[127] Jesus performed many exorcisms we are told, and they have been a favourite of the Catholic church over thousands of years. What we understand today as psychiatric disorders like schizophrenia or Tourette's syndrome, along with conditions such as epilepsy, convulsions, hallucinations, and hysteria—were viewed as devil possession.[128] In every corner of Christendom, the Church exorcised not only the devils that lived in men. They purged them out of the air … The whole second century was under the dominion of the spirit of darkness. The world and the air around it was peopled with devils; all the formalities of daily living, not merely the worship of idols, were governed by them. They sat on thrones and hovered around children's cots. The earth, God's creation though it may be, now and forever, became … hell.[129]

Even on his deathbed, St Augustine, according to the *Acta Sanctorum*, laid on hands to expel demons (the *Acta* is replete with stories of the curing of those possessed by demons).[130] The Catholic church is so convinced that people continue to be demonised that it launched a course in 2005 called Exorcism and the Prayer of Liberation, attended each year by up to 250 priests from 50 or more countries. In the week-long €300 (£260, US$370) course, priests are taught how to recognise a genuine spiritual disturbance from psychiatric illness. In a modern-day exorcism priests wear a surplice (white-embroidered tunic) and a purple stole. The person possessed is usually bound, and holy water splashed while the priest continues to make the sign of the cross. And

> In Jesus' name he asks the possessing demon to 'yield to God' and 'depart'. Once the priest is convinced the exorcism has worked, he prays to God to prevent the evil spirit from bothering the afflicted person further.[131]

Pope Francis has a thing for the devil and 'has warned many times against naiveté in the fight against Satan'.[132] As we learn in the famous *Malleus Maleficarum* (the 'Hammer and Witches') commissioned by Pope Innocent VIII and published in 1487, the devil would interfere in copulation, stealing human semen and injecting it into others. As Carl Sagan has described them, devils are 'sexually obsessive non-humans who live in the sky, walk through walls, communicate telepathically, and perform breeding experiments on the human species'. No wonder we should want them out of our bodies.[133] The official exorcist for the diocese of Rome, and founder of the International Association of Exorcists in 1994—Father Gabriele Amorth—was given the exorcist-as-superhero makeover by Russell Crowe in the 2023 film *The Pope's Exorcist* which is sure to have Catholics pleading with the church to rid them of demonic possession. Amorth claimed to have performed some 60,000 exorcisms before his death in 2016. He admitted he was 'content' if one of the possessed was 'liberated within four or five years of exorcism', but he had seen 'rare cases of liberation in a few months'.[134] For the exorcised, patience is a virtue.

Imagine No Deception—It's Easy If You Try

Has it been unfair to pick on Augustine—our bronze medal winner? Not according to Elaine Pagels, one of the most respected writers on early Christianity:

> From the fifth century on, Augustine's pessimistic views of sexuality, politics and human nature would become the dominant influence on western Christianity, both Catholic and Protestant, and color all western culture, Christian or not, ever since. Thus, Adam, Eve, and the serpent – our ancestral story – would continue, often in some version of its Augustinian form, to affect our lives to the present day.[135]

Augustine elevated the status of the Devil to that of the Lord. Witches had entered a pact with the Devil to spread evil throughout the world and he insisted that the Church promote fear as a means of dominating and controlling errant believers.[136] Catholicism 101. What if we abandon Catholicism and embrace more 'rational' varieties such as Protestantism? Unfortunately, they are all cut from the same cloth.

Monotheistic religions—such as Judaism, Christianity, and Islam—do not, as in the ancient times of Greece and Rome, allow practitioners to recognise that a multiplicity of gods might exist. It is necessary to renounce all other gods for the One True God. Such exclusivity pits those following one true god against others following their own true god. Result? It encourages one group to see others as heathens or infidels and justifies conflict and war against them.

According to Colin Wells,

Whatever its precise origins, the idea of an exclusive God was crucial for Christianity to spread among the Gentiles, because it answered so many needs at once. It appropriated the pagans' own (gods) ... at the same time it provided a resounding slap in the face to naturalism that was always implicit in Greek philosophy, even if that naturalism was being culturally swamped. Indeed, it was being swamped because, then as now, it was so threatening to religious sentiment ... Exclusivity [challenged] supernaturalism and cleared the way for divine agency, by demonizing the weakened gods and putting the one true God above them and their material realm'.[137]

Questioning the Christian God's own moral code leads to an uncomfortable conclusion. He is a nasty thug:

He routinely punishes people for the sins of others. He punishes all mothers by condemning them to painful childbirth ... in a fit of pique [He] commits genocide and ecocide by flooding the earth ... He kills all firstborn sons [in Egypt] ... He condemns the Samarians, telling them that their children will be 'dashed to the ground, their pregnant women ripped open' ... He commands us to put to death adulterers ... homosexuals ... and people who work on the Sabbath ... God repeatedly directs the Israelites to commit ethnic cleansing.[138]

Bertrand Russell makes much of the vengeance of God:

Religion is based ... mainly upon fear ... fear of the mysterious, fear of defeat, fear of death. Fear is the parent of cruelty, and therefore it is no wonder if cruelty and religion have gone hand in hand. My own view on religion is that of Lucretius. I regard it as a disease born of fear and as a source of untold misery to the human race.[139]

For Christopher Hitchens, religion 'invents a problem where none exists', calls it wicked, and then proceeds to torture those whose behaviour is unaltered. So-called sinner fairy-tales are the product of those who have no real liking of others (sociopaths) and those who derive pleasure from cruelty (psychopaths). He asks 'how did such evil nonsense ever come to be so influential?' and concludes that religious thought was formed in eras of ignorance and superstition. Belief in God is much like belief in the tooth fairy, however:

> The fans of the tooth fairy do not bang on your door and try to convert you. They do not insist that their pseudo-science be taught in schools. They do not condemn believers in rival tooth fairies to death and damnation ... They do not say the tooth fairy made the world ... They do not say the tooth fairy will order you to kill your sister if she is seen with a man who is not her brother.[140]

For Dr Tamas Pataki, an Honorary Fellow in Historical and Philosophical Studies at the University of Melbourne, his evaluation of religion emerges from closely studied texts of authors such as Feuerbach, Marx, Nietzsche, Freud, and Russell. His conclusion?

> [R]eligion springs from fear, conceit, and cruelty; it is responsible for a terrible record of moral obstruction and slaughter; it is a delusional way of confronting weakness and helplessness; it bends thought to its purposes, distorts reality, undermines reason, inhibits curiosity and imagination, obstructs self-knowledge, nourishes hubris secretly, conserves oppressive political dispensations, and forges pernicious group identities; given the opportunity, it persecutes difference and threatens the rule of law.[141]

Recently, I purchased a book entitled *Without God: Science, Belief, Morality, and the Meaning of Life*. With such a broad purview the book might have discussed the fallacies of religion, the viciousness inflicted by religions over the millennia, and might have introduced a strong justification for atheism. I was wrong. The author's sole purpose was to convince the reader that life was irrelevant and pointless without God. If there's no God, how can we make sense of the world? Without God our lives are meaningless (as Tolstoy and Dostoevsky would agree).[142] We have no moral 'compass' to determine what is good, evil, truthful, or beautiful. Without God our lives unravel.

I then recalled a passage by Penn Jillette, the famous magician (and atheist) who has spent his life showing us the secrets of deception—from levitation to bent spoons to buzz saw dissections of pretty assistants. He describes his lack of faith as liberation:

> Believing there is no God means that the suffering I've seen in my family, and indeed all the suffering of the world, isn't caused by an omniscient, omnipresent, omnipotent force that isn't bothered to help or is just testing us ... No God means the possibility of less suffering in the future. Believing there is no God gives me more room for belief in family, people, love, truth, beauty, sex, Jell-O, and all the other things I can prove and that make this life the best life I will ever have.[143]

For many people 'heaven' is construed to be one giant cosmological porky and its creator the One Great Magician. An even more interesting conclusion has been provided by Reza Aslan an Iranian-American scholar of religion and author of *God: A Human History*. After 170 pages of liturgical analysis he suggests we 'take a lesson from our mythological ancestors Adam and Eve'. We *should* 'eat the forbidden fruit'. He invites us to look in the mirror—'You need not fear God. You *are* God'.[144]

Alright, so religions are agencies of societal delusion, but should we be at all concerned if people seek and obtain solace from their teachings? Suffice it to say that religions damage society by demonising large swathes of people who don't follow a particular belief, by provoking and justifying wars and violence that have led to the deaths of millions, by opposing the tenets of science and questioning or dismissing its findings, and by promoting ideas and practices like misogyny, racism, and inequality—all, of course, in the name of some god but founded, nevertheless, upon superstition, fallacies, misconceptions, and misbelief. Religions are hindering societal progress. So, brethren, let us pray:

> O Lord, please deliver your worthy followers from the evils and tyranny of the Church. Let them live their lives in the knowledge that religiosity is a pathetic condition given to those who have been brainwashed since birth to believe in the hollow promise of eternal life in the Kingdom of Heaven. Let them reject the doctrine of Original Sin and bizarre concepts like transubstantiation. Free them from the hands of paedophile priests and ministers. Let them cut down on the use of plastics and stop them overfishing. And please keep global temperatures from rising above the expected 1.5 degree pre-industrial mark. Please stop the continued promulgation of the centuries of lies given in your name. Above all, Lord, please convince your worthy followers you don't exist.
>
> This we beseech Thee, O Lord. Amen.

Notes

1. My mother had been brought up in the Church of England and remained a Christian all her life. She was a firm believer in God-as-cosmic-architect. My father had been 'excommunicated' from the Catholic church when ten years of age when he refused to kneel before the cross stating, apparently, that he took the church at its word and would not 'bow down before any graven image'.
2. There are also many insane and unsound reasons, which is the focus of this chapter.
3. Almond, P. (2018) Friday essay: What might heaven be like? The Conversation, https://theconversation.com/friday-essay-what-might-heaven-be-like-95939.
4. Some 40,000–50,000 were burnt at the stake during 300 years of Christian persecution. See Warraq, I. (2009) The Koran, in C. Hitchens (ed.) *The Portable Atheist: Essential Readings for the Nonbeliever*, Da Capo Press, US, p. 459.
5. The quote is from the Quran—see Almond, Friday essay.
6. Quoted in Almond, Friday Essay.
7. Wikipedia. (2022) Religion, https://en.wikipedia.org/wiki/Religion.
8. Oliver, M. (2017) 10 weirdly specific gods your mythology class left out, Listverse, https://listverse.com/2017/02/09/10-weirdly-specific-gods-your-mythology-class-left-out/; Swan, T. (2021) 10 weird (and funny) gods and goddesses, Owlcation, https://owlcation.com/humanities/10-Weird-Gods-and-Goddesses.
9. The Age of Blasphemy. (2021) 101 insane, crazy and secretive beliefs of Mormons, https://theageofblasphemy.com/2012/10/08/101-insane-crazy-and-secretive-beliefs-of-mormons/; and check out Book of Mormon, The Script, https://www.allmusicals.com/lyrics/bookofmormonthe/script.htm.
10. Kuroski, J. (2019) Five of the strangest things Scientologists actually believe, ATI, https://allthatsinteresting.com/scientology-beliefs.
11. Xenophanes quoted in https://www.goodreads.com/quotes/199943-the-ethiops-say-that-their-gods-are-flat-nosed-and-black;

see also Barnstone, W. (1993) *The Poetics of Translation: History, Theory, Practice*, Yale University Press, New Haven, p. 144.

12. Frazer, J. (2020) *The Golden Bough: Abridged Edition*, Dover Publications, New York. The original was published in Britain in 1890.
13. The question would be which god—A Muslim god, perhaps? Or, a Christian God punishing the Catholic church for corruption and clerical pederasty? The cause of the blaze remains a mystery, but many Christians are blaming Muslim terrorists see Hawkins, F. (2019) What really caused the Notre Dame cathedral fire? American Thinker, https://www.americanthinker.com/articles/2019/04/what_really_caused_the_notre_dame_cathedral_fire.html; Andrade, G. (2019) An age-old question: Why would God allow Notre Dame to burn? Merion West, https://merionwest.com/2019/04/20/an-age-old-question-why-did-god-allow-notre-dame-to-burn/. The latter author considers that 'the more reasonable theologians, I believe, are the ones who shrug and, unable to find answers, simply repeat the old cliché: "The Lord works in mysterious ways." That is very close to admitting the unreasonableness of God's existence ... I would come to that conclusion on the basis that a God as defined by the great religions (omnipotent and benevolent) is likely not to exist, given the amount of evil in the world'.
14. See Ambrosino, B. (2019) Do humans have a 'religion instinct'? BBC, https://www.bbc.com/future/article/20190529-do-humans-have-a-religion-instinct.
15. Sandoiu, What religion does to your brain.
16. Marx, K. (1843) A contribution to the critique of Hegel's philosophy of right, https://www.marxists.org/archive/marx/works/1843/critique-hpr/intro.htm; also quoted in McLellan, D. (1971) *The Thought of Karl Marx: An Introduction*, Harper and Row, New York, p. 22.
17. Sandoiu, A. (2018) What religion does to your brain.
18. See Langley, M. (2022) Why rituals have been crucial for humans throughout history—and why we still need them, https://theconversation.com/why-rituals-have-been-crucial-for-humans-throughout-history-and-why-we-still-need-them-193951; Wikipedia.

(2023) Christianity and paganism, https://en.wikipedia.org/wiki/Christianity_and_paganism; OtherWorldlyOracle. (2019) Christianity's pagan roots, https://otherworldlyoracle.com/christianitys-pagan-traditions/.
19. OtherWorldlyOracle, Christianity's pagan roots.
20. Whitmarsh, T. (2011) *Battling the Gods: Atheism in the Ancient World*, Cambridge University Press, Cambridge.
21. Mathers, C. (2020) Religiosity and atheism in 2020, https://colinmathers.com/2020/09/05/religiosity-and-atheism-in-2020/.
22. World Population Review. (2021) Most atheist countries 2021, https://worldpopulationreview.com/country-rankings/most-atheist-countries.
23. Paul-Choudhury, S. (2019) Tomorrow's gods: What is the future of religion? BBC, https://www.bbc.com/future/article/20190801-tomorrows-gods-what-is-the-future-of-religion.
24. Zuckerman, P. (2008) *Society Without God: What the Least Religious Nations Can Tell Us About Contentment*, New York University Press, New York.
25. Pierotti, S. (2003) Backup of *The Protestant Ethic and the Spirit of Capitalism*: Criticisms of Weber's thesis, https://www.bxscience.edu/ourpages/auto/2014/3/11/44281781/weber%20and%20prot%20ethic.htm; Zafirovski, M. (2019) A neglected gap in the Weber thesis? The long economic lag of capitalism from Protestantism, *Social Science Information* 58(1): 3–56.
26. Ruether, R. (2014) Sexism and misogyny in the Christian tradition: Liberating alternatives, *Buddhist-Christian Studies* 34: 83–94.
27. Alba, B. (2019) If we reject gender discrimination in every other arena, why do we accept it in religion? The Guardian, https://www.theguardian.com/commentisfree/2019/mar/06/if-we-reject-gender-discrimination-in-every-other-arena-why-do-we-accept-it-in-religion.
28. Robertson, J. (2004) *A Short History of Christianity*, Third Edition, Kessinger Publishing LLC, Montana; Mitchell, P. (2013) Violence and the Crusades: Warfare, injuries and torture in medieval Middle East, in C. Knusel and M. Smith (eds.)

The Routledge Handbook of the Bioarchaeology of Human Conflict, Routledge, London, pp. 251–262; Madden, T. (2013) *The Concise History of the Crusades*, Rowman and Littlefield, Maryland.
29. Reported in Enquirer.net. (2018) 'Raisins,' not 'virgins,' Quran scholars say, Inquirer, https://globalnation.inquirer.net/163694/raisins-not-virgins-quran-scholars-say. According to one sixteenth-century Koranic scholar Al-Suyuti each time the martyr sleeps with a heavenly virgin, her virginity returns and 'the penis of the Elected never softens. The erection is eternal; the sensation that you feel each time you make love is utterly delicious and out of this world and were you to experience it in this world you would faint. Each chosen one [i.e. Muslim] will marry seventy [virgins], besides the women he married on earth, and all will have appetising vaginas'. Quoted in Warraq, I. (2002) Virgins, what virgins? The Guardian, https://www.theguardian.com/books/2002/jan/12/books.guardianreview5; see also Kristof, N. (2004) Martyrs, virgins and grapes, https://www.nytimes.com/2004/08/04/opinion/martyrs-virgins-and-grapes.html.
30. Weil, J. (2019) The Bible was used to justify slavery. Then Africans made it their path to freedom, Washington Post, https://www.washingtonpost.com/local/the-bible-was-used-to-justify-slavery-then-africans-made-it-their-path-to-freedom/2019/04/29/34699e8e-6512-11e9-82ba-fcfeff232e8f_story.html.
31. White, L. (1967) The historical roots of our ecological crisis, *Science* 155(3767): 1203–1207, https://www.cmu.ca/faculty/gmatties/lynnwhiterootsofcrisis.pdf.
32. See discussion in Faraqi, Y. (2007) Islamic view of nature and values: Could these be the answer to building bridges between modern science and Islamic science, *International Education Journal* 8(2): 461–469.
33. Van Hooft, S. (2023) What is essentialism? And how does it shape attitudes to transgender people and sexual diversity, The Conversation, https://theconversation.com/what-is-essentialism-and-how-does-it-shape-attitudes-to-transgender-people-and-sexual-diversity-203577.

34. White, The historical roots of our ecological crisis; Fortin, E. (1995) The bible made me do it: Christianity, science, and the environment, *The Review of Politics* 57(2): 197–223.
35. NPR. (2010) Do you believe in miracles? Most Americans do, https://www.npr.org/templates/story/story.php?storyId=124007551; Moschovis, P. (2005) 'Lord, I need a healing': The uneasy relationship between faith and medicine, https://journalofethics.ama-assn.org/article/lord-i-need-healing-uneasy-relationship-between-faith-and-medicine/2005-05.
36. Merriam-Webster. (2021) Miracle, https://www.merriam-webster.com/dictionary/miracle.
37. Forbes, M. and Anderson, R. (2014) Standards for sainthood: What defines a 'miracle'? The Conversation, https://theconversation.com/standards-for-sainthood-what-defines-a-miracle-26160.
38. DeLillo, D. (2011) *White Noise*, Pan Macmillan, UK, p. 318.
39. LibQuotes. (2023) Woody Allen, https://libquotes.com/woody-allen/quote/lbx7k7c; BestQuotations. (2023) Woody Allen, https://best-quotations.com/authquotes.php?auth=78. There are several versions of these quotes on record.
40. Bond, H. (2002) Who was the real Virgin Mary? The Guardian, https://www.theguardian.com/world/2002/dec/19/gender.uk1.
41. Almond, P. (2021) 5 things to know about Mary, the mother of Jesus, The Conversation, https://theconversation.com/5-things-to-know-about-mary-the-mother-of-jesus-172483.
42. Many people believe that Jesus, too, was immaculately conceived. But this is not so according to Catholicism. Mary would have been tainted with sin if she were not given the special grace of Immaculate Conception. But Jesus didn't need this—he had no stain of sin from Adam. He was born of the Holy Spirit not by grubby human propagation. See The New Theological Movement. (2011) Was Jesus immaculately conceived? http://newtheologicalmovement.blogspot.com/2011/12/was-jesus-immaculately-conceived.html.
43. Camille, A. (2019) How many times has Mary appeared in history and where? Vocation Network, https://vocationnetwork.org/en/blog/questions_catholics_ask/2019/08/how_many_times_has_mary_appeared_in_history_and_where; ArcGIS.

(2021) UFO sightings map, https://www.arcgis.com/apps/webappviewer/index.html?id=ddda71d5211f47e782b12f3f8d06246e.
44. Wikipedia. (2023) Depiction of Jesus, https://en.wikipedia.org/wiki/Depiction_of_Jesus.
45. Wikipedia, Depiction of Jesus.
46. See image at: https://en.wikipedia.org/wiki/Depiction_of_Jesus.
47. It has been dated at between 1260 and 1390, the Middle Ages. See Wikipedia. (2023) Shroud of Turin, https://en.wikipedia.org/wiki/Shroud_of_Turin.
48. The Telegraph. (2015) 21 images of Jesus and other religious figures seen in strange things and places, https://www.telegraph.co.uk/news/picturegalleries/howaboutthat/11491504/20-images-of-Jesus-and-other-religious-figures-seen-in-strange-things-and-places.html?frame=3243164.
49. Ong, C. (2017) Man trying to sell his 'Jesus Toast' on eBay for $25K, Christian Today, https://www.christiantoday.com/article/man-trying-to-sell-his-jesus-toast-on-ebay-for-25k/105294.htm.
50. Amazon. (2023) The Grilled Cheeses sandwich press, https://www.amazon.com/dp/B00DD0P0TK/?tag=097-20&ascsubtag=default.
51. 10MostToday. (2013) 10 most famous Jesus statues in the world, https://10mosttoday.com/10-most-famous-jesus-statues-in-the-world/.
52. Wikipedia. (2023) *Lux Mundi* (statue), https://en.wikipedia.org/wiki/Lux_Mundi_(statue).
53. Izzard, H. (2019) Take a look at me now: Baby Jesus statue resembles Phil Collins, The Guardian, https://www.theguardian.com/music/2019/nov/21/take-a-look-at-me-now-baby-jesus-statue-resembles-phil-collins.
54. See Wikipedia. (2021) Immaculate Conception, https://en.wikipedia.org/wiki/Immaculate_Conception. It is interesting to learn that a 'virtual civil war' broke out in the Middle Ages between the Franciscans (who believed in the immaculate conception), and the Dominicans (who didn't). The Dominican

friar, Thomas Aquinas couldn't stomach the idea of an immaculate conception. This didn't stop it eventually being adopted as a truth by the Catholic church. In 1854 Pope Pius IX it became dogma after the release of the papal bull *Ineffabilis Deus* (that is, an ineffable God—a God beyond description).

55. Medievalists. (2022) The Holy foreskin, https://www.medievalists.net/2013/12/the-holy-foreskin/; see also Wikipedia. (2022) Holy prepuce, https://en.wikipedia.org/wiki/Holy_Prepuce. The Wikipedia entry puts the number of foreskins at between 8 and 18.
56. Woods, W. (1975) *A History of the Devil*, Granada, UK, p. 204.
57. Rattray Taylor, G. (1953) *Sex in History*, Thames and Hudson, London, p. 39.
58. Rattray Taylor, *Sex in History*, p. 42; Wikipedia. (2021) Veronica Giuliana, https://en.wikipedia.org/wiki/Veronica_Giuliani.
59. Rattray Taylor, Sex in History, p. 43; Wikipedia. (2021) Christina the Astonishing, https://en.wikipedia.org/wiki/Christina_the_Astonishing.
60. Rattray Taylor, *Sex in History*, p. 48.
61. Woods, *A History of the Devil*, p. 207.
62. Rattray Taylor, *Sex in History*, pp. 70–71.
63. May, G. (1930) *Social Control of Sexual Expression*, Allen and Unwin, UK, quoted in Rattray Taylor, *Sex in History*, p. 55. I'm not sure whether mutton chops refer to facial hair of meat on Friday. Perhaps both were considered equally inappropriate?
64. Rattray Taylor, *Sex in History*, p. 55.
65. Rattray Taylor, *Sex in History*, pp. 48–51.
66. Kohanski, D. (2018) Why the Catholic church is so conflicted about sex, The Humanist, https://thehumanist.com/magazine/january-february-2019/features/why-the-catholic-church-is-so-conflicted-about-sex/; Armstrong, D. (2018) Sex and Catholics: Our views briefly explained, https://www.ncregister.com/blog/sex-and-catholics-our-views-briefly-explained. According to the latter, 'Catholics believe that sexuality has a fundamental purpose, decreed by God: procreation'.

67. Daily History. (2021) Why was St. Augustine so important in Christian history, https://dailyhistory.org/Why_was_St._Augustine_so_important_in_Christian_History.
68. Augustine's interpretation of Paul has been described as 'the most sublime "strong misreading" in the history of Christian thought'—quoted in Kohanski, Why the Catholic church is so conflicted about sex.
69. Vertical View. (2016) What did Adam and Eve eat? https://verticalviewblog.wordpress.com/2016/01/27/what-fruit-did-adam-and-eve-eat/. Etrog is a lemon-like fruit.
70. Pagels, E. (1989) *Adam, Eve, and the Serpent: Sex and Politics in Early Christianity*, Vintage Books, New York, p. 109.
71. Pagels, *Adam, Eve and the Serpent*.
72. Mabry, J. (1990) The naughty Bishop of Hippo: Disfunctional theological innovations of St Augustine, http://apocryphile.org/jrm/articles/augustine.html.
73. James, F. (2021) Augustine's sex-life change: From profligate to celibate, Christianity Today, https://www.christianitytoday.com/history/issues/issue-15/augustines-sex-life-change-from-profligate-to-celibate.html.
74. James, Augustine's sex-life change: From profligate to celibate.
75. Mabry, The naughty Bishop of Hippo.
76. Boyce, J. (2015) Don't blame the Devil: St Augustine and original sin, UTNE Reader, https://www.utne.com/mind-and-body/st-augustine-and-original-sin-ze0z1505zken/.
77. Mabry, The naughty Bishop of Hippo.
78. Quoted in Mabry, The naughty Bishop of Hippo.
79. Augustine quoted in Pagels, *Adam, Eve and the Serpent*, p. 112.
80. It appears that when Augustine decided to give up sex, he demanded everyone else do so as well.
81. Kohanski, Why the Catholic church is so conflicted about sex.
82. Livesay, C. (2019) Abused nuns reveal stories of rape, forced abortions, PBS, https://www.pbs.org/newshour/show/abused-nuns-reveal-stories-of-rape-forced-abortions; Poggioli, S. (2019) After years of abuse by priests, #NunsToo are speaking out, NPR, https://www.npr.org/2019/03/18/703067602/after-years-of-abuse-by-priests-nunstoo-are-speaking-out; Hidalgo, M.

(2007) *Sexual Abuse and the Culture of Catholicism: How Priests and Nuns Become Perpetrators*, Routledge, London; Blakely, J. (2018) Sexual abuse and the culture of clericalism, https://www.americamagazine.org/faith/2018/08/23/sexual-abuse-and-culture-clericalism.
83. Chrisafis, A. (2021) French Catholic church expresses 'shame' after report finds 330,000 children were abused, The Guardian, https://www.theguardian.com/world/2021/oct/05/french-catholic-priests-abused-children-report.
84. *Agence France-Presse*. (2023) Spanish clergy sexually abused more than 200,000 children, inquiry estimates, https://www.theguardian.com/world/2023/oct/27/spanish-clergy-sexual-abused-more-than-200000-children-inquiry-estimates.
85. The Guardian. (2021) The Guardian view on sexual abuse and the Catholic church: Contrition is not enough, https://www.theguardian.com/commentisfree/2021/oct/10/the-guardian-view-on-sexual-abuse-and-the-catholic-church-contrition-is-not-enough.
86. Stille, A. (2016) What Pope Benedict knew about abuse in the Catholic Church, New Yorker, https://www.newyorker.com/news/news-desk/what-pope-benedict-knew-about-abuse-in-the-catholic-church. Stille argues that the sainted John Paul II was the Pope most responsible for ignoring the suffering of the young and vulnerable at the hands of priests. His second in command, Joseph Ratzinger (later to become Benedict XVI) also had the ability to act but did so, during his own reign, only when the scandals broke. 'During most of his tenure [Benedict] was far too busy disciplining anyone who dared step out of line with Church teachings on personal sexuality and family planning to bother with the thousands of priests molesting children'; see also Wikipedia. (2021) Catholic Church sexual abuse cases by country, https://en.wikipedia.org/wiki/Catholic_Church_sexual_abuse_cases_by_country.
87. Mac Dougall, D. (2022) Ex-Pope Benedict XVI knew about sexual abuse as archbishop of Munich, report says, Euronews,

https://www.euronews.com/2022/01/20/ex-pope-benedict-xvi-knew-about-sexual-abuse-as-archbishop-of-munich-report-says.
88. Warraq, I. (2009) The Koran, p. 435; see also Robertson, A. (1946) *Jesus: Myth or History?* Watts & Co., London; see also Fuller, P. (1984) The Christs of faith and the Jesus of History, *New Left Review* 146 (July/August), https://newleftreview.org/issues/i146/articles/peter-fuller-the-christs-of-faith-and-the-jesus-of-history.
89. Robertson, *Jesus*, p. 93.
90. Warraq, The Koran, pp. 384–453.
91. See Warraq, The Koran, p. 437; Lester, T. (1999) What is the Koran? https://www.theatlantic.com/magazine/archive/1999/01/what-is-the-koran/304024/; see also Wikipedia. (2022) Gerd R. Puin, https://en.wikipedia.org/wiki/Gerd_R._Puin.
92. Warraq, I. (2007) The Koran: Why I am not a Muslim, in Hitchens, *The Portable Atheist*, pp. 392–395; Warraq, I. (2007) The totalitarian nature of Islam, in Hitchens, *The Portable Atheist*, pp. 445–453.
93. Warraq, The totalitarian nature of Islam, p. 452.
94. Rattray Taylor, *Sex in History*, p. 56.
95. Brakke, D. (2016) Early Christian lies and the lying liars who wrote them: Bart Ehrman's *Forgery and Counterforgery*, *Journal of Religion* 96(3): 378–390.
96. Ehrman, B. (2013) *Forgery and Counterforgery: The Use of Literary Deceit in Early Christian Polemics*, Oxford University Press, New York, p. 532.
97. Ehrman, *Forgery and Counterforgery*, p. 1.
98. Ehrman, *Forgery and Counterforgery*, pp. 3 and 529.
99. Brakke, Early Christian lies and the lying liars who wrote them, p. 381.
100. Ehrman, *Forgery and Counterforgery*, pp. 121–128.
101. Herzog, H. (2015) Why people care more about pets than other humans, https://www.wired.com/2015/04/people-care-pets-humans/.
102. One research study conducted in the US showed subjects showed more empathy towards suffering animals than suffering

humans—see Levin, J., Arluke, A. and Irvine, L. (2017) Are people more disturbed by dog or human suffering? Influence of Victim's Species and Age, *Society and Animals* 25(1): 1–16, https://doi.org/10.1163/15685306-12341440; Dodgson, L. (2017) A study has finally shown that people really do love dogs more than other humans, https://www.businessinsider.com.au/humans-love-dogs-more-than-other-humans-2017-11?r=US&IR=T.

103. Dalzell, S. (2021) Do you prefer pets to people? So do about a third of Australians, according to Australia Talks, ABC, https://www.abc.net.au/news/2021-05-29/australia-talks-pets-easing-loneliness-and-bringing-people-joy/100163858.
104. Davis, N. (2022) Dogs produce tears when reunited with owners, study finds, The Guardian, https://www.theguardian.com/science/2022/aug/22/dogs-produce-tears-when-reunited-with-owners-study-finds.
105. King, W. (2021) Do pets go to heaven? https://www.simplycatholic.com/pets-in-heaven/; Epstein, A. (2014) Who's a good boy?! https://qz.com/311346/pope-francis-says-all-pets-go-to-heaven-but-what-do-other-religions-say/. Benedict was following Augustine's dictum that since Jesus' placed evil spirits in swine (causing them to hurtle towards the sea, and drown), humankind has little responsibility for animal welfare, no duty of care.
106. Bora, M. (2010) Pigs may not fly in heaven, The Guardian, https://www.theguardian.com/commentisfree/belief/2010/jan/22/islam-animals.
107. There is uncertainty in most other religions. In Buddhism, with animals becoming humans and vice versa there is no means of separating the two, so the question of animals-in-heaven doesn't really have meaning. For Jews there are ongoing debates about concepts like 'heaven' and 'hell' with Judaism being unclear about the fate of animals. Hindus believe animals have souls and that they can enter the human plane as part of reincarnation. They move from being animals to being human in constant life-death-rebirth cycles. See Epstein, Who's a good boy?!

108. Kell, G. (2017) What happens to our pets when they die? https://www.thegospelcoalition.org/article/what-happens-to-pets-when-they-die/.
109. Wells, C. (2021) How did God get started? https://www.bu.edu/arion/archive/volume-18/colin_wells_how_did_god_get_started/.
110. Charles Freeman quoted in Wells, How did God get started?
111. Laurie, G. (2020) Who was Doubting Thomas? Bible story and verses, https://www.christianity.com/jesus/life-of-jesus/disciples/was-he-really-a-doubting-thomas.html.
112. Freud, S. (2007) The future of an illusion, in Hitchins, *The Portable Atheist*, p. 148.
113. Wells, How did God get started?
114. As British physicist William W. Bragg has argued 'Religion and science are indeed incompatible. Religion and science both offer explanations for why life and the universe exist. Science relied on testable empirical evidence and observation. Religion relies on subjective belief in a creator. Only one explanation is correct. The other must be discarded. Explanations require evidence. None exists for a creator outside the human mind … religious belief in a divinity is no more viable than belief in the now-proverbial Flying Spaghetti Monster'. Quoted in Inch Magazine. (2022) Debate: Can religion and science co-exist? https://www.ineos.com/inch-magazine/articles/issue-7/debate/.
115. Encyclopedia Britannica. (2022) Transubstantiation, https://www.britannica.com/topic/transubstantiation.
116. Christian, D. (2018) *Origin Story: A Big History of Everything*, Penguin, UK, p. 19. 'Stephen Hawking argues that the question of beginnings is just badly put. If the geometry of space-time is spherical, like the surface of the earth but in more directions, then asking what existed before the universe is like looking for a starting point on the surface of a tennis ball. That's not how it works. There is no edge or beginning to time, just as there is no edge to the surface of Earth'.

117. Matson, W. (1997) The argument from design, in P. Angels, *Critiques of God: Making the Case Against Belief in God*, Prometheus Books, New York, pp. 59–91.
118. Creation Museum. (2022) Things to do, https://creationmuseum.org/things-to-do/. See also Sundrup, E. (2018) Creationism isn't about science, it's about theology (and it's really bad theology), https://www.americamagazine.org/arts-culture/2018/01/30/creationism-isnt-about-science-its-about-theology-and-its-really-bad.
119. It is quite comprehensive—see https://arkencounter.com/jobs/statement-of-faith/.
120. Angel, W. (2022) The best 16 Creationist jokes, https://jokojokes.com/creationist-jokes.html.
121. Greenspan, S. (2009) *Annals of Gullibility: Why we get Duped and how to Avoid it*, Praeger, Connecticut, pp. 36–37.
122. Billson, A. (2010) *Rosemary's Baby*: No 2 best horror film of all time, The Guardian, https://www.theguardian.com/film/2010/oct/22/rosemarys-baby-polanksi-horror.
123. Butters, T. (2015) 10 best movie depictions of the devil, Screenrant, https://screenrant.com/best-movie-depictions-devil-satan/.
124. All quotes are from Butters, 10 best movie depictions of the devil.
125. Wikipedia. (2022) *The Last Temptation of Christ* (film), https://en.wikipedia.org/wiki/The_Last_Temptation_of_Christ_(film).
126. Dutta, D. (2020) Why *The Exorcist* is still one of the scariest horror movies ever made, Screenrant, https://screenrant.com/exorcist-scariest-horror-movie-2020-all-time-reason/.
127. McNeil, B. (2019) The centuries-old practice of exorcism is on the rise. Why now? VCU News, https://news.vcu.edu/article/The_centuriesold_practice_of_exorcism_is_on_the_rise_Why_now.
128. Woods, *A History of the Devil*, p. 9.
129. Quoted in Woods, *A History of the Devil*, p. 196.
130. Woods, *A History of the Devil*, p. 201.
131. BBC. (2018) Exorcism: Vatican course opens doors to 250 priests, https://www.bbc.com/news/world-europe-43697573.

132. Crary, D. (2020) Exorcism: Increasingly frequent, including after US protests, ABC News, https://abcnews.go.com/US/wireStory/exorcism-increasingly-frequent-including-us-protests-73942073.
133. Sagan, C. (2009) The demon-haunted world, in C. Hitchens, *The Portable Atheist*, p. 225.
134. Getten, L. (2020) How an exorcist priest came face-to-face with the devil himself, NY Post, https://nypost.com/2020/03/07/how-an-exorcist-priest-came-face-to-face-with-the-devil-himself/.
135. Pagels, *Adam, Eve and the* Serpent, p. 150.
136. James, A. (2001) *The Myth of Christianity*, Premier Publishers, Australia, p. 170.
137. Wells, How did God get started?
138. Anderson, E. (2007) If God is dead, is everything permitted? in Hitchens, *The Portable Atheist*, pp. 336–337.
139. Russell, B. (2024) in AZ Quotes, https://www.azquotes.com/quote/575216.
140. Hitchens, *The Portable Atheist*, pp. xx–xxi.
141. Pataki, T. (2007) *Against Religion*, Scribe, Melbourne, p. 13.
142. See Baier, K. (1997) The meaning of life, in Angles, *Critiques of God*, p. 322.
143. Jillette, P. (2007) There is no God, in C. Hitchens, *The Portable Atheist*, p. 350.
144. Aslan, R. (2017) *God: A Human History*, Bantam, London, p. 171.

7

The Ultimate Diversion: Sport as False Consciousness?

The media had a field day—or more accurately a field month. It was January 2022, and the Australian Tennis Open was about to commence in Melbourne. One of the arrivals—arguably the best men's tennis player the world has ever seen—had completed his paperwork and had arrived at Melbourne airport from Spain via Dubai on January 5. But this was no ordinary Grand Slam. Australia was in the grip of COVID-19, with the Omicron variant taking hold throughout the nation. Australians had been counselled by State and Federal governments to double vaccinate and to line up for a booster. Sport-loving fans wondered whether the Open would take place at all. But strict rules were put in place—fans attending the event would have to be double vaccinated and social distancing would be practised. The crowd had been limited to 50% capacity. As well, athletes entering the country were also expected to be at least double vaccinated and were tested for the virus upon arrival.

One athlete chose to refrain from vaccination. It was the Serbian Novak Djokovic, winner of nine Grand Slams in Melbourne and, on current form, the predicted winner of the 2022 men's final. Djokovic was at his fittest and healthiest but had requested a medical exemption. The exemption went before an expert panel of Australian doctors

© The Author(s), under exclusive license to Springer Nature Limited 2024
G. Lawrence, *Societal Deception*, https://doi.org/10.1057/978-1-349-96107-8_7

which included immunologists and infectious disease experts. They saw merit in Djokovic's application (stating that since he'd already tested positive to COVID-19 twice in 2021, he could be exempt from the double vax requirement), allowing it to proceed to the next, and final, stage. The so-called Independent Medical Exemption Review Panel, a government-selected expert body, reviewed the paperwork and decided the application met the guidelines of the Australian Technical Advisory Group on Immunisation (ATAGI). There are only two grounds for approval—either the player had an acute major medical condition at the time, or an underlying condition would cause him or her to experience anaphylaxis or other serious medical problems if given one of the three vaccines (AstraZeneca, Pfizer, Moderna) approved for use against COVID-19 in Australia. Strangely, while neither ground seemed to apply, his application was approved, giving him the same status as tennis players who were fully vaccinated. Tennis Australia was in raptures, the Victorian Government was overjoyed and Djokovic, surely, couldn't believe his luck.

Then things began to unravel. It appears Djokovic and his team were under the impression that his previous COVID-19 infections were sufficient grounds for entry to Australia. But what the Victorian government and Tennis Australia had ignored when giving Djokovic the green light to come into the country was that it was the Federal government which controls the nation's borders. (Tennis Australia had been reminded of this in letters from the Federal Health Minister in November of 2021 with the Minister stating that having had COVID-19 was not a legitimate reason to be excused from vaccination.) Djokovic's exemption was deemed invalid. He was sent to an immigration hotel—joining other illegal immigrants—and told to leave the country. It was clearly unedifying. Hundreds of members of Melbourne's Serbian community held a vigil outside the hotel hoping to persuade the government to allow him to take his place in the tournament. He appealed the government's decision to place him in detention. The judge agreed that he'd been poorly treated and ordered his release. Djokovic then high-tailed it to a five-star luxury hotel and began practising at Rod Laver Arena. Australia would be seeing the champ perform, after all.

7 The Ultimate Diversion: Sport as False Consciousness?

Then it was revealed that his visa paperwork had been filled out incorrectly. He had stated that he had not left his place of residence for 14 days prior to entering Australia. Yet, social media showed him to be in Belgrade, Serbia, on Christmas Day, playing handball with a friend. A second image on Twitter on January 2 showed him kicking a soccer ball with his brother Marko in Marbella, Spain. He'd also been photographed on December 17 handing over prizes to young tennis players, a day after he claimed to have tested positive for COVID-19.[1] There were no masks in sight. He then quadruple-faulted by confessing to having given an interview with a journalist from *L'Equipe*, a French sports newspaper on December 18. He'd clearly broken Australia's entry rules which some interpreted as deliberate contravention. He blamed his agent for the mistake with the entry paperwork.[2] The Federal Immigration Minister was keeping his cards close to his chest, delaying any decision on the star's final fate.

In the meantime, journalists were poking around into various online platforms, past TV interviews, and newspaper reports of his off-court behaviour. He had always been a polarising player whose on-court gamesmanship had not been seen to be in the spirit of tennis.[3] But the main and most disturbing revelation was that he had been an anti-vaxxer for years. Overnight the press had blessed him with the irresistible title 'No Vax Djokovic' and the story became an intriguing worldwide phenomenon. Aside from his dislike of being jabbed, it was revealed he believed in a string of unconventional ideas. At one time he had self-diagnosed a wheat allergy by placing a slice of bread on his tummy. He is a fan of so-called hyperbaric chambers; in an effort to reverse the ageing process, the body is sealed in a tank and exposed to three times the normal pressure of oxygen. He believes that positive thinking can make polluted water clean again (molecules in water act to human emotion) and that the humble celery stick contains transformative powers.[4] He regularly visits the so-called Bosnian pyramids to gain strength from their mystical powers (archaeologists have deemed them a cruel hoax).[5] Not all his ideas are so silly. He is a firm believer in the value of hugging trees.

The press began revealing his 'bonehead decisions', 'ghastly miscalculations', and—largely because of his hubris—the 'ill-conceived and sloppily executed maneuvers' that had led him to apply for an exemption that should never have been contemplated. He was 'perhaps even delusional' to think that the Australians 'owed' him a playing spot.[6] The Minister's word is final on these matters, and despite a second attempt by the Djoker's legal team to keep him in the country, a unanimous High Court ruling had sealed his fate. The Federal Minister finally acted, deporting him on January 16, some 11 days after the star had arrived in Australia unvaccinated.

Public opinion was on the High Court's side—in two separate surveys, between 71 and 92% of respondents in newspaper polls were against his being granted an exemption. Why, it was being asked, should a seemingly healthy but unvaccinated player be allowed into Victoria when the Melbourne population had experienced one of the longest and toughest pandemic lockdowns in the nation's two-year fight with the virus? The Immigration Minister went further, arguing that Djokovic was quickly becoming an icon of the anti-vax movement in Australia. His high-profile presence could endanger civil society by giving credence to the propaganda of anti-vaxxers, encouraging them to flout Australia's COVID-19 rules.[7]

It was not only Australia where Djokovic became a cause célèbre. The Serbian President, Aleksandar Vučić, accused the Australian government of 'not only intellectual but physical torture' against the tennis star, saying the rules of entry into Australia had been changed for the government's own political purposes.[8] For Serbian Prime Minister, Ana Brnabić, the deportation had been 'scandalous'. 'It's been incredible' she said 'to witness brutal lies, incredible lies in Australia by the representatives of the state'. The Serbian Minister of Youth and Sports said 'this is no longer a question of sport … we are talking about the breach of his liberty' and indicated that Serbia was considering what appropriate diplomatic steps it might take.[9] Srdjan Djokovic, Novak's father, accused Australia of trying to 'blackmail' his son into having a COVID-19 vaccination. Following Novak's detention, he raised the stakes—'They're keeping him in captivity. They're stomping all over Novak to stomp all over Serbia and Serbian people'. He continued, 'Jesus was crucified on the cross … but he is still alive among us. They are trying to crucify and belittle Novak and throw him to his knees'.[10] Of course, in comparing

7 The Ultimate Diversion: Sport as False Consciousness?   327

his son to Jesus Srdjan was, *ipso facto*, claiming he was God—someone we should all listen to very carefully.

Summing up the Djokovic saga, a journalist from *The Age* wrote:

> Novak Djokovic came to Australia trying to become the greatest player in the history of men's tennis. He will leave under armed guard as an undesirable alien and toxic icon of the anti-vax movement.[11]

What can we learn about sport from the Djokovic incident? There are five insights. First, sport is a global phenomenon—what happens in far-flung Melbourne, in a corner of an ex-British colony, can reverberate around the world. Sport is front and centre of popular culture worldwide and a 'media-sport-cultural-complex' has emerged to promote and commodify sport and to expose it to an ever-growing global audience.[12] (The COVID-19 pandemic has laid bare the vulnerability and fragility of global sport, with cancellations causing mayhem for organisers, broadcasters, and a public whose cheering and booing from the grandstands is the very essence of modern sporting contests.)[13] Second, sport stars are social influencers and they have particular impact with a younger age cohort (in the US one-third of 13–36-year-olds follow their favourite athletes on social media).[14] The fans form an emotional attachment with the stars, sharing an athlete's views, interests, and backstories. Novak Djokovic has 29 million devotees on social media, making him the third most followed tennis player in the world.[15] His latest tennis games, his actions, and his predilections are also heavily covered in the print and electronic media. It is little wonder that Australia's Immigration Minister considered his anti-vax sentiments provided a risk to social order. Third, on display were many of the agents, and mechanisms, of societal deception. Tennis Australia and the Victorian Government were complicit in Djokovic's illegal entry into Australia, winking and nodding that he'd be able to enter as an unvaccinated player. On all accounts he and his team had been deceived and manipulated by Tennis Australia—all in the hope that such a high-profile player would be given an exemption at the border. There was secrecy about how he was given medical approval to play in the Open. Djokovic and his team obviously lied about his activities the fourteen days before he entered the country. (Evidence showed his positive COVID-19 test most likely occurred between December 25 and 28, not December 16—with implications of impropriety by Serbian officials.)[16] Even with a Djoker in their pack, his team had played a pretty poor hand. Fourth, while we constantly hear about the importance of keeping sport free of politics, the debacle had politics written all over it. Tennis Australia and the Victorian Government, desperately wanting the star to play—for the TV exposure and the city's promotion accompanying his presence—failed to check in with (or thumbed their noses at) the Federal Government, which had the final say on whether he could enter the country. When the Federal Minister acted it was with the approval of most Australians, helping to shore up popularity at a soon-to-be announced federal election. The Serbian nation's fragile international status was on show when its President, Prime Minister, and sports minister construed Djokovic's detention and later expulsion to be an attack on the nation. Nationalism was at the fore when Novak's father believed the entire Serbian nation had been humiliated by Australia and that his son really was the Christ. (Less dramatically, one fan is on record as saying Djokovic 'is one of the best things Serbia has at the moment … you don't have, unfortunately, a lot of great things in Serbia, so Novak is the best'.)[17] Sport fosters nationalism, and nationalism is one of the ideologies that deceives people about the way the world really works: Better a class-divided nation believe in itself (we are all Serbian, or British, or French, or Italian) than understand the class differences that keep the rich rich, and the poor poor, in those countries. Fifth—but strongly linked to the fourth point—the Djokovic affair was a great diversion, turning people's attention away from mass shootings in America, Russia's invasion of Ukraine, and the melting of the Arctic and Antarctic ice caps.

After having his three-year suspension overturned, Djokovic returned to Australia in 2023. He played brilliant tennis and won the Grand Slam. Unfortunately, his father, God, was a little less brilliant, being photographed smiling with fans of Russian tennis players who were carrying a banned Russian flag bearing the face of—you guessed it—Vladimir Putin.[18]

7 The Ultimate Diversion: Sport as False Consciousness? 329

My Sporting Life

I do have a confession to make. I was never very good at sport. I think the operative word is 'hopeless' or, as the British might say 'rubbish'. In my early years coaches could be heard muttering 'District', 'State', or 'National' about the sporting potential of members of my teams—but I never saw their eyes glance in my direction. I opened the batting for our under 14s cricket club. These were the days before helmets. 'Duck' was the frequent call, in both senses of the word. I once captained a high school cricket seconds which took a pounding. Some decades later at a school reunion I was gently told by one of my friends that I'd been setting a field for a fast bowler, when all the slow-paced deliveries were being smashed over the bowlers' heads for fours and sixes. My attempts at golf were a tragedy until I finally decided that my *own* par would be double that for any hole on the card. The tensions were immediately relieved. I partly blame my poor showing to the $20 set of second-hand clubs my father bought me after he'd backed in 'You Little Beauty' at the Dapto dogs. My rugby days were no better. As a fast(ish)-running centre, my greatest moment was to score a length-of-the-field try, collapsing with exhaustion under the goal posts. Only to find out the referee had blown his whistle back on my own try line. The air in my lungs had gone; the opposition had enough in theirs to guffaw and to utter impolite comments. Humiliation was an ever-present shadow.[19] I played field hockey at university, being advised—after my third game—to focus more upon my studies. Most of my friends had at least one sporting trophy on the family mantelpiece. I boasted a red ribbon saying 'second place' for a 100-metre sprint at primary school. It sat beside my only other prize, a certificate signed by the headmaster for 'best mechanical toy' when I was eight and in my fourth year of school. It was a tin submarine. Perhaps I should have thrown away my sporting paraphernalia and enlisted in the Navy.

My performance in sport turned out to be inversely proportional to my fascination for it. I've managed to enjoy some wonderful sporting moments—attending a season of the Wisconsin Badgers ice hockey and football teams, being on the sidelines for a Superbowl game in New Orleans, and watching the Blue Jay's battle it out with Orioles at the Rogers Center in Toronto. I've been at Ashes cricket tests between Australia and England, rugby games too numerous to mention, and have visited Olympic venues in Montreal, Lillehammer, Seoul, and Melbourne. With my family, I was in the stands when Australia's Cathy Freeman won the women's 400 metres race at the 2000 Sydney Olympics. As Chauncey Gardner (Peter Sellers) once remarked in the movie *Being There*, 'I like to watch'.

I've done some remarkable watching over the decades. I've seen advertisers colonise major sporting competitions, rewriting the rules to allow longer breaks in play to display their wares on television. I've seen wealthy media barons turn sports into lucrative money-making spectacles. Athletes have become living display units, their jerseys emblazoned with the brands of gas and oil companies, car makers, fast-food corporations, international banks, and gambling establishments.[20] I've noted how game commentators have increasingly emphasised the more brutal, boorish, and controversial aspects of sport to entertain and win an audience. I've observed changes in stadia, with ribbons of electronic advertising replacing picket fences, playing surfaces bearing painted logos, and huge screens erected to saturate the fans with the colourful images and commentary promoting corporate products—all part of the 'spectacularisation' and 'Americanisation' of global sport.[21] Russian oligarchs have entered the scene, buying and selling football clubs at whim, as members of a Billionaire's Club that is increasing its control of international sport.[22] I've seen politics insinuate itself in major sporting events—from black-power salutes to Israeli athlete deaths to political boycotts to crass jargonistic nationalism at the Olympics and, in other sports, to apartheid sanctions, to ethnic clashes in football, to athletes taking a knee to protest racism and police violence, to sports heroes endorsing Presidential candidates, to bodybuilders becoming politicians (think Arnie), to politicians looking for courtside exposure and glory. Sport diplomacy is on the rise as well, with nations such as China, Russia, Australia and Saudi Arabia building stadiums in foreign lands, and subsidising training, in order to curry favour with the locals. According to sociologist David Rowe

7 The Ultimate Diversion: Sport as False Consciousness?

Despite the persistent delusion of some that politics should be kept out of sport, it has always been suffused with political calculations and meanings. The major question is not whether but what kinds of politics will be played and by whom.[23]

Sports betting is a particularly insidious element that has emerged in recent decades, with sport being used as a

> marketing platform to deploy huge investments of money by sports betting operators to recruit and retain customers through advertising, merchandising and celebrity endorsements that incorporate sport products, images, usages and icons.[24]

Sports betting adverts have become embedded in virtually all televised sporting events and feature heavily on mobile devices and social media platforms, with sports betting companies targeting not only professional sports, but also community-based sports and sport involving minors.[25] Advertising by the betting companies has been shown to normalise gambling among young males where it is promoted as a harmless, skill-based, activity providing fun and pleasure. In reality, the 'gamblification' of sport has resulted in young people being pressured by peers to become involved in betting, along with the significant growth of problem gambling throughout society.[26] At the same time the gambling companies are increasing their revenues from sport, governments are picking up the tab for the associated relationship breakdowns, health problems, psychological distress, and criminal activity.[27]

But it would be wrong to leave out other important observations. Women's involvement in sport has increased at both junior and elite levels; prize money for women's events is rising; women are challenging the various myths and stereotypes that have previously befallen them; women's sporting events are usually more inclusive spaces for children and families than are the stadia suffused with toxic masculinity; and, elite women's sports are leading the way in combating climate change effects of long-distance travel.[28] Coverage and empowerment are coming through sporting involvement. People of colour can gain social elevation, high earnings, status, and prestige through sport—although rags-to-riches stories are few, and white middle-class men from privileged backgrounds enjoy greater social mobility via sport.[29] Despite organised and sometimes vicious campaigns of denigration, LGBTQIA+ athletes are becoming increasingly accepted in competitive sports—at all levels.[30] Athletes with disabilities are being given more funding and more media exposure, with sport transforming community ideas about disability, helping to lessen stigma and discrimination.[31]

Of course, to get to the top it might be necessary to suffer a little hard disciplining at the hands of coaches. The abusive and controlling behaviour of parents and coaches has become 'normalised', with one Australian study reporting one in three people had been abused during their time in amateur/community sport. Such abuse included 'excessive criticism, insults and humiliation, [and] excessive training to extreme exhaustion/vomiting'.[32] When that didn't work, they would be cold-shouldered until their performance improved. Elite athletes who have reported parental abuse include David Beckham, Tiger Woods, and Andre Agassi. As the British public were reminded in 2022, their Olympic gymnasts had been regularly subjected to mental, physical, and sexual abuse, denied food, water, and toilet breaks during training, and bodily shamed as part of a culture of mistreatment, a medals-at-all-costs mission.[33] And let us not forget the misogyny that is rampant in many sporting bodies. Some organisations are addressing this, of course. Take the Welsh Rugby Union (WRU). Saddled with claims of sexism and discrimination in its treatment of women administrators, and women athletes, the WRU acted swiftly, banning the singing of a crowd favourite—Tom Jones' *Delilah* (about a jealous lover stabbing to death his adulterous partner)—at all future rugby internationals.[34] Can't say they're not responding to criticism …

Sport can be seen to demolish myths, while strengthening others. It should be recognised that:

> Myths are not total delusions or utter falsehoods, but partial truths that accentuate some versions of reality and marginalize or omit others. They embody fundamental cultural values and character-types and appeal to deep-seated emotions. Myths depoliticize social relations by ignoring the vested interests surrounding those stories that become ascendant in a

7 The Ultimate Diversion: Sport as False Consciousness?   333

given culture. And critically, myths disavow or deny their own conditions of existence: they are forms of speech that derive from specific sites and power relations, but are passed off as natural and eternal verities.[35]

The sporting media entertain the masses, reproducing favoured cultural myths and legends, while ultimately promoting the consumption of the products that bring profits to their sponsors. A 'bread and circuses' understanding of sport could easily follow—with capitalists as the new Roman emperors manipulating public attitudes and behaviour for their own benefit. There is a partial truth here—Big Sport is big business is big profit; the sports apparel, sports equipment, and athletic footwear markets totalled US$407 billion in 2024, with online gambling on sport worth an additional US$63 billion.[36] But people have social agency and they are free to accept or reject what they listen to, read, and view. They are no dummies. So, what is sport?

    Ultimately, sport is a diversion. One of the first uses of the term 'sport' in the English language was by Geoffrey Chaucer (1342–1400) who described it as a distraction from work, and from other serious matters.[37] It is about play, pleasure, entertainment. Sport can encourage and foster blissful ignorance—at the very heart of societal deception. I say 'foster' because sport is much more than advertisers manipulating 'signs' to make us buy, more than the media cosying up to sport celebrities, and certainly more than the confirmation of national pride (or humiliation). Sport-as-agent-of-social-control is a seductive trope and fits nicely with Marx's notion of religion as an 'opium of the people'.[38] And while Marx never uttered the phrase 'false consciousness' many of his followers have. They view entertainment, such as sport, as diverting people's attention from the real issues in life—in particular inequality, oppression, and exploitation. The sporting afficionado's complete indulgence in sports events—from the often brutal competition, to the elation of the goal or home-run, to the ritual of pouring over the game's statistics, to speculation about an athlete's calf or groin injury—is a preoccupation that prevents them seeing the true nature of exploitation under capitalism. Their false consciousness results in an unquestioning acceptance of the status quo, and with it the continuation of an unfair system based on social class. Sport also promotes ideologies that sit nicely with capitalism—the importance of competition, of a neutral umpire, of self-discipline, of knowing that there will always be winners and losers, and so forth. Sport's main roles are to have fans identify with, and support, capitalist culture, while producing fit bodies for the assembly line.[39]

But to suggest such greatly understates, and distorts, sport's complexity. It is best to view sport as a social phenomenon embedded in, and reproducing, structures and cultures that nurture and display competitive physical competition in particular ways—ways that inculcate certain modes of thinking among competitors and fans. It promotes important cultural myths while providing pleasure and enjoyment (sometime exquisite entertainment) for a wide spectrum of society. For example, rugby union followers believe rugby is 'the game played in heaven'—the most perfect example of athletic skill, strength, teamwork, and competitiveness. The angels in this case, though, are not so much ethereal, winged, compassionate beauties as brick-shaped men sporting broken noses and cauliflower ears. Rugby might turn out to be the game played in Hades.

In the Beginning …

Virtually every visitor to Crete, Greece, visits the Great Palace of Knossos, the most significant Bronze Age site on the island and considered by some to be the oldest city in Europe. It is a Neolithic site and centre of the Minoan civilisation which, at the height of its political and cultural rule during 1700 BCE, supported a population of some 100,000 people. On sabbatical in 2011 I was fortunate to visit the site and take in the splendour of its architecture, frescos, and cobbled streets. One of Knossos' most famous frescos, now located at the Heraklion Archaeological Museum some six kilometres from the Palace towards the coast, depicts the sport of bull leaping. Dated at around 1400 BCE, the fresco shows a young man performing a somersault over a charging bull. He is captured in the painting mid-air but, in motion, would have grabbed the charging bull's horns, have been flung by the bull backward into the air, and have been caught by an open-armed compatriot running behind. (So incredibly exhilarating the experience must be, that a slightly different

7 The Ultimate Diversion: Sport as False Consciousness? 335

version continues to be performed in isolated regions of France, Spain, and India.)[40]

Some view bull leaping as a ritual, a ceremonial rite, practised by both sexes; some view it as a sport. It was probably a mixture of both—as were many other activities of the ancients. It was essential that spring would follow winter, with games and sports helping to ensure that outcome. The Wichita tribe of Oklahoma invented a game not unlike modern field hockey which was a symbolic contest between spring and winter (played with the profound hope that the former would ultimately win). The Inuit had seasonal games as well. In spring a cup and ball were used to 'catch' the sun; in autumn with the sun low on the horizon, a tangled web made from the intestines of seals was pointed towards the sun to capture it and slow its progress south. For the desert-dwelling tribe, the Zuni (part of the Pueblo peoples of America's southwest) early games were developed to convince their three most powerful deities—the Earth Mother, Sun Father, and Moonlight-Giving Mother—to bring rain for the spring crops. (Unfortunately, by the 1400s many of the Zuni settlements had disappeared because of on-going drought.)[41] Further south, Aztecs were building settlements around this same time period. The first thing they would do was to construct a shrine to the god Huitzilopochtli; the second was to build, next to it, a ball court where opposing teams could play the game *ullamaliztli*. The court was long and narrow and surrounded by two-metre-high rock walls, allowing spectators to look down at the play. At either end were suspended stone hoops through which players would attempt to lodge a large solid-rubber ball (the Aztecs had been using rubber for thousands of years before the Spanish conquest).[42] During play, the ball had to be in the air at all times—requiring considerable physical endurance. The game would last hours and, at the end the losing coach—and perhaps the entire team—might be sacrificed (human blood was necessary to ensure the sun moved across the sky). The losers would not complain—it was an honour to be sacrificed to the gods.[43] A little less dramatic were Nigerian wrestling contests held to help generate growth in crops through 'sympathetic magic'. Large crowds would gather to watch the tussle and would intervene 'should either of the fighters show weakness, anger, or fatigue, lest these deficiencies cause any ill-effect on the reproductive forces of nature'.[44] Most of the primitive sports were played to induce the gods to bring about favourable weather for the growing season. In those games rules were strict and there was no need for an umpire—why would anyone think of cheating on the gods?

The athletic activities of the ancient Greeks were also based upon mythology and religion. Games accompanied festivals which blended prayer, sacrifice, music, dancing, and feasting.[45] The whale bones, sticks, stakes, and rocks of the ancients had given way to weapons of war—weapons that needed to be mastered to ensure the mind and body were fit and ready for battle. Included in the first Olympics held in 776 BCE were the disciplined sports of running, wrestling, jumping, javelin throwing, and chariot racing. Initially, it was mainly the sons of wealthy Greek families who competed, requiring considerable family financial support to pay for trainers, coaches, and travel. As the Olympics grew in popularity, various city-states throughout Greece recognised the political pride that could be gained through successful competition at the games. Healthy slaves and robust youth from the *hoi polloi* were pressed into service for the city. Others were handpicked by wealthy patrons and were paid to train for the Olympics. Upon winning, successful competitors received prize payments that guaranteed them a (usually short) period of freedom to continue to train, compete, and earn their keep at the Olympics and other sporting events. While amateurism was lauded at the time, many athletes viewed themselves as professionals.[46] And with 'professionalism' came an increasingly strong desire to win. Despite having sworn an oath (on slices of boar's flesh) that they would not sin against the Olympics, some found it necessary to take bribes, bend the strict rules associated with training, and in other ways violate the Olympic code. When caught, they were fined, with proceeds used to place additional statues (or Zanes) of Zeus, the patron of the Games, at Olympia. As a warning to others each Zane bared an inscription that outed the athlete caught cheating.[47]

According to sport sociologist Jay Coakley and his co-writers, while the early Games have been romanticised for their contribution to mind–body harmony, this was not the case:

7 The Ultimate Diversion: Sport as False Consciousness?

Athletes were maimed and killed in the pursuit of victories and the rewards that came with them ... fairness was not as important as honour; and athletic contests were connected with a cultural emphasis on warfare.[48]

And, as their training also took the performers away from intellectual pursuits, Greek philosophers believed the Games were 'brutal and dehumanising and the athletes ... useless and ignorant'.[49] Very unlike today's sports and sporting champions.

When in Rome, do as the Greeks do. Learning from the Greeks, the Romans embraced sporting contests as a means of training male bodies for war, and for mass spectacles. And they were much more inclusive than the Greeks—women could watch from the stands. With slaves doing most of the heavy lifting in the Roman economy, public holidays were aplenty, occupying about 50% of the year. Boxing and chariot races held public attention but more was needed to entertain and distract. What could be better than bear baiting; bull baiting; men-and-women fighting lions, tigers, and panthers; and, lions, tigers, and panthers fighting each other? Criminals and 'undesirables' were forced to wear sheepskins before facing a half-starved lion, while gladiators fought each other to the death. Such activities served two main purposes—'they entertained an idle populace and disposed of ... people such as thieves, murderers, unruly slaves and Christians'.[50] Folk games also became popular and were often played in church grounds with the blessing of the local priest. A thousand years later, in medieval times, such rudimentary examples of what would later become soccer, rugby, bowling, and curling were growing in popularity. But early football in Britain was not quite the game it is today. It was disorganised, violent, spontaneous, and involved an unspecified number of players:

Frequently, games took the form of a heated contest between whole villages - through streets and squares, across fields, hedges, fences and streams. Kicking was allowed, as in fact was almost everything else. Sometimes kicking the ball was out of the question due to the size and weight of the sphere being used - in such cases, kicking was instead limited to taking out opponents.[51]

The upper classes were content to tolerate village games. While a good number of peasant sports were deliberately organised to maim humans or kill animals, the upper classes nevertheless recognised their capacity to contain festering public anger over taxes, land ownership, and concentrated wealth.[52] Sports served their purpose well.

Writing the Rules

The Industrial Revolution, commencing in the mid-1700s, disrupted both rural and urban life—including the games and sports in those locations. In Britain people were forced into cities as common lands were seized by landowners during the enclosure movement. The new urban proletariat worked long hours and had little time to engage in sports. Few parks were provided for recreation. The political and business elite feared workers might gather in such spaces and get up to no good—that is, form unions to oppose bosses and argue for better working conditions.[53] By the 1850s—a time when the industrial revolution was altering the face of Britain forever, entrenching capitalism and its worker/boss relations—the strict rules imposed upon factory workers were also being generalised throughout the economy. Any leisure time was to be a structured, productive, time with sports needing to be 'contained' and rationalised.[54] The Puritanism at the root of this was palpable—Puritans eschewed revelry, with sport and many other leisure activities viewed as encouraging drunkenness, licentiousness, and debauchery. Playing sport on the sabbath was a profanation. With such views in abundance was sport to wither on the vine?

A number of developments ensured this was not to be. Puritan orthodoxy had begun to founder; the Puritans had lost the battle of trying to force the Church of England to abandon rituals and other influences (decorations, religious garb, crucifixes, vestments) that were remnants of Catholicism. And as Puritanism waned more moderate and tolerant branches grew. The leaders of the new Anglican congregations—along with the captains of industry—were detecting that growing economic prosperity in industrial nations like Britain and the US was producing

7 The Ultimate Diversion: Sport as False Consciousness?

a more sedentary, less fit, proletariat. Enter, stage right, muscular Christianity. The wealthy had long considered that moral virtues could be instilled and honed through organised physical exercise, and through contest on the playing field. The Church, educational bodies, and humanitarian organisations began to agree. Young, healthy, athletic, bodies were important for industry and war but—as well—minds sharpened by sporting adventure would embrace leadership, teambuilding, perseverance, and fortitude.[55] Organised physical activity offering structure and discipline could build the 'right' character and, with it, self-esteem, fairness, and respect. Sport was to 'provide a means by which a new capitalist class sought to "civilise" and morally educate' the children and youth of the working class.[56] In fact, for sociologist Norbert Elias a 'civilising process' was underway before and during the nineteenth century which created new standards of behaviour. Less disorderly and less crude, it was becoming more self-restraining and more temperate with social life being increasingly regulated through self-control.[57]

There were other influences in this civilising process. Technological developments such as railways encouraged travel, and teams could venture beyond town boundaries to engage in contest. But many of the emerging sports were literally 'unruly'—they were devoid of agreed-upon regulations. How could Aston Villa play Nottingham Forest or the Boston Red Stocking play the Philadelphia Quakers, if they could not agree on the rules of engagement? It was here that nascent sporting organisations began to formalise codes of conduct and practice for players. In England, the mayhem of the village-based shin-kicking game of football gave way to a more standardised form when clubs were formed from 1820. The rules became established in Cambridge in 1848. This was the same year—some 25 years after a young William Webb Ellis 'with disregard for the rules of football … first took up the ball and ran with it'—that a meeting of schools drafted the code for rugby union. There were 20 players a side and the score was decided by goals alone (scoring a 'try'—or touchdown—meant, literally, that a side could 'try' to kick a goal). Scoring points for a 'try' was added in 1875. Early American football followed in the tradition of soccer and so embraced the rules established by the London Football Association. In 1874, the ball running of rugby was added to the mix. Then, in 1891 Walter

Camp, a member of the Intercollegiate Football Association, added some new features (an 11-man team, the scrimmage line, and offensive signal calling)—and the rules for gridiron were firmly established.[58] Although the rules for cricket were scrawled upon a silk handkerchief at London's Star and Garter pub as early as 1744, overarm bowling and other features of the modern game were not introduced until 1864.[59] In 1845 Alexander Cartwright is credited (sometimes not credited) with writing a set of rules for the Knickerbocker baseball club in New York which were adopted widely and provided the original platform for the game, while Albert Spalding (of sporting goods fame) established a National League in 1876.[60] Sports were being standardised, rationalised, and bureaucratised much like other aspects of life under modernity. There was an underlying logic to the changes being wrought—they were not haphazard. Rather, they followed the prescriptions of those who saw an opportunity to make money from sport, as is noted below.

A third feature was the penetration of capitalist ideals and finances into what at the time were largely amateur sporting contests. It was clear that sports were popular with the public. To expand public participation, grounds and venues needed to be prepared, sporting goods needed to be manufactured, tickets sold, and clothing, shoes, and other paraphernalia developed and distributed. Sponsorship was both demanded and welcomed by teams and athletes to provide economic certainty from season to season. In the period up to the start of the twentieth century we can identify the beginnings of the commodification of sport—turning sport into a commodity, a vehicle for consumption and exchange. Entrepreneurs were ever at the ready, building new and grand sporting arenas and spruiking the 'latest' technological breakthroughs in bats, balls, shoes, and clothing. In 1855 Charles Goodyear created soccer balls made from vulcanised rubber, the first commercially-produced baseballs appeared in 1858 and, in 1865, baseball bat manufacturers began using ash and hickory in place of heavier woods. New sports were founded—softball in 1887, basketball in 1891, volleyball in 1895 and, while a form of tennis had been played since the Middle Ages, it did not become lawn tennis until its rules—set out by London's Marylebone Cricket Club—were written in 1875.[61]

7 The Ultimate Diversion: Sport as False Consciousness?

A fourth element at work in guiding the development of sport was internationalisation—the spreading of people, ideas, products, and services across multiple nations. By the beginning of the twentieth century the world was becoming increasingly integrated. Colonial conquests had led to the establishment of a variety of (usually male-oriented) sports—notably cricket, rugby, football, and tennis—in distant nations. There was an appetite for international competition, which was fuelled by nationalistic stirrings and by an eager print media. One important development was the birth of the modern Olympics. It had been a long time since the last winning athlete at Olympus had been crowned with a wreath of leaves taken from a sacred olive tree that grew close to the temple of Zeus. It was 1,503 years, to be precise. The Frenchman Baron Pierre de Coubertin, a fan of muscular Christianity, argued for the games' revival. An aristocrat fascinated by sociology, history, and education, de Coubertin—with considerable backing from others—founded the International Olympic Committee in 1894. The Olympic ideal was, ostensibly, about the noble pursuit of developing young bodies to help improve young minds. Healthy minds in healthy bodies.[62] But much more was at stake. De Coubertin had lived through the French defeat in the Franco-Prussian war of 1870 and saw the need to improve the tenacity and physical strength of his compatriots. After lengthy periods in Britain, he'd decided that British success in warfare was based largely upon encounters on the sporting fields of Eton, Harrow, and Rugby. If France were again to be glorious it must train its young men to be battle-ready. The Olympics would prove to be just the thing and he sought to make his Olympic dream a reality. According to sportswriter, Frank Deford, few of the people de Coubertin approached for support initially shared his dream:

> For that matter, some found it absolutely screwball. Notwithstanding, the baron was indefatigable; in today's world he would have been a lobbyist. He was forever establishing shadow committees and setting up meetings or high falutin gatherings he billed as 'congresses'.[63]

Olympic participants were expected to be gentlemanly amateurs who had neither competed for money, nor worked for a wage in physical instruction. His vision was of the Olympics being an 'oasis of honour and camaraderie', one that would 'build a more valiant, more scrupulous and gracious humanity'.[64] A gracious humanity of men, that is. Recall that the Victorian woman was expected to be gentle in nature, delicate in constitution, and always submissive. While the Games extolled Citius, Altius, Fortius (Faster, Higher, Stronger), such goals should only be for men. Throughout his life de Coubertin opposed women's participation in elite track and field events. When questioned about women's possible involvement he suggested it would be 'impractical, uninteresting, unaesthetic and incorrect'.[65] The Olympic motto was updated in 2021 to that of Citius, Altius, Fortius—Communiter (Faster, Higher, Stronger—Together) to suggest solidarity and inclusivity.[66] That still might be a little way off.

The first Olympic Games of the modern era were held in Athens in 1896. Some 280 athletes from 12 nations competed in over 40 events including track and field, swimming, gymnastics, cycling, weightlifting, wrestling, tennis, fencing, and shooting. The atmosphere was 'festive' featuring parades and banquets and, importantly, all the competitors were amateurs—drawn from the wealthy leisured classes (including university students and members of top-notch athletic clubs).[67] At the time it was the largest sporting event ever held in the modern era and was deemed a great success.

The next two games were held only because they were attached to world fairs. In Paris in 1900 the Games were held over a five-month period and featured events such as dousing a fire, ballooning, and swimming through an obstacle course. St Louis in 1904 added some new events—climbing a greasy pole and mud fighting among them. It was part of a grand carnival—the Louisiana Purchase Exhibition.[68] The athletic venues were of a poor standard and the events were disorganised (officially-agreed rules were yet to be established). It was nearly the demise of the emerging Olympic movement. With bravado and ceaseless lobbying of his rich mates, Englishman William Grenfell (later Lord Desborough of Taplow) showed, in the London Games of 1908, how a 'modern' Olympics should be run. Business backing, strong political approval, and the blessing of newspaper magnates were a recipe for success. De Coubertin died in Geneva in 1937. His body was buried in Lausanne, but his heart was taken to Mount Olympus and interred in a memorial stone column. He went to his grave confidently believing that 'democracy and internationalism would be a strong enough moral force to keep the Games "from sinking into the slough of commercialism"'.[69] His confidence was matched only by his naivety.

Deceptive Moves

There is obviously deception in sport; it would be difficult to imagine sport functioning otherwise. Player's deceptive actions are aimed at disguising true intentions—in the hope of fooling the opposition and gaining advantage. Misleading cues include basketballers' head fakes— passing to the right side when looking to the left, for example. In volleyball servers hide, as much as possible, their intention of delivering a smash or a lob into the opponent's court. In cricket, spinners will flight the ball using topspin or backspin, while seam bowlers use the seam (stitching) of the ball to produce a random deviation when it hits the pitch. Swing bowlers rely upon the difference in the flow of air either side of the seam, having greatest effect when one side of the cricket ball has been 'polished' (by spittle and rubbing) and the other side left 'roughed' (left untouched after hitting the grass). Baseball and softball pitchers have several ways of throwing a 'curveball'. Imparted with spin, the ball deviates from its expected path, fooling the batter. Then there is shielding the baseball—disguising the delivery—for which Oakland's Yusmeiro Petit is a master:

> Sometimes you'll have pitchers that throw really hard, but they show you the ball the whole time they're throwing so you can kind of follow it ... The longer you see [the ball] the easier it is to decide, to recognize, to figure out what's happening ... He's shortened that amount of time ... You can't really pick up anything from someone like Petit.[70]

He'd produced the so-called invisiball. And if that won't work for you maybe try the seam-shifted wake, spin mirroring, or the vertical approach angle. The one thing that batters find extremely difficult is detecting deception.[71] In basketball, if you can't deceive, why not resort to the 'barking dog'? Just before a ball is put into play a member of one team will get onto all fours and bark like rover to distract the opposing team.[72] Not illegal, but slightly silly. The 'sideline hangout' in American football is a bit more devious. An in-field player stands close to his out-of-bounds teammates pretending to be part of that group—he doesn't seem to be in the game. The play resumes and hey presto! our on-field hero catches, runs, and throws, fooling the enemy.[73] If you are a soccer player you could bend the ball like Bekham. Or, if you find yourself close to the opposition's goal post you might develop an uncontrollable desire to fall over. If one of your opponents is then blamed for a 'trip', your team has a very good chance of scoring a goal from a penalty. This somewhat mysterious medical condition—a contagious and some say incurable disease—is known as 'flopping' or 'diving'.[74]

Stealing Gold

The St Louis marathon of 1904 has gone down as one of the most bizarre events ever to have been held. Two South Africans, in town for an exhibit (as part of the World Fair), turned up for the race in bare feet. A Cuban runner, Felix Carbajal, who'd received money to attend the Games from supporters by staging running events in Havana, lost it all in a game of craps after he arrived in the US. Unperturbed, he hitchhiked to St Louis, arriving at the starting line in what he considered appropriate attire for such an auspicious occasion. He wore long dark trousers, white shirt, beret, and black lace-up shoes for the 40-kilometre run. An American discus competitor took pity on Felix and, with the runner's permission, scissored his pants at the knee.[75] It was a good thing, too. Set over some steep and unfriendly terrain (including an obstacle course of cobble stones, delivery vans, railroad crossings, trolley cars, and wild dogs), the athletes faced unbearably hot and humid conditions. Support vehicles with trainers and doctors travelled close to the athletes—kicking up dust

7 The Ultimate Diversion: Sport as False Consciousness?

and filling exhausted lungs with debilitating debris. There was only one drink stop on the entire route. After some 14ks, US runner Fred Lorz had succumbed to cramp. He managed to cadge a lift in a spectator's car for another 11ks. When its engine failed, Lorz disembarked and, feeling re-invigorated, resumed his run, turning up at the finishing line to claim victory. It was short-lived once news got out about his unpaid Uber ride.

So, who did win? It was US athlete Thomas Hicks. Although collapsing from exhaustion on several occasions Hicks was able to be revived with brandy, egg whites, and strychnine. The latter stimulated his motor neurons thereby increasing muscle performance. Of course, strychnine is also a rat poison so must be used in very small doses. And it was. After a second small dose, Hicks crossed the finish line. 'Crossed' doesn't mean with his feet on the ground. His coaches, realising his distress, held him upright while his legs moved in a pseudo-running motion.[76] He was declared the winner (gulping drugs or not having your feet on the ground were not issues at the time). Hicks was too exhausted to collect his medal and never competed in another marathon (but did live until 76 years of age, one year more than the lifespan—in human years—of the average rat).[77] For those interested in Olympics trivia, only 14 of the original 32 runners completed the race, with Cuban Felix Carbajal finishing a plucky fourth. And, despite later being declared a banned substance, strychnine was detected in the blood of Chinese volleyball player Wu Dan in 1992 (the Barcelona Olympics)—given to her in a capsule by the team doctor, apparently without her knowledge. In 2016 Kyrgyzstan weightlifter Izzat Artykov was stripped of his bronze medal when he tested positive to strychnine. It's hardly a plague among athletes but strychnine has been a serious drug-of-choice of Olympians and bike riders.[78]

Other cheats have been detected. Ukrainian Boris Onischenko was favoured to do well (to 'medal' in current parlance) in the pentathlon at the Montreal Olympics in 1976. During his fencing bout with a British competitor, it was noticed that he was being awarded points for striking his opponent when it was apparent his épée was nowhere near the target. Apparently, Onishchenko (and/or members of his team) had wired his sword so that he could press a button to falsely register a hit:

Diabolical in design, Mr. Bean in execution. Onischenko could register a hit at will, but inept timing beggared belief in the touches. Maybe he choked under Olympic pressure, but a more practiced trickster wouldn't have pushed the button with his sword pointed skyward. On the biggest stage, Onischenko was as convincing as the schoolboy who signs a failing report card "My Mom."[79]

He was unceremoniously removed from the Games. As was the entire Tunisian pentathlon team at the 1960 Olympics in Rome. They were not a well-honed unit, falling off their horses, one athlete nearly drowning, and another in the shooting event pointing his pistol at the judge. When the fencing event began, they sent out their best swordsman masked and ready for competition. Then they sent out their second-best swordsman, masked and ready for competition, and then their third. But the ploy was quickly unmasked: It was the same athlete on all three occasions.[80] Exit the Tunisians.

There's more. In the 1988 Seoul Games, US boxer Roy Jones was defeated by South Korean boxer Park Si-Hun despite the former having landed 86 punches to the latter's 32. The Korean had registered two standing eight-counts and had received two referee's warnings. He won, nevertheless, and seemed somewhat embarrassed by the decision. At the ceremonies, Jones pulled the silver medal from his neck and refused to acknowledge it again. It later transpired that an Argentinian judge had been offered a bribe by the Korean boxing authorities, but the IOC later ruled 'there is no evidence of corruption in the boxing events in Seoul'.[81]

At least the Korean boxer was not on drugs. If we can possibly forgive and forget the earlier strychnine episodes, it is hard to go past the illegal use of drugs by athletes as the biggest cheating scourge of the modern Olympics. We've all been taken for a ride when athletes, standing on the dais with joyful smiles and tears of success, have knowingly taken drugs to enhance their performances and to defeat the opposition. It is clear that in many Olympic sports, success sometimes comes down to being hundredths of a second faster than the competition. And when Olympic success brings endorsements, sponsorships, careers in the media, fame, and fortune—while providing the bonus of a heavy dose of nationalistic pride—there are undeniable and inbuilt drivers to win at all costs. Those hundredths of a second are precious.

Drugs were formally banned from Olympic competition in 1967 and then first imposed at the Mexico Games in October 1968. Since then, some 150 medals have been stripped from athletes.[82] Athletics events are the big winner—some 51 medals including 19 gold having been stripped. Weightlifting comes second with 50 medals, including 14 gold. The main culprits? Russia and its post-soviet allies which, together, accounted for some 90% of the total.[83] The Moscow Olympics of 1980 has been singled out as a hotbed of cheating, with *The Bulletin* stating:

> There is hardly a medal-winner at the Moscow Games, certainly not a gold-medal winner, who is not on one sort of drug or another: usually several kinds. The Moscow Games might as well have been called the Chemists' Games, for in many events it will not be the athlete who is naturally the strongest or fastest who wins, but the athlete with the best bag of drugs.[84]

Soviet whistleblowers Vitaly and Yuliya Stepanov outlined their nation's doping programme in a revealing German-produced documentary in 2014. More claims were made in the Netflix film *Icarus*.[85] Russian doctors were issuing athletes with banned substances and were doing so with the blessing and encouragement, in recent times, of Vladimir Putin, and the federal security agency. One biomedical specialist's role was to mask the substances being used and to make hormonal 'corrections' to athletes to maximise performance. They were 'swimming in steroids'.[86] Some 99% of Russian Olympic competitors were involved in the programme.[87] It paralleled what East Germany had successfully achieved in the 1970s and 1980s—largely involving anabolic steroids. The Russian government, led by Putin, also sanctioned doping at the 2014 Sochi Winter Olympics. Russian intelligence agents and former KGB agents were involved in switching 'dirty' urine samples of athletes with 'fresh' samples taken months before. In what could have been a *Get Smart* episode, athletes would pass their urine samples to the Russian operatives through a discrete hole in the wall of a hidden room in the testing laboratory.[88] When the cheating was discovered 13 of the 33 medals won by the Russians were stripped, and some 43 athletes were disqualified for their actions.

China had a state-sanctioned doping programme in place during the Los Angeles, Seoul, and Barcelona Olympics. It was modelled on the 'scientific training' of athletes in eastern Europe. Children as young as 11 years were involved in 'compulsory doping', with over 10,000 officials, trainers, and doctors dealing out the dollies. Complaining was tantamount to requesting a jail sentence. When asked to explain China's growing success at the Games, officials pointed to the combination of hard, physical, training in the mountains of Tibet, the blood of turtles, and caterpillar fungus.[89] This is in keeping with Chinese medicine which asserts that the Qi, the vital force of life (and excellent scrabble word), flows through the body and that ingesting natural substances can provide the energy for remarkable health—especially at the Olympics.

While there are literally hundreds of different illegal substances available to athletes and their coaches, the most popular fall into three main categories. The first can promote endurance by improving muscle gain and blood flow (stimulants, anabolic steroids, and growth hormones). The second category can produce more efficient, less fatigued bodies (metabolic modulators that speed up or slow down the body's chemistry). Female Russian figure skater, Kamila Valieva, tested positive for the drug trimetazidine at the Beijing Winter Olympics of 2022 later claiming that she must have accidentally imbibed the drug by drinking from a glass used by her grandfather. He was on medication for a heart condition. Valieva openly admitted having taken two other (legal) heart medication drugs, when the substances were discovered in her blood sample.[90] She was 15 years of age at the time. The third group of drugs increases energy and attention, keeping athletes alert and improving reaction time (these are the stimulants including cocaine, amphetamines, and caffeine).[91]

All three varieties have been ingested with great verve and boundless success, with drug taking for both the Eastern Bloc and western nations having been systemic. It was at the 1988 Seoul Olympics where Canadian Ben Johnson beat US Carl Lewis in the men's 100-metre sprint. He won in an amazing world best time of 9.79 seconds (a record only surpassed some 25 years later by Usain Bolt from Jamaica in 9.58 seconds). Johnson kept the title for three days—until the wonder drug stanozolol, a banned anabolic steroid derived from testosterone, showed up in his urine sample. Stanozolol improves strength and speed without adding to body weight, making it the perfect go-to drug for top athletes. Johnson's gold medal was stripped from him and given to second place getter Carl Lewis—who was subsequently also shown to have taken drugs for performance enhancement. While initially denying any fault, Johnson later admitted to being on an illegal drug regime for years. Why did he do it? Because everybody else did, he said.[92] Something similar is occurring at the paralympic games—the third biggest sporting event in the world. The exaggeration of impairment can place an athlete in a classification where he or she has more chance of winning. Feigning impairment is 'almost like an inside joke' among Paralympians.[93]

With all this cheating and subterfuge, it should come as no surprise that a new alternative Olympics has been proposed. Creator of the 'Enhanced Games', London-based Aussie entrepreneur Aron D'Souza is encouraging athletes to take as many enhancement-performing drugs as they wish—'bodily autonomy is a human right', he argues. He frowns at today's 'corrupt Olympics'. His alternative competition, where athletes will be paid to perform, has one simple goal—to have athletes beat current world records, no matter what it takes. The 100 metres dash will be the 'showcase' event and be designed to 'maximise entertainment value'.[94] This sports spectacle should be on our screens by 2025.

La tromperie de France

Poor Lance. In many interviews he has claimed he's been hurt, and badly done by, through the negative publicity that has come from his doping confessions. Just like Ben Johnson before him his defence for taking drugs was that everyone else was doing it. So why make such a big fuss of Lance? Three factors stand out—his high profile as an elite athlete, his continual and forceful denials that he was a doper, and the elaborate lies and deceptions that were at the core of his cheating practices.

Lance Armstrong was a very talented young athlete. At the age of 11 he swam in a Texas State 1,500 metre freestyle event, coming fourth. Switching to triathlons, he became a US sprint-course champion at the age of 16. At 19 he was ranked the nation's number-one triathlete. At 21 he turned to professional bike riding, joining the Motorola Cycling Team, winning events in the US, Europe, and the UK.[95] Then, in 1996, it appeared his riding career was over. He was diagnosed with an advanced form of testicular cancer that had spread to his abdomen, lungs, and brain. Doctors gave him virtually no chance of survival.[96] His diseased testicle was removed and he was placed on a cocktail of anti-cancer drugs. Later, his necrotic brain lesions were removed by surgery. But the young Lance was strong and responded well to chemotherapy. One month after his final treatment in December 1996, he was back on his bike, riding in a 100-kilometre event at Lille in France.[97] Two years later he won the Tour of Luxembourg. Then came the first of his wins in the Tour de France. It was 1999 and he won the event convincingly, including four stages. He won again in 2000, then 2001—in fact he won the gruelling event every consecutive year up to and including 2005—seven wins in a row. In 2005 his average speed in the race was a shade under 42 kilometres per hour—the highest in the race's 92-year history. He had covered 21 stages, riding a distance 3,593 kilometres. He was a fit, elite, athlete at his peak. He also said that 2005 would be his last Tour—he wanted to retire to spend time with family and to concentrate his efforts in helping cancer sufferers through his charity the Lance Armstrong Foundation (now the Livestrong Foundation). He came out of retirement in 2009 and rode for the company RadioShack in the 2010 Tour de France, only to be plagued by crashes in the race. He came in at 23rd and then announced in early 2011 that his professional racing career was over. Nobody before or after Armstrong has won seven Tour de France events, let alone seven in a row.[98]

There had been claims, throughout much of his professional career, that Armstrong was doping. A former teammate, Floyd Landis, said Armstrong would pause midway through a race where his own blood, previously taken from him, would be transfused back into his body. Blood doping is an illicit means of improving physical endurance by oxygenating tired muscles. A transfusion of one's own blood is a simple means of doing this. Another is use of the hormone erythropoietin (EPO) that increases the production of red blood cells. Synthetic oxygen carriers are yet another means of improving endurance. And they can be supplemented with other useful accessories. The human growth hormone, testosterone, and cortisone were among other favourites in the Armstrong medikit.[99]

How could he have cheated for so long without being detected? It relied on team bullying from Armstrong, deceptive practices during the race, along with the ethically dubious actions of smart doctors. His trainer of choice was Dr Ferrari. That should have told us something immediately about Lance's upcoming performances. Here's what happened. EPO was regularly injected by Armstrong and his riding team. They would do so intravenously and at night (avoiding surprise tests). In the morning the synthetic EPO would have been absorbed and could not be detected. (It is important to mention that EPO was not a measured substance before 2000—it could not be distinguished from its naturally occurring cousin. Similarly, human growth hormone used by athletes was not tested until after Armstrong's retirement in 2005.) Then there was saline—a saline solution was always on hand to dilute a rider's blood, should there be any likelihood of detection. The US Anti-Doping Agency's (USADA) 2012 report on Armstrong claimed that during blood transfusions EPO was used to stimulate production of immature blood cells—to counter the high level of red blood cells injected during the transfusion.[100] It also claimed that the entire team was on a low-dose regime of testosterone (helping in building muscle and helping muscles to recover). A team doctor had 'perfected' a way of delivering testosterone via an olive-oil-based mixture that would be trickled under a rider's tongue during a race without detection. Finally, there were the corticosteroids:

> These chemicals ... can be used by athletes to ease inflammation and promote muscle recovery. Armstrong tested positive in 1999, the year of his first Tour de France win. The USADA says a team doctor then fabricated and backdated a prescription of the cortisone to excuse the positive result, claiming that Armstrong had been using the cortisone to treat a 'saddle sore'.[101]

The sport of long-distance cycling puts huge stress on a rider's body. Why would riders not look to substances that improve performance and recovery? In fact, there is an argument that athletes should be free to choose whatever they like to—it's a free world, and it's their bodies. Chemical concoctions are part of normal life:

> The majority of adults in most wealthy, high-tech societies use tranquillisers, pain controllers, mood controllers, antidepressants, decongestants, diet pills, birth control pills, insulin, caffeine, nicotine, sleep aids and alcohol ... Why should athletes be tested and denied access to substances, when others [in society] are often encouraged to take similar substances?[102]

This is a good question and goes to the issue of the social construction of sport and sporting contests. If sport is about winning at all costs, wouldn't you go to any lengths to win? In such circumstances you might risk being detected—to give yourself the best chance of winning. But if sporting competition is viewed as requiring fairness and allowing skills, training, dedication, and fortitude to decide events—not substances that artificially create advantage—then it is clear a regime of drug testing is necessary to catch those guilty of cheating.

That said, it is important to remember the social milieu in which elite athletes perform. There are coaches to please. Sponsors will gravitate to the most successful performers. Fans and teammates will be angry if failures are regular:

> Elite sports today emphasise control, especially control over the body ... The desire to control one's body plus the need to meet performance expectations [are] powerful incentive[s] to do whatever it takes to remain an elite athlete.[103]

This is important in explaining Armstrong's behaviour:

> It turned out that Armstrong had a years-long, meticulously designed plan for doping. It wasn't just personal; he browbeat his teammates into following suit ... Armstrong even paid out bribes to keep positive tests under wraps.[104]

7 The Ultimate Diversion: Sport as False Consciousness?

In 2012 USADA accused Armstrong of doping and trafficking in drugs and brought formal charges later that year. Armstrong did not appeal the findings and was subsequently stripped of all his wins from August 1998 including, of course, his seven Tour de France titles.[105]

Did he ever show remorse for his actions? In 2013 Armstrong famously agreed to an (apparently unpaid) interview with chat show host Oprah Winfrey. With millions of Americans glued to their screens the show went close to breaking the viewing record for a Winfrey interview.[106] Armstrong admitted to drug taking throughout his career and to using EPO, testosterone, and blood transfusions to win the Tour de France races. He said he'd stopped doping in 2005. He said he'd been a bully at times. He acknowledged he was a 'jerk' and 'arrogant prick'. But according to senior editor of *The Week*, Peter Weber, Armstrong had 'flunked the sincerity test' by coming over as cold and calculating, lacking sincerity. He was 'weaselly with the word "cheat"' saying the doping occurring in cycling made it a level playing field for him and all other riders. And he 'refused to believably apologise' to the people he had bullied.[107] In other words he had 'botched his big national shot at the beginning of redemption'.[108] Five years after the Winfrey interview he went on the *Today* show to deny publicly that he was a fraud. Unfortunately, the 'blind ego and arrogance' in his interview came through yet again, demonstrating 'exactly why Armstrong remains so reviled'.[109] 'No athlete in history has ever cheated the system so methodically or behaved in such an unethical manner'.[110] Armstrong not only forfeited his titles but has also experienced damning public humiliation and an amazing fall from grace. It is estimated that cheating cost him millions in sponsorship deals (some $75 million in one day), and many more millions in funds from lawsuits brought by former promoters and sponsors. After the USADA revelations he was banned, for life, from competing in all sports.[111] He was later forced to resign from the charity he founded. He eventually acknowledged that he's been using performance-enhancing drugs since the age of 21, rationalising that doping for athletes was the equivalent of having 'air in our tires, or water in our bottles'.[112]

Armstrong did not perform his deceit as a lone wolf. It was a social compact from start to finish—the doctors, the teammates, the support staff, the trainers, drug smugglers, and numerous and unidentified others who kept the 'Myth of Lance' alive and ticking.[113] It was societal deceit comprising a tightly-knit array of dubious characters whose mission was to fool officials and the public. We were all taken on one long, memorable, and entirely duplicitous ride.

Sportswashing—Cleaning the Image

Whitewashing, a term that has been in vogue since the sixteenth century, is literally the painting of walls, floors, and fences with a coating of thin white plaster made from lime and water. It is a simple and inexpensive way to cover up blemishes, faults, and marks without actually fixing them. Problems are whitewashed away. While it has several meanings in popular culture,[114] whitewashing usually refers to the use of propaganda to gloss over an inconvenient issue, or to cover up a situation that, if exposed, would cause a person, group, company, or nation considerable embarrassment. We saw in Chapter 4 how 'greenwashing' has been used to describe how companies continue with practices that harm the planet, while falsely claiming that their products are environmentally friendly. 'Sportswashing', the latest addition to the washing vocabulary, refers to the investment in sporting individuals, teams, or events designed to cover up the untoward practices of the investor. The aim is to win public approval, or to improve a tarnished reputation, while failing to deal with the causes or consequences of actions that disadvantage particular groups in society. It is an attempt to launder an image, to distract an audience.[115] As such it is a form of societal deception.

One obvious example of sportswashing was the attempt by Hitler's Nazi Party to promote 'Nordic supremacy' and other racist ideologies at the 1936 Olympic Games in Berlin. Jewish athletes were banned from representing Germany, and competing nations were encouraged not to send Jewish or black athletes.[116] With extensive funding having been provided to train its athletes, the German team performed well, winning some 89 medals, 23 more than the US team, and four times the number of any other nation.[117] As is widely known, African American runner Jesse Owens achieved greatness winning four gold medals, allowing people to question the superiority of 'whiteness' in sport. The

7 The Ultimate Diversion: Sport as False Consciousness?

International Olympic Committee believes the Berlin games represented a victory over prejudice, given Hitler's failure to demonstrate the superiority of the Aryan race.[118] A different interpretation is that holding the Games in Germany gave legitimacy to Nazi ideals and showcased the organisational capabilities of the German state in successfully mounting a 'compelling' and successful sporting event.[119] The introduction of the torch relay at the Berlin games has been viewed as 'a celebration of [Nazi] claims to have inherited the tradition of European culture and civilisation from the time of the Greeks'.[120] Hitler also had his moment when England visited Berlin two years later to play the Germans at football. England won, but not before the English team had lined up at the start of the game to join the hosts in a Nazi salute (on instructions from the British Foreign Office).[121] A nice little gift for der Führer.

Italian media owner, Silvio Berlusconi, purchased A. C. Milan in 1986—a clever move as it turned out. The club competed well, lifting the owner's profile and status. With popularity and high public standing he was elected Italy's Prime Minister in 1994. He then decided to use his privileged position to engage in bribery, corruption, cronyism, and clientelism (passing laws favouring his own businesses). Sex scandals were a particular favourite.[122] But sport was key to his rise and continued success:

> A.C. Milan was always more than a toy, a trophy asset, in [Berlusconi's] eyes: He did not bankroll the club to five European Cups and eight Italian championships as an end in itself; he did it, at least in part, in pursuit of real power … It was no coincidence that when Berlusconi formed his political party in 1993, he borrowed its name from soccer's lexicon: "Forza Italia!" The label echoed a terrace chant, a deliberate attempt to leverage Milan's success in the minds of voters. It worked.[123]

Sportswashing is a beloved practice of authoritarian political regimes that hope to improve their images while engaging in human rights violations, racism, ethnic cleansing, and state corruption. Elite sport is a global phenomenon and its up-beat formatting and commercialisation by PR firms and the media helps ensure its success in capturing enthusiastic worldwide audiences.[124] In 2020 a US$65 million deal was signed between Formula One (F1) and Saudi Arabia to allow the Middle Eastern kingdom to host the race for ten years. Amnesty International was quick to label this as an attempt to airbrush quite serious human rights issues in the nation which included the humanitarian disaster of Saudi Arabia's war with Yemen, and its continued home-based repression of women's rights activists, intellectuals, and would-be reformers.[125] When Cristiano Ronaldo joined the Saudi Arabian team Al Nassr in 2023 for some £177 million a year he became the highest paid soccer player in history. He was obviously not thinking about the nation's horrendous human rights record when he described the nation as 'amazing'.[126] And, although Lionel Messi is yet to join a Saudi team, he remains the nation's tourist ambassador, receiving an estimated €22.5 million over three years for social media posts and sundry appearances.[127]

In another deal described as classic sportswashing, Saudi Arabia's sovereign wealth fund, PIF, paid £300 million for an 80% share of football club Newcastle United in 2021. Here, the glamour associated with a Premier League club provides a soft-power mechanism to elevate the status of the Saudis (and potentially to improve the image of PIF's Chair, Mohammed bin Salam, the Crown Prince of the kingdom, implicated in the 2018 murder of journalist Jamal Khashoggi). In his book *The Billionaire's Club*—an exposé of the oligarchs and sundry billionaires who have purchased premier football clubs throughout the world—author James Montague claims a major motive for club ownership is to increase visibility and enhance the profile of owners and nations. He says 'nothing promotes a country better than football. And nothing launders a reputation more thoroughly than football'.[128]

Or is it golf? The Saudis were at it again in 2022, using hundreds of millions of dollars from their Public Investment Fund to 'buy' the world's best golfers for their LIV tournament. (LIV are the Roman numerals for 54—representing 54 holes of golf to be contested rather than the usual 72 for most professional events.) According to *Washington Post* journalist Fred Bowen,

> By taking Saudi money instead of standing up for what is right … [participating golfers including Phil Mickelson and Dustin Johnson] have lost

7 The Ultimate Diversion: Sport as False Consciousness?

their good reputation. From now on they will not be known as champions but as men who could be bought.[129]

But none of the participating golfers seemed to care, and the Saudis sought to deflect criticism—allowing their sportswashing to continue unabated. The LIV tour was designed to alter the nation's 'conservative oil image' to make it 'progressive', like Dubai, to 'increase Saudi Arabia's power on a global scale and expand its Western reputation', and to launder the reputation of the Chair of the Saudi Public Investment Fund, Mohammed bin Salam.[130] And then, in June 2023—in a surprise move to many—the American-based PGA and LIV kissed and made up. Golf was again united and, in a massive new sportswash, Saudi money is now bankrolling professional men's golf. This has angered some in the US who are at pains to remind the golfing fraternity that Saudi terrorists were largely responsible for the 9/11 attacks.[131] In a two-and-a-half-year period—from early 2021 until July 2023—the Saudis spent over US$6 billion on sportswashing activities aimed at distracting attention from the nation's 'brutal, blood-soaked human rights record'.[132]

At a time when China was holding up to two million Uyghurs and Turkic Muslims in mass detention in the western Xinjiang region, while razing mosques, imposing restrictions on religious practice, re-educating detainees, and practising cultural genocide, the torch-lighting ceremony at the commencement of the 2022 Beijing Winter Olympics featured a photogenic and very happy cross-country skier of Uyghur origin, Dilnigar Ilhamjan.[133] Earlier, in the 2008 Olympics, another Uyghur torchbearer, Kamalturk Yalqun, remarked that 'for decades, the stereotypical "happily dancing Uyghur" has served as a puppet of propaganda for China's "ethnic unity and harmony" narrative'.[134] Not surprisingly, President Xi Jinping said the Beijing Winter Games would present China as a 'positive, prosperous and open nation committed to building a community with a shared future' for humankind.[135]

We have seen fossil fuel companies line up to sponsor sports, hoping to improve their reputations in the process.[136] The Russian gas monopoly Gazprom has probably the highest profile, owning three football clubs in Europe and sponsoring the Union of European Football Associations (UEFA) Champions League. Saudi Arabia's tiny neighbour, Qatar, has also joined the fray using sport as a means of portraying the nation as progressive and international.[137] Doha regularly hosts international tennis, cycling, gymnastics, and football events including the FIFA World Cup in November/December 2022. It is a nation with major violations against humanity, from the slave-like conditions experienced by its migrant workers under the 'kafala' system of employment, to restrictions on free speech, criminalisation of same-sex relations, abuse of women, and violence against minorities.[138] During the soccer World Cup, players protesting against Qatar's discrimination against LGBTQIA+ communities planned to wear 'OneLove' rainbow armbands during the matches but were threatened with an immediate yellow card if they did so. FIFA's position? It warned competing nations to refrain from 'handing out moral lessons'. This is despite its claim to be 'committed to respecting all internationally recognised human rights'.[139] Meanwhile, before and during the World Cup, David Beckham's face lit up Qatar's billboards and screens. He was the iconic ambassador for Qatar and believed the tournament would be a 'platform for progress, inclusivity and tolerance'.[140] He received an estimated £150 million for those nice thoughts.

Clearly, while sportswashing represents an *attempt* to put a positive spin on a tarnished reputation, gloss over past indiscretions, and mask assorted wrongdoings, it is not always clear that it *works*.[141] After all, the ownership and patronage of high-profile teams and events put the individual, corporate, or national sponsor's profile smack-bang into centre view. As soon as Qatar, Saudi Arabia, or some Russian plutocrat puts billions into currying favour with a sport-mad fan-base, a host of journalists, academics, and commentators are at the fore, quick to reveal the very practices their sporting investments seek to disguise. As we learn more about the carbon industry's impact on human health, the environment, and climate, the more likely we are to see athletes, sporting bodies, and fans questioning sponsorship deals from the major polluters.[142]

It is refreshing to see the efforts of green lobby groups in exposing the sport advertising practices of some of the largest emitters of carbon pollution. According to the *New Weather Institute*, the global sports industry is worth around US$470 billion, with some 258 sport sponsorship deals 'promoting high-carbon products, services and lifestyles'.[143] Football is

7 The Ultimate Diversion: Sport as False Consciousness?

the sport most targeted—there are 57 sponsorship deals with high-carbon polluters. (Toyota, with 31 deals is the polluter most involved in sport sponsorship, followed closely by Emirates with 29 deals.)[144] In nearly every major sport, money from polluters helps pay the bills. Sports include football, gridiron, cricket, tennis, golf, motor racing, rugby, basketball, sailing, athletics, golf and, of course, the Olympics.[145] The Institute argues that allowing sponsors implicated in carbon pollution to continue to be involved in sport is tantamount to endorsing the debilitation and potential death of athletes and the sports in which they are involved. Increasing snow melts are causing havoc with many winter sports. Heatwave temperatures are impacting upon athletes' health and performance. Increased flooding damages sporting grounds and leads to the abandonment of flagship events. Air pollution caused by burning forests chokes lungs, and so on. Climate change will impact negatively on many African nations where training will be compromised by increased heat and drought. The ethos of sport is linked to health and vitality, the very things compromised by global warming to which the polluting sponsors contribute.

Sponsorship from polluters contradicts the very notion of societal well-being and flies in the face of sporting clubs' supposed commitment to the United Nations Sports for Climate Change Framework, focused upon reducing sport's substantial climate footprint.[146] It is for good reason that the sponsorships tainted with fossil fuel dollars are being compared to tobacco advertising of the 1980s—with tobacco company advertising having now been banned in many nations.[147] As we cheer athletes on TV and in the stands, we should be highly conscious of the corporate half-truths, sleights-of-hand, spin, and lying that accompany the dollars sponsoring sport.

Notes

1. Adair, D. (2023) The 2023 Australian Open pauses a year of profound political tensions in tennis, https://theconversation.com/the-2023-australian-open-pauses-a-year-of-profound-political-tensions-in-tennis-197397.

2. Bodo, P. (2022) The tarnished legacy of Novak Djokovic, https://www.tennis.com/news/articles/the-tarnished-legacy-of-novak-djokovic.
3. Taking toilet breaks at times when he was losing momentum, exaggerating injury, and unruly court behaviour are among the accusations, see Adair, D. (2022a) Novak Djokovic has long divided opinion. Now, his legacy will be complicated even further, https://theconversation.com/novak-djokovic-has-long-divided-opinion-now-his-legacy-will-be-complicated-even-further-174531.
4. Adair, D. (2022b) Secrecy surrounding Djokovic's medical exemption means star can expect a hostile reception on centre court, https://theconversation.com/secrecy-surrounding-djokovics-medical-exemption-means-star-can-expect-a-hostile-reception-on-centre-court-174331; Matthey, J. (2020) Novak Djokovic criticised for 'dangerous conspiracy theory', https://www.foxsports.com.au/tennis/novak-djokovic-criticised-for-dangerous-conspiracy-theory/news-story/feca8fc6999d357ab6986759ec8572d3.
5. Minn, H. (2022) DOUBLE FAULT: Inside Novak Djokovic's scandal-hit life—cheating rumours, £50K sextortion plot, dodgy toilet breaks and anti-vax row, https://www.thesun.co.uk/sport/17238542/novak-djokovic-australian-open-cheating-rumours-scandals/; Wikipedia. (2022) Bosnian pyramids claims, https://en.wikipedia.org/wiki/Bosnian_pyramid_claims.
6. Bodo, The tarnished legacy of Novak Djokovic.
7. Groch, S. (2022) Djokovic is gone. How did the case unfold and what does it mean for Australia's border rules? https://www.theage.com.au/sport/tennis/djokovic-has-lost-his-fight-to-stay-in-australia-how-did-the-case-unfold-and-what-happens-now-20220115-p59oif.html.
8. Rimmer, M. (2022) Novak Djokovic's father fuming after deportation of Serbian tennis player, https://www.yourlifechoices.com.au/government/federal-government/djokovics-father-fuming-after-deportation-of-serbian-tennis-player/.

9. Rimmer, Novak Djokovic's father fuming after deportation of Serbian tennis player.
10. Ryan, S. (2022) Unpacking the incredibly stupid Novak Djokovic fiasco in 10 easy steps, https://www.golfdigest.com/story/novak-djokovic-australian-open-COVID-19-visa-vaccination-tennis-grand-slam.
11. Le Grand, C. (2022) Djokovic goes from greatest to anti-vax icon, https://www.theage.com.au/sport/djokovic-goes-from-greatest-to-anti-vax-icon-20220116-p59omt.html.
12. Rowe, D. (1999) *Sport, Culture and the Media: The Unruly Trinity*, Open University Press, Buckingham; Miller, T., Lawrence, G., McKay, J. and Rowe, D. (2001) *Globalization and Sport: Playing the World*, Sage, London.
13. Rowe, D. (2020) Subjecting pandemic sport to a sociological procedure, *Journal of Sociology* 56(4): 704–713. During the pandemic some sporting events featured cardboard cut-outs of fans, and canned sounds to simulate a sporting atmosphere—see Pavlidis, A. and Rowe, D. (2021) The sporting bubble as gilded cage: Gendered professional sport in pandemic times and beyond, *M/C Journal* 24(1), https://doi.org/10.5204/mcj.2736.
14. YPulse. (2022) From Athletes to Influencers: How social media has changed the game for Pro Sports stars, https://www.ypulse.com/article/2019/07/02/athletes-to-influencers-how-social-media-has-changed-the-game-for-pro-sport/.
15. Fan's Arena. (2022) Novak Djokovic fans, stats, polls, and social media ranking, https://www.fansarena.in/novak-djokovic-fans-follower-count-polls-and-social-media-rank-2/.
16. ABC. (2022) BBC investigation raises doubts over timing of Novak Djokovic's positive COVID test, https://www.abc.net.au/news/2022-01-29/bbc-investigation-raises-doubts-timing-novak-djokovic-covid-test/100790060.
17. Quoted in Rimmer, Novak Djokovic's father fuming after deportation of Serbian tennis player.
18. Adair, The 2023 Australian Open pauses a year of profound political tensions in tennis.

19. Fortunately, I didn't fare as badly as my friend and co-author, Toby Miller, who recalls 'wandering around rugby fields being hit and kicked by opponents and shouted at by their parents. 'Kill the Protestants' was a typical … refrain'. See Miller, T. (2010) *Sportsex*, Temple University Press, Pennsylvania, p. 2.
20. Lawrence, G. and Rowe, D. (eds) (1986) *Power Play: The Commercialisation of Australian Sport*, Hale and Iremonger, Sydney; Rowe, D. and Lawrence, G. (eds) (1990) *Sport and Leisure: Trends in Australian Popular Culture*, HBJ, Sydney; Miller, Lawrence, McKay and Rowe, *Globalization and Sport*.
21. Miller, Lawrence, McKay and Rowe, *Globalization and Sport*; Whannel, G. (2009) Television and the transformation of sport, *Annals of the American Academy of Political and Social Sciences* 625(1): 205–218.
22. Montague, J. (2018) *The Billionaires Club: The Unstoppable Rise of Football's Super-rich Owners*, Bloomsbury, London.
23. Rowe, D. (2023) Penalties, passes, and a touch of politics: the Women's World Cup is about to kick off, https://theconversation.com/penalties-passes-and-a-touch-of-politics-the-womens-world-cup-is-about-to-kick-off-209050.
24. Hing, N. (2014) *Sports Betting and Advertising*, AGRC Discussion Paper No. 4, Australian Gambling Research Centre, Melbourne, p. 4.
25. McGrath, P. and Curnow, S. (2023) Gambling companies Sportsbet, TAB and bet365 taking bets on cricket matches involving minors, https://www.abc.net.au/news/2023-01-20/gambling-companies-offering-bets-on-matches-involving-minors/101872892.
26. Hing, *Sports Betting and Advertising*, pp. 1–8; Livingstone, C. (2023) Sport is being used to normalise gambling. We should treat the problem just like smoking, https://theconversation.com/sport-is-being-used-to-normalise-gambling-we-should-treat-the-problem-just-like-smoking-205843.
27. Thomas, S., Pitt, H. and McCarthy, S. (2023) Premier League's front-of-shirt gambling ad ban is a flawed approach. Australia should learn from it, https://theconversation.com/premier-leagues-front-of-shirt-gambling-ad-ban-is-a-flawed-approach-australia-should-learn-from-it-204105; Victorian Responsible

Gambling Foundation. (2022) Gambling in Victoria, https://responsiblegambling.vic.gov.au/resources/gambling-victoria/.
28. Symons, K. and Bowell, P. (2023) 'Felt alienated by the men's game': How the culture of women's sport has driven record Matildas viewership, https://theconversation.com/felt-alienated-by-the-mens-game-how-the-culture-of-womens-sport-has-driven-record-matildas-viewership-211524; Women's soccer teams are offsetting the carbon emissions caused by long haul flights and advocating for other action on climate change—see Sethna-McIntosh, K. (2023) Women's World Cup players launch football's biggest climate campaign, https://www.theguardian.com/football/2023/jul/13/womens-world-cup-players-launch-footballs-biggest-climate-campaign.
29. Spaaij, R. and Ryder, S. (2022) Sport, social mobility and elite athletes, in L. Wenner (ed) *The Oxford Handbook of Sport and Society*, Oxford University Press, New York, pp. 668–684.
30. There is evidence of public backlash against LGBTQIA+ via 'heteroactivism'—an attempt to assert heterosexuality and vilify those not conforming to orthodox gender norms and behaviours. See Storr, R. (2023) What is 'heteroactivism'? How sports became a battleground for opposing LGBTIQ+ progress, https://theconversation.com/what-is-heteroactivism-how-sports-became-a-battleground-for-opposing-lgbtiq-progress-208015.
31. Hardwicke, J., Anderson, E., Parry, K. and Magrath, R. (2021) LGBTQ+ athletes: Why more sportspeople than ever are coming out, https://theconversation.com/lgbtq-athletes-why-more-sportspeople-than-ever-are-coming-out-168010; Gray, M. and Verdonck, M. (2016) The Paralympics is changing the way people perceive disabilities, https://theconversation.com/the-paralympics-is-changing-the-way-people-perceive-disabilities-65407.
32. Woessner, M., Parker, A. and Pankowiak, A. (2023) What the David Beckham documentary tells us—and what it doesn't—about controlling parents in sport, https://theconversation.com/what-the-david-beckham-documentary-tells-us-and-what-it-doesnt-about-controlling-parents-in-sport-215437.

33. Ingle, S. (2022) Child gymnasts abused and denied water, food, and toilet breaks—the damning report on British Gymnastics, https://www.theguardian.com/sport/2022/jun/16/british-gymnastics-report-anne-whyte-review-uk-sport-gymnasts-abused.
34. Martin, A. (2023) Bye, bye, bye Delilah: Wales rugby choirs banned from singing Tom Jones hit, https://www.irishtimes.com/sport/rugby/2023/02/01/six-nations-2023-bye-bye-bye-delilah-wales-rugby-choirs-banned-from-singing-tom-jones-hit/; The Guardian. (2023) WRU facing allegations of sexism and discrimination in BBC investigation, https://www.theguardian.com/sport/2023/jan/23/welsh-rugby-union-wru-facing-allegations-sexism-discrimination-bbc-investigation.
35. Miller, Lawrence, McKay, and Rowe, *Globalization and Sport*, p. 3.
36. Statista. (2024) Global sports market—statistics and facts, https://www.statista.com/topics/8468/global-sports-market/#topicOverview.
37. Word Histories. (2022) Origin and history of the word 'sport', https://wordhistories.net/2016/07/31/sport/.
38. Marx, K. (1844) Critique of Hegel's philosophy of right, https://www.marxist.com/classics-critique-of-hegel-s-philosophy-of-right/introduction.htm; another view is that sport is 'a prison of measured time' where players and spectators alike are trapped within an ideology that celebrates and reproduces discipline, competition, chauvinism, racism, and sexism. See Brohm, J-M. (1978) *Sport—A Prison of Measured Time*, Ink Links, London.
39. Brohm, *Sport—A Prison of Measured Time*.
40. Wikipedia. (2022) Bull-leaping, https://en.wikipedia.org/wiki/Bull-leaping.
41. Muscato, C. (2021) The Zuni People, https://study.com/academy/lesson/zuni-tribe-facts-history-culture.html.
42. Wikipedia. (2022) Mesoamerican rubber balls, https://en.wikipedia.org/wiki/Mesoamerican_rubber_balls.
43. Aztec-History. (2022) Aztec ball game, http://www.aztec-history.com/aztec-ball-game.html.

44. Brasch, R. (1986) *How Did Sports Begin? A Look at the Origins of Man at Play*, Fontana, Sydney, p. 3.
45. Coakley, J., Hallinan, C., Jackson, S. and Mewett, P. (2009) *Sports in Society: Issues and Controversies in Australia and New Zealand*, McGraw-Hill, Sydney, p. 59.
46. Coakley, Hallinan, Jackson and Mewett, *Sport in Society*, p. 60.
47. Phippen, W. (2016) A brief history of cheating at the Olympics, https://www.theatlantic.com/news/archive/2016/08/cheating-at-the-olympics/495938/; Perseus Project. (2022) Frequently asked questions about the ancient Olympic Games, http://www.perseus.tufts.edu/Olympics/faq9.html.
48. Coakley, Hallinan, Jackson and Mewett, *Sport in Society*, p. 80.
49. Coakley, Hallinan, Jackson and Mewett, *Sport in Society*, p. 80.
50. Coakley, Hallinan, Jackson and Mewett, *Sport in Society*, p. 81.
51. FIFA. (2022) History of football—Britain, the home of football, https://web.archive.org/web/20150908052207/http://www.fifa.com/about-fifa/who-we-are/the-game/britain-home-of-football.html.
52. Freedman, P. (1998) Peasant anger in the Middle Ages, in B. Rosenwein (ed.) *Anger's Past: The Social Uses of an Emotion in the Middle Ages*, Cornell University Press, Ithaca, pp. 171–190.
53. Coakley, Hallinan, Jackson and Mewett, *Sport in Society*, p. 69.
54. Miller, Lawrence, McKay, and Rowe, *Globalization and Sport*; Wagg, S., Brick, C., Wheaton, B. and Caudwell, J. (2009) *Key Concepts in Sports Studies*, Sage, Los Angeles.
55. Rowe, *Sport, Culture and the Media*; Miller, Lawrence, McKay and Rowe, *Globalization and Sport*.
56. Wagg, Brick, Wheaton and Caudwell, *Key Concepts in Sports Studies*, p. 19.
57. Elias, N. (1982) *The Civilizing Process*, Pantheon, New York; see also Dunning, E. and Sheard, K. (1979) *Barbarians, Gentlemen and Players: A Sociological Study of the Development of Rugby Football*, Australian National University Press, Canberra. This is very similar to Foucault's notion of governmentality—mentalities, rationalities, and techniques that control social behaviour. See Foucault, M. (1991) Governmentality, in G. Burchell, C.

Gordon, and P. Miller (eds) *The Foucault Effect: Studies in Governmentality*, Harvester Wheatsheaf, London, pp. 87–104.
58. Brasch, *How Did Sports Begin?*, p. 153; Encyclopedia Britannica. (2022) Walter Camp: American sportsman, https://www.britannica.com/biography/Walter-Camp.
59. Mark, D. (2019) Cricket's laws were written long before the Ashes began, but are still a 'work in progress', https://www.abc.net.au/news/2019-07-30/the-long-and-complicated-history-of-the-rules-of-cricket/11358826.
60. Tyrrell, I. (1979) The emergence of modern American baseball c. 1850–1880, in R. Cashman and M. McKernan (eds) *Sport in History: The Making of Modern Sporting History*, University of Queensland Press, Brisbane, pp. 205–226; Wikipedia. (2022) Origins of baseball, https://en.wikipedia.org/wiki/Origins_of_baseball.
61. Harle, W. (2011) The history of sporting equipment, https://www.sportsrec.com/358231-the-history-of-sporting-equipment.html; Wikipedia. (2022) History of tennis, https://en.wikipedia.org/wiki/History_of_tennis.
62. Whannel, G. (1983) *Blowing the Whistle: The Politics of Sport*, Pluto, London, p. 18.
63. Deford, F. (2012) The little-known history of how the modern Olympics got their start, https://www.smithsonianmag.com/history/the-little-known-history-of-how-the-modern-olympics-got-their-start-138117709/.
64. Beamish, R. (1996) Peirre de Coubertin's shattered dream, *Queen's Quarterly* 103(3): 489–501.
65. Of course, the suffragettes had much to say about this, leading to the Women's Olympiad during the 1920s and the Women's World Games during the 1920s and 1930s. Despite de Coubertin's dislike of female competition, some 22 of the 972 athletes in the Paris games of 1900 were women; Wikipedia. (2022) 1896 Summer Olympics, https://en.wikipedia.org/wiki/1896_Summer_Olympics; International Olympic Committee. (2022) When did women first compete in the Olympic

Games? https://olympics.com/ioc/faq/history-and-origin-of-the-games/when-did-women-first-compete-in-the-olympic-games.
66. International Olympic Committee. (2021) 'Faster, Higher, Stronger—Together'—IOC Session approves historic change in Olympic motto, https://olympics.com/ioc/news/faster-higher-stronger-together-the-ioc-publishes-2021-annual-report-and-financial-statements.
67. Encyclopedia Britannica. (2022) Athens 1896 Olympic Games, https://www.britannica.com/event/Athens-1896-Olympic-Games.
68. It was held to acknowledge and celebrate the centennial of the 1803 Louisiana Purchase. See Deford, The little-known history of how the modern Olympics got their start.
69. Tomlinson, A. and Whannel, G. (1984) *Five Ring Circus: Money, Power and Politics at the Olympic Games*, Pluto Press, London, p. 93.
70. Lindbergh, B. (2021) Yus your illusion: Yusmeiro Petit and the well-hidden power of pitcher deception, https://www.theringer.com/mlb/2021/9/28/22695180/yusmeiro-petit-deception-pitching-delivery-velocity-biomechanics-invisiball.
71. Lindbergh, Yus your illusion.
72. Bowen, J. (2015) Deception and trickery in sport: The Patriots' 'Formation Gate' 2015, https://law.scu.edu/sports-law/deception-and-trickery-in-sport-the-patriots-formation-gate-2015/.
73. Bowen, Deception and trickery in sport.
74. Flopping/diving has been termed 'simulation', or 'successful deception of a match official', by the Football Association and carries a two match ban for the offender. See George-Miller, D. (2017) New FA rules to retroactively punish simulation beginning next season, https://cartilagefreecaptain.sbnation.com/2017/8/2/16081290/premier-league-news-fa-retroactive-punishment-simulation-diving-fake-injury.
75. Abbott, K. (2012) The 1904 Olympic marathon may have been the strangest ever, https://www.smithsonianmag.com/history/the-1904-olympic-marathon-may-have-been-the-strangest-ever-14910747/; Phukan, S. (2022) Felix Carvajal and the Saint

Louis Olympics, https://drsatyakamphukan.wordpress.com/felix-carvajal-and-the-saint-louis-olympics/.
76. Abbott, The 1904 Olympic marathon may have been the strangest ever; Wikipedia. (2022) Athletics at the 1904 Summer Olympics—men's marathon, https://en.wikipedia.org/wiki/Athletics_at_the_1904_Summer_Olympics_%E2%80%93_Men%27s_marathon; for a witty summary of the event see O'Reily, T. (2020) *Cheat: The Not-so-subtle Art of Conning Your Way to Sporting Glory*, Michael Joseph, UK.
77. Harkup, K. (2016) The cocktail of poison and brandy that led to Olympic gold, https://www.theguardian.com/science/blog/2016/jul/21/the-cocktail-of-poison-and-brandy-that-led-to-olympic-gold-strychnine; Rat Health Notes. (2022) How old is a rat in human years? http://www.ratbehavior.org/RatYears.htm.
78. Shine, O. (2016) Weightlifter stripped of medal for doping with rat poison, https://www.reuters.com/article/us-olympics-rio-doping-artykov-idUSKCN10T1NQ.
79. Farber, M. (2020) The curious case of the electrified épée, https://www.si.com/olympics/2020/07/21/greatest-olympic-cheater-boris-onischenko-1976-olympics.
80. SkyHistory. (2022) 9 famous Olympic cheaters, https://www.history.co.uk/article/9-famous-olympic-cheaters.
81. Jenkins, S. (2020) The devastating way Roy Jones Jr. lost the gold medal at the 1988 Olympics, https://www.sportscasting.com/the-devastating-way-roy-jones-jr-lost-the-gold-medal-at-the-1988-olympics/.
82. Wikipedia. (2022) List of stripped Olympic medals, https://en.wikipedia.org/wiki/List_of_stripped_Olympic_medals.
83. Wikipedia, List of stripped Olympic medals.
84. Quoted in Australian Government. (1989) *Drugs in Sport: Interim Report of the Senate Standing Committee on the Environment, Recreation and the Arts*, Australian Government Publishing Service, Canberra, p. 10, https://repositories.lib.utexas.edu/bitstream/handle/2152/3255/huntt51425.pdf?sequence=2.
85. The documentary was called *Secret Doping Dossier: How Russia Produces its Winners*, see Savage, N. (2019) A nation of cheats:

Russian doping scandal explained, https://www.news.com.au/sport/olympics/a-nation-of-cheats-russian-doping-scandal-explained/news-story/1f2b5aa31c4d92485f7084f7cd931440.
86. Tikkanen, A. (2022) 8 Olympic cheating scandals, https://www.britannica.com/list/8-olympic-cheating-scandals.
87. Savage, A nation of cheats; Finkel, J. (2014) The 'Michael Jordan of Creatine' talks Soviet sports, steroids and Rugenix, http://www.thepostgame.com/blog/gold-standard/201402/dr-moris-silber-soviet-creatine-steroid-olympics-cortisol-rugenix.
88. Carozza, D. (2018) A doping dichotomy, https://www.fraud-magazine.com/cover-article.aspx?id=4295002404.
89. Ingle, S. (2017) China 'compulsorily doped' athletes in 1980s and 90s, claims whistleblower, https://www.theguardian.com/sport/2017/oct/22/china-compulsory-doping-olympic-athletes-claims-whistleblower-athletics.
90. Landsverk, G. (2022) 6 types of drugs banned by the Olympics, and how they affect athletic performance, from marijuana to trimetazidine, https://www.businessinsider.in/science/health/news/6-types-of-drugs-banned-by-the-olympics-and-how-they-affect-athletic-performance-from-marijuana-to-trimetazidine/articleshow/89649346.cms; DW. (2022) Kamila Valieva: Grandfather's heart medication in glass of water, claims team, https://www.dw.com/en/kamila-valieva-grandfathers-heart-medication-in-glass-of-water-claims-team/a-60767142.
91. Landsverk, 6 types of drugs banned by the Olympics, and how they affect athletic performance, from marijuana to trimetazidine.
92. Hunt, K. (2012) History of cheating at the Olympics, https://www.kylehuntfitness.com/history-of-cheating-in-the-olympic-games/; ESPN. (2022) Ben Johnson: drug cheat, http://en.espn.co.uk/onthisday/sport/story/283.html. 'He was sent back in disgrace to an angry Canada that had embraced its adopted son only to feel humiliated in the eyes of the world. Johnson left for Seoul as a Canadian and returned Jamaica-born'. See Montague, J. (2012) Hero or villain? Ben Johnson and the dirtiest race

in history, https://edition.cnn.com/2012/07/23/sport/olympics-2012-ben-johnson-seoul-1988-dirtiest-race/index.html.
93. Four Corners. (2023) Paralympics in crisis as international and Australian athletes game the system, https://www.abc.net.au/news/2023-04-03/paralympic-games-classification-system-exploited-australian/102165924.
94. Mac Ghlionn, J. (2023) Performance-drugged 'Olympics' to launch in 2024 and pay athletes, https://nypost.com/2023/08/02/performance-drug-enhanced-games-to-launch-in-2024-pay-athletes/.
95. Wikipedia. (2022) Lance Armstrong, https://en.wikipedia.org/wiki/Lance_Armstrong.
96. Wikipedia, Lance Armstrong.
97. Wikipedia, Lance Armstrong.
98. Four riders have won the Tour de France five times—Jacques Anquetil (France), Eddy Merckx (Belgium), Bernard Hinault (France), and Miguel Indurain (Spain).
99. Mojica, A. (2020) How exactly did Lance Armstrong cheat? https://www.sportscasting.com/how-exactly-did-lance-armstrong-cheat/.
100. Live Science. (2012) How did Lance Armstrong avoid a positive doping test? https://www.livescience.com/23932-lance-armstrong-doping-tests.html.
101. Live Science, How did Lance Armstrong avoid a positive doping test?
102. Coakley, Hallinan, Jackson and Mewett, *Sport in Society*, p. 191.
103. Coakley, Hallinan, Jackson and Mewett, *Sport in Society*, p. 193.
104. Live Science, How did Lance Armstrong avoid a positive doping test?
105. Wikipedia, Lance Armstrong.
106. There were some 3.5 million people tuned in to the March 2012 interview with the late Whitney Houston's daughter, Bobbi Kristina. See Levin, G. (2013) Oprah gets huge ratings with Lance Armstrong interview, https://www.usatoday.com/story/life/tv/2013/01/18/oprah-lance-armstrong-ratings/1845373/.

107. Rowe, D. (2013) Lance Armstrong begins his confession—but why Oprah? https://theconversation.com/lance-armstrong-begins-his-confession-but-why-oprah-11688; Weber, P. (2015) 5 ways Lance Armstrong flubbed his Oprah confessional, https://theweek.com/articles/468563/5-ways-lance-armstrong-flubbed-oprah-confessional.
108. Weber, 5 ways Lance Armstrong flubbed his Oprah confessional.
109. Armour, N. (2018) Lance Armstrong doesn't get it and until he does he won't get any sympathy, https://www.usatoday.com/story/sports/columnist/nancy-armour/2018/12/06/lance-armstrong-interview-cheating-arrogance/2228468002/; Stump, S. (2018) Lance Armstrong: 'I don't feel like a failure' in wake of doping scandal, https://www.today.com/news/lance-armstrong-i-don-t-feel-failure-wake-doping-scandal-t144620.
110. Ask, M. (2013) Lance Armstrong is the dirtiest cheater in sports history, https://bleacherreport.com/articles/1516420-lance-armstrong-is-the-dirtiest-cheater-in-sports-history.
111. Ethics Unwrapped. (2022) Armstrong's doping downfall, https://ethicsunwrapped.utexas.edu/video/armstrongs-doping-downfall; Wikipedia, Lance Armstrong.
112. Hersh, A. (2013) Armstrong doping confession: Key quotes, https://www.triathlete.com/culture/news/armstrong-doping-confession-key-quotes/.
113. Armour, Lance Armstrong doesn't get it and until he does he won't get any sympathy; Ethics Unwrapped, Armstrong's doping downfall.
114. There are two other uses of the term. The first describes keeping an opposing team scoreless in a match—your win has been a 'whitewash'; also, a sporting series can be a whitewash if the opposition fails to win a match in that series. The second is the attempt to disparage or ignore people of colour by, for example, writing their history out of a book or movie script, or by choosing white actors to play roles designed for black actors. The result is purposeful misrepresentation.
115. Chadwick, S. (2018) Sport-washing, soft power and scrubbing the stains: Can international sporting events really clean up a

country's tarnished image? https://www.policyforum.net/sport-washing-soft-power-and-scrubbing-the-stains/; Miller, T. (2018) *Greenwashing Sport*, Routledge, London.
116. Lang, S. (2018) Why Boris Johnson was right to compare Vladimir Putin's World Cup with Hitler's Olympics, https://theconversation.com/why-boris-johnson-was-right-to-compare-vladimir-putins-world-cup-with-hitlers-olympics-93922.
117. Coakley, Hallinan, Jackson and Mewett, *Sport in Society*, p. 417.
118. Wagg, Brick, Wheaton and Caudwell, *Key Concepts in Sports Studies*, p. 156.
119. Wagg, Brick, Wheaton and Caudwell, *Key Concepts in Sports Studies*, p. 156.
120. Lang, Why Boris Johnson was right to compare Vladimir Putin's World Cup with Hitler's Olympics.
121. Lang, Why Boris Johnson was right to compare Vladimir Putin's World Cup with Hitler's Olympics.
122. Wikipedia. (2022) Sportswashing, https://en.wikipedia.org/wiki/Sportswashing.
123. Smith, R. (2020) For Silvio Berlusconi, new colors and a new cause, https://www.nytimes.com/2020/02/28/sports/soccer/silvio-berlusconi-monza.html.
124. Miller, Lawrence, McKay and Rowe, *Globalization and Sport*; Naess, H. (2019) Sociology and the ethnography of human rights at mega-sport events, *Current Sociology* 68(7): 972–989.
125. Zidan, K. (2022) Could 2022 be sportswashing's biggest year? https://www.theguardian.com/sport/2022/jan/05/sportswashing-winter-olympics-world-cup.
126. Martin, A. (2023) Amnesty urges Ronaldo to speak out over human rights in Saudi Arabia, https://www.theguardian.com/football/2023/jan/04/amnesty-international-christian-ronaldo-human-rights-saudi-arabia.
127. Sripad. (2023) How much money does Lionel Messi earn from lucrative contract to promote Saudi Arabia tourism? Astonishing fee and details explored, https://www.sportskeeda.com/football/news-how-much-money-lionel-messi-earn-lucrative-contract-promote-saudi-arabia-tourism-astonishing-fee-details-explored.

128. Quoted in Weiner, D. (2021) Toon takeover: What is sportswashing? https://sport.optus.com.au/articles/os32790/sportswashing-newcastle-united.
129. Bowen, F. (2022) Golfers cash in on Saudi-funded tour but hurt their legacies, https://www.washingtonpost.com/kidspost/2022/06/16/golfers-liv-participation-hurts-legacy/.
130. Everett, L. (2022) The Cheap Seats: Why the Saudi Arabia-backed LIV Golf tour has led to ethical concerns, rivalry with PGA tour, https://www.thedartmouth.com/article/2022/08/everett-liv-golf-tour; Helfand, Z. (2022) Will the Saudis and Donald Trump save golf—or wreck it? https://www.newyorker.com/magazine/2022/10/24/will-the-saudis-and-donald-trump-save-golf-or-wreck-it.
131. Although the US concluded that the Saudi government did not commit the 9/11 atrocities, some 15 of the 19 terrorists were Saudis. And, of course, Osama bin Laden belonged to one of Saudi Arabia's wealthiest families. See NPR. (2023) Who really benefits from the PGA-LIV merger? https://www.npr.org/2023/06/11/1181590531/who-really-benefits-from-the-pga-liv-merger.
132. The quote is from Felix Jakens of Amnesty International. See Michaelson, R. (2023) Revealed: Saudi Arabia's $6bn spend on 'sportswashing', https://www.inkl.com/news/revealed-saudi-arabia-s-6bn-spend-on-sportswashing.
133. Clarke, M. (2022) Can China use the Beijing Olympics to 'sportwash' its abuses against the Uyghurs? Only if the world remains silent, https://theconversation.com/can-china-use-the-beijing-olympics-to-sportwash-its-abuses-against-the-uyghurs-only-if-the-world-remains-silent-175922.
134. Kashgarian, A. (2022) What happens to Uyghurs after competing in the Olympics? https://www.voanews.com/a/what-happens-to-uyghurs-after-competing-in-the-olympics-/6450163.html.
135. Clarke, Can China use the Beijing Olympics to 'sportwash' its abuses against the Uyghurs?
136. Hutchins, B. (2022) Time for a reckoning: Cricket Australia, fossil fuel sponsorship and climate change, https://theconversation.com/time-for-a-reckoning-cricket-australia-fossil-fuel-sponsorship-and-climate-change-176707.

137. Two books telling the story of Qatar's strategic use of sport are McManus, J. (2022) *Inside Qatar: Hidden Stories from One of the Richest Nations on Earth*, Icon Books, London; Brannagan, P. and Reiche, D. (2022) *Qatar and the 2022 FIFA World Cup: Politics, Controversy, Change*, Palgrave Macmillan, London.
138. Zidan, Could 2022 be sportswashing's biggest year? See also Rowe, D. (2022) The Qatar men's FIFA World Cup 2022: Free kick or body check for human rights, https://www.internationalaffairs.org.au/australianoutlook/the-qatar-mens-fifa-world-cup-2022-free-kick-or-body-check-for-human-rights/; Adair, D. (2022) Why is the Qatar FIFA World Cup so controversial? https://theconversation.com/why-is-the-qatar-fifa-world-cup-so-controversial-192627.
139. Quotes taken from King-Hill, S. (2022) World Cup 2022: Fifa's clampdown on rainbow armbands conflicts with its own guidance on human rights, https://theconversation.com/world-cup-2022-fifas-clampdown-on-rainbow-armbands-conflicts-with-its-own-guidance-on-human-rights-194485.
140. Quoted in Boffey, D. (2022) 'A gay icon no more': will David Beckham's Qatar role kill his brand? https://www.theguardian.com/football/2022/nov/18/will-david-beckham-qatar-role-kill-his-brand-world-cup.
141. Whiteaker, J. (2021) What is sportswashing and does it really work? https://www.investmentmonitor.ai/analysis/what-is-sports washing-and-does-it-really-work.
142. Sherry, E., McCullough, B. and Bramley, O. (2022) Out of bounds: How much does greenwashing cost fossil-fuel sponsors of Australian sport? https://theconversation.com/out-of-bounds-how-much-does-greenwashing-cost-fossil-fuel-sponsors-of-aus tralian-sport-192720; Morgan, A. (2022) Should athletes just shut up and play ball? No—society is changing and sport sponsorship must too, https://theconversation.com/should-athletes-just-shut-up-and-play-ball-no-society-is-changing-and-sport-spo nsorship-must-too-192959.
143. New Weather Institute. (2021) Sweat not oil: Why sports should drop advertising and sponsorship of high carbon

polluters, https://static1.squarespace.com/static/5ebd00802 38e863d04911b51/t/605b60b09a957c1b05f433e2/161660127 1774/Sweat+Not+Oil+-+why+Sports+should+drop+advertising+ from+high+carbon+polluters+-+March+2021v3.pdf.
144. New Weather Institute, Sweat not oil.
145. New Weather Institute, Sweat not oil.
146. United Nations. (2022) Addressing climate change through sport, https://www.un.org/development/desa/dspd/2022/02/addressing-climate-change-through-sport/.
147. Hutchins, Time for a reckoning.

8

The Future: Confronting the Culprits

Andromeda is a hungry galaxy. It has been on something of a feeding frenzy during the past billion years and is on course to devour the Milky Way. 'It will eat us' warned the UK's *Express*, presumably hoping to put fear into the hearts of its already nervous readers.[1] Being cannibalised by a hostile galaxy is a rather scary thought. There is some comfort, however. Although the Milky Way will succumb to its near neighbour's avaricious demands in 4.5 billion years, our very own planet will have already been heated to such a level that liquid water will have disappeared. In a billion years from now the sun will have become so hot it will have weathered the earth's crust which, in turn, will trigger removal of carbon dioxide from the atmosphere thereby starving plants of their source of energy. They die and with them all the birds, reptiles, ruminants, and mammals dependent upon them. Even if some species adapt at the time, the solar brightening will have vaporised the earth's water (a runaway greenhouse event) around 600 million years from now.

So that's it. No more McDonald's, no more Murdoch press, no more QAnon—just nothingness. We could pray, of course, that the cosmic collision with Andromeda won't occur, but it is unlikely to alter the course of events. We're dead. In any case, mammalian species don't seem to last long (species extinction occurs every 100 million years or so—a lot closer than 600 million years). Or is 250 million years a better bet? The world's tectonic plates are nudging closer to each other. They will form a supercontinent—Pangea Ultima—one which will experience extreme temperatures, volcanic eruptions, collapsing food systems, and ultimately mass extinction.[2]

In his prophetic tome *End Times*, Bryan Walsh has written:

> Our species has always lived under the shadow of existential risk – we just didn't know it. At least five times over the course of our planet's … history, life has been virtually wiped out in great extinction waves, often punctuated by a natural catastrophe that struck on a planetary scale. Asteroid impacts, supervolcanic eruptions, even gamma rays from space – the universe is not a safe space.[3]

How long do we have? As evolutionary biologist Nicholas Longrich has written, 'The fossil record shows everything goes extinct, eventually. [Of all] the species that ever lived, over 99.9% are extinct'. Longrich gives us around 250,000 years.[4] Before his death, Stephen Hawking concluded that nuclear war and/or climate disaster would see us all gone within the next 1,000 years.[5] In his 2008 book *The End of the World*, philosopher John Leslie forecast there is a one in three chance our species will be extinct within 500 years. Noted virologist Professor Frank Fenner said it was more likely to be 100 years. Ecologist and evolutionary biologist Guy McPherson has modelled our present course and predicts humans will be extinct this decade.[6]

Of course, we should take some relief knowing that previous predictions have been, to say the least, a little wide of the mark. Johannes Stöffler, a mathematician and astrologer from Germany, predicted in 1499 that the world would end in February 1524, with a huge flood engulfing the planet. Apparently, the planets would align under the water sign of Pisces, dumping huge volumes of water (quite possibly containing fish?)[7] and flooding the earth. Pamphlets were spread far and wide with boat builders reaping substantial benefits. One Count von Iggleheim had a three-story ark constructed on the Rhine. On the day of judgement—a day which started with light rain—Germans gathered in their masses, fighting for a seat on the boat. Hundreds perished in the melee and the Count was stoned to death for refusing to allow anyone on board. Unfazed by his embarrassing prophetical blunder, Stöffler subsequently revised his prediction to 1528.[8] Noah was not needed—the floods stayed away.

That would-be global circumnavigator, Christopher Columbus, believed the world had been created in 5343 BCE and would end in 1658. The Protestant reformer Martin Luther predicted the world would end before 1600. Members of the British Christian sect, the Shakers (so-called because of their propensity to shimmy and shake during services) knew the world would end in 1792. The Jehovah's Witnesses calculated that, since 1975 marked 6,000 years since the creation of humankind, that would be the year of worldly destruction. (1975 was actually celebrated for the release of the film *One Flew Over the Cuckoo's Nest*, gaining a bag of Oscars the following year.)[9] That hymn writer extraordinaire and founder of the Methodists, Charles Wesley, told his followers to be ready for the 'Great Beast of Revelation' that would arrive in 1794. US preacher, televangelist, and conservative pastor Jerry Falwell predicted the world would end on 1 January 2000, as did Sun Myung Moon of the Unification Church. Grigori Rasputin—the famous 'lover of the Russian Queen' if you can believe *Boney M*—believed a massive fire would ravage the world on 23 August 2013.[10] Maybe he foresaw global warming?

Others have tried their hand. The not-so-innocent, Pope Innocent III, believing that Mohammad was the devil, calculated that the world would end in the year 1284—exactly 666 years after the founding of Islam. Historian David Montaigne, after examining the Mayan calendar and precise star arrangements, said earthquakes and tidal waves would destroy the world on 28 December 2019.[11] US Psychic Jean Dixon, famous for predicting president Kennedy's death in 1963, said Armageddon would begin in 2020 with Jesus returning to earth to fight the devil. When he wasn't busy discovering the laws of motion, Isaac Newton would pore over the Holy Bible for clues as to our final demise. Conclusion? The year 2060.[12] For Hon-Ming Chen, founder of the True Way sect, on 25 March 1988 God was to appear on US channel 18 to announce the end of the world. Devil spirits would appear the following year, along with devastating floods which would wipe out the human race. Spaceships, masquerading as clouds, would descend from the heavens to save the faithful.[13] More recently, in 2015, Pope Francis told a congregation that end times, as described in Mark, Chapter 13, were nigh. Hearing his message, the editors of *Catholic Online* proclaimed 'may we be ready to meet our Lord, Jesus Christ … The Year of Great Jubilee is upon us'.[14]

Disappearing Acts

In their examination of existential threats to the planet, scientists have been much less fanciful, and a great deal more sober, than preachers and psychics. That doesn't mean their predictions are any less scary. Here are some of the main threats and their likelihoods.

Asteroids might pummel the planet. They have done so before. Most of us know that the death of the dinosaurs some 66 million years ago was caused by an asteroid landing in Yucatan, Mexico. Estimated to have been some 10 kilometres wide, it impacted with high velocity creating a crater 180 kilometres in diameter and 20 kilometres in depth. The so-called Chicxulub crater is the second largest on earth. The asteroid vaporised in the enormous heat generated upon impact. Massive tidal waves and fires followed, with the soot and debris blasting into the atmosphere blocking the sun's rays. The planet's ecosystem began to collapse—plant life could not photosynthesise and began dying. Herbivores starved, along with the carnivores that fed on them. Fortunately, not all plants and animals became extinct, with many species we see today surviving the asteroid's impact. Could we still face species extinction from asteroids? Yes—with 100% certainty.[15] There are millions of asteroids and comets shooting throughout the solar system, many the size of that which created the Chicxulub crater. Asteroid 2022 AP7 was discovered in November 2022. Its diameter, at 1.5 kilometres, is much smaller than the one that wiped out the dinosaurs; nevertheless, it has been designated a future 'planet killer'. Its trajectory will sync with the Earth's orbit in a few centuries time.[16] This should not be surprising—a 'monster' asteroid is expected to crash into our planet every 100 million years or so.[17] NASA was so concerned with the prospect of such an event that it launched the Double Asteroid Redirection Test (DART) mission in 2021 to determine whether human intervention might be able to throw an asteroid off its course. The NASA spacecraft hit the asteroid Dimorphos on 26 September 2022 and did as predicted—nudging it off its normal orbit.[18] Are we now safe from future devastation? Don't count on it—we simply don't know which of the hundreds of millions of asteroids in the solar system might have its eye on planet Earth.

Global interconnectivity has ensured that **diseases** spread rapidly throughout human populations—think of the outbreaks of Severe Acute Respiratory Syndrome (SARS), bird flu, and COVID-19. Viruses multiply quickly and some—the zoonotic diseases like SARS—jump species barriers, beginning in animals like palm civets and finding their way into humans. As Bryan Walsh has written:

> Nothing has killed more human beings through history than the viruses, bacteria, and parasites that cause disease. Not natural disasters like earthquakes and volcanoes. Not even war. By one estimate half of the human beings who ever lived have been killed by one disease, malaria.[19]

In his much-lauded book *Pathogenesis: How Germs Made History* health sociologist Jonathan Kennedy demonstrates how some of the most minute lifeforms on the planet have orchestrated profound change in human and animal populations throughout time.[20] It is microbes, not humankind, that have shaped the world. Some 200 million people are estimated to have perished in the Black Death in the fourteenth century, smallpox has dispatched more than 300 million people during the twentieth century, and up to 50 million died during the influenza pandemic that began in 1918. (It was called The Spanish Flu, but that appears to be a misnomer, with the first infections discovered in American servicemen on their way to Europe to serve in the First World War.)[21] The Human Immunodeficiency Virus (HIV)—another zoonotic disease thought to have infected the human population, this time through the consumption of monkey meat—has afflicted some 80 million people worldwide, with close to half this number having died. HIV causes AIDS which damages the immune system, preventing bodies from fighting off other diseases.[22] Antiretroviral treatments limit its progression in the body, but it has no cure.

The virus on everybody's lips, as it were, is the human coronavirus, COVID-19. Believed to have jumped to humans from an infected animal in a 'wet market' (an open-air market trading animals, many exotic) in Wuhan, China, the virus has infected over 774 million people worldwide, and killed more than 7 million.[23]

There is much debate about the origins of COVID-19. Should we pin it on a pangolin? Pangolins (scaly anteaters) are a food delicacy in countries like China and Vietnam. Although they are an endangered species, their meat is highly sought after and their scales provide over 60 commercially-available pharmaceuticals for use in traditional medicine, treating everything from poor circulation, asthma, ulcers, rheumatism, stroke, venereal diseases, to mental illness.[24] It doesn't matter that their scales are very much like human fingernails and have about the same medicinal benefit (read: zilch). For many Asians they have 'magical' properties, and that is all that matters.[25] Pangolins are the most trafficked mammal species in the world and—along with bats—are carriers of coronaviruses.[26] They could be the culprit.

Or was it the so-called raccoon dog, another delicacy of the Chinese and readily available in wet markets?[27] Or did COVID-19 arise from China's Wuhan Institute of Virology (WIV)? For over a decade WIV scientists have been collecting and researching coronavirus samples from bats which live in mine shafts in the region. Could they have unintentionally 'leaked' the virus into the community? According to classified US intelligence, three WIV researchers had been hospitalised in November 2019—just prior to infections being found among the residents of Wuhan. There seems to be a link. Or is there? Results from investigations have been inconclusive.[28]

Yet another, more sinister, possibility is that the Chinese laboratory was being used to manufacture weapons for future use in biological warfare, and that the virus accidentally escaped.[29]

We do know one thing for certain—the early years of the COVID-19 pandemic brought the conspiracy theorists out of their closets, with the then director of the US National Institute of Allergy and Infectious Diseases, Dr Anthony Fauci, being roundly vilified. He was accused of opposing hydroxychloroquine as a possible treatment for the disease (against Trump's strong, but unscientific, endorsement of the drug).[30]

Apparently, Fauci's aim was to have the virus spread, hoping a new vaccine would be developed—and be named after him. He was held directly responsible for the funding of 'gain-of-function' research at the Wuhan lab—research that would impart increased potency on viruses, including the development and release of COVID-19. The escape of the virus meant Fauci was 'culpable for the entire pandemic'.[31] Websites carried the damning words 'Fauci Lied, Millions Died'.[32] And, of course, he was working for Big Pharma—which is why, after his retirement in 2022, he accepted a lucrative position at Pfizer.[33] He wasn't, and he didn't. What this sad episode confirms is the growing ability of those who would use social media for malicious purposes to deliberately create and circulate disinformation, and for gullible members of the public to uncritically accept conspiracy theories generated by misinformed ideologues.

As we saw in Chapter 3, **genetic engineering** is being gleefully employed to create novel plants, animals, and viruses—this is nothing new. What is new is 'synthetic biology', the name given to the science of precisely altering the genes of living things. With CRISPR technology[34] genes can be readily spliced and then rearranged, removed, or new genes added to DNA strands. It is a 'molecular scalpel for genomes'.[35] It is allowing geneticists to alter cellular processes that cause diseases like Parkinson's and Alzheimer's. It will aid in the development of new drugs. It has already been used in China to increase meat and wool output in farm animals. The humble chicken has been turned into a bioreactor, producing therapeutic drugs and human antibodies.[36] More controversially, CRISPR will allow human gene editing and the creation of designer babies.[37] Once a technology for the scientific elite in top research universities, CRISPR is becoming available to a growing number of people, worldwide:

> do-it-yourself CRISPR kits are available commercially for less than $150. In the wrong hands, these simple but powerful tools are a cause for alarm. Terrorists targeting the food supply could alter the avian influenza genome and engineer a large bird flu epidemic [and] design [and employ other] bioweapons.[38]

Or, as Bryan Walsh has written:

> We're scared of disease outbreaks and we're scared of terrorism – put them together and you have a formula for chaos … biotechnology has rewritten what [is] possible in creating new weapons, while also increasing the range of people capable of carrying out such attacks. That's a fatal combination, one that plausibly threatens the future of humanity like nothing else.[39]

Like nothing else? In fact, it may not be a lone terrorist who poisons our drinking water or ravages our food supply. Biotechnology is being weaponised, with over 17 nations currently experimenting with genetically engineered biological agents which, if released, could wreak havoc. Biohacking is on the rise, with gene editing having been officially listed by US Intelligence as a potentially new weapon of mass destruction.[40]

Then there's the threat of **nuclear annihilation**—something Robert Oppenheimer predicted would inevitably occur because of his, and his 'Manhattan collaborators', success in developing the first atomic bomb which landed on the Japanese city of Hiroshima in August 1945. Nuclear warfare has been back on the agenda since Russia invaded Ukraine in February 2022, with Vladimir Putin threatening to use nuclear force against any foreign country daring to interfering in his military campaign.[41] Russia's nuclear arsenal consists of 6,257 nuclear weapons including cruise missiles and short-, medium-, and long-range ballistic missiles—capable of launching 'an all-out nuclear war'. (By way of comparison the US admits to having 5,550 nuclear warheads.) North Korea's Kim Jong-un has promised that he will have developed the world's most powerful nuclear arsenal during this century,[42] while South Korea's President Yoon Suk-yeol publicly declared in January 2023 that his nation might be forced to build nuclear armaments if South Korea's security were to be threatened by Kim's regime in the North.[43] The mushroom clouds are gathering. And it's not just Putin's paranoia about NATO and its intentions, or unease on the Korean Peninsula. There are nine nations with nuclear arsenals—Russia, the US, the UK, China, France, Israel, North Korea, India, and Pakistan.

For some analysts, the most likely nuclear war will be that between the last two nations. Why? In that quaint phrase of Charles Dickens— 'not to put too fine a point on it'—they simply 'hate each other'.[44] How might that have come about? When Britain ceased its rule in India in 1947 it bestowed a lasting colonial gift—it partitioned the country into 'India' and 'Pakistan', the former largely Hindu, the latter Muslim. Mayhem, dislocation, and conflict followed, particularly in the region of Kashmir where a Hindu leader ruled over a predominantly Muslim population. Result? More chaos, with wars igniting in 1947, 1964, 1971, and 1999. One prediction for the nuclear face-to-face is for a 10-day war with around 30 15-kiloton bombs being launched. About 20 million people would die instantly, with radiation exposure killing many more. If 100 15-kiloton bombs were dropped up to 26 million Indians and 18 million Pakistanis would perish, with subsequent firestorms killing millions of others.[45] Radioactive fallout would spread across the world. Smoke and ash from the explosion would screen much of the sun's rays from entering, temperatures would fall, the cereal growing season would be shortened by up to 40 days. With global yields declining, famine would set in. A worldwide food crisis would last for more than a decade and hundreds of millions of human beings would starve to death.[46] Up to 30% of the ozone layer would be removed, with the increased radiation killing plankton and other marine life. The sun's rays would be highly dangerous to all animal life. It is important to remember:

> These are outcomes for a 'light' nuclear winter scenario, not a full slugging match between the Russian and U.S. arsenals.[47]

What about a Russian/US 'slugging match'? It would be as good as anything coming out of Hollywood. But not even Dwayne (The Rock) Johnson would be able to save the world this time around. Hundreds of rockets would be launched more-or-less instantaneously across the US, Russia, and Europe. Then they would detonate. Microseconds into the detonation of just one 30-kiloton bomb, a fireball of superheated air would kill all life in a 13-kilometre radius. The blast wave from the explosion would raze all buildings and infrastructure.[48] Radioactive fallout would impact thousands of square kilometres, killing most living things. Hundreds of millions of people would die within the first week. Soot would reach the stratosphere, staying there for years and reducing both precipitation and global temperatures—the latter dropping by as much as 8 °C, triggering a new ice age.[49] The increasing amount of UV light entering the planet would fry the skins of those unable to escape exposure, and cause havoc with food production—there would be mass food shortages across most nations. Output from the world's fisheries would be reduced by half.[50] Two years following the conflagration over five billion human beings would have perished.[51] The so-called preppers will have wasted their money. As an editor of the Bulletin of the Atomic Scientists stated plainly 'there is nowhere to hide'.[52] Any upsides? Nuclear annihilation would certainly stem global warming.

If the nukes don't kill us all, perhaps **climate change** will. As was discussed in Chapter 4, human-induced climate change is responsible for major damage to people and the planet.

In 2015 some 196 Parties (nations and territories) across the globe signed the United Nations Framework Convention on Climate Change—the so-called Paris Agreement. It proposed that global temperatures should be kept at well below 2 °C above pre-industrial times—and hopefully not exceed 1.5 °C—as the only way to prevent disastrous climate change impacts. The 1.5 °C figure was written in stone and became the agreed-upon international target to be pursued by nations attending the various Conference of the Parties (COP) meetings.

During 2023 there was widespread consensus that the planet was sitting at 1.2 °C above pre-industrial temperatures. But a 2024 study published in *Nature Climate Change* indicates we have already moved beyond the 1.5 °C limit and we are currently sitting at 1.7 °C and, at this rate, we are likely to hit 2.0 °C by the start of 2030.[53] The outcomes have been, of course, melting ice sheets, prolonged droughts, more intense cyclones and hurricanes, horrendous bushfires, and the loss of countless lives through these disasters, and from subsequent disease and starvation. 'Time-travelling' pathogens, once frozen in Antarctic ice and Siberian permafrost, will emerge—with the prospect of ecosystem collapse and 'catastrophic extinctions'.[54] With predicted temperature increases the world will become 'sicker, hungrier, poorer, gloomier and way more dangerous' than today.[55]

Carbon dioxide in the atmosphere is now over 420 parts per million. If it gets to 1,000 parts per million by 2100—as has been predicted—the air people breathe will poison their brains, lowering their cognitive ability by 20%.[56] (On a positive note, maybe they won't have the intellectual capacity to worry about climate change?) If the planet's atmosphere is not progressively decarbonised it is possible that temperatures could soar to some 3 °C above the pre-industrial average turning cropping and grazing lands to deserts, rising sea levels, acidifying the oceans, creating millions of climate change refugees, and destroying entire ecosystems. Chaos would prevail and would herald, according to one report, 'the end of human civilization and modern society as we have known it'.[57] This will occur as early as 2050 if drastic action is not taken soon.[58] But some can't wait. As comedian Conan O'Brien lamented:

> Yesterday, a group of scientists warned that because of global warming, sea levels will rise so much that parts of New Jersey will be under water. The bad news? Parts of New Jersey won't be under water.[59]

Rather unhappily, the UN has predicted that if nations stick to their currently agreed-upon levels of emissions, and no additional actions are taken, the global temperature is expected to reach 2.8 °C above pre-industrial levels by 2100.[60] That's just a little under the temperature associated with the 'chaos' scenario, above. Melting asphalt is not a secure road to the future.

Meanwhile, world consumption of heating gases has hit an all-time high, including an 'alarming' surge in the emission of the potent greenhouse gas, methane.[61] And Russia's invasion of Ukraine has triggered a 'fossil fuel goldrush' as European nations seek new energy supply options.[62] At the very time the dire climate change predictions were being made the fossil fuel industry's profits doubled to US$4 trillion in one year.[63] As climate change scientist Professor Simon Lewis, from University College London, said:

> The situation is serious and bleak ... The solution is to do everything we can to defeat the fossil fuel industry – they stand between us all and a prosperous future.[64]

But there *is* an immediate solution. As comedian Jimmy Kimmel once joked, if Americans really wanted to lower the temperature dramatically, they could do so 'just by switching from Fahrenheit to Celsius'.[65] That's the spirit.

There are other culprits in the list of world-ending disasters—super-volcanic explosions, artificial intelligence (robotic ascension), gamma-ray bursts, and ecosystem collapse. (Some would also include alien or zombie invasions, as we learnt in Chapter 1.)[66] There's also the 'snowball effect'—one disaster building upon another. Here, global warming might increase the number of pathogens; biotechnology comes to the rescue killing the pathogens, only to find the pathogens remaining build resistance and become stronger, destroying bodies, or food supplies, or the entire environment.[67] 'Welcome to the world of the polycrisis' writes academic Adam Tooze.[68] It is a 'world where global crises are interconnected, entwining and worsening one another' and for which there are no straightforward solutions.[69] It is little wonder that, in 2024, the second hand on the famous Doomsday Clock sits now only 90 seconds away from midnight—the closest the world has ever come to catastrophe.[70]

'Apocalypticism' is the rather ungainly name given to the belief that the world is about to end, brought about by a tumultuous and catastrophic global event.[71] It is often the religiously-minded who fondly embrace the idea—not surprising considering how firmly it is entrenched in their sacred texts:

> The story of apocalypse is an old one, one of the oldest humans tell. In ancient religious traditions beyond Christianity — including Judaism, Islam and Buddhism — it is a common narrative that arises in moments of social and political crisis, as people try to process unprecedented or shocking events.[72]

One US poll, for example, showed that some 44% of voting-age respondents believed the COVID-19 pandemic was either 'a wake-up call to faith, a sign of God's coming judgement or both'.[73] Indeed, some 48% of US Christians believe that Christ will 'definitely' or 'probably' return to earth in their lifetime.[74] The belief of Jesus' return is widespread, of course. (Perhaps somewhat strangely, over 60% of people in Tunisia,

Turkey, and Iraq also think that Jesus will return in their lifetime.) In one survey of 23 Muslim nations, more than half of the adult respondents believed the Mahdi (the Guided One in Muslim teachings) would return during their time on earth.[75] The faithful just can't seem to wait.

If we manage to avoid the asteroids, diseases, and nuclear bombs—and limit the effects of climate change—surely, in a sane world, humanity will be safe? No. Even if we accept the unlikely premise that we are living in a 'sane' world, there are plenty of groups and individuals motivated to cause harm. In his book *Morality, Foresight, and Human Flourishing: An Introduction to Existential Risks*, New York-based biologist Phil Torres provides us with a brief list of possible miscreants:

> apocalyptic terrorists, psychopaths, psychotics, misanthropes, ecoterrorists, anarcho-primitivists, eco-anarchists, violent technophobes, militant neo-Luddites and even 'morally good people' who maintain, for ethical reasons, that human suffering is so great that we would be better off not existing at all.[76]

And don't forget Russian, or US, or North Korean, presidents who just might possess some of the traits of those in the list above. Yet many others want to put up the good fight—to save the planet and its inhabitants, with plenty of examples provided below.

One of the main arguments in this book is that the actions of existing power regimes—whether they be in the form of corporate capitalism, post-soviet oligarchies, absolute monarchies, or countless cronies and dictators are—knowingly or unknowingly—killing the planet. Current regimes use both soft force (artifice, beguilement, deceit, and trumpery) and hard force (bullets, bombs, and torture) to shore up their power, wealth, and privilege. They are creating a world of growing economic inequality, social malaise, authoritarian politics, illiberalism, environmental degradation, and climate devastation. Yet citizens have **social agency**—the desire and capacity to rally against institutions, structures, and ideologies that constrain and oppress. People form action groups to resist oppression. They come together to picket, rally, riot, and revolt in efforts to overthrow corrupt regimes, and to create new (and hopefully more beneficial) social and political structures.

Facing the Future

In the following section, we will examine the many social movements, protest groups, and political organisations which are attempting to 'jump off' the merry-go-round of societal deception. Let's start with the media.

Information Flows

'Houston, we have a problem' was an ironic understatement made by astronaut Jack Swigert as he told mission control that an on-board explosion had crippled the Apollo 13 spacecraft.[77] 'Humanity, we have a problem' might be an apt phrase in today's world where half-truths, distortions, and lies permeate the entire mediascape. In Chapter 6, religion was revealed as one of the most potent agencies of societal deception not only packaging superstitions as heavenly 'truths', but also reproducing sexism, racism, and xenophobia in ways that justify prejudices and injustices. But next in line come politics and the media. The public finds it difficult to fathom what is true and untrue when, for ideological and political reasons, elected representatives fabricate the 'truth', the right-wing media deliberately present falsehoods, and when Think Tanks seek to manipulate public opinion to serve some corporate agenda.[78] The term 'media capture' describes the influence of vested interests as they use their money and power to control public discourse and, more insidiously, to ensure political decisions conform with their own interests and demands.[79] Being 'captured' prevents the media from performing

> their Fourth Estate functions of providing increased accountability, government monitoring, and [incorporating] feedback from citizens. Instead of producing a vital public good – high-quality, relevant, and verifiable news and information – captured media produce propaganda, distractions and scandal that serve the interest and ambitions of a select group of powerful elites.[80]

Lies are employed because of their 'power to halt progress and justify political positions that would otherwise seem cruel, irrational or extreme'.[81] Moreover,

8 The Future: Confronting the Culprits 391

Lies are socially sticky, and even after one has been thoroughly debunked, it will still have advocates among those whose worldview it justifies. These zombie lies continue to rise from the dead again and again, impacting political debate and swaying public opinion on a variety of issues.[82]

According to *Lies, Incorporated* author Ari Rabin-Havt,

> **lies**, along with **money** and **lobbying**, constitute three essential elements that distort our policy making process. Like a barstool of corruption, each of its three legs offers support to groups that fight on behalf of financial or ideological interests.[83] (My emphasis)

As Chapter 1 demonstrated, it is not only the media and Think Tanks that are mendacious, wilfully perverting the truth; we have a range of other powerful players—from PR firms, to lobbyists, to supposed 'experts', along with influencers, bots, cyborgs, and sock puppets. Rabin-Havt described the background to the undermining of policies during Obama's reign as President:

> paid experts produced fake research that was converted into talking points and memes, then repeated on television by paid shills [stooges] and spread through social media and, when necessary, hammered into the public consciousness through paid advertising campaigns ... [The rationale?] if facts don't support your argument, make up your own facts.[84]

Of course, when they spot what they believe to be disinformation, social media platforms can, and do, remove it. Or they will attach a label, warning readers that the post is false or disputed. According to media analyst Ed Coper, author of *Facts and Other Lies*, this can be counterproductive. Labelling has become

> a 'badge of honour' for many in the right-wing ecosystem who fit it within their worldview that social media platforms are out there to censor their 'truth'.[85]

If that's not bad enough, there is also a significant time lapse between the identification of false or inaccurate content and the labelling of that information:

> By one count, it takes Facebook (Meta) an average of 28 days to label false content ... By the time any content is labelled it may have been viewed millions of times ... As debunked and labelled posts get removed, dozens of 'clones' appear in their place, sometimes with very minor changes to avoid detection ... The [anti-vaxxer, conspiracy theory] film *Plandemic* had racked up over 7 million views [on YouTube] before it was taken down.[86]

Coper suggests that one tactic to limit disinformation is 'prebunking'. This means (1) alerting the public to the intentions of those distributing false content, (2) eroding the public's confidence in these sources by exposing their true identities and interests, and (3) being the first to spread the truth. '[R]ather than repeat the disinformation to negate it, positively tell the opposite factual truth'.[87]

Maybe easier said than done. How else might we counter lies and deception? For many analysts the answers are improved media governance and increased regulation (not self-regulation, which has been exposed as a near-total failure).[88] Citizen activism, including the rise of civil society organisations, is viewed as crucial in challenging those who would seek to distribute false information. Examples from West Africa and Latin America demonstrate that local actors can link arms, metaphorically, across jurisdictions to challenge media hegemony. And what are some of their demands?

- public broadcasting should be independent,
- media ownership should be open and transparent,
- an agreed-upon set of standards for media regulation must be adopted,
- free and impartial information has to be guaranteed during elections, and
- protection of media freedom and human rights are to be assured.[89]

But others are less sanguine that such initiatives will prevail, pointing to the 'death of media regulation' in the face of the largely uncontrolled

8 The Future: Confronting the Culprits 393

growth of mega-giants such as Facebook/Meta, Google, and Amazon.[90] Meanwhile, journalists are on a 'hamster wheel', running faster and faster to produce and publish content. 'The digital diktat [has] warped journalistic incentives, causing a rush toward "volume without thought", "news panic", and "a recalibration of the news calculus"'. Journalists no longer have the time to think as they 'churn out content … for digital ad revenue'.[91] How could this be challenged? In Hungary, a funding stream for NGOs and civic actors has been created via a 1% tax on incomes. The funding pool allows progressive organisations to support independent journalism and to create a 'counternarrative to the government's propaganda'.[92] In the US, reporters expose crime and corruption leading to the yearly seizure of billions of dollars. It has been suggested if even 10% of those funds were deposited in a suitable trust, it could provide a huge boost for investigative journalism.[93]

Deplatforming is another means of robbing liars of their place to speak. Donald Trump enjoyed using his Twitter account to put forward his latest ideas and commentary, escaping any fact-checking in the process. But when Trump messaged his followers 'Statistically impossible to have lost the 2020 Election. Big protest in D.C. on January 6th. Be there, will be wild', he was accused of inciting violence. His site @realDonaldTrump was taken down by Twitter and later by other social media platforms including Facebook, Snapchat, YouTube, and Reddit.[94] (When Elon Musk purchased Twitter for US$44 billion in October 2022, he quickly reinstated Trump's account. Hate speech immediately returned to the site as did misinformation.)[95] Deplatforming is an effective way of punishing users who resort to hate speech and other offensive material to provoke their audiences. It would be a good step to hold social media companies liable for user-generated disinformation and hateful material; presently, there are no internationally-binding regulations that make social media companies accountable for content on their platforms.[96]

Others pin their hopes on various **independent non-profit organisations** involved in investigative reporting, whose aim is to hold governments responsible for their actions. They have 'redefined journalism' in places like Armenia, Burkina Faso, Kyrgyzstan, Peru, Romania, and Serbia. The Philippine Center for Investigative Journalism's exposure of the corrupt behaviour of President Estrada in the 1990s leads to his later impeachment.[97]

Then there's **the personal approach**—becoming adept at spotting disinformation and misinformation. Remember, Google and Facebook/Meta receive a great deal of their income from clickbait providers. These clickbait providers are eager to access personal Internet Protocol (IP) addresses, along with information about people's preferences, habits, consumption patterns, and whatever other savoury or unsavoury information users have divulged to the web-based world. Each time we talk to Siri and Alexa, 'pin', or left-or-right swipe, we give important clues to those who would like to blend seamlessly into our personal lives. In the age of the algorithm, we can all be highly cyber smart while being highly cyber vulnerable, especially to computational propaganda. To help counter this, Mozilla has produced a doco *Misinfo Nation: Misinformation, Democracy, and the Internet*[98] It is helpful in letting us know what is going on, and why. A 'Disinformation Toolkit' has been developed by the international NGO InterAction to help civil society organisations and NGOs identify and address false and misleading information following any online attack.[99] *NewsGuard* scrutinises the web for fake news, blatant errors, hoaxes, conspiracy theories, and political propaganda. It issues a 'reliability score' for media sites—allowing online readers to ascertain the likelihood of those sites being able to be trusted, or otherwise.[100]

A very useful approach is SIFT—a strategy to assist in judging the trustworthiness of online media content. Developed by Vancouver-based academic Michael Caulfield, it encourages the viewer to:

Stop
Investigate the source
Find better coverage
Trace claims, quotes, and media to their original context.[101]

Beware of cookies—especially the electronic type. Cookies increase our exposure to unwanted targeted advertisements. Turnoff options are available in Chrome, Safari, and Internet Explorer. Mozilla's Facebook Container limits how much of your data media organisations can retrieve. The major browsers also have a setting called 'incognito' which will prevent cookies spying on your browsing habits.[102] The 'Learn to Discern: Media Literacy Trainer's Manual' is a go-to website for educators. It allows people of all ages to recognise disinformation and misinformation including hate speech, fake news, clickbait, and half-truths. Its aim is to teach audiences to identify, and reject, manipulative content.[103] Before posting on social media, double check the info. Importantly, don't spread anything that doesn't pass the bullshit test.[104] It is useful to remember that

> post-truth amounts to a form of ideological supremacy, whereby its practitioners are trying to compel someone to believe something whether there is good evidence for it or not.[105]

As we saw in Chapter 1, deepfakes (images that have been doctored to misrepresent a person—an electronic form of face-swapping) are another web-based form of trickery. As with other synthetic media, their aim is to:

> create a zero-trust society, where people cannot, or no longer bother to, distinguish truth from falsehood. And when trust is eroded, it is easier to raise doubts about specific [claims].[106]

New York-based Witness Media Lab has (in association with the Google News Initiative) produced the video 'Prepare, Don't Panic: Synthetic Media and Deepfakes' which explores how 'deepfakes' and other AI-generated synthetic media are being employed to deceive the public via altered imagery, fake news, and hoaxes.[107]

A final option for avoiding misinformation and disinformation is to **refrain from using the media platforms**. But for most of us, that is not a realistic option. We want to learn more about Sarah's new *Tinder* boyfriend, join the 150 million followers of Khaby Lame on TikTok, or get the latest world news instantaneously. Online news is a crucial source of information around the globe. More than 80% of Americans rely upon smartphones, computers, or tablets to access their daily news, as do over 50% of people in 15 surveyed nations, worldwide.[108] Furthermore, social media sites are addictive. Our lives have become an 'electronic text', where it becomes imperative to participate in online activities. We are disadvantaged if we don't—we will literally drop out of the conversation, a no–no in the era of social media.[109] A 2015 study tried to establish why people who try to leave social media platforms are largely incapable of doing so:

> For those who are curating a self, social media notifications work as a form of clickbait. Notifications light up the reward centres of the brain … The addictive aspect of this is similar to the effect of poker machines or smartphone games. [It is part of] the 'gamification of capitalism' [where] the machine always wins.[110]

If it is hard to control the content of the electronic media, it might be even harder to control our own desire for more of it. It is not surprising that some 41 States in the US have filed lawsuits against Facebook/Meta, claiming the platform deliberately employs deceptive strategies (such as the 'infinite scroll') to keep young people hooked.[111] Web sites are 'irresistible', and we have become obsessed.[112]

Turning Down the Thermostat

As was outlined earlier in this chapter and in Chapter 4, runaway climate change is one of the existential threats to life on this planet. The earth is warming, and the cause is anthropogenic. It is our doing. We are releasing too much greenhouse gas into the atmosphere—something which needs to be addressed urgently if temperatures on earth are to be held below 1.5 °C above the pre-industrial level. In fact, some 80% of presently known fossil fuel deposits must be kept in the ground if we are to keep to that target. That's US$20 trillion in corporate profits which cannot be realised.[113] What would you say about this if you were the CEO of, or a shareholder in, ExxonMobil, Shell, ConocoPhillips, or BP? You would fight like a Trojan to ensure you were not holding on to 'stranded assets'. It's your fortune against the planet's future. And

8 The Future: Confronting the Culprits 397

you don't want to lose. So, what can be done, and by whom, to address climate change?

Some excellent ideas have been put forward—impose a carbon tax, increase taxes on the rich (the richest 1% of the population, owning the majority of resources, contributes twice as much carbon pollution as the poorest 50%), go solar, shut down coal plants, and expose the fraud of the media's 'both-sidesism' which gives voice to anti-science. Place bans on ads by fuel companies. And, of course, protest, protest, protest![114] But it is also important to look for ultimate causes. In his book *Climate Change as Class War*, geography professor Matthew Huber explains how fossil fuel production is embedded in a system where a rich and powerful capitalist class exert a huge influence over governments, aimed at entrenching their profligate consumption and production patterns. They drive a system which affords them differential benefits—even if they are destroying the Earth to protect their own interests. A massive public struggle on a global level, he argues, will be necessary to bring about a **Green New Deal**. The Deal would include public ownership and control of all energy markets.[115] In the US the aim is to cut emissions to net zero by 2030 by replacing current polluting power sources with clean, renewable. It calls for the government to create millions of new jobs through investment in public services and infrastructure.[116] But there's a great deal to overcome—including 'fossil fuel hegemony', the ideology carefully cultivated by corporations and politicians that endless economic growth is essential for future prosperity and that it will require a fossil fuel industry to drive it.[117] Writer George Monbiot has gone further:

> There are just two actions needed to prevent catastrophic climate breakdown: leave fossil fuels in the ground and stop farming animals. But, thanks to the power of the two industries, both aims are officially unmentionable. Neither of them has featured in any of the declarations from the 26 climate summits concluded so far.[118]

The United Nations *is* trying, with some desperation, to bring countries to a consensus about the causes and impacts of climate change, and to identify the steps that must be taken to halt further greenhouse gas emissions. It has been calling for action for the past thirty years, yet the latest figures demonstrate that fossil fuel emissions are at an all-time high and will continue to grow.[119] The UN Framework Convention on Climate Change—which was ratified in 1994—aimed to stabilise atmospheric greenhouse gas levels. But high-polluting nations rejected mandatory cuts. Forward three years to Japan and the Kyoto Protocol. Some 42 nations promised to reduce their emissions by 5% from 1990s levels.[120] The US pulled out. Paris, in 2015, held promise. But agreements were not legally enforceable, and the flimsy 'pledge and review' mechanism has meant that promises could readily be broken. The Paris Agreement has been described as a 'fraud'.[121]

At the COP27 meeting in Egypt in 2022 it was revealed that 'nationally determined contributions' (NDCs) aimed at addressing climate change were grossly inadequate. Even if the agreements were implemented in full, emissions would *increase* by 10.6% by 2030, in place of the much-needed *decrease* of some 45% to stop global temperatures from rising. Climate depredation is already costing the poorer, more vulnerable, nations billions of dollars each year, but the richer nations have been reluctant to sign up to what is potentially a trillion dollar 'loss and damage' demand by the Global South.[122] A commitment to do so was made at the COP27, but the mechanisms remain undecided.[123] (There have been pledges from the Global North of some US$700 million. But this falls a little short of the US$400 billion that is estimated to be required each year.)[124] Just as importantly, the meeting failed to commit to a fossil fuel phase-out.[125]

Perhaps unsurprisingly, the follow-up COP28 meeting in Dubai 'played out like a dystopian satire'.[126] Host, Sultan Al Jaber began by claiming that science did not support an ending of fossil fuel extraction. Present at the meetings were 2,456 representatives of the oil and gas industries. The agri-food and agri-chemical industries were represented by over 100 lobbyists whose primary task was to prevent new climate measures from being enacted.[127] They told of their plans for 'regenerative agriculture'—supposedly sustainable but built on polluting agricultural inputs. The carbon offset lobby was highly vocal—despite the growing evidence that offsetting allows polluters to continue with business-as-usual.[128] And just like the year before at the COP27 climate activists faced tight security, harassment, intimidation, and surveillance. In Dubai they were forbidden from taking their protests to the street.[129] The meeting ended with 'The UAE consensus' which calls for the world to 'move away from' fossil fuels, much weaker wording than the 'phase out' that many climate scientists and environmentalist had hoped for. It was a 'limp and vague' response in a world of climate-related disasters.[130]

The polluting nation-states seem utterly incapable of shutting self-interested geopolitics outside the negotiating door.

> Some would argue that trying to get 197 countries to agree on anything is a fool's errand ... [But] the sticking point was – and still is – what the US government, and the business lobbies behind it, would find acceptable ... [W]hat has happened – straightforward veto power by the US of anything that would look like real action – remains with us today, and it doesn't help to pretend otherwise.[131]

It is estimated that since 1990 greenhouse gas emissions from the US alone have caused more than US$1.9 trillion in damages to other nations, mostly in the Global South.[132] So, why not try something radical? *A Debt for Climate* movement has sprung into life to demand compensation for damage wrought by climate change. George Monbiot explains.

> Rich nations owe a massive climate debt to poorer nations ... Yet they have no intention of paying for the loss and damage they have caused. Poor nations are deemed to owe massive financial debts to the rich nations, yet they cannot pay them without destroying their economies and their ecosystems. The proposal is simultaneously to cancel both the climate and the financial debts, liberating the money poorer nations need to take climate action.[133]

Brilliant. But for some mysterious reason the proposal does not seem to sit well with the nations of the Global North, which show on-going reluctance to compensate the South, and whose economies gain continuing financial benefits from the interest on outstanding loans.

There are other excellent initiatives going on behind the scenes—some 15 international organisations (including the OECD, the Asian Development Bank, and the European Bank for Reconstruction and Development) have committed to climate neutrality by reducing their emissions. Actions undertaken by these organisations include installing solar panels, upgrading insulation, fitting efficient cooling and heating systems, recycling waste, and so forth.[134] Then there are the organisations involved in global governance, in civil society, and in green investment (including the IPCC, UNEP, Green Climate Fund, 350.org, and Climate Leadership Group, among others). They are all pushing for strong action to reduce greenhouse gases via a move to renewables.

It is particularly encouraging to see major corporations committing to reductions in greenhouse gas emissions. But are they, really? What lurks in the background is that favourite of business—the greenwash. As was shown in Chapter 4, companies want to prove they are operating in environmentally sustainable ways, while ensuring profits are generated through business-as-usual activities. Greenwashing allows companies to claim they are helping the planet, while they pursue policies that result in the opposite. It is often very costly for firms to alter existing practices; it is much easier to hire some dubious PR firm to lie to the public on their behalf. Or, to use creative accounting to seemingly reduce their carbon footprint. Shell has employed 'accounting tricks' to overstate its emission reductions from rice farms in China, affording it 'a license to pollute at the expense of small farmers'.[135] Similarly, IKEA includes in its emissions reductions the solar panels it sells to customers. It also

> counts the carbon stored in some of its furniture. However, there is a slight snag here. For that stored carbon to make a difference to the climate, it will have to remain in IKEA's chairs and beds for centuries.

For some reason, IKEA products don't seem to last that long. Then there is the problem with phrases like 'net zero' and 'carbon neutral', 'fuel efficient' and 'earth-friendly'. These elastic, ambiguous, and nebulous terms have become invaluable friends of the greenwashers.[136]

The UN has finally exposed the scam of companies pledging net-zero emissions while expanding their fossil fuel dependency. It has called for greater regulation of business by governments setting 'firm rules'—especially for 'high-impact corporate emitters'[137] including fossil fuel, electricity, transport, and manufacturing companies. As things stand:

> Two-thirds of the [world's] largest listed businesses still lack a net zero pledge, and of the one-third that do, only a portion have committed to an independent voluntary initiative. The majority of privately-listed businesses and state-owned enterprises have no net zero target at all.[138]

There is also state-sponsored greenwashing, with governments allowing companies to use carbon offsets to make up for all their emission reductions—without any changes to actual carbon generation or usage.[139] According to Greta Thunberg 'we've been greenwashed out of our senses', while for UN Secretary-General Antonio Guterres, greenwashing is nothing but 'rank deception', a 'toxic cover-up' that could 'push our world over the climate cliff. The sham must end'.[140] But will it?

Chandra Bhushan—one of India's foremost public policy experts—says it is imperative to force the private sector to act:

> Many would argue that the Paris Agreement engages the private sector. But private-sector engagement ... is voluntary and doesn't add up to much. To push [the] private sector, we will have to make climate change a fiduciary duty of corporations and hold them accountable for polluting the climate.[141]

The latter is a very sensible option. But it would not sit well with the current batch of global neolibs who want government as far away from business as possible. And big business has the courts at its disposal—fossil fuel companies regularly use legal processes to block legislation that would curtail their activities. Thunberg again:

> Beyoncé was wrong. It is not girls who run the world. It is run by politicians, corporations and financial interests – mainly represented by white, privileged, middle-aged, straight ... men. And it turns out most of them are terribly ill suited for the job. This may not come as a big surprise. After all, the purpose of a company is not to save the world – it is to

make a profit. Or, rather, it is to make as much profit as it possibly can in order to keep shareholders and market interests happy.[142]

In her book *The Carbon Club*, Marian Wilkinson exposed a 'greenhouse mafia'—a network of energy CEOs, right-wing politicians, PR lobbyists, and climate change sceptics who have deliberately worked to delay action on climate change in Australia.[143] In the US the notoriously conservative Heritage Foundation has funded 'Project 2025'—a coalition of over 400 right-wing economists and policy 'experts' which has provided details of the legal and administrative tools to be used to dismantle that nation's climate policy, should the Republicans again come to power.[144] As we saw in Chapter 4, despite the stellar work being done by technologists to bring down the costs of renewable energy sources like wind, hydro, and solar, powerful networks exist on a global plane and have had remarkable success in frustrating attempts to confront the current, unsustainable, carbon trajectory.

Meanwhile, we are seeing growing protests worldwide from activists, young and old, aimed at exposing the hypocrisy of the polluters, of the greenwashers, and of the governments that harbour them. To alert the public to the severity of the climate crisis, demonstrators have organised a global climate 'strike'. Protesters in their thousands, banging drums and chanting, have marched through the streets of London, Paris, and New York in (largely) peaceful civil disobedience. The more hardened Extinction Rebellion activists have chained themselves to roadways, bridges, and cars to cause pandemonium and bring attention to the climate plight.[145]

Art has become a target. Just Stop Oil activists have hurled cakes at the wax figure of King Charles at Madame Tussauds in London. Cakes have landed on the enigmatically smiling face of the Mona Lisa at the Louvre.[146] In 2024 it was pumpkin soup, with protesters from Riposte Alimentaire ('food counterattack') demanding the right to healthy, sustainably produced, food.[147] Campaigners have glued themselves to Botticelli's 'Spring' at the Uffizi Museum in Florence and have tried (unsuccessfully) to do the same to Johannes Vermeer's 'Girl with a Pearl Earring' at the Mauritshuis Museum in The Hague. They have scribbled graffiti on Warhol's 'Campbell's Soup 1' at Australia's National

Gallery in Canberra. Gustav Klimt's 'Death and Life' was sprayed with an oily black liquid at the Leopold Museum in Vienna. Activists have thrown mash onto Claude Monet's 'Haystacks', in Potsdam (although a more deserving target might have been Van Gough's 'The Potato Eaters', in Amsterdam).[148]

Vandalism or valour? The major aim of groups like Extinction Rebellion is to obtain widespread media coverage with slogans including 'climate chaos = war + famine', 'just stop oil', 'coal kills', and 'one earth, one chance'.[149] Their straightforward call is for the end to further coal, oil, and gas exploration and production. Justifying their attacks on artworks, a spokesperson for an Italian protest group said 'if the climate collapses, the entire civilization as we know it collapses. There will be no more tourism, no museums, no art'. And, for one UK-based activist 'art and the public gallery is a contested space, it does not exist and cannot exist outside of the wider debate and arguments taking place in society … Ending new oil and gas is a demand that needs to be made both inside and outside the gallery'.[150]

Protests and civil disobedience remain key actions in the fight to limit the climate damage wrought by carbon polluters and their misguided allies in governments, PR firms, think tanks, and the media. Maybe we should take the lead from California and sue firms which have knowingly deceived the public about the long-term effects of fossil fuel production? The State of California has filed a suit against ExxonMobil, Shell, BP, ConocoPhillips, and Chevron for having misled the public about the risks of oil exploration and production. It wants to create an 'abatement fund', paid for by the oil companies, to address the future climate change-related damages resulting from their activities and their disinformation campaigns.[151] Legal challenges to fossil fuel policies—so-called climate accountability lawsuits—are on the rise throughout the US.

Earthly Preoccupations

In Chapter 4, the negative health and environmental impacts of plastics and pesticides were discussed, along with the unsustainable consumption patterns of people in the Global North. Resource depletion is a direct result of unsustainable production and consumption. Farming activity has caused major problems, with some 40% of the earth's surface having now been classified as degraded.[152] According to the Food and Agriculture Organisation, 10 million hectares of forests have been destroyed each year since 2015 to make way for commercial farming (cattle ranching and soy and palm oil production) and—to a lesser extent—subsistence agriculture.[153] The habitats of insect, plant, and animal species are being destroyed in the process, leading to dramatic reductions in biodiversity, and to species extinctions.

Trees stabilise the soil and reduce the soil's vulnerability to wind and water erosion. They also help to control flooding. Where large-scale deforestation has taken place—for example, in Haiti—there has been ecological devastation and hundreds of human lives have been lost.[154] And when you eat your next chocolate bar, give a thought to the rainforests of West Africa. In the last seventy years the planting of cocoa beans—largely for chocolate consumption in the Global North—has been implicated in the loss of some 65% of the forests in Ghana, and some 90% of the forest area of Côte d'Ivoire. Then there's the issue of forced child labour in these nations ...[155]

Two other processes associated with resource depletion are acidification and desertification. The former occurs when farmers soak the soil with ammonium-based fertilisers, acidifying the environment and reducing plant growth. The latter occurs as a result of deforestation and other vegetation removal. With no plant roots to keep it intact, soil washes away in rains and blows away in winds, taking valuable land out of production at the very time more land is needed to produce food. Prolonged and more severe droughts, resulting from climate change, exacerbate the problem. One billion hectares of land—about the size of China—has experienced desertification. An additional 200,000 hectares—an area larger than Senegal—are affected each year.[156] Food resources are depleted resulting in economic ruination, starvation, and the forced migration of hundreds of millions of people. For the UN:

> Land resources – soil, water, and biodiversity – provide the foundation for the wealth of our societies and economies ... Conserving, restoring,

and using our land resources sustainably is a global imperative: one that requires moving to a crisis footing.[157]

Scientists have identified many **tipping points** that would hasten disaster for life on earth. For example, planetary interconnections mean that if the Amazon rainforests continue to be logged at their present rate it will increase global warming, impacting negatively on coral reefs, on the Greenland ice sheet, on Antarctic ice sheets, on the Gulf Stream current, and on regions of permafrost.[158] The big danger is that the crossing of one tipping point could 'cascade', meaning other tipping points will be crossed and there will be no way back for the planet.[159]

It is now possible to calculate the extent to which resources are being exploited. An interesting, if not slightly controversial,[160] measure developed by scientists is that of humankind's **ecological footprint** upon the earth. The footprint is the amount of resources used in producing the goods people consume, along with the environment's ability to assimilate the associated wastes. In simple terms, it is 'the amount of the environment necessary to produce the goods and services necessary to support a particular lifestyle'.[161] It is a measure of how much a nation consumes compared to how much that nation has available for consumption. If the footprint exceeds a nation's biocapacity it is running a deficit. If biocapacity exceeds its footprint, it is running a surplus. And the results?

> Today, more than 80 percent of the world's population lives in countries that are running ecological deficits, using more resources than their ecosystems can generate.[162]

To support their lifestyles the US population is consuming the equivalent of 5.1 planet Earths each year. To support their lifestyles Australians consume 4.5 Earths, Russians 3.4, Germans 3.0, the British 2.6, and the Chinese 2.4. For the entire world population? It is 1.8 planets.[163] Given we only have one planet—Earth—upon which to live, what does all this mean? It means that we are polluting (largely producing carbon dioxide) in much larger quantities than our planet can absorb. Citizens of the planet are placing enormous pressure on the environment to absorb the wastes created by current lifestyles, and the environment can't take it. We are crapping in our own nest. We are 'borrowing nature' from generations to come—literally consuming their future.[164]

What is being done to address this unsustainable situation? Beginning with its 'Earth Summit' in Rio de Janeiro in 1992, the UN has been working with its member nations to develop an Agenda for Sustainable Development. It has produced a list of 17 **Sustainable Development Goals** (SDGs) including Affordable and Clean Energy, Reduced Inequality, Responsible Consumption and Production, and Life on Land. The latter, 15th Goal, is to 'protect, restore and promote sustainable use of terrestrial ecosystems, sustainably manage forests, combat desertification, and halt and reverse land degradation and halt biodiversity loss'.[165]

The UN reports yearly on progress in meeting its Goals. In 2022 it reported that the world's forested areas continue to shrink, the risk of species extinction is 'increasing at a rate unprecedented in human history' and that spending on biodiversity has been 'largely neglected'.[166] Oops. Despite 196 of the 198 members of the UN having signed its convention on biological diversity (the US and the Holy See are the pariahs)[167] these nations have done nowhere near enough to protect the planet. The UN has no mechanism to police their actions. The UN did hold a successful COP15 nature summit in 2022, having Parties agree to the Kunming-Montreal Global Biodiversity Framework. The Framework commits Parties to some 23 targets aimed at limiting extinctions including a so-called 30 × 30 target of protecting 30% of the world's terrestrial and marine (freshwater and ocean) habitats by 2030, with the ultimate goal of having people living in harmony with nature by 2050.[168] Restoring degraded ecosystems was also a primary goal, along with protecting the rights of indigenous peoples. Importantly, it endorses tougher regulations to reduce pesticide use and plastic pollution of the environment (without, unfortunately, providing targets). The production of non-biodegradable plastics can simply not continue.[169] But while the Framework represents a significant advancement it falls short in several ways. It aims to stem what is being called the 'sixth mass extinction event' by 2050. That will be some 28 years after the signing of the agreement.[170] This is too slow—'28 years of more species loss will leave the biodiversity of life depleted, undermining our environments, food systems, culture and way of life'.[171] The Framework ensures that only the largest corporations will need to disclose their impacts on the environment, letting most businesses off the hook. The document contains no statements about the need for changes in global diets, ignoring the finding that the consumption of beef will need to fall drastically (by up to some 90% in western nations) to limit climate change.[172] And, of course, it will be up to nations to pursue goals in the Framework—yet commitments are not binding and in past years governments have failed to meet targets.[173]

Not-for-profit organisations are taking the initiative where governments have failed. The Climate Action Fund is financing community-led activities which promote sustainable use of resources in places like Malaysia, Guatemala, Mexico, Peru, and Kenya. The Rainforest Alliance has developed programmes for farmers in over 40 countries which teach sustainable agricultural practices and provide alternatives to deforestation. Seed Programs International engages with women throughout Africa to promote ecologically-sound gardening practices which counteract desertification.[174] Scores of university centres around the world are working with local communities to address environmental degradation. Conservation groups, such as Amazon Watch, Conservation International, Rainforest Action Network, and Trees for the Future, assist communities and governments in reducing deforestation and restoring degraded lands.

Then there are the **radical protest groups**. Despite being labelled by the FBI as eco-terrorists, members of the Earth Liberation Front employ various disruptive tactics to damage the property of polluters to draw attention to global ecological destruction. The Elves, as they are known, have active cells in over 17 countries.[175] We should also recognise the force of direct public action. In 2019 trade union members walked off their jobs, doctors and nurses left hospitals, and students marched out of schools to join hundreds of millions of protestors worldwide urging governments to reduce global carbon emissions and prevent further global warming.[176] Such protests directly confront today's free-market authoritarianism, along with its unwanted siblings—ultranationalism and anti-environmentalism.[177] Action is occurring, even if the positive environmental benefits have been slow coming.

Our Daily Bread

There is something fundamentally wrong with our food and farming systems. As Chapters 3 and 4 disclosed, the much-vaunted technical breakthroughs that have boosted agricultural output have caused untold damage to the natural environment, poisoning soils and waterways while promoting an industrial form of farming dependent upon ecologically destructive monocultures and highly polluting Concentrated Animal Feeding Operations (CAFOs). The food system—including livestock production, cropping, land-use, and food-chain processing and transportation—generates some 25% of the world's yearly greenhouse gas production.[178] If we add in food waste, the agri-food sector's carbon emissions grow to some 31% of total greenhouse gases. But rather than look for immediate ways to reduce this footprint, agribusiness argues that the present system reflects the growing demand for animal protein and industrially-produced foods. Market forces must be obeyed.

Meat production has doubled in the past twenty years and is on steep upward curve. Global consumption of meat is currently 317 million tonnes per year. It is expected to reach some 517 million tons by 2050—a 63% increase over 25 years.[179] This means more CAFOs, more methane emissions, more animal waste, and the increased use of grain for animal feed, rather than human consumption (about half of the world's grain harvest is fed to animals).[180] Meat has the worst ecological footprint of any food, requiring greater amounts of energy, water, and land than any other form of food production, with animal production accounting for some 57% of emissions from the entire global food system.[181] As bioethics professor Peter Singer wryly noted 'we are gambling with the future of our planet for the sake of hamburgers'.[182]

To solve the land problem the Chinese have come up with a brilliant solution—CAFOs on steroids. The Chinese have a penchant for pigs and if land is in short supply why not build skyscrapers to house the animals? After all, 'vertical farming' (the production of vegetables in stacked shelves in controlled indoor environments) has been lauded as the future for agriculture.[183] In Ezhou in China's Hubei province two 'apartment buildings', some 26 stories high, are being constructed to grow and slaughter 1.2 million pigs each year—China's very own 'porkopolis'.[184] We are told that it will be an 'efficient', 'biosecure', and 'sustainable' production system. But for the pigs there's no view of the countryside, and they can't ride the lifts to visit their sisters (they are all sows) on other levels—they are trapped on one floor for their entire lives. To enhance biosecurity, workers will only be allowed to leave the site once per week. Yet, scientists in the west are already pointing to the likely spread of infectious diseases, and to further negative impacts on the climate.[185] The high-rise animal factories are not an isolated feature on the Chinese landscape. Six have already been erected in the Guangxi region, and thirteen in the Sichuan province.[186] Homer Simpson would have a field day—'porkchops and bacon, my two favourite animals'.

Is anything being done to confront factory farm developments such as these? While Chinese citizens are not taking to the streets in protest, others are. There is much more at stake than the welfare of animals and climatic impacts. Human health is also at stake. People living in rural communities close to CAFOs are expected to get used to the smell of rotten egg gas emanating from pig dung. And, if they drink water from local sources, it is highly likely they are consuming pathogens, heavy metals, and antibiotics along with the H_2O. If they are wheezing, rubbing their eyes, continually blowing their noses, displaying increased blood pressure, and suffering mental stress, no one should be surprised.[187] And it is a good idea to use the clothes drier for their whites and undies as a fine 'mist of manure' descends from heaven upon an unsuspecting clothesline.[188] Protests occur throughout the world, but concerns are rarely recognised and acted upon. Some suggest getting in early—as soon as a CAFO is mooted, bring pressure on governments to stop the development (of course, you are likely to be protesting to the very government that approved the application).

Something more radical is needed to save the planet and this is where alternatives to industrial agriculture are of increasing significance. **Regenerative agriculture** (also called 'climate smart agriculture') is a form of farming which uses crop rotation, cover crops, and no-till methods, to capture carbon. Companies such as McDonald's, Pepsico, Nestle, and General Mills are pumping billions of dollars to make regenerative agriculture the start of their food production chains. But altering farming methods to capture carbon—as a means of offsetting their overall carbon emissions—does nothing to reduce those emissions along the rest of their supply chains. Much of the effort of the companies promoting regenerative agriculture is aimed at 'sustainable intensification', including the use of genetically engineered crops.[189] At present regenerative agriculture looks a lot like another corporate greenwash.[190] **Organic farming** (or biological farming) is a system of production that eschews manufactured fertilisers and pesticides relying, instead, upon the use of compost, green manure, and other natural soil-enhancing processes such as crop rotation, along with companion planting to control insects. Organic farming methods are practised in 187 nations. There are over 72 million hectares of agricultural land managed by over 3 million farmers. Importantly, there is strong demand for organic products from consumers wary of the health-compromising effects of agro-chemicals.[191] The global organic food market is growing by 12% each year and is expected to reach some US$497.3 billion by 2030.[192] The International Federation of Organic Agriculture Movements (IFOAM) assists conventional farmers to convert to organics. It spreads word about the need for farmers to become environmentally sustainable, and lobbies governments to enact laws conducive to the expansion of organic farming methods.[193]

Agroecology is another realistic alternative to Big Ag. Defined as 'the science of applying ecological concepts and principles to the design and management of food systems',[194] agroecology confronts the agribusiness 'model' of maximising production at the expense of workers, the environment, the climate, and cultures. Its strongest advocate is the peasant-based organisation **La Via Campesina**. Formed in 1993, La Via Campesina is a social movement which brings together peasant farmers, small and medium-sized farmers, indigenous peoples, fishers, migrant farmworkers, and others, to advance peasant-driven agroecology. It comprises over 180 local and national organisations in over 80 nations, representing some 200 million small-scale food producers.[195] Its claims are that peasant farming not only feeds over half the world's population, but that it does so by cooling the planet (employing methods that capture, rather than release, carbon).[196] And that it is a more energy-efficient way of producing food.[197] Women are the world's main food producers (growing and supplying some 70% of all food, globally) and the movement pays particular attention to women's rights, including gender equality.[198]

For La Via Campesina, agroecology is viewed as the only alternative farming system that can reduce hunger, malnutrition, poverty, pollution, and global warming.[199] The organisation calls for the dismantling of corporate agribusiness, the disbanding of industrial-scale farming, and the implementation of policies and laws that foster sustainable agricultural practices and the local consumption of foods.[200] Its focus is upon 'food sovereignty'—the principle that people are entitled to healthy and culturally-appropriate foods produced in sustainable ways. Those producing, distributing, and consuming food are placed at the centre of the food system, not on the margins as is the case for corporate, neoliberal, global food markets.[201] La Via Campesina can claim success on a number of fronts—being the strong and influential voice of diverse and otherwise marginalised farmers, having 'food sovereignty' written into the constitutions of many nation-states (including Ecuador, Venezuela, Mali, Senegal, and Egypt), and persuading the UN to pass a declaration that its member States 'shall respect, protect and fulfil the rights of peasants and other people working in rural areas'.[202]

There are many other groups seeking alternatives to our unsustainable corporate agri-food system. **GRAIN international** has informed social movements and NGOs around the world about agribusiness and its discontents. It has revealed the characteristics of today's 'climate-killing food system' and has proposed solutions, including challenging corporate control of the food chain, and promoting food sovereignty. It champions bio-diverse small farms, and community-controlled food systems, along with exposing 'land grabbing' throughout the world.[203]

The National Resources Defense Council (NRDC) has more than 3 million members worldwide, many of whom are activists. They work with scientists, legal teams, and policy experts to advocate for the decrease of chemicals in food and the environment, reduction in food waste, and more sustainable farming systems. It fights the oil and gas companies responsible for increasing CO_2 emissions.[204] **Greenpeace**, mentioned earlier, is one of more than 20 global not-for-profit organisations seeking to tackle climate change and expose the power plays of corporate agribusiness.

In relation to food quality and supply, agribusiness corporations use direct lobbying of politicians and government officials to ensure that any food-related legislation does not affect profits. Powerful corporations have spent billions of dollars fighting the introduction of 'traffic light' food labelling and opposing taxes on soft drinks and unhealthy (junk) food products.[205] They have lobbied state politicians to pass laws that prevent local governments legislating against them—a tactic called 'pre-emption'.[206] They have also spent money 'individualising' the obesity issue, deflecting criticisms that the fast-food companies have been responsible for creating, and promoting, obesogenic diets.

But there is ample evidence that opposition to unhealthy foods is growing. Groups that lobby governments for greater control and regulation of the food industry have sprung up around the globe, largely in response to the surge in diet-related Type 2 diabetes. In 2020 in the state of Oaxaca, Mexicans blocked roads to prevent trucks delivering ultra-processed foods and drinks to retail outlets. Later, the Oaxaca parliament banned the sale of these products to minors. Mexico's Federal Senate then got into the act, banning junk foods in school meals and preventing their sale near school grounds. More than 50 jurisdictions in Mexico now tax soda pop (curbing people's enthusiasm for sugary drinks, while raising funds for public health campaigns).[207] The Republic of South Korea has developed a National Food Plan to ensure its people have access to healthy diets (including removing dog meat from the menu).[208] At the global level, representatives of over 100 nations met in Rome in 2021 to discuss ways they could work to transform their food systems to meet the UN Sustainable Development Goals by 2030,[209] while at the local level many activist groups have developed 'alternative food plans' to counter the influence of the food corporations. An example, here, is that of the Australian Food Sovereignty Alliance. Following public forums and interviews with over 600 people, the Alliance has developed a detailed, 83-page 'People's Food Plan' which aims to build a fair and just food system through small-scale businesses and new social enterprises. Nutrient recycling, re-localisation of food production and consumption, and serious waste reduction are some of the underlying principles.[210] We should all take heed of Black Eyed Peas singer Will.i.am's profound pronouncement:

Waste isn't waste until it is wasted.[211]

Numerous 'community food system plans' have been developed throughout the world as a means of bringing consumers closer to producers and helping ensure healthy, nutritious, and locally-sourced foods are widely available to community members. In the US there is a 'food-is-medicine' movement that promotes healthy eating and exposes the impact of food intake on health.[212] There are calls to tax the advertising of ultra-processed foods and to curb the power and influence of the corporations responsible for their manufacture.[213] Meanwhile, the 'nose-to-tail' (!!!) New Nordic movement is persuading consumers to abandon the supermarkets and helping to transform Scandinavia 'from a land of herring cured in lye' to the 'gastronomic centre of the world'.[214] Move aside Paris.

We should not forget the importance of the thousands of **farmers' markets** in most large cities that provide an alternative to the meats, fruits, and vegetables on supermarket shelves. In selling food directly to customers, farmers can capture revenue that would otherwise go to wholesalers and retailers. Consumers gain by having locally-sourced, fresher, foods (foods that spend less time in transit) available to them. The saving in energy that would normally have been used in transporting, storing, processing, and refrigerating foods is a bonus for the environment. Other benefits are less tangible but include the fostering and maintenance of local social ties and supporting a community of small farmers. My research with colleagues has demonstrated that in times of natural disasters, such as flooding, short food chains (supplying locally produced foods) are more resilient than long food chains (supplying foods sourced at a great distance and sold via supermarkets).[215] COVID-19 is seen to have exposed many problems with the global food system, not the least of which is its lack of resilience. With little health cover, and working in exploitative conditions, migrant farm workers have been particularly vulnerable to COVID-19 which has compromised their well-being while also reducing the volume of food destined for the marketplace.[216]

Community-supported agriculture is another example of a short food chain. Here, farmers box a variety of seasonal foods which are then delivered to consumers on a weekly or bi-weekly basis. Small farmers benefit from a regular and reliable income—allowing them to stay on the land; consumers receive fresh, (mostly) high-quality produce, on a regular basis. Money circulates in the district, helping to build the regional economy.

Another group challenging the corporate food system is the **Slow Food movement**. Appropriately bearing a snail logo, the movement is opposed to everything 'fast' about modern life. In Bra, northern Italy in 1986, a group of friends—food journalists and philosophers among them—were appalled with the opening of a McDonald's restaurant close to the famous Spanish Steps in Rome (the golden arches are still there, by the way). A national petition was launched and there were peaceful demonstrations at the site. Three years later Carlo Petrini and Folco Portinari developed a manifesto for the Slow Food movement. It counteracts the hectic modern life where food is simply fuel and little is known, understood, or appreciated about local cultures and traditions. 'Slow Food envisions a world in which all people can access and enjoy food that is good for them, good for those who grow it and good for the planet'.[217] All Slow Fooders are members of a 'convivium' or local chapter. There are now over 1,500 Slow Food convivia, globally, which organise events to promote the movement's principles—GOOD (quality foods that are flavoursome and healthy), CLEAN (free of chemicals and produced in sustainable ways), and FAIR (reasonably priced food for consumers, and fair pay for producers).[218]

Unfortunately, despite their ability to confront Big Ag and Big Food (and the Big Finance which runs both)[219] many of these positive initiatives are either below the radar of time-poor city-dwelling consumers, or are considered quaint and fanciful in a world dominated by corporate agribusiness and supermarkets. Perhaps we will eventually find salvation in the industrial-produced plant-based products that 'bleed' like meat and look and taste like the real thing. Or maybe we'll be filling our plates with healthy helpings of insects and fungi?[220]

Capital Ideas

Modern economics is replete with fallacies—as described in Chapter 2. These include the myths of perfect competition, the 'rational' actor, comparative advantage, along with free trade's supposed benefits for all. It is sold as a 'science'—one that uses sophisticated formulae to help us understand the workings of the marketplace and thereby control the economy's direction. Only to find out—as we saw in the GFC of 2008—that it has very little predictive power and even less ability to find socially-beneficial solutions to market mayhem. Its assumption that capitalism is underpinned by a stable, self-equilibrating, economy is laughable, given the turbulence of recessions and depressions. Its economic modelling is faulty, and it is based upon a language of deception. In his book *Econobabble: How to Decode Political Spin and Economic Nonsense*, Richard Denniss highlights the ways 'the market' has become reified—we forget that it is a human creation, not some monumental force controlling us. For Denniss

> The high priests of econobabble often tell us that 'the markets', like the gods of cultures past, can be angry. They can be vengeful. And they can punish nonbelievers ... [Yet] it is absurd to suggest [markets] have 'feelings', 'needs', or 'demands'.[221]

We need to look at who gains advantage from treating 'the market' as some overwhelming, controlling, force that must be obeyed:

> regardless of their form, markets never have feelings. Ever. Rich people, on the other hand, do have feelings. And rich people who own billions of dollars' worth of shares in a company often have strong feelings. They have feelings about government policies, and they have feelings about tax rates.[222]

It is they, and friendly economists in business, government, and right-wing think tanks, who use 'the market' as a battering ram to force a gullible public to agree to tax cuts for the wealthy at the same time as approving reductions in spending on public services for the poor.

Can orthodox economics be salvaged? Hardly. Its purpose is to justify the present system of 'rational irrationality' which lies at the heart of capitalism.[223] While we have been lured into believing that free-market capitalism provides the best economic outcomes for society, we know, instead, that neoliberal globalisation is producing billionaires while impoverishing large sections of the world's population. Its theories justify greed while lamenting the average worker's ability to be 'entrepreneurial'—it is poor training, or laziness, or both that leads to deteriorating life conditions for workers. Orthodox economics is an ideology and practice creating and justifying continued economic and social inequality.

What Can Be Done?

Fortunately, there is an alternative to orthodox economics. Heterodox economics exists outside the mainstream, with **critical political economy** one of its most important branches. Building upon concepts and theories derived largely from Marx, Keynes, post-Keynesians, and institutional economics, critical political economists do not see the economy, society, and politics as separate entities. The three are interwoven. While this makes analysis complex, it provides a richness that allows us to see

> What is happening? Why? Who gains; who loses? Does it matter? If so, what can be done about it, and by whom?[224]

When these questions are asked about important human and planetary phenomena—economic production, social reproduction, environmental change, dietary intake, and so forth—it is possible to discern a common pattern. In a system characterised by the fundamental social division between those owning and controlling resources, and those who don't, there is persistent economic and social antagonism. As discussed in Chapter 2, when workers—those creating the goods and services necessary for life—have little or no say over what is produced, how it is produced, and where it goes, they are simply cogs in a machine controlled by capitalists. And capitalists place the need to generate profit over human need. The state can control and regulate them to an extent but, ultimately, the state trusts in capitalists to drive the economy forward and refrains from hindering 'progress'. Again, as we saw in Chapter 2, those with capital will do their utmost to avoid paying for the full costs of production. They don't like paying for the 'externalities' generated by their operations. And they don't like paying taxes or increasing workers' wages—both affect their bottom line and reduce the income they and their shareholders receive. What this adds up to is constant struggles between capital and labour, increased pollution, resource depletion, environmental damage, runaway climate change—all being overseen by a compliant state whose police, military, and legal system intervene to keep the wheels of an unsustainable system of production turning. Critical political economists view these problems as systemic. The system must change for those problems to be overcome. To the question 'What can be done about it, and by whom?' the answer is clear. Those who are oppressed, who face discrimination, who have their land 'grabbed', and who are becoming impoverished in the workplace, need to mobilise to challenge the hegemony and power of the ruling classes that are responsible for their subjugation. And, because capitalism is a global system, it is crucial that those oppressed by that system organise themselves internationally.

It is easy to see why the ideas embedded in political economy would fall foul of the rich and powerful and their allies. It is also easy to understand why critical political economy remains largely marginalised in academia, in government, and in business; it does not conform to—indeed, diametrically opposes—present structures of economic ownership and control, including the power of transnational corporations. It is taught in many universities throughout the world but suffers the great misfortune of being a little unpopular with the captains of industry and their friends in government. That said, political economists are contributing in creative and positive ways to many social movements, including feminism, environmentalism, animal welfare, and indigenous land rights, helping groups in their struggles to find social justice.[225]

There are also independent organisations challenging orthodox economics. The **New Economics Foundation** (NEF) in the UK has developed practical measures to foster co-production (cooperative workplaces eliminating the boss/worker dichotomy) and ethical investment, and to alter ownership of resources. It recommends a **wealth tax** to raise government revenue and to address the wealth inequalities entrenched in society. NEF has also produced manifestos for a polity that will recognise environmental limits. One, mentioned earlier, is A Green New Deal which places government at the centre of investments aimed simultaneously at cutting carbon emissions and boosting employment.[226] In the US, one legacy of the GFC has been the formation of workers' self-directed enterprises (WSDEs). The workers become their own boards of directors deciding what to produce, where and how—along with how income is distributed.[227] According to political economist Richard Wolf, movements such as Occupy Wall Street are directly targeting capitalism as the culprit in economic chaos and social inequality, with 'public opinion polls show[ing] widespread antipathy toward "capitalism" and equally remarkable positive attitudes toward "socialism"'.[228] While overwhelmed by the industry-funded think tanks that promote neoliberalism, the small independent think tanks provide a range of alternative and compelling ways of conceptualising and confronting the excesses of capitalism. Oxfam, for example, has provided an eloquently simple three stage means of undermining corporate power—revitalise the state, regulate corporations, and reinvent business so competition is genuine, and shareholder interests are secondary to societal well-being.[229]

Universities, as focal sites where knowledge is generated and disseminated, have a central role to play in educating students and the general public about the causes of many of the problems faced by the world. Today, subject to the destructive market-driven forces of neoliberalism, and experiencing assorted 'culture wars' aimed at proving the superiority of western social values over competing ideas, academic freedoms are often curtailed. The pursuit of factual evidence, the application of critical reasoning, and the presence of healthy debate are readily compromised in such environments. The generation of reliable knowledge—about our society, economy, climate, and so forth—is often a casualty. Academics have a duty to explain the existential threats faced by humanity and to show how they can be addressed. Public education was originally established, we should remember, to foster progressive social change.[230]

Fortunately, a number of critical thinkers are developing practical strategies for economic transformation. Yanis Varoufakis, a former Greek finance minister and heterodox economist, believes we are living in a world of 'technofeudalism'. It is a world where power resides with the 'Lords'—those controlling digital platforms. 'Cloud capitalism' thrives and has undermined the two pillars of traditional capitalism, those of markets and profits. He proposes that the digital companies should be democratised and run by 'employee-shareholders'. He demands control of central banks, argues for a universal basic income, along with the creation of a Bill of Digital Rights—to protect citizens in their online activities.[231] Other radical options can be found in The **Real Utopias Project** initiated by the late Eric Olin Wright at the University of Wisconsin-Madison. In a series of workshops, and through the publication of books, radical social alternatives have been canvassed—including universal basic incomes (to replace social welfare), a coupon-based form of 'market socialism', deepening democracy through new forms of participation, new means of redistributing resources such as housing and education, and new institutions to promote gender egalitarianism.[232]

Creating a **degrowth (steady state) economy**, or a **circular economy** which eliminates waste, are other ideas being canvassed by heterodox economists. Both options would mean living a simpler life—producing less and consuming less—but saving the planet.[233] Some excellent ideas are provided by academic Mark Diesendorf and science writer Rod Taylor in their book *The Path to a Sustainable Civilization* and include: Reducing the political influence of corporations; transitioning from fossil fuels; attacking rampant consumerism; and ending neocolonialism.[234] Ecologists believe that, given our current trajectory, degrowth is 'inevitable'.[235] In her book **Doughnut Economics** Oxford University economist Kate Raworth proposes that human society must live within the outer and inner boundaries of a hypothetical doughnut. The breaching of an ecological ceiling on its outer rim will be disastrous, while not providing a strong social foundation (food, water, energy, health, housing, and so forth) as its inner rim, will result in increased poverty, inequality, and social malaise. A much more regenerative and distributive economic system must be built to ensure the needs of people are met—but without overshooting ecological boundaries.[236] The book promotes sustainable development while challenging the system of capitalist production and distribution.

There is also a plethora of **left-leaning journals** analysing and debating alternatives to capitalism and the best ways that can be achieved. They include *Capital and Class, Critical Sociology, Historical Materialism, Journal of Political Ecology, Marxism Today, Monthly Review, New Left Review, Radical Philosophy, Rethinking Marxism,* and *Theory, Culture and Society.* Radical newspapers, magazines, and websites are also important sources of information (there are 90 such outlets in the UK alone).[237] Publishers of radical books include *Verso, Monthly Review, Haymarket Books,* and *Pluto Press.* Palgrave Macmillan's website emphasises it is 'the natural home for cutting-edge, provocative and definitive content that strives to interpret and challenge the society we live in'.[238]

Dangling Democracy

And the future of democracy? On 6 January 2021 tens of thousands of US citizens, believing Trump was right in claiming he'd won the 2020 federal election—only to have it 'stolen'—protested at the Capitol building in Washington DC to prevent Congress from certifying Joe Biden as the 46th President of the United States. Over 1,000 people were arrested.[239] Trump's tweet in the early hours of the morning was designed to inflame his followers—including members of the Proud Boys, the Oath Keepers, and others with right-wing extremist leanings. It was modern-day vigilantism. Members of these groups were later charged with sedition and Trump, himself, was accused by the US House of Representatives panel investigating the break-in, of obstruction and insurrection in igniting the riot. (Trump became a convicted felon in May 2024, found guilty on 34 counts of falsifying business records.)[240]

Election-loss-denial made its way into South America in 2023 with right-wing nationalist President of Brazil, Jair Bolsonaro, declaring that he was the victim of electoral fraud. His followers took to the streets, blocking roads, and demanding military intervention to stop left-wing Luiz Inácio Lula da Silva from being sworn in as President. Bolsonaro supporters posted details, on Telegram channels, giving details of when and where 'liberty caravans' would pick up would-be protestors and carry them to the capital, Brasilia. It was there where these so-called freedom fighters subsequently vandalised the nation's Congress, Supreme Court, and presidential palace.[241] Just as with the Capitol attacks in the US, powerful right-wing organisations used the pretext of an 'unfair' election to attack public institutions. Hardly democracy at work. It was fuelled, as *New York Times* journalist Jack Nicas wrote, by an 'insidious, deeply rooted threat: mass delusion',[242] with social media blamed for provoking much of the turmoil.[243]

Is democracy on the ropes? It has been said that

> democracy relies upon the public agreeing on a body of reliable knowledge and information. Two aspects of shared knowledge are particularly important: First, confidence in the processes by which power is distributed, foremost among them the electoral process. Second, reliable information about the evidence in support of different policy options … [In the US] both aspects have been eroded by widespread disinformation and misinformation.[244]

Every year the V-Dem Institute in Gothenburg, Sweden, publishes a report on democracy. Its latest report shows that dictatorships are becoming more prevalent. Approximately 70% of the world's population—some 5.4 billion people—live under dictatorships. This is up from 49% in 2011[245] Autocratisation (or democratic backsliding) is on the rise globally, characterised by growing inequalities, social tensions, populist politics, and refusal—in the case of Trump and Bolsonaro—to admit defeat and allow for a smooth transition of power.[246] Anti-pluralist parties are driving autocratisation in nations such as Brazil, Hungry, India, Serbia, Turkey, and Poland, with governments regularly using misinformation and disinformation to shape their domestic and foreign agendas.[247] In the US, Trump's anti-democratic core belief has been that of White Supremacy which is 'now informally the ruling ideology of the Republican Party'.[248] For Barbara Walter, author of *How Civil Wars Start*,

> Where is the United States today? We are a factionalized anocracy [a degenerating democracy] that is quickly approaching the open insurgency stage, which means we are closer to civil war than any of us would like to believe.[249]

She blames social media for democratic decay. Social media firms want people to use their platforms; whether or not those online get truthful content is largely immaterial to them. And, as seen in Chapter 1, the algorithms that are employed drive users to identify extreme content as normal—they reinforce prejudices. Indeed,

> those who speak to the algorithm achieve the widest circulation of their ideas. This is akin to large-scale social engineering … Algorithmic audiencing has a material effect on public discourse [driving] the proliferation of harmful comment.[250]

The outcome is increasing 'ethnic, social, religious and geographic divisions' that create conditions for social foment, particularly white violence against coloured minorities.[251] Neoliberalism has promoted both financialisation (helping those at the top end of town) along with deindustrialisation (affecting millions of workers and helping to promote reactionary political options as a way forward).[252] Fascism sits calmly on the side, biding its time. According to sociologist Phil McMichael neoliberalism has mutated into 'neo-illiberalism' where the state fosters and accommodates 'billionaire classes across the world, generating sociopolitical discontent as a seedbed of national fascisms'.[253] We are moving towards 'vigilantism' where supremacist political ideologies create ethnoracial tensions in societies, leading to the normalising of fascist ideals and hostilities.[254] This is a huge threat to democracy.

Of course, not everyone believes in the virtues of democracy—rule by the people. That great defender of slavery and doubter of the intellectual abilities of women, Aristotle, did not want the poor and uneducated anywhere near a ballot box. He favoured 'the rule by the best over the rest', believing that elite rule would produce optimal outcomes for society.[255] Plato agreed—imagine a world in which an ignoramus had the same voting rights as a scholar? In his book *Leviathan*, Enlightenment philosopher Thomas Hobbes was less than enlightened when he vehemently supported absolute sovereignty of the monarchy, rather than democratic rule.[256] Swiss-born philosopher Jean-Jacques Rousseau—who made the insightful observation that people 'will never be free until the last king is strangled with the entrails of the last priest'—believed representative democracy to be a sham. Elected representatives were fallible human beings who could never be trusted to do the bidding for their supporters—if you are represented by another, you are no longer a truly 'free' citizen.[257]

Similarly, for Marx, bourgeois democracy was a charade—it was nothing more than government-by-the-ruling-class. A democratic society could only be achieved by the destruction of classes. After revolution there would be a 'dictatorship of the proletariat'—an interval called 'socialism'. Socialism would then be replaced by communism, and the state would 'wither away' allowing citizens of all nations to be truly liberated.[258] (Unfortunately for Marx, the form of government that emerged from the revolution in Russia prohibited any opposition, strengthened the state bureaucracy and military, and controlled personal and public life. It was a form of transitional 'socialism' that was totalitarian, ruled—as we saw in Chapter 5—by the brutal dictator Stalin.) In more recent times political commentator Noam Chomsky has argued that, for the US, there is a strong correlation between people's wealth and their political influence, to such an extent that some 70% of the nation's people—the lower-middle income earners and the poor—are effectively disenfranchised: They have no influence in policy-making at all.[259]

Then there are the modern 'charges' against democracy—it is characterised by political instability, by frequent elections that promote short-termism in decision-making, by pathways to power lined with corruption, by manipulation of voters via political and media propaganda, and so on. But many people would choose to live in a world of capitalist excesses rather than contemplate a world of totalitarian kleptocracy. Should democracy be saved?

Voters are well aware of its supposed desirable features. It encourages citizen participation in government, affords minorities a degree of protection under the law, makes office holders (largely) accountable to the people, allows for political change via regular elections, embraces civil liberties including freedom of association and expression, and—in theory at least—has a court system independent of government.

Many socialist movements and parties throughout the world embrace these features of democracy—and have misgivings about a future 'one party' state that could readily become authoritarian and bureaucratic. Most importantly, they also recognise the need for an alternative, radical, approach to economic management—one endorsing public ownership of the means of production, one which focuses upon cooperation rather than competition, one built upon sustainability rather than wanton environmental destruction, one which empowers minorities rather than marginalising them, and one built upon cooperative planning rather than economic chaos. A recent count indicates that there are over 50 nations with political parties, often with strong links to trade unions and the labour movement, dedicated to the pursuit of **democratic socialism**.[260] In his book *A Brief History of Equality*, political economist Thomas Piketty discusses the possibility of creating

> a democratic and federal socialism, decentralized and participatory, ecological and multicultural, based on the extension of the welfare state and progressive taxation, power-sharing in business enterprises, post-colonial reparations, the battle against discrimination, [and including] educational equality ... carbon [reduction], the gradual decommodification of the economy, guaranteed employment and an inheritance for all, the drastic reduction of monetary inequalities, and finally, an electoral and media system that cannot be controlled by money.[261]

That's a great list of progressive options. Of course, it still doesn't answer the burning question of whether capitalism can be reformed from within. Socialists have forever been torn between the options of reform or revolution as the key to progressive social change. Perhaps a revolution will be required to defeat those leading our planet towards catastrophe. At the present time I can't seem to identify a social or political movement capable of revolution on a global scale. (There *is* a strong global movement against climate change, but it's largely uncoordinated and its general intentions are not to destroy the state through revolution.) Still, we should not give up. As one of my former students wrote in her evaluation of my undergraduate sociology course:

> One thing I've learned this semester is that if we want to create a better world it is super important to build our future on the ideas of Karl Marx and The Marx Brothers.

Largely correct—on both counts.

Notes

1. Dassanayake, D. (2014) 'It will EAT us' Earth and Milky Way galaxy will be SWALLOWED by our galactic neighbour, https://www.express.co.uk/news/nature/512868/End-of-the-world-Earth-Milky-Way-Andromeda.
2. Watts, J. (2023) 'Supercontinent' could make Earth uninhabitable in 250m years, study predicts, https://www.theguardian.com/science/2023/sep/25/supercontinent-could-make-earth-uninhabitable-in-250m-years-study-predicts.
3. Walsh, B. (2019) *End Times: A Brief Guide to the End of the World*, Seven Dials, Great Britain, p. 6.
4. Longrich, N. (2020) Will humans go extinct? For all the existential threats, we'll likely be here for a very long time, https://singularityhub.com/2020/05/08/will-humans-go-extinct-for-all-the-existential-threats-well-likely-be-here-for-a-very-long-time/.
5. See Torres, E. (2017) It's the end of the world as we know it: Scientists in many disciplines see apocalypse, soon, https://www.salon.com/2017/04/30/its-the-end-of-the-world-and-we-know-it-scientists-in-many-disciplines-see-apocalypse-soon/.
6. See Smith, C. (2021) Climate Cassandra Guy McPherson makes a case that scientists, IPCC, and media underplay the crisis, https://www.straight.com/news/climate-cassandra-guy-mcpherson-makes-a-case-that-scientists-ipcc-and-media-underplay-crisis.
7. ScaleClimateAction. (2023) Fish rain: The science behind fish falling from the sky, https://scaleclimateaction.org/guides/fish-rain-the-science-behind-fish-falling-from-the-sky/.
8. Cole, R. (2022) 10 failed Doomsday predictions, https://www.britannica.com/list/6-fictional-languages-you-can-really-learn; Wikipedia. (2022) List of dates predicted for apocalyptic events, https://en.wikipedia.org/wiki/List_of_dates_predicted_for_apocalyptic_events; Alexander, R. (2015) 10 embarrassing mistakes

historical figures want you to forget, https://listverse.com/2015/03/28/10-embarrassing-mistakes-historical-figures-want-you-to-forget/.
9. Events History. (2022) What happened in history year 1975, http://www.eventshistory.com/date/1975/.
10. Wikipedia, List of dates predicted for apocalyptic events.
11. Morris, I. (2019) End of the world: Biblical prophecy predicts Rapture in 2019, https://www.mirror.co.uk/science/end-world-biblical-prophecy-predicts-13799960.
12. James, G. (2011) 14 fools who predicted the end of the world, https://www.cbsnews.com/media/14-fools-who-predicted-the-end-of-the-world/.
13. Cole, 10 failed Doomsday predictions; Wikipedia. (2022) Chen Tao (UFO religion), https://en.wikipedia.org/wiki/Chen_Tao_(UFO_religion).
14. Catholic Online. (2016) 'I HAVE GIVEN YOU FULL WARNING.' Dark days—Did Pope Francis just predict the END OF THE WORLD? https://www.catholic.org/news/hf/faith/story.php?id=65625.
15. English, N. (2020) What are the chances of an asteroid hitting Earth? https://www.underluckystars.com/blog/what-are-the-chances-of-an-asteroid-hitting-earth.
16. Tingay, S. (2022) Astronomers have detected another 'planet killer' asteroid. Could we miss one coming our way? https://www.theguardian.com/science/2022/nov/01/huge-planet-killer-asteroid-discovered-and-its-heading-our-way.
17. Lloyd, J. (2022) What is the chance of an asteroid hitting Earth? https://www.sciencefocus.com/space/what-is-the-chance-of-an-asteroid-hitting-earth/.
18. Williams, A. (2020) Nasa confirms DART impact changed asteroid's motion in space, https://www.electronicsweekly.com/news/nasa-confirms-dart-impact-changed-asteroids-motion-in-space-2022-10/.
19. Walsh, *End Times*, p. 182.
20. Kennedy, J. (2023) *Pathogenesis: How Germs Made History*, Transworld Publishers, London.

21. Hemmings, J. (2019) Wiped Out up to 50 Million, Spanish Flu Carried to Europe by US Troops Heading for the Trenches of WWI, https://www.warhistoryonline.com/instant-articles/wwi-soldiers-buried-in-denmark.html.
22. HIV Talk. (2022) How Many People Have Died From HIV, https://www.hivtalk.net/how-many-people-have-died-from-hiv/.
23. Wikipedia. (2024) COVID-19 pandemic, https://simple.wikipedia.org/wiki/COVID-19_pandemic.
24. Bale, R. (2019) Pangolin scale medicines no longer covered by Chinese insurance, https://www.nationalgeographic.com/animals/article/pangolin-traditional-medicine-not-covered-insurance.
25. Davidson, S. (2022) Why do people want pangolin scales? https://wildanswers.com/people-want-pangolin-scales-060ff/.
26. Bale, R. (2020) Trafficked pangolins can carry coronaviruses closely related to pandemic strain, https://www.nationalgeographic.com/animals/article/pangolins-coronavirus-covid-possibility.
27. Sample, I. (2023) New data links Covid-19's origins to raccoon dogs at Wuhan market, https://www.theguardian.com/society/2023/mar/17/covid-19-origins-raccoon-dogs-wuhan-market-data.
28. WebMD. (2022) Coronavirus history, https://www.webmd.com/lung/coronavirus-history.
29. Craig, E. (2022) Covid 'Was engineered in a lab': Study dismisses natural origin theory, https://www.msn.com/en-gb/health/other/covid-was-engineered-in-a-lab-study-dismisses-natural-origin-theory/ar-AA13k5Of.
30. Hydroxychloroquine was the anti-malaria drug promoted by Trump as a potential cure for COVID-19. Instead, those taking the drug became 11% more likely to die from the virus than those not using the treatment. That's close to 17,000 people. See Vargas, A. (2024) Malaria drug Trump touted as COVID-19 cure increased chance of death—Study, https://www.theguardian.com/world/2024/jan/12/hydroxychloroquine-covid-increase-chance-death-trump.

31. This is a claim made by Republican Senator Rand Paul in May 2021. See Gore, D. (2022) Correcting misinformation about Dr. Fauci, https://www.factcheck.org/2022/08/correcting-misinformation-about-dr-fauci/.
32. Jamieson, K. (2021) How conspiracists exploited COVID-19 science, *Nature Human Behaviour* 5: 1464–1465; Gore, Correcting misinformation about Dr. Fauci.
33. Reuters. (2021) No evidence Fauci is stepping down to accept a position at Pfizer, contrary to online claims, https://www.reuters.com/article/factcheck-fauci-niaid-pfizer-idUSL1N3O01HQ/.
34. CRISPR is short for 'clustered regularly interspaced short palindromic repeats'. It is a genetic engineering technology that allows bio-scientists to selectively modify the DNA of any living organism. See National Human Genome Research Institute. (2022) CRISPR, https://www.genome.gov/genetics-glossary/CRISPR.
35. Park, S. (2016) How CRISPR could change the world—and why that frightens many of us, https://geneticliteracyproject.org/2016/10/04/crispr-change-world-frightens-many-us/.
36. Cyriac, S., Churchil, R. and George, T. (2012) Transgenic chicken: Methods and applications, *Journal of Indian Veterinary Association* 10(2): 67–71.
37. Crawford, M. (2017) 8 ways CRISPR-Cas9 can change the world, https://www.asme.org/topics-resources/content/8-ways-crisprcas9-can-change-world.
38. Acharya, A. and Acharya, A. (2017) Dangerous combination: Is CRISPR a potential weapon for terrorists? https://geneticliteracyproject.org/2017/06/08/dangerous-combination-crispr-potential-weapon-terrorists/.
39. Walsh, *End Times*, pp. 204–205; Prasad, A. (2017) Genomics and genetic engineering, in J. Al-Khalili (ed.) *What's Next? Even Scientists Can't Predict the Future—or Can They?* Profile Books, London, pp. 58–69.

40. WION. (2020) What are biological weapons? Here is a list of countries that possess them! https://www.wionews.com/science/what-are-biological-weapons-here-is-a-list-of-countries-that-possess-them-330033.
41. Gollom, M. (2022) Putin implies nuclear attack if West interferes in Ukraine. Why it's not just an empty threat, https://www.cbc.ca/news/world/putin-ukraine-nato-nuclear-weapons-1.6362890.
42. Phelan, J. (2022) How many nuclear weapons exist, and who has them? https://www.livescience.com/how-many-nuclear-weapons-exist; Gollom, Putin implies nuclear attack if West interferes in Ukraine; on North Korea see *The Guardian*. (2022) Kim Jong-un daughter inspects another ICBM as leader hails North Korea's nuclear power, https://www.theguardian.com/world/2022/nov/27/kim-jong-un-daughter-inspects-another-icbm-as-leader-hails-north-koreas-nuclear-power.
43. Bernal, G. (2023) 'If the problem becomes more serious': South Korea talks going nuclear, https://www.lowyinstitute.org/the-interpreter/if-problem-becomes-more-serious-south-korea-talks-going-nuclear.
44. Doyle, L. (2019) Pakistan vs India: Why do Pakistan and India hate each other? Where is Kashmir? https://www.express.co.uk/news/world/1093314/Pakistan-India-conflict-explained-why-india-pakistan-war-where-is-Kashmir.
45. Roblin, S. (2021) The entire world would suffer from an Indian-Pakistani nuclear war, https://nationalinterest.org/blog/reboot/entire-world-would-suffer-indian-pakistani-nuclear-war-177550.
46. Heneghan, R. (2022) Even a 'limited' nuclear war would starve millions of people, new study reveals, https://phys.org/news/2022-08-limited-nuclear-war-starve-millions.html.
47. Roblin, The entire world would suffer from an Indian-Pakistani nuclear war; Krajick, K. (2020) Even a limited India-Pakistani nuclear war would bring global famine, says

study, https://news.climate.columbia.edu/2020/03/16/even-limited-india-pakistan-nuclear-war-would-bring-global-famine/.
48. Diaz-Maurin, F. (2022) How a nuclear war would kill you—and almost everyone else, https://www.globalresearch.ca/nowhere-hide-how-nuclear-war-would-kill-you-almost-everyone-else/5797124.
49. Diaz-Maurin, How a nuclear war would kill you—and almost everyone else.
50. Diaz-Maurin, How a nuclear war would kill you—and almost everyone else.
51. Diaz-Maurin, How a nuclear war would kill you—and almost everyone else.
52. Diaz-Maurin, How a nuclear war would kill you—and almost everyone else.
53. McCulloch, M., Winter, A., Sherman, C. and Trotter, J. (2024) *Nature Climate Change* 14: 171–177.
54. Bradshaw, C. and Strona, G. (2023) Ancient pathogens released from melting ice could wreak havoc on the world, new analysis reveals, https://theconversation.com/ancient-pathogens-released-from-melting-ice-could-wreak-havoc-on-the-world-new-analysis-reveals-209795.
55. Borenstein, S. (2022) Landmark UN climate change report: 'Parts of the planet will become uninhabitable', https://whyy.org/articles/un-ipcc-climate-change-report-uninhabitable-planet-code-red/.
56. Wallace-Wells, D. (2017) The uninhabitable earth, https://nymag.com/intelligencer/2017/07/climate-change-earth-too-hot-for-humans.html.
57. Spratt, D. and Dunlop, I. (2019) Existential climate-related security risk: A scenario approach, https://docs.wixstatic.com/ugd/148cb0_b2c0c79dc4344b279bcf2365336ff23b.pdf, p. 10.
58. Spratt and Dunlop, Existential climate-related security risk, p. 8.
59. Dunagan, C. (2014) Amusing Monday: To laugh about climate change, https://pugetsoundblogs.com/waterways/2014/06/09/amusing-monday-to-laugh-about-climate-change/.

60. United Nations Environment Programme. (2022) *Emissions Gap Report 2022: The Closing Window—Climate Crisis calls for Rapid Transformation of Societies*, UNEP, Nairobi, p. xvi.
61. Carrington, World close to 'irreversible' climate breakdown, warn major studies.
62. Fisher, J. (2022) Climate change: Ukraine war prompts fossil fuel 'gold rush'—Report, https://www.bbc.com/news/science-environment-61723252.
63. Carrington, World close to 'irreversible' climate breakdown, warn major studies.
64. Quoted in Carrington, World close to 'irreversible' climate breakdown, warn major studies.
65. Dunagan, Amusing Monday.
66. Lowth, M. (2020) Top 10 reasons the Zombie Apocalypse could really happen! https://listverse.com/2020/02/22/top-10-reasons-the-zombie-apocalypse-could-really-happen/; Walsh, *End Times*.
67. See, for example, Ghose, T. (2013) Doomsday: 9 real ways the earth could end, https://www.cbsnews.com/news/doomsday-nine-real-ways-the-earth-could-end/.
68. Tooze, A. (2022) Welcome to the world of the polycrisis, https://www.ft.com/content/498398e7-11b1-494b-9cd3-6d669dc3de33.
69. Lawrence, M. (2022) 'Polycrisis' may be a buzzword, but it could help us tackle the world's woes, https://theconversation.com/polycrisis-may-be-a-buzzword-but-it-could-help-us-tackle-the-worlds-woes-195280. 'Polycrisis' was Collins Dictionary's word of the year for 2022.
70. Sepasspour, R. (2024) The Doomsday Clock is still at 90 seconds to midnight. But what does that mean? https://theconversation.com/the-doomsday-clock-is-still-at-90-seconds-to-midnight-but-what-does-that-mean-221871.
71. Wikipedia. (2022) Apocalypticism, https://en.wikipedia.org/wiki/Apocalypticism.
72. Dias, E. (2020) The Apocalypse as an 'unveiling': What religion teaches us about the End Times, https://www.nytimes.com/2020/04/02/us/coronavirus-apocalypse-religion.html.

73. Dias, The Apocalypse as an 'unveiling'.
74. Pew Research Center. (2013) U.S. Christians' views on the return of Christ, https://www.pewresearch.org/religion/2013/03/26/us-christians-views-on-the-return-of-christ/.
75. Pew Research Center. (2012) Chapter 3: Articles of Faith, https://www.pewresearch.org/religion/2012/08/09/the-worlds-muslims-unity-and-diversity-3-articles-of-faith.
76. Torres, E. (2017) It's the end of the world and we know it: Scientists in many disciplines see apocalypse, soon, https://www.salon.com/2017/04/30/its-the-end-of-the-world-and-we-know-it-scientists-in-many-disciplines-see-apocalypse-soon/.
77. Wikipedia. (2022) Houston, we have a problem, https://en.wikipedia.org/wiki/Houston,_we_have_a_problem. Swigert actually used the words 'Okay, Houston, we've had a problem here', but it has since been popularised into the shorter form.
78. Rabin-Havt, A. and Media Matters for America. (2016) *Lies, Incorporated: The World of Post-truth Politics*, Anchor Books, New York, p. 16.
79. Schiffrin, A. (2021) Introduction, in A. Schiffrin (ed.) *Media Capture: How Money, Digital Platforms, and Governments Control the News*, Columbia University Press, New York, p. 5.
80. Nelson, M. (2021) A global strategy for combating media capture, in Schiffrin, *Media Capture*, p. 213.
81. Rabin-Havt and Media Matters for America, *Lies, Incorporated*, p. 189.
82. Rabin-Hart, and Media Matters for America, *Lies, Incorporated*, p. 190.
83. Rabin-Havt and Media Matters for America, *Lies, Incorporated*, p. 4.
84. Rabin-Havt and Media Matters for America, *Lies, Incorporated*, p. 7.
85. Coper, E. (2022) *Facts and Other Lies: Welcome to the Disinformation Age*, Allen and Unwin, Sydney, p. 264.
86. Coper, *Facts and Other Lies*, pp. 264–265.
87. Coper, *Facts and Other Lies*, pp. 279–280.

88. Leitch, S. and Pickering, P. (eds) (2022) *Rethinking Social Media and Extremism*, ANU Press, Canberra.
89. Nelson, A global strategy for combating media capture, p. 227.
90. Nelson, A global strategy for combating media capture, p. 220.
91. Starkman, D. and Chittum, R. (2021) The hamster wheel, triumphant: Commercial models for journalism are not working; let's try something else, in Schriffin, *Media Capture*, pp. 236–237.
92. Starkman and Chittum, The hamster wheel, triumphant, p. 252.
93. Sullivan, A. (2021) Building trust (and a Trust), in Schriffin, *Media Capture*, p. 262.
94. Coper, *Facts and Other Lies*, p. 285; Wikipedia. (2022) Deplatforming, https://en.wikipedia.org/wiki/Deplatforming.
95. Angus, D. and Graham, T. (2022) Thinking of breaking up with Twitter? Here's the right way to do it, https://theconversation.com/thinking-of-breaking-up-with-twitter-heres-the-right-way-to-do-it-195002.
96. Honigberg, B. (2021) Why deplatforming just isn't enough, https://www.csis.org/blogs/technology-policy-blog/why-deplatforming-just-isnt-enough,
97. Sullivan, Building trust (and a Trust), p. 268.
98. See: https://blog.mozilla.org/en/internet-culture/deep-dives/misinfo-nation-misinformation-democracy-internet/.
99. InterAction. (2022) Who we are, https://www.interaction.org/about-interaction/. Access to the tool can be found here: https://www.interaction.org/disinformation-toolkit-2-0/.
100. NewsGuard. (2023) Introducing: NewsGuard, https://www.newsguardtech.com/how-it-works/.
101. Wayne State University Library System. (2024) SIFT: Stop, Investigate, Find, Trace: What is SIFT? https://guides.lib.wayne.edu/sift.
102. Dangerfield, K. (2018) Facebook, Google and others are tracking you. Here's how to stop targeted ads, https://globalnews.ca/news/4110311/how-to-stop-targeted-ads-facebook-google-browser/.
To stop ads on Facebook and Google, visit this site: https://www.allconnect.com/blog/how-to-stop-google-and-facebook-ads.

103. See https://www.irex.org/resource/learn-discern-media-literacy-trainers-manual.
104. See Bergstrom, C. and West, J. (2020) *Calling Bullshit: The Art of Scepticism in a Data-Driven World*, Allen Lane, UK.
105. McIntyre, L. (2018) *Post-truth*, MIT Press, Massachusetts, p. 13.
106. Sample, I. (2020) What are deepfakes—and how you can spot them, https://www.theguardian.com/technology/2020/jan/13/what-are-deepfakes-and-how-can-you-spot-them.
107. Witness Media Lab. (2022) Prepare, don't panic: Synthetic media and deepfakes, https://lab.witness.org/projects/synthetic-media-and-deep-fakes/; DeepFake. (2022) What is a deepfake? Everything you need to know, https://deepfake.com/knowledge-center/what-is-a-deepfake/.
108. Shearer, E. (2021) More than eight-in-ten Americans get news from digital devices, https://www.pewresearch.org/fact-tank/2021/01/12/more-than-eight-in-ten-americans-get-news-from-digital-devices/. See also Statistica. (2022) Share of adults who use social media as a source of news in selected countries worldwide as of February 2022, https://www.statista.com/statistics/718019/social-media-news-source/.
109. Seymour, R. (2019) The machine always wins: What drives our addiction to social media, https://www.theguardian.com/technology/2019/aug/23/social-media-addiction-gambling.
110. Seymour, The machine always wins. Also see Patella-Rey, P. (2014) Gamification and post-Fordist capitalism, in S. Walz and S. Detering (eds) *The Gameful World: Approaches, Issues and Applications*, MIT Press, Massachusetts, pp. 277–295.
111. Manwaring, K. and Narrain, S. (2023) 41 US states are suing Meta for getting teens hooked on social media. Here's what to expect next, https://theconversation.com/41-us-states-are-suing-meta-for-getting-teens-hooked-on-social-media-heres-what-to-expect-next-216914.
112. According to US psychologist and author Adam Alter, over half the US population has an internet-related addiction—the technology is literally 'irresistible'. See Alter, A. (2017) *Irresistible:*

The Rise of Addictive Technology and the Business of Keeping Us Hooked, Penguin, New York.
113. Williams, C. (2014) The UN's dismal failure on climate change, https://socialistworker.org/2014/09/17/dismal-failure-on-climate-change.
114. Goodell, J. (2022) The climate fight isn't lost. Here are 10 ways to win, https://www.rollingstone.com/politics/political-commentary/climate-change-earth-day-solutions-solar-coal-1323853/. See other recommendations in UNEP. (2022) *Emissions Gap Report 2022: The Closing Window—Climate Crisis Calls for Rapid Transformation of Societies*, UN Environment Programme, Nairobi, p. xxiv; Gayle, D. (2022) To solve the climate crisis, we must rein in the wasteful wealthy, https://ecosocialistsvancouver.org/article/solve-climate-crisis-we-must-rein-wasteful-wealthy.
115. Huber, M. (2022) *Climate Change as Class War: Building Socialism on a Warming Planet*, Verso, London.
116. D'Souza, D. (2022) Understanding the Green New Deal & what's in the climate proposal, https://www.investopedia.com/the-green-new-deal-explained-4588463.
117. Wright, C., Nyberg, D. and Bowden, V. (2022) A technologically advanced society is choosing to destroy itself. It's both fascinating and horrifying to watch, https://theconversation.com/a-technologically-advanced-society-is-choosing-to-destroy-itself-its-both-fascinating-and-horrifying-to-watch-192939.
118. Monbiot, G. (2022) There's one big subject our leaders at Cop27 won't touch: Livestock farming, https://www.theguardian.com/commentisfree/2022/nov/09/leaders-cop27-livestock-farming-carbon-budget-governments.
119. Canadell, P. (et al.)(2022) Global carbon emissions at record levels with no sign of shrinking, new data shows. Humanity has a monumental task ahead, https://theconversation.com/global-carbon-emissions-at-record-levels-with-no-signs-of-shrinking-new-data-shows-humanity-has-a-monumental-task-ahead-193108.
120. Williams, The UN's dismal failure on climate change.

121. Hudson, M. (2019) Don't bet on the UN to fix climate change—it's failed for 30 years, https://theconversation.com/dont-bet-on-the-un-to-fix-climate-change-its-failed-for-30-years-123308.
122. Peel, J. (2022) It's the big issue of COP27 climate summit: Poor nations face a $1 trillion 'loss and damage' bill, but rich nations won't pay up, https://theconversation.com/its-the-big-issue-of-cop27-climate-summit-poor-nations-face-a-1trillion-loss-and-damage-bill-but-rich-nations-wont-pay-up-194043. 'Loss and damage' relates to the impacts that climate change is having on people and the environment—impacts that can no longer be avoided such as increased flooding, more intense droughts, biodiversity loss, and rising sea levels. Given rich nations' carbon pollution is causing most of the damage, the poorer nations are demanding financial compensation.
123. See discussions in King, A., Kimutai, J., Harrington, L. and Grose, M. (2023) Poorer countries must be compensated for climate change. But how exactly do we crunch the numbers? https://theconversation.com/poorer-countries-must-be-compensated-for-climate-damage-but-how-exactly-do-we-crunch-the-numbers-202387.
124. Lakhani, N. (2023) $700m pledges to loss and damage fund at Cop28 covers less than 0.2% needed, https://www.theguardian.com/environment/2023/dec/06/700m-pledged-to-loss-and-damage-fund-cop28-covers-less-than-02-percent-needed.
125. McDonald, M. (2022) COP27: One big breakthrough but ultimately an inadequate response to the climate crisis, https://theconversation.com/cop27-one-big-breakthrough-but-ultimately-an-inadequate-response-to-the-climate-crisis-194056.
126. Bennett, E. (2023) Dystopian satire: COP28 conference hosted by petrostate, https://australiainstitute.org.au/post/dystopian-satire-cop28-conference-hosted-by-petrostate/.
127. Sherrington, R., Carlile, C. and Healy, H. (2023) Big meat and dairy lobbyists turn our in record numbers at Cop28, https://ground.news/article/big-meat-and-dairy-lobbyists-turn-out-in-record-numbers-at-cop28; Watts, J. (2023) Cop28's winners and losers: from fossil fuel firms to future

generations, https://www.theguardian.com/environment/2023/dec/14/cop28-winners-and-losers-fossil-fuel-climate-crisis.
128. GRAIN. (2023) Regenerative agriculture was a good idea, until corporations got hold of it, https://grain.org/en/article/7067-regenerative-agriculture-was-a-good-idea-until-corporations-got-hold-of-it; GRAIN. (2023) Stop carbon offsetting now! https://grain.org/e/7071.
129. Green, G. (2023) Environmental campaigners filmed, threatened and harassed at Cop28, https://www.theguardian.com/environment/2023/dec/20/threats-intimidation-creating-climate-of-fear-un-cop-events.
130. Watts, J. (2023) World looks back at 2023 as a year humanity exposed its inability to tackle climate crisis, scientists say, https://www.theguardian.com/environment/2023/dec/29/world-will-look-back-at-2023-as-year-humanity-exposed-its-inability-to-tackle-climate-crisis.
131. Hudson, M. (2019) Don't bet on the UN to fix climate change—it's failed for 30 years.
132. Reported in Milman, O. (2022) Nearly $2tn of damage inflicted on other countries by US emissions, https://www.theguardian.com/environment/2022/jul/12/us-carbon-emissions-greenhouse-gases-climate-crisis.
133. Monbiot, G. (2022) There's a simple way to unite everyone behind climate justice—and it's within our power, https://www.theguardian.com/commentisfree/2022/jun/24/rich-nations-climate-debt-cancelling-debts-emissions-global-debt-swap-campaign. See also Jubilee Debt Campaign. (2021) Debt and the climate crisis: A perfect storm—Why climate justice must include debt justice, https://jubileedebt.org.uk/wp-content/uploads/2021/09/Debt-and-the-Climate-Crisis-a-Perfect-Storm.pdf.
134. Hill, J. (2018) 15 leading international organizations announce joint climate neutrality commitment at COP24, https://cleantechnica.com/2018/12/14/15-leading-international-organizations-announce-joint-climate-neutrality-commitment-at-cop24/.

135. GRAIN. (2023) Carbon rice farming: A license to pollute at the expense of small farmers, https://grain.org/en/article/7009-carbon-rice-farming-a-license-to-pollute-at-the-expense-of-small-farmers.
136. Diab, K. (2022) Why do corporations greenwash? The system is loaded against the climate and the environment, https://www.aljazeera.com/opinions/2022/3/5/why-do-corporations-greenwash; Clendaniel, M. (2022) Seven ways that companies greenwash, https://www.fastcompany.com/1678896/seven-ways-that-companies-greenwash.
137. United Nations' High Level Expert Group. (2022) *Integrity Matters: Net Zero Commitments by Businesses, Financial Institutions, Cities and Regions*, UN, Geneva, p. 33.
138. United Nations' High Level Expert Group, *Integrity Matters*, p. 33.
139. Readfearn, G. and Morton, A. (2022) Australia risks being a 'state sponsoring greenwashing' if it relies on carbon offsets, expert warns, https://www.theguardian.com/environment/2022/nov/13/australia-risks-being-a-state-sponsoring-greenwashing-if-it-relies-on-carbon-offsets-expert-warns; Real Farming Trust. (2023) The pressure to capitalise on nature, https://realfarming.org/news-features/the-pressure-to-capitalise-on-nature/.
140. Quoted in Lo, J. (2022) 'Toxic cover-up': UN blasts oil majors' fake net zero pledges, https://www.climatechangenews.com/2022/11/08/toxic-cover-up-un-blasts-oil-majors-fake-net-zero-pledges/.
141. Bhushan, C. (2019) After 25 years of failure, we should abandon the UNFCCC, https://www.climatechangenews.com/2019/03/27/25-years-failure-abandon-unfccc/.
142. Thunberg, G. (2022) Greta Thunberg on the climate delusion: 'We've been greenwashed out of our senses. It's time to stand our ground, https://www.theguardian.com/environment/2022/oct/08/greta-thunberg-climate-delusion-greenwashed-out-of-our-senses.

143. Wilkinson, M. (2020) *The Carbon Club: How a Network of Influential Climate Sceptics, Politicians and Business Leaders Fought to Control Australia's Climate Policy*, Allen and Unwin, Sydney.
144. See details at Noor, D. (2023) 'Project 2025': Plan to dismantle US climate policy for next Republican president, https://www.theguardian.com/environment/2023/jul/27/project-2025-dismantle-us-climate-policy-next-republican-president; Project 2025, https://www.project2025.org/policy/.
145. Nicholls, P. and Serrapica, I. (2019) 'Sorry, this is an emergency': Climate protesters block streets around the world, https://www.reuters.com/article/us-climate-change-protests-idUSKBN1WM1JP.
146. Riga, J. (2022) Soup on a Van Gough, mashed potatoes on a Monet: Why are activists throwing food on priceless art? https://www.abc.net.au/news/2022-10-28/why-are-activists-throwing-food-on-art/101589870.
147. Butt, M. (2024) Mona Lisa painting targeted by protesters who throw pumpkin soup at da Vinci painting in Paris, https://au.news.yahoo.com/mona-lisa-painting-targetted-protesters-103320573.html.
148. Grieshaber, K. and The Associated Press. (2022) Another day, another climate activist attacking a masterpiece: Now it's a black oily liquid on a Klimt, https://fortune.com/2022/11/15/gustav-klimt-painting-climate-activists-oily-liquid-death-and-life-glued/; Dalton, A. (2022) Superglued to van Gogh: Why climate protesters are targeting art, https://www.smh.com.au/culture/art-and-design/superglued-to-van-gogh-why-climate-protesters-are-targeting-art-20221010-p5boh8.html. No real damage has been done to the paintings targeted. As most art aficionados know, all major works are kept safely behind glass, as a protection from UV rays as well as from those wanting to make public statements.
149. Benzine, V. (2022) Here Is every artwork attacked by climate activists this year, From the 'Mona Lisa' to 'Girl With a Pearl

Earring', https://news.artnet.com/art-world/here-is-every-art work-attacked-by-climate-activists-this-year-from-the-mona-lisa-to-girl-with-a-pearl-earring-2200804.

150. Quoted in Suliman, A. (2022) World's museums urge climate activists targeting 'irreplaceable' art to stop, https://www.washingtonpost.com/lifestyle/2022/11/11/climate-change-protesters-art-museums/.

151. Sahagun, L. (2023) California sues five major oil companies for 'decades-long campaign of deception' about climate change, https://www.latimes.com/california/story/2023-09-16/california-sues-five-major-oil-companies-for-lying-about-climate-change.

152. Quoted in Harvey, F. (2022) UN says up to 40% of world's land now degraded, https://www.theguardian.com/environment/2022/apr/27/united-nations-40-per-cent-planet-land-degraded.

153. FAO. (2020) The state of the world's forests 2020, https://www.fao.org/state-of-forests/en.

154. The Human League. (2021) Effects of Deforestation on humans and the environment, https://thehumaneleague.org/article/effects-of-deforestation.

155. Hart, W. (2023) The real cost of your chocolate habit: New research reveals the bittersweet truth of cocoa farming in Africa's forests, https://theconversation.com/the-real-cost-of-your-chocolate-habit-new-research-reveals-the-bittersweet-truth-of-cocoa-farming-in-africas-forests-206082.

156. UIA. (2022) Desertification, http://encyclopedia.uia.org/en/problem/135018.

157. United Nations Convention to Combat Desertification. (2022) The Global Land Outlook, Second Edition, UNCCO, Bonn, p. ix; Harvey, F. (2023) UN says up to 40% of world's land now degraded, https://www.theguardian.com/environment/2022/apr/27/united-nations-40-per-cent-planet-land-degraded.

158. Carrington, D. (2022) World on brink of five 'disastrous' climate tipping points, study finds, https://www.theguardian.com/environment/2022/sep/08/world-on-brink-five-climate-tipping-points-study-finds.

159. Wikipedia. (2022) Tipping points in the climate system, https://en.wikipedia.org/wiki/Tipping_points_in_the_climate_system.
160. McDonald, C. (2015) How many Earths do we need? https://www.bbc.com/news/magazine-33133712.
161. WWF. (2022) What is ecological footprint, https://wwf.panda.org/discover/knowledge_hub/teacher_resources/webfieldtrips/ecological_balance/eco_footprint/.
162. Global Footprint Network. (2022) How the Footprint works, https://www.footprintnetwork.org/our-work/ecological-footprint.
163. Earth Overshoot Day. (2022) How many Earths? How many countries? https://www.overshootday.org/how-many-earths-or-countries-do-we-need/; McDonald, C. (2015) How many Earths do we need?
164. The World Counts. (2022) Number of planet Earths we need, https://www.theworldcounts.com/challenges/planet-earth/state-of-the-planet/overuse-of-resources-on-earth.
165. United Nations Department of Economic and Social Affairs. (2022) Sustainable Development Goals, https://sdgs.un.org/goals#implementation.
166. United Nations. (2022) The Sustainable Development Goals Report 2022, https://unstats.un.org/sdgs/report/2022/The-Sustainable-Development-Goals-Report-2022.pdf.
167. Monbiot, G. (2022) The US is a rogue state leading the world towards ecological collapse, https://www.theguardian.com/commentisfree/2022/dec/09/us-world-climate-collapse-nations. In this article Monbiot lists other international treaties the US has failed to sign, including bans on cluster bombs and landmines, the nuclear test treaty ban, the convention on discrimination against women, the convention on hazardous waste, the statute on international crimes, and the convention on the rights of persons with disabilities.
168. United Nations Environment Programme. (2022) Convention on Biological Diversity, Kunming-Montreal Global biodiversity

framework, https://www.cbd.int/doc/c/e6d3/cd1d/daf663719a03902a9b116c34/cop-15-l-25-en.pdf; United Nations environment Programme. (2022) Convention on Biological Diversity, Long-term Strategic Directions to the 2050 Vision for Biodiversity, https://www.cbd.int/doc/c/0b54/1750/607267ea9109b52b750314a0/cop-14-09-en.pdf.

169. Mah, A. (2022) *Plastic Unlimited: How Corporations are Fuelling the Ecological Crisis and What we can do About it*, Polity, UK.
170. Bekessy, S., Wintle, B., Pascoe, J., Fitzsimons, J., Morgain, R. and Spindler, R. (2022) The historic COP15 outcome is an imperfect game-changer for saving nature. Here's why Australia did us proud, https://theconversation.com/the-historic-cop15-outcome-is-an-imperfect-game-changer-for-saving-nature-heres-why-australia-did-us-proud-196731.
171. Bekessy et al., The historic COP15 outcome is an imperfect game-change for saving nature.
172. Carrington, D. (2018) Huge reduction in meat-eating 'essential' to avoid climate breakdown, https://www.theguardian.com/environment/2018/oct/10/huge-reduction-in-meat-eating-essential-to-avoid-climate-breakdown.
173. Weston, P. (2022) Cop15 in Montreal: Did the summit deliver for the natural world? https://www.theguardian.com/environment/2022/dec/20/cop15-montreal-did-it-deliver-for-natural-world-aoe.
174. The Climate Action Fund. (2022) The Climate Action Fund: A new approach, https://www.globalgiving.org/climate-action-fund/?rf=learn; Forest, N. (2019) Meet 4 nonprofits dedicated to defeating drought, https://www.globalgiving.org/learn/listicle/defeating-drought-and-desertification.
175. Wikipedia. (2022) Earth Liberation Front, https://en.wikipedia.org/wiki/Earth_Liberation_Front.
176. Laville, S. and Watts, J. (2019) Across the globe, millions join biggest climate protest ever, https://www.theguardian.com/environment/2019/sep/21/across-the-globe-millions-join-biggest-climate-protest-ever.

177. Baer, H. (2023) Climate change and capitalism, climate dystopia, and radical climate futures, *Journal of Australian Political Economy* 91: 107–127.
178. Richie, H. (2020) Sector by sector: Where do global greenhouse emissions come from? https://ourworldindata.org/emissions-by-sector.
179. The World Counts. (2022) Globally, we consume around 350 million tons of meat a year, https://www.theworldcounts.com/challenges/consumption/foods-and-beverages/world-consumption-of-meat.
180. The World Counts, Globally, we consume around 350 million tons of meat a year.
181. Carrington, D. (2023) Meat, dairy and rice production will bust 1.5C climate target, study shows, https://www.theguardian.com/environment/2023/mar/06/meat-dairy-rice-high-methane-food-production-bust-climate-target-study
182. Singer, P. (2023) 'We are gambling with the future of our planet for the sake of hamburgers': Peter Singer on climate change, https://theconversation.com/we-are-gambling-with-the-future-of-our-planet-for-the-sake-of-hamburgers-peter-singer-on-climate-change-207605.
183. Newman, L. and Fraser, E. (2021) 3 technologies poised to change food and the planet, https://theconversation.com/3-technologies-poised-to-change-food-and-the-planet-153852.
184. Pig Progress. (2022) Under construction: A 26 storey pig house, https://www.pigprogress.net/the-industrymarkets/market-trends-analysis-the-industrymarkets-2/under-construction-a-26-storey-pig-house/; Of course, the Americans can never be outdone. One small midwestern town in the US raises and slaughters some 7 million pigs each year. It has been termed 'Porkopolis'—see Blanchette, A. (2020) *Porkopolis: American Animality, Standardized Life and the Factory Farm*, Duke University Press, North Carolina.

185. *The Guardian.* (2022) China's 26-storey pig skyscraper ready to slaughter 1 million pigs per year, https://www.theguardian.com/environment/2022/nov/25/chinas-26-storey-pig-skyscraper-ready-to-produce-1-million-pigs-a-year.
186. Butler, G. (2020) China Is Building a City of Pig Apartments to Protect Their Herds from Swine Flu, https://www.vice.com/en/article/g5bxgy/china-is-building-a-city-of-pig-apartments-to-protect-their-herds-from-swine-flu; LaScaLa. (2019) Sichuan province, China: 13 large-scale pig farms under construction, https://www.largescaleagriculture.com/home/news-details/sichuan-province-china-13-large-scale-pig-farms-under-construction/.
187. Nicole, W. (2013) CAFOs and Environmental Justice: The Case of North Carolina, *Environmental Health Perspectives* 121(6): a182–a189.
188. Nicole, CAFOs and Environmental Justice.
189. Harris, J., Anderson, M., Clement, C. and Nisbett, N. (2019) The Political economy of food, *IDS Bulletin* 50(2): 89–109.
190. Peters, A. (2022) Is regenerative agriculture the future of farming or the next greenwashing fad? https://www.fastcompany.com/90796487/is-regenerative-agriculture-the-future-of-farming-or-the-next-greenwashing-fad. For a more detailed discussion of 'climate smart agriculture' see Clapp, J., Newell, P. and Brent, Z. (2018) The global political economy of climate change, agriculture and food systems, *The Journal of Peasant Studies* 45(1): 80–88.
191. FAO. (2021) Family farming knowledge platform, https://www.fao.org/family-farming/detail/en/c/1378841.
192. GlobeNewswire. (2022) Organic food market size to hit around USD 497.3 billion by 2030, https://www.globenewswire.com/en/news-release/2022/07/12/2478115/0/en/Organic-Food-Market-Size-to-Hit-Around-USD-497-3-Billion-by-2030.html.
193. IFOAM. (2022) About us, https://www.ifoam.bio/.
194. Quoted in Price, M. et al. (2022) Agroecology in the North: Centering indigenous food sovereignty and land stewardship in agricultural 'frontiers', *Agriculture and Human Values* 39: 1195.

195. La Via Campesina. (2022) The international peasants' voice, https://viacampesina.org/en/international-peasants-voice/; see also McMichael, P. (2013) *Food Regimes and Agrarian Questions*, Fernwood, Halifax.
196. La Via Campesina. (2007) Small scale sustainable farmers are cooling down the earth, https://viacampesina.org/en/small-scale-sustainable-farmers-are-cooling-down-the-earth/.
197. Woodhouse, P. (2010) Beyond industrial agriculture? Some questions about farm size, productivity and sustainability, *Journal of Agrarian Change* 10(3): 437–453.
198. La Via Campesina, The international peasants' voice.
199. La Via Campesina, The international peasants' voice.
200. GRAIN. (2012) *The Great Food Robbery: How Corporations Control Food, Grab Land and Destroy the Climate*, Pambazuka Press, Cape Town, p. 112.
201. Patel, R. (2009) What does food sovereignty look like? *The Journal of Peasant Studies* 36(3): 663–706; Edwards, F. (2023) *Food Resistance Movements: Journeying Through Alternative Food Networks*, Palgrave Macmillan, Singapore.
202. RightDocs. (2018) United Nations Declaration on the Rights of Peasants and Other People Working in Rural Areas, https://www.right-docs.org/doc/a-hrc-res-39-12/.
203. GRAIN. (2022) About us, https://grain.org/; GRAIN. (2016) *The Great Climate Robbery: How the Food System Drives Climate Change and What we can do About it*, GRAIN, Barcelona.
204. NRDC. (2022) About us, https://www.nrdc.org/about.
205. Sacks, G. (2014) Big Food lobbying: Tip of the iceberg exposed, https://theconversation.com/big-food-lobbying-tip-of-the-iceberg-exposed-23232.
206. Waters, R. (2017) Soda and fast food lobbyists push State preemption laws to prevent local regulation, https://www.forbes.com/sites/robwaters/2017/06/21/soda-and-fast-food-lobbyists-push-state-preemption-laws-to-prevent-local-regulation/?sh=79a7633f745d.

207. NDCAlliance. (2021) Turning the table: Fighting back against the junk food industry, https://ncdalliance.org/news-events/blog/turning-the-table-fighting-back-against-the-junk-food-industry.
208. Humane Society International. (2022) Seoul city council proposes bill to ban dog meat consumption, https://www.hsi.org/news-media/seoul-proposes-bill-to-ban-dog-meat-consumption/.
209. United Nations. (2021) More than 100 countries discuss visions for national food futures to accelerate global action ahead of September Summit, https://www.un.org/en/food-systems-summit/news/more-100-countries-discuss-visions-national-food-futures-accelerate-global.
210. Australian Food Sovereignty Movement. (2013) The People's Food Plan: A common-sense approach to a fair, sustainable and resilient food system, https://afsa.org.au/wp-content/uploads/2012/11/AFSA_PFP_WorkingPaper-FINAL-15-Feb-2013.pdf.
211. See Twitter post at: https://twitter.com/Fash_Rev/status/633536180542377984.
212. Stevens, A. (2024) If the government recognises that 'food is medicine', why aren't they taking hunger more seriously? https://www.salon.com/2024/02/01/if-the-government-recognizes-that-food-is-medicine-why-arent-they-taking-hunger-more-seriously/.
213. Wood, B., Williams, O., Baker, P. and Sacks, G. (2023) Behind the 'creative destruction' of human diets: An analysis of the structure and market dynamics of the ultra-processed food manufacturing industry and implications for public health, *Journal of Agrarian Change*, https://doi.org/10.1111/joac.12545.
214. Morris, K. (2020) What Norma did next: How the 'New Nordic' is reshaping the food world, https://www.theguardian.com/food/2020/feb/28/what-noma-did-next-new-nordic-food-rene-redzepi-claus-meyer-locavore-foraging.
215. See McMahon, A., Smith, K. and Lawrence, G. (2014) Connecting Resilience, Food Security and Climate Change? Lessons from Flooding in Queensland, Australia, *Journal of*

Environmental Studies and Sciences https://doi.org/10.1007/s13 412-015-0278-0; Singh-Peterson, L. and Lawrence, G. (2014) Insights into Community Vulnerability and Resilience Following Natural Disasters: Perspectives with Food Retailers in Northern NSW, Australia, *Local Environment*, 1–14, https://doi.org/10.1080/13549839.2013.873396; Smith, K. and Lawrence, G. (2014) Flooding and Food Security: A Case Study of Community Vulnerability and Resilience in Rockhampton, *Rural Society* 23(3): 216–228.
216. Clapp, J. and Moseley, W. (2020) This food crisis is different: COVID-19 and the fragility of the neoliberal food security order, *The Journal of Peasant Studies* 47(7): 1393–1417.
217. Slow Food. (2022) About us, https://www.slowfood.com/about-us/where-we-are/.
218. Slow Food, About us.
219. Ashwood, L., Pilny, A., Canfield, J., Jamila, M. and Thomson, R. (2022) From Big Ag to Big Finance: A market network approach to power in agriculture, *Agriculture and Human Values* 39: 1421–1434.
220. Guthman, J. and Biltekoff, C. (2021) Magical disruption? Alternative protein and the promise of de-materialization, *Environment and Planning E: Nature and Space* 4(4): 1583–1600; Livingstone, K. and Marchese, L. (2022) Is fake meat healthy? And what's actually in it? https://theconversation.com/is-fake-meat-healthy-and-whats-actually-in-it-187532.
221. Denniss, R. (2021) *Econobabble: How to Decode Political Spin and Economic Nonsense*, Black Inc, Victoria, p. 14.
222. Denniss, *Econobabble*, p. 15.
223. Bonefeld, W. (2014) *Critical Theory and the Critique of Political Economy*, Bloomsbury Publishing, London; Diesendorf, M. and Taylor, R. (2023) *The Path to a Sustainable Civilization: Technological, Socioeconomic and Political Change*, Palgrave Macmillan, Singapore.
224. Stilwell, F. (2002) *Political Economy: The Contest of Economic Ideas*, Oxford University Press, Victoria, p. 4.
225. Stilwell, *Political Economy*, pp. 304–305.

226. Welsh, M. (2022) Five steps towards a Green New Deal, https://neweconomics.org/2022/01/five-steps-towards-a-green-new-deal; New Economics Foundation. (2019) Change the rules: New rules for the economy, https://neweconomics.org/uploads/files/newrules2020.pdf.
227. Wolf, R. (2013) Alternatives to capitalism, *Critical Sociology* 39(4): 487–490.
228. Wolf, Alternatives to capitalism, p. 487.
229. Oxfam International. (2024) *Inequality Inc: How Corporate Power Divides our World and the Need for a New Era of Public Action*, Oxfam International, Oxford, UK, pp. 12–13.
230. Diamond, J. and Ehrlich, P. (2022) Failure of the universities: The culture gap is now near lethal, https://mahb.stanford.edu/library-item/failure-of-the-universities-the-culture-gap-is-now-near-lethal/; Connell, R. (2019) *The Good University: What Universities Actually do and why it's Time for Radical Change*, Monash University Press, Melbourne; Hil, R., Lyons, K. and Thompsett, F. (2022) *Transforming Universities in the Midst of Global Crisis: A University for the Common Good*, Routledge, New York. What constitutes 'progressive' will be forever debated, of course.
231. Varoufakis, Y. (2023) *Technofeudalism: What Killed Capitalism*, Penguin Random House, London.
232. Wright, E. (2010) The Real Utopia Project: A general overview, https://www.ssc.wisc.edu/~wright/OVERVIEW.html. Other ideas for reducing economic inequality can be found in Stilwell, F. (1993) *Economic Inequality: Who Gets What in Australia*, Pluto Press, Sydney, pp. 83–88.
233. Alexander, S. (2014) Life in a 'degrowth' economy, and why you might actually enjoy it, https://theconversation.com/life-in-a-degrowth-economy-and-why-you-might-actually-enjoy-it-32224; Saito, K. (2023) *Capital in the Anthropocene*, Cambridge University Press, Cambridge, UK; Diesendorf and Taylor, *The Path to a Sustainable Civilization*, pp. 176–178.
234. Diesendorf and Taylor, *The Path to a Sustainable Civilization*, pp. 214–218.

235. See arguments in Joy, M. (2023) Critics of 'degrowth' economics say it's unworkable—but from an ecologist's perspective, it is inevitable, https://theconversation.com/critics-of-degrowth-economics-say-its-unworkable-but-from-an-ecologists-perspective-its-inevitable-211496.
236. Raworth, K. (2017) *Doughnut Economics: Seven Ways to Think Like a 21st-Century Economist*, Penguin, London.
237. Wikipedia. (2022) List of left-wing publications in the United Kingdom, https://en.wikipedia.org/wiki/List_of_left-wing_publications_in_the_United_Kingdom.
238. Palgrave Macmillan. (2024) Sociology, https://www.palgrave.com/gb/social-science.
239. Newsweek. (2023) Full list of Capitol rioters jailed so far and the sentences they are serving, https://www.newsweek.com/full-list-capitol-rioters-jailed-sentences-january-6-1826075.
240. Zengerle, P. and Warburton, M. (2022) Trump should face insurrection, obstruction charges, Jan 6 panel says, https://www.reuters.com/world/us/us-house-jan-6-capitol-riot-probe-consider-trump-criminal-referral-2022-12-19/; https://www.bu.edu/articles/2024/trump-convicted-felon-what-does-that-mean/.
241. Brito, R., Ellsworth, B. and Gaier, R. (2022) Brazil's Bolsonaro does not concede to Lula, but authorises transition, https://www.reuters.com/world/americas/brazilian-court-orders-roadblocks-cleared-bolsonaro-silent-election-loss-2022-11-01/. Telegram messaging is one-way communication which does not allow users to reply to the message.
242. Nicas, J. (2023) What drove a mass attack on Brazil's capital? Mass delusion, https://www.nytimes.com/2023/01/09/world/americas/brazil-riots-bolsonaro-conspiracy-theories.html.
243. Dwoskin, E. (2023) Come to the 'war cry party': How social media helped drive mayhem in Brazil, https://www.washingtonpost.com/technology/2023/01/08/brazil-bolsonaro-twitter-facebook/.
244. Lewandowsky, S., Ecker, U., Cook, J., van der Linden, S., Roozenbeek, J. and Oreskes, N. (2023) Misinformation and the

epistemic integrity of democracy, *Current Opinion in Psychology* 54, https://doi.org/10.1016/j.copsyc.2023.101711, p. 1.
245. V-Dem Institute. (2022) *Democracy Report 2022: Autocratization Changing Nature*, https://v-dem.net/media/publications/dr_2022.pdf.
246. Wikipedia. (2023) Democratic backsliding, https://en.wikipedia.org/wiki/Democratic_backsliding.
247. V-Dem Institute, *Democracy Report 2022*, p. 7.
248. Bello, W. (2022) Do we need another Goliath? https://www.networkideas.org/featured-articles/2022/10/do-we-need-another-goliath/.
249. Quoted in Bello, Do we need another Goliath?
250. Reimer, K. and Peter, S. (2022) Wrong, Elon Musk: The big problem with free speech on platforms isn't censorship. It's the algorithms, https://theconversation.com/wrong-elon-musk-the-big-problem-with-free-speech-on-platforms-isnt-censorship-its-the-algorithms-182433.
251. Gamrath, D. (2022) First slow, then FAST: Expert in the field predicts how the second U.S. civil war could begin, https://www.realchangenews.org/news/2022/07/07/first-slow-then-fast-expert-field-predicts-how-second-us-civil-war-could-begin.
252. See for example, Fraser, N. (2023) From progressive neoliberalism to Trump—and beyond, in M. Leger (ed.) *Identity Trumps Socialism*, Routledge, New York, chapter 7.
253. McMichael, P. (2023) Critical agrarian studies and crises of the world-historical present, *Journal of Peasant Studies* https://doi.org/10.1080/03066150.2022.2163630.
254. McMichael, Critical agrarian studies and crises of the world-historical present. Noam Chomsky has stated that the future of the US is 'racist, right-wing Christian nationalism controlled by state power over independent thought and institutions'. See Chomsky, N. (2022) The Proto-fascist guide to destroying the world, https://www.bostonreview.net/articles/the-proto-fascist-guide-to-destroying-the-world/.

255. Baggini, J. (2018) Aristotle's thinking on democracy has more relevance than ever, https://www.prospectmagazine.co.uk/philosophy/aristotles-thinking-on-democracy-has-more-relevance-than-ever.
256. Wolfenden, K. (2010) Hobbes' Leviathan and views on the origins of civil Government: Conservatism by covenant, http://www.inquiriesjournal.com/articles/349/2/hobbes-leviathan-and-views-on-the-origins-of-civil-government-conservatism-by-covenant.
257. Britannica. (2023) Rousseau, https://www.britannica.com/topic/democracy/The-value-of-democracy.
258. Britannica. (2023) Dictatorship of the proletariat, https://www.britannica.com/topic/dictatorship-of-the-proletariat.
259. Reported in Rosenmann, A. (2016) Noam Chomsky: America is only a democracy for the 1%, https://www.salon.com/2016/06/22/noam_chomsky_america_is_only_a_democracy_for_the_1_percent_partner/. See also Allott, N., Knight, C. and Smith, N. (2019) *The Responsibility of Intellectuals: Reflections by Noam Chomsky and Others After 50 Years*, University College London Press, London.
260. Wikipedia. (2022) Socialist Party, https://en.wikipedia.org/wiki/Socialist_Party.
261. Picketty, T. (2022) *A Brief History of Equality*, The Belknap Press, Massachusetts, p. 237.

Index

A
advertisements 3, 54, 125, 126, 185, 221, 394
advertisers 5, 8, 12, 24, 99, 120, 133, 330, 333
agribusiness 105, 110, 251, 408, 410–412, 414
agrichemicals 107
agriculture
  community supported agriculture 413
  corporate 101, 186
  family farm 101
  organic 155
  peasant and subsistence 248
agroecology 410, 411
algorithms 81, 82, 234, 422
Amazon company 165, 218, 287, 393, 407

American War of Independence. *See* wars
'Americanisation'. *See* sport
anti-vaxxers 326
apocalypticism 388
Armstrong, Lance 315, 349–353, 370, 371
artificial intelligence (AI) 19, 21, 30, 31, 388
atheism 279, 307

B
banking 8, 75, 83
belief 20, 27, 29, 54, 63, 81, 229, 236, 239, 272, 275–278, 280, 281, 291, 300, 303, 307, 308, 346, 388, 421
Biden, Joe 13, 21, 176, 233, 420
Big Ag. *See* agriculture, corporate

Big Bang 301
biofuels 107, 109, 247
biotechnology. *See* genetic engineering
Brexit 15, 61, 230, 231
Buddhism. *See* religion
Bush, George W. 12, 23, 160, 211, 212, 225, 226

C

capitalism 20, 53, 64, 66–68, 72, 74, 75, 77, 84, 86, 132, 156, 179, 186, 224, 239, 251, 280, 333, 338, 389, 396, 415–420, 424
carbon tax 397
Catholicism. *See* religion
Cato Institute 183, 184
ChatGPT 30, 31
cheating. *See* sport
Chicago School. *See* economics
Christianity. *See* religion
'civilising process'. *See* sport
climate change
  denial 183
  effects 331, 389
  fossil fuels 181, 182, 397, 399
  greenhouse gases 173, 187
  ocean warming 171
  temperatures 170, 173, 386, 387, 396
climate change denial. *See* climate change
Cold War. *See* wars
colonialism 238–240, 246
communism 75, 181, 183, 223, 423
Community Supported Agriculture. *See* agriculture

Concentrated Animal Feeding Operations (CAFOs) 104, 408
conspiracy theories 15, 182, 217, 383, 394
consumerism 419
Corona virus. *See* COVID-19
corporate farming. *See* agriculture
COVID-19 130, 232, 323, 327, 382, 383
cricket. *See* sport
CRISPR technology 383
Cromwell, Oliver 243, 265
Crusades 282

D

dark advertising 21, 43
Darwin, Charles 283, 301
'dashboard dining'. *See* food
DDT. *See* agrichemicals
deepfakes 395
deforestation. *See* environment
degrowth economy 419
democracy 10, 15, 16, 19, 20, 29, 70, 74, 77, 179, 189, 220, 223, 234, 419–423
democratic socialism 424
deregulation. *See* economics
derivatives. *See* economics
desertification. *See* environment
disinformation. *See* misinformation/disinformation
Djokovic, Novak. *See* sport
doping. *See* sport
droughts. *See* environment

E

ecological footprint. *See* environment
economics
    Chicago School 69
    comparative advantage 58, 59
    deregulation 9
    derivatives 77
    externalities 63, 69
    hedge funds 77, 78, 80
    heterodox 416, 418, 419
    industry concentration 111
    inequality 10, 63, 67, 74, 77, 389, 416, 418, 419
    monetarist theory 71
    orthodox 52, 64, 416, 417
    securitisation 80
    structural adjustments 60
    taxation 61, 245
    'too big to fail' 78
    trickle-down theory 75, 93
ecosystem collapse. *See* environment
environment
    deforestation 249, 250, 404, 407
    desertification 404
    destruction 111, 174, 251, 424
    droughts 172, 404
    ecological footprint 408
    ecosystem collapse 388
    fracking 177
    land degradation 174, 406
    oil drilling 166, 177
    oil spills 166
    pollution 58, 104, 154, 174, 176, 249, 406, 417
    resource depletion 403, 404, 417
    tipping points 405, 441
exorcism. *See* religion

extinction 152, 159, 170, 172, 378, 386, 406
    causes 159, 380, 402
    dinosaurs 380
    human 152, 159
    planetary 378
    species 152, 159, 170, 172, 378, 380, 404, 406
Extinction Rebellion 188, 402, 403

F

Facebook/Meta. *See* social media
factory farming. *See* agriculture, corporate
fake news 2, 27, 28, 30, 231–234, 394, 395
false consciousness 280, 333
farmers' markets 413
far right. *See* politics
fast food. *See* food
fertilisers 103, 156, 183, 404
feudalism 66
financialisation 75–77, 101, 110, 422
fires. *See* climate change, effects
First Nation peoples 244
First World War. *See* wars
flags of the world 237
flooding. *See* climate change, effects
food
    'dashboard dining' 132, 134
    fabrication of trust 118, 119
    fast food 101, 124–126, 129, 131
    frankenfoods 128
    horsemeat scandal 142
    hot dogs 129–130
    industrial diet 126, 127, 132
    junk food 126, 127, 130, 412

organic 152, 156, 410
poisoning 103, 114–116, 154, 408
regulation 117, 412
retailers 101, 117–119, 413
scares 114
security 102, 172, 248, 249, 251
ultra-processed 126, 130, 132, 412, 413
food commodity traders 67, 75, 108
football/soccer. *See* sport
fossil fuels. *See* climate change
Fox News. *See* media, companies
fracking. *See* environment
Frankenfoods. *See* food
free trade 58–60
Friedman, Milton 69, 71, 75

G

gamblification. *See* sport
Genetically Modified Organisms (GMOs). *See* genetic engineering
genetic engineering 105, 151, 161, 164, 383
Global Financial Crisis (GFC), 2008 246, 415, 418
global food crisis 246
Global North 103, 174, 247, 398, 399, 403, 404
Global South 59, 103, 155, 156, 174, 247, 248, 398, 399
global warming. *See* climate change
Glyphosate. *See* agrichemicals
Google 81, 393–395
Great Depression (from 1929) 63, 75
greenhouse effect 173

greenhouse gasses. *See* climate change
Green New Deal 397, 418, 448
Greenpeace 168, 194, 411
Green Revolution 102, 103
greenwashing 178, 354, 400, 401

H

heatwaves. *See* climate change, effects
heaven. *See* religion
hedge funds. *See* economics
herbicides. *See* agrichemicals
Heritage Foundation 8–10, 183, 188, 402
heterodox economics. *See* economics
High Fructose Corn Syrup (HFCS). *See* food
high-tech agriculture. *See* agriculture, corporate
Hinduism. *See* religion
Hitler, Adolf 23, 159, 214, 215, 217, 355
hoax 2, 179, 325, 394, 395
Hudson Institute 151, 159–161
Hussein, Saddam 23, 212, 224, 225

I

Ideology 54, 64, 283, 284, 397, 416
Indigenous communities. *See* First Nation peoples
Industrial revolution 284, 338
industry concentration. *See* economics
inequality. *See* economics
influencers 3, 5, 16, 18, 20, 119, 161, 164, 234, 327, 391

Instagram. *See* social media
Intergovernmental Panel on Climate Change (IPCC) 170, 173, 184, 400
Iraq war. *See* war
Islam. *See* religion

Jesus Christ. *See* religion
Jewish persecution 296
Judaism. *See* religion
junk foods. *See* food

Kentucky Fried Chicken (KFC) 19, 124, 131, 133
Keynes, Milton 416
Koch Brothers 180, 183, 184
Kroc, Ray 121–123
Kyoto Protocol 186, 398

land degradation. *See* environment
land grabbing 76, 248, 250, 411
La Via Campesina 410, 411
LGBTQIA+ community 9
liberalism 68
lies 3, 13, 20, 22, 24, 27, 29, 168, 187, 230–234, 242, 276, 308, 326, 349, 390–392, 416
lobbying 8–10, 106, 160, 161, 177, 182, 186, 342, 391, 412, 445
logos 7, 118, 125, 131, 178, 330
lying. *See* lies

Mao Zedong 218
Marx, Karl 280, 281, 307, 333, 423, 424
masculinities 96
mass media. *See* media
McCarthyism 222
McDonald's 7, 99, 100, 122–124, 131, 134, 135, 144, 377, 409, 414
'McJobs' 8
'meatification' 152
media
 companies 28, 188, 393
 mass 11
 power 11
Microsoft 7, 31, 94, 183
Middle Ages 4, 66, 114, 289–291, 314, 340
military-entertainment complex 227, 228
military-industrial complex 227
miracles 284, 285
misinformation/disinformation 2, 15, 28–31, 182, 186–188, 217, 224, 231, 239, 383, 391–393, 403, 421
misogyny 281, 308, 332
Mohammed. *See* religion
monetarist theory. *See* economics
Monsanto 110, 161–165
movies. *See* popular culture
Murdoch media. *See* media, companies
Murdoch, Rupert 11–16, 160
Muscular Christianity. *See* sport
Musk, Elon 28, 231, 261, 393
myths 62, 301, 331–334, 415

N

Nazi Party 214, 354
neoliberal globalisation. *See* neoliberalism
neoliberalism 61, 71, 72, 76, 221, 418, 422
New Economics Foundation (NEF) 417, 418
News Corporation. *See* media, companies
not-for-profit organisations 407, 411
nuclear disasters 169, 378
nuclear power 159, 166–168, 181, 189
'nudging effect' 5
nuns. *See* religion

O

obesogenic diet 128–133, 412
ocean warming. *See* climate change
oil drilling. *See* environment
oil spills. *See* environment
Olympic games. *See* sport
organic farming. *See* agricullture
organic food. *See* food
orthodox economics. *See* economics

P

Packard, Vance 6, 35
paganism 278, 279, 284, 311
Paris Agreement 175, 176, 182, 203, 386, 398, 401
peasant and subsistence agriculture. *See* agriculture
perfect competition 55, 56, 415
pesticides. *See* agrichemicals
petrochemicals 157, 173
petroleum industry 157
Piketty, Thomas 74, 93, 424
plastic 24, 112, 152, 153, 157–159, 192–194, 308, 403, 406
politics 11, 12, 15, 17, 65, 161, 177, 232, 259, 277, 305, 328, 330, 331, 362, 389, 390, 416, 421
  far right 160
  revolution 424
politics and sport. *See* sport
Pollan, Michael 131, 133, 148, 149
pollution. *See* environment
Popes. *See* religion
popular culture 85, 327, 354
  movies 229
  television 218
population 10, 34, 60, 62, 66, 68, 74, 102–104, 106, 108, 130, 151, 152, 154, 159, 167, 174, 216, 219, 237, 242, 244, 247, 248, 250, 279, 311, 326, 334, 381, 385, 397, 405, 410, 416, 421, 434
post-truth 1, 15, 28, 29, 47, 232, 395
private equity (PE) 76, 84, 246
productivity 54, 56, 57, 67, 81, 102, 103, 105, 106, 108, 138, 152, 250, 270, 445
propaganda
  Chinese 219, 220
  history 25, 222
  Soviet Union 217, 222
  United States 222
propaganda posters 256
Protestantism. *See* religion, Christianity

protests 10, 143, 220, 235, 239, 246, 260, 330, 390, 393, 399, 402, 403, 407, 409, 442
Proud Boys 420
public relations (PR) 3, 21, 26, 164, 185, 208, 220
Putin, Vladimir 218, 232, 254, 328, 347, 372, 384, 429

Q

QAnon 21, 44, 377

R

Reagan, Ronald 8, 12, 69, 71, 73, 91, 128, 160
regenerative agriculture 186, 398, 409, 410, 437, 444
religion
   ancient 276, 277, 305
   and science 283
   Buddhism 272, 281, 284, 319
   Christianity 238, 240, 272, 276, 283, 285, 305
      Catholicism 240
      Protestantism 281
   exorcism 272
   forgeries 271, 295–298
   heaven 273, 276, 308
   Hinduism 272, 281, 284
   Islam 272, 276, 284, 285, 305
   Jesus Christ 380
   Judaism 272, 276, 285, 305
   Mohammad 379
   nuns 285
   Popes 379
   Scientology 276
   sexual abuse 295
   the Devil 276
   Virgin Mary 286
resource depletion. *See* environment
revolution. *See* politics
right wing 9, 10, 13, 42, 415, 420
rugby. *See* sport

S

Satan. *See* religion, the Devil
science and religion. *See* religion, and science
Scientology. *See* religion
Second World War. *See* wars
'securitisation'. *See* economics
self-interest 53–55, 224, 242
sexual abuse and the church. *See* religion
shock jocks 3, 16–18, 42
slavery 65, 240, 242, 312, 422
Slow Food movement 414
Snapchat. *See* social media
social agency 333, 389
social class 333
socialism 75, 92, 220, 418, 423, 424
social media
   Facebook/Meta 2, 19, 21, 125
   Instagram 21, 231, 232
   Snapchat 125, 393
   Telegram 29, 420
   TikTok 234, 395
   Twitter/X 28, 231, 232
   YouTube 18, 232, 393
societal deception-definition 2
species extinction. *See* extinction
spectacularisation. *See* sport
spin 26, 27, 46, 77, 164, 194, 209, 343, 344, 358, 359

sponsorship. *See* sport
sport
   Americanisation 330
   and politics 328, 330, 331
   Armstrong, Lance 349–353
   cheating 336, 346, 347, 349, 352, 353
   'civilising process' 339
   cricket 329, 341, 343, 359
   Djokovic, Novak 323, 324, 326–328
   doping 348–350, 352, 353
   football/soccer 330, 337, 339, 340, 344, 356–359
   'gamblification' 331
   history 327, 353
   muscular christianity 339
   olympic games 330–359
   rugby 330, 332, 334, 337, 339, 341, 359
   rules 323, 326, 330, 336, 338–340
   sexual abuse 332
   'spectacularisation' 330
   sponsorship 346, 353, 358, 359
   tennis 324–328, 340, 342, 358
sporting rules. *See* sport
sportswashing 354–358
Stalin, Joseph 216, 217, 423
St Augustine of Hippo 292–293, 304
structural adjustment. *See* economics
Sunak, Rishi 178, 204
Supermarketisation 140
supermarkets 101, 111–114, 117, 119, 120, 125, 127, 131, 133, 413, 414
Super Size Me 124, 144, 145
supply chains 116, 119, 157, 410

Sustainable development goals (SDGs) 406

taxation. *See* economics
tax havens 12
Tea Party 184
television. *See* media
tennis. *See* sport
terrorism 384
Thatcher, Margaret 12, 71, 72, 93
the Amazon 111, 249, 405
the Devil. *See* religion
the industrial diet. *See* food
think tanks 3, 8–10, 64, 69, 161, 183, 251, 390, 391, 403, 415, 418
Third World. *See* Global South
Thunberg, Greta 188, 401
TikTok. *See* social media
'too big to fail'. *See* economics
totalitarianism 11, 216, 297, 423
trickle-down theory. *See* economics
Trump, Donald 9, 13, 15, 21, 24, 29, 57, 74, 85, 160, 175, 176, 179, 180, 184, 187, 188, 232, 233, 238, 382, 393, 420, 421
Twin Tower bombings (9/11) 160, 225, 226

ultra-processed food. *See* food
United Nations (UN) 41, 195, 375, 397, 441
universities 106, 222, 383, 417, 418

V

Vietnam War. *See* wars
Virgin Mary. *See* religion

W

Wall Street 77, 82–85, 418
wars
   American War of Independence 244
   Cold War 222
   First World War 221, 381
   Iraq 252, 257
   Israel-Hamas 260, 261
   Second World War 71, 126, 127, 214, 221
   Ukraine 431
   Vietnam 229
Weapons of mass destruction (WMD) 23, 211, 225
Weber, Max 280, 281

X

Xi Jinping 220, 357

Y

YouTube. *See* social media

Z

zombies vii–viii, 86, 218, 388, 391

GPSR Compliance
The European Union's (EU) General Product Safety Regulation (GPSR) is a set of rules that requires consumer products to be safe and our obligations to ensure this.

If you have any concerns about our products, you can contact us on

ProductSafety@springernature.com

In case Publisher is established outside the EU, the EU authorized representative is:

Springer Nature Customer Service Center GmbH
Europaplatz 3
69115 Heidelberg, Germany

www.ingramcontent.com/pod-product-compliance
Lightning Source LLC
LaVergne TN
LVHW040730250326
834688LV00031B/227

9 781349 961061